A Friendship in Twilight

JACK MILES

MARK C. TAYLOR

# A Friendship in Twilight

## LOCKDOWN CONVERSATIONS
## ON DEATH AND LIFE

Columbia University Press / New York

Columbia University Press
*Publishers Since 1893*
New York   Chichester, West Sussex
cup.columbia.edu
Copyright © 2022 Jack Miles and Mark C. Taylor
All rights reserved

Library of Congress Cataloging-in-Publication Data
Names: Miles, Jack, 1942– author. | Taylor, Mark C., 1945– author.
Title: A friendship in twilight : lockdown conversations on death and life /
Jack Miles, Mark C. Taylor.
Description: New York : Columbia University Press, [2022] |
Includes bibliographical references and index.
Identifiers: LCCN 2021048812 (print) | LCCN 2021048813 (ebook) |
ISBN 9780231205948 (hardback) | ISBN 9780231205955 (trade paperback) |
ISBN 9780231556248 (ebook)
Subjects: LCSH: Death. | Death—Religious aspects. | Future life. | Miles, Jack, 1942– |
Taylor, Mark C., 1945– | COVID-19 (Disease)—Miscellanea.
Classification: LCC BD444 .M47 2022 (print) | LCC BD444 (ebook) |
DDC 128/.5—dc23/eng/20211104
LC record available at https://lccn.loc.gov/2021048812
LC ebook record available at https://lccn.loc.gov/2021048813

Columbia University Press books are printed on permanent
and durable acid-free paper.

Printed in the United States of America

Cover design: Lisa Hamm
Cover photo: Photograph by Edwin I. Stearns. Cambridge, MA, 1968.
Courtesy of Mark C. Taylor.

*In my letter to you*
*I took all my fears and doubts*
*In my letter to you*
*All the hard things I found out*
*In my letter to you*
*All that I've found true*
*And I sent it in a letter to you.*

—Bruce Springsteen, "Letter to You"

# Contents

# *A Note to Our Readers*

"WILL ALL THIS EVER BE BEHIND US?" Over the past months, we, like you, have found ourselves often asking this question and sometimes wondering whether our lives will end before any real answer arrives. People around us have been more than eager to believe that it will all be behind us quite soon, or even that it is already behind us. Others whom we respect, armed with impressive research, project themselves mentally into the future, look back on the present, and warn us that we must take drastic action or else. But the two of us, now in our seventies, do not have decades to live, only countable years. We worry, of course, and intensely about our children, grandchildren, great-grandchildren, but what are we or they to do *now*?

And, prior to that question, there comes, of course, a more basic question—namely, "What are we to think?" Knowledge counts, but knowledge is not the same as wisdom. Early in life, we two were eager for knowledge, eager for experience, raking it in from all sides, from all sources. Now, late in life, we find ourselves yearning more for wisdom than for further increments of knowledge, wondering how to place ourselves spiritually in our world, wherever it may be headed, and, above all, how to do this in only the time remaining to us.

\* \* \*

"Wherever it may be headed," we just wrote, but where *is* the world headed? If someone could actually come back from the distant future—from the world of Kim Stanley Robinson's futuristic "climate fiction" novel *2312*, for example—to answer that question and "wise us up," would that kind of wisdom make the crucial difference? It might, but it might not. Skepticism about whether wisdom brought back from the future can make much difference is as old as the Bible. Jesus, for example, told this parable, where unbelievers can easily substitute a messenger from the future for a messenger from the afterlife:

> There was a rich man who was dressed in purple and fine linen and who feasted sumptuously every day. And at his gate lay a poor man named Lazarus, covered with sores, who longed to satisfy his hunger with what fell from the rich man's table; even the dogs would come and lick his sores. The poor man died and was carried away by the angels to be with Abraham. The rich man also died and was buried. In Hades, where he was being tormented, he looked up and saw Abraham far away with Lazarus by his side. He called out, "Father Abraham, have mercy on me, and send Lazarus to dip the tip of his finger in water and cool my tongue; for I am in agony in these flames." But Abraham said, "Child, remember that during your lifetime you received your good things, and Lazarus in like manner evil things; but now he is comforted here, and you are in agony. Besides all this, between you and us a great chasm has been fixed, so that those who might want to pass from here to you cannot do so, and no one can cross from there to us." He said, "Then, father, I beg you to send him to my father's house—for I have five brothers— that he may warn them, so that they will not also come into this place of torment." Abraham replied, "They have Moses and the prophets; they should listen to them. He said, "No, father Abraham; but if someone goes to them from the dead, they will repent." He said to him, "If they do not listen to Moses and the prophets, neither will they be convinced even if someone rises from the dead."

Classic Christianity regards every ordinary human lifetime as just a test, a probationary period for the world to come—a test that one passes not by acquiring wealth but by doing good, avoiding evil, and trusting in the Lord. Yet reading between the lines and thinking now of the future more than of the afterlife, the story that Jesus tells has a sobering but instructive second meaning: that a messenger from the future, however stunning his message, might only too easily be ignored or scorned.

Our world is ablaze with a virus that is both biological and political. Yesteryear's visionary prophets have become today's sober scientists, who warn that the apocalypse is now. Yet those in power and those who lust for it continue to hoard false treasure, while the world burns around them, and there is no water to quench the growing thirst. Like the five doomed brothers in Jesus's parable, they have been provided all the knowledge they need but possess neither the will nor the wisdom to act on it.

\* \* \*

But where, finally, does that leave you or us? When we began writing the letters that fill this book, we had fifty years of friendship behind us, and the fifty had been filled with learning, but now the time was growing short. In the dwindling years remaining, we had no choice: we had to seek wisdom with only the knowledge that we had already on hand. Given our respective comorbidities, the pandemic might take either of us at any moment. Such was our fear as we began. Then, halfway through the year, we began to fear that our nation's political survival was in as much danger as its physical survival. Death was now threatening us, you might say, in two different disguises, and how would we respond?

The Danish philosopher Søren Kierkegaard once wrote, "Death is a good dancing partner." While at some level we all realize that our ticket for life is stamped by death, we typically push the prospect or our own death and the deaths of those closest to us into the distant future. As the dark winter of 2020 lengthened into the darker summer, this strategy of avoidance no longer worked for the two of us. A virus that had infected a single individual on the other side of the globe had spread like wildfire both around the world and, mercilessly, around our beloved country. The more urgent the warnings of scientists and medical experts became, the louder the denials of politicians and their credulous followers grew. But, as the numbers exploded and the bodies piled up, it became clear that death could not be denied in either its medical or its political guise. Rather than turn from it, we realized after a while that we were dancing with it, learning not from the future but from the present and from each other the lessons that it had to teach us about living well and even about dying well. In this book, we invite you to join us in that dance.

INDEPENDENCE DAY, 2021

# A Friendship in Twilight

# Introduction

Friendship always matters, and during the worst of the 2020 pandemic it began to matter more than ever to millions locked down at home wondering what lay ahead. Jack Miles and Mark Taylor, whose friendship began at Harvard University in 1968 and continues to this day, had been in the habit for years of exchanging almost daily email messages, often with extensive attachments. Both were widely published writers, but they had never collaborated for publication. When the pandemic erupted, Mark proposed to Jack that now might be the moment for them to attempt something together. Jack countered with the suggestion that they simply expand their existing epistolary habit, exchanging more serious letters once a day and determining only after the fact what the longer exchange might amount to.

Mark agreed, and between March 15, 2020, and January 6, 2021, they produced an electronic text of fully 475,000 words (1,700 pages)—the equivalent of several published volumes. *A Friendship in Twilight: Lockdown Conversations on Death and Life* is a substantial selection from what they wrote, offered as an invitation to enter their friendship as you might enter a private home and listen to the conversation around the dinner table. But who are these two guys conversing so volubly across the table—or, to begin with, who were they when they first met half a century ago?

\* \* \*

Jack Miles (b. 1942) arrived at Harvard in 1967 as an improbable candidate for a doctorate in Near Eastern languages and literatures. What made his candidacy improbable was that he did not have a conventional American bachelor's degree. What made it plausible was that he was a Jesuit, and the

Harvard professors who taught Near Eastern languages and literatures had taught Jesuits before him. They knew that Jesuit intellectual formation, though hopelessly anachronistic in many ways (at the Pontifical Gregorian University—where Jack had studied philosophy for two years—textbooks, lectures, and examinations were all in Latin), was paradoxically perfect for the study of ancient literatures like the Hebrew Bible. Jack had spent the 1966–1967 academic year at the Hebrew University of Jerusalem studying archaeology and the Hebrew language but, outside of class, learning much about Jews and Israelis that was not taught in any university but that would change the course of his life. The final chapter in that pivotal year was the Six-Day War, which he lived through in Haifa, initially in a bomb shelter.

Mark Taylor (b. 1945) arrived at Harvard in 1968 as a star candidate for the doctorate in theology at the Harvard Divinity School. He had excelled as an undergraduate at Wesleyan University, where he first read and studied the works of Søren Kierkegaard, the Danish thinker rightly honored as the father of existentialism. Raised as a cultural Protestant (nominally Presbyterian), Mark never aspired to be a minister but was already en route to a lifelong engagement with extrareligious paths to meaning and even to transcendence. At Harvard, while deepening his understanding of Kierkegaard, whose work would provide the subject matter for two of his earliest books, he began a lifelong and ultimately more challenging attempt not just to master the thought of G. W. F. Hegel, Kierkegaard's intellectual nemesis, but even to become a latter-day Hegel himself, as Jack, who edited Mark's transitional *Journeys to Selfhood: Hegel and Kierkegaard*, would later characterize his friend's emergent ambition. Hegel, who famously defined philosophy as "its time comprehended in thought," addressed in his voluminous work nearly every area of intellectual endeavor alive in his early nineteenth-century world. Mark, while never publishing a book exclusively devoted to Hegel, has, like Hegel, addressed at book length subjects as varied as art, architecture, science, technology, finance, literature, and even medicine.

Miles and Taylor met in the fall of 1968 when Mark and Dinny Taylor, newly married, rented an apartment on the second story of the same Cambridge three-decker where Miles and two other Jesuits had rented the third. 1968 was a year of exceptional national trauma and social transformation. As 2020 unfolded, it was impossible for the two friends not to draw best-of-times/worst-of-times parallels with the year when they first met.

True, the world was not being ravaged in 1968 by a new and lethal disease equivalent to 2020's COVID-19, but there was a pervasive background fear that nuclear war might not just take millions of lives, but also plunge the planet into the apocalyptic darkness of a new ice age. The Nuclear Nonproliferation Treaty was signed midway in 1968, but this was a far cry from nuclear disarmament. The fear remained.

The murder of George Floyd in 2020, followed by massive, nation-wide Black Lives Matter (BLM) demonstrations, brought sadly to mind the murder of the Rev. Dr. Martin Luther King Jr. in 1968. It was the Rev. Dr. John Maguire—King's roommate during a fateful conference at Crozier Theological Seminary and thereafter his lifelong friend—who at Wesleyan had simultaneously introduced Mark to Kierkegaard and to the paramount importance of personal, moral, self- and life-defining *choice*, the kind that can sometimes change the world. King's murder had been followed by violent uprisings in Washington, DC, Chicago, and elsewhere. (Jack's father, a blue-collar worker, narrowly escaped harm in the Chicago riots.) Yet the late Rep. John Lewis, a civil rights activist who died in 2020 (and whose casket lay in state in the Capitol Rotunda), declared himself hugely encouraged by the scope, order, and interracial breadth of the BLM demonstrations. 1968 was the year when Thurgood Marshall became the first Black justice appointed to the U.S. Supreme Court, and the year when the historic Civil Rights Act was passed, ending legal segregation for good. 2020 was the year when Stacey Abrams and Georgia Black activists like her delivered the two Democratic senators needed for a Democratic Senate majority: one of them, Rev. Raphael Warnock, the first African American elected to the Senate in Georgia's history; the other, Jon Ossoff, the first Jew. The Miles family handwrote some hundreds of postcards to build the Democratic turnout in Georgia.

1968 and 2020 were, of course, starkly different in many particulars, and yet there was in both a similar sense that one reality was staring us in the face, while our government was proclaiming another, with the American people caught weirdly in the middle. Through 1968, as the United States suffered one spectacular setback after another in Vietnam (the siege of Khe Sanh, the Tet Offensive, the Viet Cong invasion of the U.S. embassy in Saigon) while President Lyndon Johnson and General William Westmoreland continued to insist that victory was just around the corner, the result was a mounting sense that the American government had somehow lost its mind and was falling apart. In 2020, as deaths from COVID-19 climbed into the thousands and then into the hundreds of thousands while President Donald J. Trump and Vice President Mike Pence kept claiming, insanely, either that the pandemic was not serious or that it was about to end, Jack and Mark shared an uncanny and unwelcome sense of déja vu: two realities once again competing, each with its own committed constituency, one delusional, one not.

As 2020 drew to a close, President Trump, defeated in the November presidential election and bluntly or rudely rebuffed in every judicial attempt to reverse his defeat, continued to rally his millions of supporters around the slogan "Stop the Steal!" Where would this end? This seemed the darkest moment in American political history since the outbreak of the Civil War. But, at the same time, a scientific triumph was at hand: the stunningly rapid development of a powerfully effective vaccine against COVID-19. That triumph prompted Mark to recall another moment of scientific triumph and hope, one that came at the very end of 1968, specifically on

Christmas Eve, when, from Apollo Seven, astronaut William Anders took the incomparably beautiful and moving photo of planet Earth as seen from space. Yes, after a chaotic 1968 presidential campaign, Richard M. Nixon was about to be inaugurated as president, and where would that end? But science, even the same science that produced intercontinental ballistic missiles, could still inspire and sometimes even save.

\* \* \*

Mark's recalling in 2020 that the "whole Earth" image was first seen at the end of 1968 bespoke his respect for science as the son of a high school science teacher in prosperous Westfield, New Jersey. Both his parents were teachers (his mother taught literature), and, "in our family," as he wrote in 2007, "school was church and books were scripture. More Protestant than they ever realized, my parents always assumed that teaching was a vocation. It took me many years to understand that this is one of the primary reasons teaching has always been so important to me." No surprise, then, that after completing his doctorate at Harvard in 1973, Mark was immediately hired by prestigious Williams College, where he would raise his family and remain as professor of religion for twenty-four years plus a further decade—in a tribute to the widening breadth of his academic output—as Cluett Professor of Humanities. A dedicated teacher like his parents, he was named National Professor of the Year in 1995 by the Carnegie Foundation for the Advancement of Teaching, an award that acknowledged his pioneering contribution to online education. Twenty years before schools and colleges went virtual overnight, Mark cofounded Global Education Network, which was dedicated to delivering high-quality online education in the liberal arts, humanities, and sciences.

Jack, neither of whose parents had attended college, had no sacral sense at all about teaching. Teaching, even university teaching, was just a job for him. One wanted to do it well, to give good value, but there, spiritually, it ended. And, rather as Mark was drawn to cultural expressions of religion outside houses of worship, so Jack was drawn to the intellectual life as pursued free of the strictures of teaching and academe—as pursued, more specifically, in journalism. Hired by Loyola University of Chicago while still technically a Jesuit and still completing his 1971 doctorate, he was terminated four years later (for "confidential reasons," he was told) after giving a talk in which he outlined how, consistent with Catholic tradition, the pope could license abortion as an instance of religiously sanctioned killing. After all, in a tradition that had sanctioned just war (the Crusades) and capital punishment (even in the Papal States), such a development was far from as inconceivable as it would be in a tradition like Jainism, in which the taking of life, *all* life, even insect life, was sinful.

After that reversal, easing out of Catholicism and more or less giving up on academe, Jack moved into book publishing for ten years in New York (Doubleday) and California (University of California Press) and then into journalism for ten more years with the *Los Angeles Times.* Years earlier, before his head was turned in his last year at a Jesuit high school by the romance, sophistication, internationalism, and esprit de corps of the Society of Jesus, journalism had been his initial ambition. His father, who worked installing and removing industrial and institutional electricity meters for Chicago's Commonwealth Edison Company, never passed a day without carefully reading the newspaper. With only two years of technical training himself, he told Jack, "The daily newspaper is a liberal education," and the remark had stayed with him. Journalists are professional generalists. So are acquiring editors in book publishing houses; they are "like the Rio Grande," an old saying has it, "a mile wide and an inch deep." As the *Times*'s book review editor and then a member of its editorial board, writing anonymously on international relations as well as on "ideas," Jack found his own way, in hundreds of shorter pieces, to a shallower but even broader version (two miles wide and half an inch deep?) of the same breadth that Mark was pursuing at concentrated philosophical depth in books as varied as *Disfiguring: Art, Architecture, Religion* (1992), *Imagologies: Media Philosophy* (1994), and *Hiding* (1996)—this last an extraordinarily designed medical-cultural-philosophical meditation on, of all things, *skin.*

Mark's cultural exploration, however wide-ranging, never left behind a Hegelian determination to pursue cultural developments to their spiritual taproot. His *Speed Limits: Where Time Went and Why We Have So Little Left* (2014) is in that one regard his most striking book, tracing as it does the contemporary experience of time shortage and hyperactive busy-ness back to, of all people, Martin Luther. As regards religion itself, religion in the usual sense of the word, his grounding in Hegelian thought enabled him to recognize early on that that French *déconstruction* was a revival and extension of Hegel's logic, a derivation that Jacques Derrida himself readily admitted. In Mark's hands, Derrida applied theologically became *Erring: A Postmodern A/Theology* (1984), in which he makes Hegel's implicit atheism explicit without rendering theology by any means superfluous. *Erring,* which would be translated both into French and, interestingly, into Japanese, began a trajectory that would end in 2007 with *After God,* his culminating statement, specifically on the phenomenon of religion and the winner, that year, of the American Academy of Religion's Award for Excellence.

Between 1974 and 1995, Jack published nothing of book length other than his arcane doctoral dissertation (involving Ge'ez, the classical language of Ethiopia), but in that last year he surprised everyone with *God: A Biography*, which won the Pulitzer Prize for biography in 1996, became a *New York Times* best seller, and was translated into sixteen languages, twice into Chinese. Although journalism is sometimes called history's first draft, and biography is sometimes considered a branch of history, this book was in fact character-centered literary criticism: a literary engagement with the books of the Old Testament read as the Tanakh, the Jewish Bible, in the canonical Jewish order and, of course, without the New Testament. Methodologically, historians—and history was the regnant discipline in the study of the Bible at Harvard—cannot and do not speak directly of God at all, only of other humans who believed in or wrote about God. For Jack, the literary product of biblical study thus historically undertaken, whatever its high merit as history, was defective as literary appreciation. It was *Hamlet* without the prince.

But a more experiential component fed into *God: A Biography* as well. Thanks to the extreme insularity of his lower-working-class Catholic background in Chicago, an insularity only deepened by his early Jesuit formation, Jack had, in effect, encountered the Jews first as a majority in Israel and only later as a minority in his own country. Living through the Six-Day War in a state of acute identification with the Israeli cause, hearing Moshe Dayan over the radio speaking at the Western Wall late on the last day of the war a Hebrew prayer that by then he knew by heart, Jack had arrived at Harvard with an intensified if scarcely rationalized sense of the specifically *religious* importance of the Holy Land, the God-promised land, *'eretz yisra'el*, to the Jews. The loss of the land, for those engaging the Bible as history, was an endless ordeal for the Children of Israel as they were brutalized in turn by the Egyptians, the Assyrians, the Babylonians, the Persians, the Greeks, and, finally, the Romans. Yet that same ordeal, once the Bible was engaged as literature, could be seen as an ordeal for the God who made the original promise and then failed to keep it, a series of crises for him as his initial glorious victory over Pharaoh's Egypt was followed by one humiliating defeat after another. Did these defeats not make him a failed God, centuries before the Nazi Holocaust?

The same stance of studied critical naïveté enabled a sequel five years later, an engagement with the Gospel as the story of Yahweh the Jew, the erstwhile divine warrior arriving to resolve his greatest crisis—the Roman destruction of his Temple and Rome's reenslavement of his chosen people—by renouncing war at long last and being crucified by the Romans, mistakenly, as a seditious rebel. *Christ: A Crisis in the Life of God* (2002)—reviewed on the cover of the Sunday *New York Times Book Review* on Christmas Eve 2001—was swallowed up along with much of the entire New York book trade by the crisis of 9/11. In retrospect, Jack regretted not giving his second trade book the simpler title *God in Crisis*. But, as it happened, another kind of crisis had complicated the completion of the book that should have had that title and, with one more draft, probably would have had it.

Mark's best-selling book on religion, though neither his most personal nor his most radical, is the edited volume *Critical Terms in Religious Studies* (1998), for which Jack was initially to write the entry on "God" but finally chose not to. As a guide to the most forward-looking thought in American religious studies at the end of the twentieth century, *Critical Terms* was already widely influential in college-level religious studies when in 2007 Mark left Williams to chair the venerable Religion Department at Columbia University and to cofound and direct for six years Columbia's Institute for Religion, Culture, and Public Life.

Around the time that Mark was publishing *Critical Terms*, Jack accepted an invitation from Caltech to spend a guest year as Mellon Visiting Professor of Humanities. He had been warned not to teach about relations between religion and science, and he did not: he taught only a "straight" introduction to world religions over two semesters, plus a tutorial in biblical Hebrew. The subject of religion and science had been on his mind, however, ever since his tenure at Loyola University of Chicago—put there not by Loyola but by two books published in the 1970s: *Le hasard et la necessité* (1970) by molecular biologist and Nobel laureate Jacques Monod, and *The Limits to Growth* (1972), also called the Club of Rome report. *The Limits to Growth* portrayed industrial civilization, the child of science, as on a path to its own suicide, even if the catastrophe of nuclear self-annihilation could be avoided. Monod's *Chance and Necessity*, which Jack found both admirably rigorous and profoundly moving, nonetheless threw into relief for him how ill-equipped organized science was to assume the social burdens traditionally carried by organized religion and, thus, also, how ill-equipped to lead an effective response to the ecological Armageddon that *The Limits to Growth* saw encroaching on several different fronts.

Jack's Caltech course was popular; one student calculated that Jack was teaching one-quarter of the freshman class. At the end of that year, the Associated Students of Caltech presented him with the association's annual teaching award, rather to the astonishment of all. But, facing unemployment, Jack was more than relieved to accept a surprise offer to become senior advisor to the newly appointed president of the J. Paul Getty Trust, Barry Munitz, a friend from the time when Jack was editorializing on education for the *Times* and Munitz was head of the California State University system.

The year 2020 brought several new words into use (think "unmute") and others into new prominence (think "comorbidity"). "Comorbidity" is a word that Mark and Jack found themselves using in the earliest of their lockdown letters, and for good reason. In 1988, at the age of forty-three, Mark had developed adult-onset diabetes that would grow more acute with each passing year, diabetes being a condition, of course, that brings in its train its own special set of comorbidities. One of Mark's very last books before *A Friendship in Twilight* was *Intervolution: Smart Bodies Smart Things* (2020), in which he engages artificial intelligence through the computer brain in the artificial pancreas that he wears at his waist, a brain that is networked through the manufacturer with other brains directing other smart things (artificial pancreases) in other smart bodies so as to deliver to each just the right amount of insulin at just the right moment. The technology is dazzling, but what happens when the tiny computer brain crashes in the middle of the night? What happens if it is hacked?

In 1999, at the age of fifty-seven, just after joining the J. Paul Getty Trust, Jack suffered a heart attack and underwent triple-bypass coronary surgery, hugely disrupting the completion of *Christ: A Crisis in the Life of God*. Meanwhile, thanks, apparently, to twenty-five years breathing in the polluted air of Pasadena and of the Los Angeles freeways that led from there through long commutes to the *Times* and the Getty, he was developing chronic obstructive pulmonary disease (COPD), an ongoing comorbidity that became a grave concern with COVID-19 threatening. It is a truism that old cronies speak of nothing but their ailments, but during the 2020 pandemic it was not old cronies alone who began talking every day about the risk of infection and death. In 2003, Jack came near to death again after suffering a perforated colon. In 2005, Mark came far nearer to death by sepsis after a botched cancer biopsy. He claims, in fact, that he truly *did* die, briefly, before he was revived. Jack recalls only Dinny's phone call: "We almost lost him."

"Sad mortality o'ersways our powers," as Shakespeare wrote. He could not escape the topic, and neither could the two old friends through 2020, as they wrote their lockdown letters. In 2002, Jack had been notified that he would be a MacArthur Fellow for the years 2003-2007, but why? At the time, he could only wonder. It could scarcely have been because of his then most recent, less-than-satisfactory book. Was it perhaps because of something else he had published around the same time: "Global Requiem: The Apocalyptic Moment in Art, Science, and Religion" Something in the way the announcement was phrased vaguely suggested as much. That essay led by circuitous paths to his becoming the sole humanist joining a team of fifty University of California scientists and social scientists to produce *Bending the Curve: Ten Scalable Solutions for Carbon Neutrality and Climate Stability*, a report commissioned by then-governor Jerry Brown for his use at the 2015 COP 21 climate change conference in Paris.

Death—political, civilizational, ecological, personal—is a recurrent topic in the letters that fill this book. As we write, Jack is retired after ten years (2007-2017) at the University of California, Irvine, appointed distinguished professor at age sixty-five having never before lasted more than four years at any university. He aspires to embrace retirement as the third, dharma stage in Hinduism's classic four-part life trajectory, taking the orange grove and tranquil home of his second wife, Kitty, as his ashram. Mark, for his part, hesitates to retire from Columbia to the enveloping quiet and deeper isolation of his permanent home outside Williamstown. He knows how much he will miss his unbroken conversation with generations of students.

Prospero, foreseeing his retirement to Milan, says in *The Tempest* that his every third thought will be the grave. Mark published two books in 2018 whose revealing titles are *Last Works: Lessons in Leaving* and *Abiding Grace: Time, Modernity, Death*. Mark has a son born in 1972 and a daughter born in

1976 as well as four grandchildren; Jack has a daughter born in 1985. More than of the grave, their every third thought in 2020 was of their children and grandchildren. Mark—no longer, if ever, a Christian—did not have his children baptized. Jack, who once characterized himself as a "pious agnostic" and now refers to himself pointedly as a "*practicing* Episcopalian," did have his daughter baptized. The agnosticism took; the baptism did not.

The master plot of the modern world begins for Mark with the Protestant Reformation, as the progenitor of the Western, secular, scientific civilization that, for better or worse, he sees as having conquered the world. For Jack the master plot begins, rather, with the Renaissance and with the contemporaneous self-relativization of the West that began with the Iberian explorations of Asia and the Americas and may end with the triumph of China well before we all perish in the Last Great Extinction.

Mark and Jack both like to quote Samuel Beckett's line "I can't go on, I'll go on." Neither has quite stopped going on. In 2015, W. W. Norton published *The Norton Anthology of World Religions* in six volumes and more than four thousand pages. Jack was its general editor, and a revised edition of his general introduction appeared in 2020 as *Religion as We Know It: An Origin Story*. In between the two, he wrote *God in the Qur'an* (2018) as the third and final volume of his trilogy, billed by its publisher, Knopf, as "God in Three Classic Scriptures."

Mark—whose meditative art criticism has engaged over the years Anselm Kiefer, Mark Tansey, Michael Heizer, Joseph Beuys, Matthew Barney, James Turrell, and Andy Goldsworthy—has latterly become a sculptor and landscape architect himself, creating at substantial expense on the eight remote acres around his home a sculpture garden celebrating Hegel, Kierkegaard, and (his other philosophical hero) Nietzsche. Called Nexus, this art-and-thought garden is quintessentially modern and yet, in the manner of Native American mound art, it reveals some of its secrets only from above—only, as it were, to the eye of God. Once he leaves Columbia University and a hollowed-out Manhattan behind, Mark's institutional anchor, if he has one at all, may be Williamstown's Clark Art Institute, or perhaps the Massachusetts Museum of Contemporary Art in nearby North Adams.

Will *A Friendship in Twilight* be for each of the two his last work? Neither really wants that. Each has other books, other ventures, planned. "Old age hath yet his honour and his toil," as Tennyson wrote in "Ulysses,"

Death closes all: but something ere the end,
Some work of noble note, may yet be done,
Not unbecoming men that strove with Gods.

What do professors of religious studies do if not strive with gods? Mark sees his work as a single large oeuvre and strives always to make the parts cohere even as the whole expands. Jack experiences his own work as a series of piecemeal interruptions, strategic retreats, and expedient recoveries, Odysseus perhaps to Mark's intellectual Achilles. He is resigned that the last interruption is likely to come with some perhaps significant work left unfinished; in fact, he expects something comparable for human thought as a whole when the species itself succumbs at last to its inevitable extinction. Be all that as it may, when Mark wrote Jack that he would be happy if *Twilight* should actually be their last published words—spoken this way, privately, to each other, amid danger but out of love—Jack was taken aback but then, after a long moment, agreed.

# The Ides of March

## MARCH 15–17: MARK BEGINS.

*The plague in the classroom (what to say?) and in the church . . . first masks . . . first (not last) mention of Albert Camus,* The Plague *. . . a young Muslim comes to the rescue . . . a cousin writes from Ireland . . . love, old age, and encroaching death in the novel* This Is Happiness *. . . statistical odds that Trump or a rival will die before the election.*

---

*March 15*

Dear Jack:

At such a moment, light might seem insignificant, or it might seem to be more significant than ever. I always get up in darkness to watch first light fall on the mountain. Dawn perpetually renews the moment of creation. This morning the light was special. While trees are in spring blossom elsewhere, the mountains here are still bare and the last traces of snow and ice remain along the drive. As the sun rises in the east, it casts an indescribable lavender light on the top of the western mountains. Rather than the light falling from the outside, it is as if it shines from within the bare branches of the trees. I happened to glance up from my desk at the precise instant the light first appeared. Within a few seconds the aura suddenly lost its richness and depth, and the light quickly grew pale. Then, in a flickering moment, the light was gone. With sickness and death spreading across the world, darkness seems to be winning the diurnal struggle. And yet there are instants when light seems sublime. This daily ritual will continue long after not only I but the human race is gone. In such moments, I often recall Nietzsche's question: "Is midnight also midday?"

Mark

*March 15*

Dear Mark:

Yesterday, CA Gov. Newsom instructed all Californians sixty-five or older to stay at home until further notice. We have enough regular food on hand for a short while as well as a set of Mormon-produced survival bins that can stave off starvation for a much longer while, but, still, the moment when we heard the governor speaking on the radio, clearly under huge stress, was frightening.

Today, Church of the Messiah, Santa Ana, where we are members, had canceled services, but Grace Church, Newton, where we attended while I was guest prof at Boston College last year, prepared a simple podcast in lieu of its canceled service. We played it at our breakfast table this morning. An Old Testament reading (Exodus: water in the desert); a Gospel reading (Jesus promising "living water" to the Samaritan woman at the well); a Psalm that we joined in to read responsorially; and a brief excerpt from Paul to the Romans.

Rev. Regina Walton—a poet as well as a priest, with a small, clear, and I think rather beautiful speaking voice—lingered over Paul's "And not only that, but we also boast in our sufferings, knowing that suffering produces endurance, and endurance produces character, and character produces hope, and hope does not disappoint us, because God's love has been poured into our hearts through the Holy Spirit that has been given to us." What mattered rather than any discipline of suffering was the thought, the sense, of God's love poured into our hearts. Despite my regular churchgoing, this is not a frequent or usual feeling for me, but it came over me at that moment.

We had made tea before we settled at the table and were looking out into our garden, wet with the rain of an unseasonably cold and damp California March. The service began and ended with J. S. Bach played quietly on the piano. Afterward, we did not plan to read further scripture, but we did want to hear some more Bach, and later in the day we did.

Jack

*March 16*

Dear Jack:

I am glad it is "spring break" and I am not teaching today. I need more time to see how fast this disaster is going to cascade. It will be hard to try to pick up classes as if it were business as usual—especially when teaching Kierkegaard, Hegel, Nietzsche, Heidegger. One of the questions I've wrestled with over the years is how far into the darkness to take young people. Another way to put the problem is how honest I should be with them. Students are understandably frustrated, disappointed, and anxious, so need some reassurance. They also need a safe place to express those concerns. How do you offer reassurance and perhaps hope without being dishonest? If you are honest and share your deep concerns with them, you might plunge them into despair.

One of the many things disease has taught me over the years is humility. Disease, like death, is a great leveler. What makes this crisis so devastating is that we have a president who is allergic to humility but not to the virus. Disease mocks the will to power and the will to mastery by undeniably showing that nature is beyond humankind's notions of good and evil. Disease teaches us that sometimes our greatest strength is the ability to admit our weakness.

Mark


*March 16*

Dear Mark:

How far in the darkness to take young people and how honest to be with them . . .

Today, Kathleen phoned to strategize with me about the new situation facing us. As we spoke, she seemed to feel—and maybe she was half-right—that she had to drive home to her father how very grave the situation was going to get. She read to me a grim story just posted in the *New York Times* about corpses piling up in Lombardy, especially in Bergamo. To convince her that, yeah, I had indeed grasped the core, statistical gravity of the threat, and indeed before reading that article, I shared with her that I had written you recently that this might well be the disease that would take you or me, maybe both of us. At that, she started weeping and couldn't speak for several minutes. She had called me distressed over protecting her mother, and here she was even more distressed about her father! Her first reaction was to schedule a visit here in Santa Ana while there was still time, while I was still alive.

After a while, she calmed down, we did agree on what she should urge on her mother, and as for a father-daughter meeting, we have now taken advice I found in the *Atlantic* and scheduled (for this Thursday) a video dinner—Kathleen and Brian in their apartment, Jack and Kitty in our house, connected by Zoom, eating separate meals but together in face, voice, and spirit.

And as for my fears yesterday about food, an angel has appeared. This morning at breakfast, I received a text message from a young Syrian-born Muslim whom I met by chance at a local UPS. He heard me speak my name to the cashier and came rushing up to clasp my hand and tell me with great feeling how wonderful he found *God in the Qur'an* and how it had brought peace to him and his Christian wife. Later, Kitty and I visited them during the Christmas season and met their charming teenage children. All this as background. The text this morning included this: "Remember that you have a son by the name of _____ who can help you with anything and bring you anything you need if you prefer to stay home these days."

Kitty and I had tears in our eyes. I replied, in part: "I ask your father for permission to be your American father and you my American son. Yes, we do need someone to buy food for us, not now but soon." Two or three further exchanges followed, and we may ask them to help us as soon as tomorrow. My friend's father and older brother live in Europe in a heavily Arab district. As ISIS expanded, the family managed to sell some of their assets and flee, leaving much behind. I'm leaving out many vivid details, Mark, but this is a family that has been to hell and back, and I, with no son, am happy now to have one as American circles downward.

So, yes, and thank you, Friedrich, midnight is also midday.

Jack

*March 17*

Dear Jack:

Once again this morning I find myself thinking about light here on Stone Hill. With the switch to daylight savings time last weekend, the days getting longer, and the sun higher in the sky, you can feel spring approaching. But this year there are no rituals of renewal. I watch the president surrounded by blossoming trees making announcements in the Rose Garden, but this morning when I woke up, I was greeted by snow-covered fields and mountains that seem to portend the long winter that lies ahead.

As this crisis deepens not only with individuals, but also towns, cities, states, and countries quarantined, I continue to struggle with how to help my students deal with this disruption. The question is not only how to teach online, but what to teach. Late last night, I reached a conclusion about how to proceed when classes start again next Monday. Here is the email I sent to my students this morning:

> When last we met, I recalled our first class when I asked, why study the Philosophy of Religion? Why study it now? I repeated my answer: I think it's important to study such demanding writers because the difficult issues they probe bear directly on critical problems everyone must face in life. I also quoted Hegel, who wrote, "Philosophy is its time comprehended in thought." Needless to say, I did not anticipate this pandemic, but I continue to believe in the value of these challenging writings today more than ever. Kierkegaard, commonly regarded as the "father of existentialism," has much to say about the crisis we are facing. In view of this unexpected turn of events, I have decided to defer our discussion of his work so we can read a book by one of his twentieth-century followers—Albert Camus, *The Plague*. I am sure you will find this novel remarkably prescient. Consider, for example, the following passage:
>
>> A pestilence isn't a thing made to man's measure; therefore we tell ourselves that pestilence is a mere bogy of the mind, a bad dream that will pass away. But it doesn't always pass away and, from one bad dream to another, it is men who pass away, and the humanist first of all, because they haven't taken their precautions. Our

townsfolk were not more to blame than others; they forgot to be modest, that was all, and thought that everything was still possible form them; which presupposed that pestilences were impossible. They went on doing business, arranged for journeys, and formed views. How should they have given a thought to anything like the plague, which rules out any future, cancels journeys, silences the exchange of views. They fancied themselves free, and no one will ever be free so long as there are pestilences.

I know it is difficult to think and talk about these issues honestly and openly, but keeping your thoughts to yourself is a strategy of avoidance. Sharing our frustrations, anxieties, and anger can help all of us get through this crisis together.

Mark

*March 17*

Dear Mark:

Well, today is St. Patrick's Day, and the sun is shining beautifully on our orchard, the sky a bright blue but with billowing clouds, constantly changing: an Irish sky. More about Ireland and St. Paddy's later.

My main commitment today, as chairman of the Committee to Bridge the Gap, was chairing our annual board meeting. Daniel Hirsch founded CBG fifty years ago at the time of the Cambodia invasion and the Kent State massacre: students at that time (Dan was at Harvard) were reaching out to their elders, whence the name.

Over the years, CBG has evolved into a nuclear safety watchdog. Today, we reviewed progress on three fronts:

—moving high-level nuclear waste out of storing ponds a hundred yards from the Pacific at the now-decommissioned San Onofre Nuclear Generating Station (forty-five minutes south of our house), putting it in dry casks of solid glass, and moving it across the Pacific Coast Highway and uphill into a different part of the now-closed Pendleton Marine Base. Sea level is rising. No one in his right mind should want this poison underwater.

—halting, until the necessary and costly cleanup takes place, of a huge residential and commercial development planned for the now-closed Hunters Point naval base on the Pacific south of San Francisco. At Hunters Point, ships rendered highly radioactive during atomic bomb tests in the Pacific were sand-blasted clean, but all the thus-removed radiation remains now in the soil. The site is officially a Superfund site, but the developer is the wealthiest in the United States and perfectly willing to use its influence to falsify test results, sidestep environmental impact, and so forth.

—cleaning up the Santa Susana Field Laboratory, a nuclear weapons development site in the Santa Susana Mountains just north of LA. Here, a small nuclear plant actually went into meltdown at one point during the Cold War. At the time, the news was suppressed. More recently, the catastrophic Woolsey Fire, the one that swept through Malibu in 2017, began far east at SSFL, and, of course, carried some unknown degree of radiation with it. Boeing now owns the site but has been a scofflaw regarding its cleanup operations.

We conducted our meeting, which lasted more than ninety minutes, by conference call. Honestly, I think a live meeting of the same length would have been far easier. I was exhausted afterward. A kind of bottom line: realizing that while all press and governmental attention is rightly now focused on the coronavirus, malign interests do not go to sleep but capitalize on the chance to close backroom deals when no one is watching. So, for good reason, expect no major positive action now, but let the bad guys know we are still on their case.

Back to St. Patrick's Day. We had a late (in Galway's day) message from my second cousin Eamonn Cannon, recalling cheerily that he was with us here in Santa Ana a year ago. What a difference a year has made! There's been a lot of fun exchange of messages in the Miles family throughout the day, much of it about either our mother or our Irish grandmother. Mike remembered the time when he asked Mom to read Yeats's "The Fiddler of Dooney" as part of one of his shows, wondering whether she was up to it.

She surprised him by actually memorizing the poem (it ain't short!), delivering it with great aplomb, and then seizing the mic to add a little Irish blessing of her own:

> May those who love us love us,
> And those who don't, may God turn their hearts,
> And if he doesn't turn their hearts, may he turn their ankles
> So we'll know them by the limp.

My contribution was recalling that our Irish grandmother known in youth as Kitty Campbell but in married adulthood as Kate Murphy, believed or half-believed or didn't quite disbelieve in leprechauns. She actually had a small yellowed news clipping that she carried in her purse purporting to be a photograph of a leprechaun. When I was a boy, she showed this to me one time, and—how I'll never know—I lost it. She was disconsolate, but only for a little while. No use crying over a lost leprechaun.

While living through our indefinite lockdown here, Kitty (my Kitty) and I have sweetened the evenings by listening to some music after dinner. Lately, we're working our way through the Mozart piano concertos—first the last, then the first, then the second last, etc., all in a lovely recording by Murray Perahia. And then, after the music, I read a chapter or two, thanks to you, from Niall Williams's wonderfully rhetorical *This Is Happiness*. I did a bit of research, and learned that Williams is sixty years old, same age as Christy in the novel. So, conceivably, this story of a man returning to his ancestral village in search of his lost but now widowed love could be Williams's own story. But he very artfully distances himself from the story by telling it in the voice of a seventy-eight-year-old remembering himself as an alert seventeen-year-old atheist fresh from an expelling seminary and merely *observing* Christy, the sixty-year-old returning prodigal. I relish the cunning of that POV, that narrative tactic.

Last night, in the chapter I was reading, aged Noe says of youthful Noe assessing Christy's romantic quest to win anew his lost love:

> It was too big an idea for me to digest at the time. People's lives were small and everyday, I thought, the last great gestures of heart probably vanishing with Yeats.

Well, I took that stray reference to Yeats and the grand love-gesture as a clue. My favorite Yeats poem is "La Belle Dame Sans Merci":

When you are old and grey and full of sleep
And nodding by the fire, take down this book
And slowly read and dream of the soft look
Your eyes had then and of their shadows deep.
How many loved your moments of glad grace
And loved your beauty with love false or true!
But one man loved the pilgrim soul of you
And loved the sorrows of your changing face.
And bending down beside the glowing bars
Murmur a little softly how love fled
And paced upon the mountains overhead
And hid his face amid a crowd of stars.

I don't actually have many entire poems committed to memory, but I have that one, or close to it. The speaker in the poem knows that he has lost his love. All he really hopes for, even in her old age, is that she will remember him. Christy's scheme, you will recall, is to "accidentally" have Annie Mooney notice him at the communion rail on Easter Sunday. It doesn't work, but ever-observant young Noe observes that Annie has aged beautifully, although—ah, another clue!—there is a shadow of sorrow in her face.

At the moment, of course, what the world is mostly breaking is not my heart but my portfolio. At such a moment, does even Sheldon Adelson want the current Republican crew watching over the American economy? But then how long will Donald be with us? Kitty and I were to have attended a private dinner in my honor hosted by John Maguire's second successor at the Claremont Graduate University. Bob Klitgaard had been head of research at the RAND corporation, and I thought he was nuts to leave that job for the presidency of cash-strapped CGU. I did what I could to gently dissuade him, but he came anyway and then stepped down a few years later. He and I have remained loosely in touch, and he reads what I write. Our planned dinner (mostly about *God in the Qur'an*) is off, another coronavirus casualty, but along the way Bob shared the following calculation with me of the one-in-seven chance that one of our three presidential candidates will die of the coronavirus:

> So, the chance of at least 1 getting the virus and dying is 1–p (not get or get and not die) cubed. So, it's not get = p (0.5) plus (get and not die) = 0.5 x 0.9 = 0.95 cubed, or 0.857.

> 1–0.857 = 0.143 or about 1/7.

> With this simple model, there's a one in seven chance that one of our three presidential candidates will die from this virus.

> One has to think their chances of surviving if they get COVID-19 will be higher, given these people's salience and quality of care.

> Enough!

> Back to grading midterms.

> Your friend,

> Bob

Who knows whether it is this or another surprise that awaits us, but don't you have the sense that, good or bad, "Something's Coming," as in the classic *West Side Story* song? Yes, it could be either of our deaths, or Bernie's or Joe's or Donald's or Mike Pence's, but there are so many, many other surprises that this wildly volatile moment could deliver us.

Jack

* * *

## MARCH 19–24: JACK BEGINS.

*First Zoom dinner . . . reports of hoarding staples and toilet paper . . . fear of martial law . . ."a noose is tightening around us" . . . philosophy of boredom . . . a 1982 basketball game relived in rerun . . . talking philosophy with the coach . . . Kafka,* COVID, *and the climate crisis . . . Wallace Stevens on "the nothing that is not there and the nothing that is" . . . and now, "How then can I be happy?" . . ."the luxury of time" after retirement, even in lockdown.*

---

*March 19*

Dear Mark:

I find myself in agreement with you that "positive feedback networks" operate in a "formally similar way." I certainly see the formal similarity between an enforced pause in the "contagion" of a mass market-selloff and the virtually enforced pause in coronavirus contagion through social distancing. Generically, these actions can all be called regulation. Culturally Confucian societies (China, Korea, Japan) seem vastly more disposed to accept regulation than our culturally Christian or perhaps post-Christian/ Enlightenment societies. In his now-daily press conferences, Trump finds occasion repeatedly to boast that his stellar response to this crisis has taken the form of eliminating crippling Obama-administration regulations. But just now to scorn regulation is to welcome mass death.

Your shaping impulse, Mark, your ambition, is always to *understand* and this always in the most inclusive way possible. I myself instinctively and in advance despair of such undertakings. I chicken out preemptively and gravitate toward narrower and more practical engagements, waxing only as theoretical as absolutely necessary and, wherever possible, invoking art (usually literature) rather than theory.

Last night was a rough night for me. I haven't been able to shake Dan Hirsch's fear that Trump and company will use the coronavirus to stay in office past November 2020 by canceling or delaying sine die the election that might bring Joe Biden and a wave of Democrats into power. As the son of refugees from Nazi Germany, Dan has an almost genetic readiness for the worst, and I've learned to use his forebodings to correct my own complacency. The recent spate of state-delayed primary elections lays the groundwork for more than a little anxiety. I caught Sen. McConnell, with a smile that I found unsettling, asserting that "extraordinary times require extraordinary remedies." They do, and perhaps he had only emergency financial aid in mind, but I could not help but think ahead to this other kind of manipulation.

And that was not all. Last night, I got up to pee at 2:30 a.m. and instead of slipping back to sleep as usual, I began imagining scenarios. Example: Trump announces that the election will be postponed; Gov. Newsom counters that the regulation of elections is the responsibility of the states and that California will conduct its election on schedule. A cascade of blue-state governors follows Gavin's lead, while the red-state governors line up behind the president and postpone their elections indefinitely. Trump remains president in the red states; Biden becomes president in the blue states. And then? From whom does the Pentagon take its orders?

Add to that, in the middle of the night, talk that supermarkets may begin to ration the number of shoppers allowed in at a time. True, this could better guarantee social distancing among them and between them and staff, but there is a step beyond that. Stores may cease normal retail operations altogether, take only online orders, and deliver to vehicles as they arrive. In my nightmarish imagining, this scenario was full of parking lot road rage and ominous chaos. There are reports that the California produce industry lacks guest workers to do the harvesting. Other reports predict disruption to food shipments into New York City, where the coronavirus infection graph already terrifyingly matches that of Italy.

Today, Kitty transferred some funds to Edward and Holly, her son and daughter-in-law in Brooklyn. Edward's work has entirely dried up; Holly's continues but perhaps only for a while. I myself sent money to my friend Hector, newly unemployed, at home in Riverside with his wife, Lupita, who is employed but injured, and their two grown sons, one unemployed, one still working. And these are the luckier cases. Millions, not just thousands, are down to their last dollar. For them, isn't the choice now steal or starve? Given that choice, what would you do? Hoard-shopping may soon give way to desperation shoplifting as the desperate become true desperados. And what about Kitty and me, with our open-gated orchard, full of unguarded ripe fruit? Will we suddenly have uninvited visitors? And once they're through the gate, why stop at just the fruit?

At 3 a.m., I whispered to Kitty, "Are you awake?" She was. I started sharing these imaginations. She minimized them, offered more benign scenarios, finally offered to and did give me a long back rub as we each lay on our sides. In the morning, she remembered the grandfather clock striking 4 a.m. Today has been a good day. She made a batch of chocolate chip cookies. We went for a walk in rain gear, just in case, though it didn't rain. I cooked a rough approximation of arroz con pollo for dinner, and we joined Kathleen and Brian by Zoom as we ate.

Just before dinner, I messaged friends of ours who have just moved to Jackson Hole, to see how they're holding up. Wyoming, as you may know, is one of the states taking no official cognizance at all of the pandemic. My friend messaged that they are well and safely provisioned but that, anyway, there is a run on toilet paper and staples in the local stores, the ski lodges have just closed, all the restaurants are shutting down, and tourism-dependent Jackson Hole is facing an economic Armageddon. One cannot say of COVID-19 that there's no denying it. The denials, alas, are still spread far and wide. But despite them, there is no escaping it. Gov. Newsom said today that 50 percent of California may contract COVID-19. A noose is tightening around us.

You noted, c/o your friend, that today is Philip Roth's birthday and that the dramatization of his *The Plot Against America* is starting tonight on HBO. In that work, in my recollection, Philip had Sinclair Lewis's *It Can't Happen Here* in mind, not that his debt to it is at all large. As for Camus and *La Peste,* he had that in mind as he wrote his last work, *Nemesis,* his only work specifically about a plague. Could polio in the 1950s have been called a pandemic? My vague sense is that the word was not in general usage, but polio existed worldwide, did it not? If Philip were in New York now, he wouldn't be in New York. He would have fled by now to rural Connecticut, where he and I first met and where my memories of him are still most vivid.

Jack

*March 22*

Dear Jack:

The harsh reality of what Michel Foucault, writing of another time and place, aptly labeled "the great confinement" is beginning to sink in. As early reassurances about quick fixes and easy cures are exposed as deceitful lies, people are starting to realize that we are in this mess for the long haul. To make matters worse, the usual diversions—concerts, museums, theaters, sporting events, bars, and restaurants—have been shut down. People are not only indoors, but are also forced to turn inward, where all too often they discover a void. Years of conditioning by the busyness of business and madness of media have left an emptiness they do not know how to fill. When days turn into weeks, and weeks into months, boredom will become overwhelming.

No one has understood boredom better than Kierkegaard. The musings of Heidegger and Roland Barthes do little more than elaborate insights Kierkegaard proposed a century earlier. Spring break is over and I suspect students are already getting bored and will be glad to get back to classes. On Tuesday, we will discuss selections from the first volume of *Either-Or*, which includes an essay entitled "The Rotation Method." This is, to my knowledge, the first philosophical analysis of boredom. Kierkegaard concludes the first paragraph of the essay: "Boredom is the root of all evil. It is very curious that boredom, which itself has such a calm and sedate nature, can have such a capacity to initiate motion. The effect that boredom brings about is absolutely magical, but this effect is not one of attraction but repulsion." His proposal for overcoming boredom is a variation of the agricultural method of crop rotation. Rather than changing the soil, Kierkegaard proposes that one changes what one does or where one does it. "One is weary of living in the country and moves to the city; one is weary of one's native land and goes abroad; one is weary of Europe and goes to America." Kierkegaard's most insightful comments about boredom are focused on the issue of time. What makes boredom so dreadful is what Nietzsche describes as "the eternal return of the same." When tomorrow is just like today, there is no future—or, more precisely, the future is already the past. This unexpected inversion leads to another reversal. As the future becomes the past and thereby erases expectation with repetition, the past becomes the future, which, strangely, must be remembered forward. "The more resourceful one can be in changing the method of cultivation, the better," Kierkegaard writes,

> but every particular change still falls under the universal rule of the relation between *recollecting* and *forgetting*. It is in these two currents that all life moves, and therefore it is a matter of having them properly under one's control. Not until hope has been thrown overboard does one begin to live artistically; as long as a person hopes, he cannot limit himself.

When "hope has been thrown overboard" we return to the past for diversion more than consolation. Boredom empties the present of its meaning and purpose. To fill this void, we attempt to return to the past to remember and relive what was pleasant and forget and repress what was unpleasant.

This week I had expected to be enjoying the national spring ritual of the Final Four. Seeking diversion from growing ennui yesterday, I turned on the TV and started channel surfing. Changing channels or websites is today's equivalent of the rotation method. I discovered that CBS, which usually covers the Final Four, is filling the void in their programming by rebroadcasting past championship games. Yesterday they were replaying the memorable 1982 final between Georgetown, led by a young John Thompson, and North Carolina, coached by the legendary Dean Smith, who, in spite of his Hall of Fame career, had never won a national championship. It was a classic game featuring three players who would later be named among the fifty greatest NBA players of all time—Georgetown's Patrick Ewing and North Carolina's James Worthy and freshman sensation Michael Jordan. The game, like the uniform short shorts, was a throwback to an earlier and slower time—no thirty-second clock, which had been instituted largely as a result of Dean Smith's four-corner offense, and no three-point line. In the opening minutes, Georgetown looked unbeatable, with Ewing blocking five Carolina shots, but by the end of the first half it was a one-point game. With one minute left, there had been fifteen lead changes, when Sleepy Floyd hit a jumper to put Georgetown ahead 62–61. Carolina called a timeout; Worthy had been unstoppable, and Smith, predicting that Georgetown would double team him, told point guard Jimmy

Smith to get the ball to Jordan. As so often over the years, Smith was right—doubling Worthy left Jordan open on the left wing. Black passed him the ball and Jordan hit a jumper with seventeen seconds left. Rather than call a time-out, Georgetown tried to move the ball up court fast, but in his haste guard Fred Brown mistook Worthy for a teammate and passed him the ball. Worthy was fouled, and the future LA Laker hall of famer missed both foul shots. With two seconds left, time ran out and Dean Smith had his first national championship.

Reliving this game was sheer bliss, and precisely the diversion I needed. But a few minutes into the second half my pleasure was interrupted by Breaking News—President Trump and his bobble-head vice president staging what currently passes as a press conference to reassure the country that everything is going well and all will be fine. The effect of this daily ritual is, of course, the opposite of what they intend—the more Trump says everything is under control, the more people believe everything is spinning out of control. Reality TV is no match for the reality of the coronavirus.

As you may recall, one year after Carolina won the championship, I was a fellow at the National Humanities Center, where I wrote the book that changed my career —*Erring: A Postmodern A/Theology*. Our family lived in Chapel Hill, and Aaron and I became avid North Carolina basketball fans. Several years later, when I was trying to persuade colleges and universities to try online courses, the University of North Carolina chancellor, Michael Hooker, who was one of the few people who understood what I was attempting to do, tried very hard to persuade me to move to UNC. Somehow he found out I was a big Tarheel fan and, as part of the recruiting process, arranged an hour-long visit for me to visit with Dean Smith. In North Carolina at that time, Dean Smith was closer to God than Jesus Christ. I was thrilled as I entered his office tucked away in the Dean Dome eager to talk about basketball, but Dean refused. He knew I had written extensively about Kierkegaard, and all he wanted to do was discuss his philosophy. So, for an hour we discussed the intricacies of Kierkegaard's existentialism surrounded by Carolina memorabilia. I suppose it is fitting that the favorite philosopher of one of the greatest college basketball coaches in history (if not the greatest) is Kierkegaard, who is best known for the leap of faith.

Several years later, I taught at UNC for a semester. By that time, Dean had retired from coaching and Bill Guthridge had taken over. Dean, I had learned, was an avid reader of philosophy and theology. He and I reconnected and met every week to discuss Kierkegaard, Paul Tillich, and Reinhold Niebuhr. Throughout the semester he could not have been more generous. He gave me precious tickets to all home games in the chancellors' box and he and his wife invited Dinny and me to dinner my last week in Chapel Hill. I was deeply impressed by how serious he was and by how carefully he read and thought about questions that truly matter. But I was even more impressed by how he put his beliefs into action. Dean was a profoundly religious and moral person, who devoted his life to promoting social justice. When Charlie Scott agreed to play at UNC, Dean integrated the Atlantic Coast Conference and, when local merchants refused to serve his players, he sat with them at lunch counters and refused to leave before they were served. Dean also was an outspoken critic of the death penalty. When Kirsten betrayed her family by attending Duke Law School, she was involved in a death penalty clinic, and wrote an article for the law school newspaper. Dean met with her in his Dean Dome office for an hour to discuss his views for her article.

There are few people I admire more than Dean Smith. His letters, all signed in Carolina blue ink, are among my most valued possessions. Sometimes a game is more than a game, and sometimes the game of life needs leaders like Dean Smith. Wherever he is, I hope Dean and Kierkegaard are discussing the texts I am teaching Tuesday.

Mark


*March 24*

Dear Mark:

A wonderful letter, and a perfect illustration from your own life of at least one of the points you will be teaching from *Either/Or.* You had to forget that fabulous Georgetown-UNC game in order to be able to recollect—relive it—as you did seeing it rerun on TV. And boredom, I'm sure, is the perfect subject for your students to be discussing from their respective confinements. Confinement is not all that constricting, honestly, for people at our age, pleasantly housed, and in good health. But for twenty-year-olds?

I am brought up short, I confess, at the thought of Kierkegaard, the nonpareil phenomenologist of despair and, by and large, its moral scourge, counseling, "Not until hope has been thrown overboard does one begin to live artistically." I take the point easily enough, but then is my "counseling" the right word for what he is doing? Kierkegaard had his reservations about life lived artistically. And he was, of course, the most ironic of all philosophers. How seriously is his "advice" to rotate the crops of the mind really to be taken? My question is not rhetorical: how would you answer it? I think of Horace's famous line, "Caelum mutant, non animum": "They change the sky above but not the mind within." Kierkegaard wouldn't disagree, so—if he *were* truly advising—what would he advise?

His point that one must close off the future—in effect, stop time—to live artistically confirms what I said, quoting Auden, about fiction as "feigned history." A brilliant novel (like *This Is Happiness,* which I am still reading aloud each evening, one or two chapters at a time) can seem oh so real, but then it ends, and the ending—indispensable to the novel as a work of art—is also the point where the feint becomes recognizable as feint. History does not stop, hope cannot actually be thrown overboard, even in the face of death. Both go on whether we will it or no, and both at once escape art and fail as art. This is why, as you pointed out earlier, our diary violates the first rule of writing as you have taught it to your children and your students: it has and will have no outline, and what it speaks of will go on after we stop writing about it.

Honestly, though, I find myself almost as ready to argue against this line of thinking as for it. The classic advice to Christians in the Middle Ages, and well beyond, was "Memento mori." If you live your life as if prepared at any and every moment to have it end, then you have made art and at least one concept of sanctity coincide for you. Yeats wrote, "The intellect of man must choose / Perfection of the life or of the work." But the saint, whose choice is indeed perfection of the life, may still be said to have made an aesthetic choice by virtue of thinking of his *earthly* life as a start-to-finish whole, even while insisting that that earthly life is not to be confused with life as such. One frequently honored form of sanctity was heroic fasting, but Franz Kafka wrote a celebrated short story called "Der

Hungerkunstler" about a man who went, or was taken, from town to town to be exhibited in a kind of tiger cage as he starved himself. The show was a freak show exhibiting how wondrously little one could eat and yet remain alive. Finally, if I recall the ending correctly (and I may be quite confusedly recalling it), the hunger artist dies, and the story ends. The point? As always with Kafka, readers can argue for hours about that, but surely it has something to do with the strange kinship or isomorphism of the disciplines of art and holiness. Shakespeare's *The Tempest*, his last play, is commonly taken also to be a kind of artistic last will and testament, with Prospero, the magisterial magician, standing in for the playwright. At a peak moment, Prospero speaks the famous lines, "We are such stuff as dreams are made on / And our little life is rounded with a sleep." Rounded with a sleep means bounded at either end by the sleep of life before birth and the sleep of life after death. By seeing life as thus bound, one can engage it artistically. Or refuse to do so.

I was interrupted in writing the previous paragraph by the arrival of my Syrian son with our latest food order. When I sent him my latest order, I added this quote, Qur'an 2:110:

Any good deed you do, laid by for your souls in this life,
You shall surely find with God.
God sees full well what you do.

My friend countered with 92:19-20:

Seeking no favor in return,
Only seeking the acceptance of his Lord, the Most High.

When he arrived with the delivery, he had good news: his daughter has been accepted at University of California at Irvine. He thinks she might be eligible for a scholarship but does not know how to begin exploring. I'll see if I can help him, but my niece, Ellen, whose twins are just home from interruptions of their freshman years at, respectively, Iowa and Arizona State, may be able to help too. She's fresh from the same quest.

My rescuer, who says he follows the news only loosely, asked me if it was true that half of the United States might contract the coronavirus. I said that Gov. Newsom has said that half of *California* might contract it; I couldn't cite a comparable estimate for the United States. He then quoted the Qur'an again: "No one can add a day or even a minute to his lifespan. Allah alone decides." I thought of Jesus in Matthew 6:27: "Which of you by thinking can add one cubit unto his stature?" No doubt you've heard by now that Rand Paul has tested positive for COVID-19 and that Angela Merkel, in quarantine herself, has urged Germans to congregate in no group larger than *two* outside the family. Jon Segal, my old friend and my editor at Knopf, decided to join his wife, Haidi, at their home in the South of France rather than remain in New York. There, Haidi, who suffers advanced dementia, has two caretakers who together watch over her 24-7. But when Jon showed up, from plague-ridden New York, the caretakers refused to come any longer to their house out of fear of contagion! We're watching a fire leap from room to room in a burning house.

I fear the worst on several fronts. I fear the breakdown in the supply chain of basic life-needs, not just of the special medical needs that you wrote about in the *Wall Street Journal*. I fear the massive breakdown of hospital care and the death of many of the health care providers. I fear the breakdown of public order. (We hear so much about how hospitals are coping but nothing about how police departments are coping.) I fear, as I've said, that Republicans will attempt (are already attempting) to seek the suppression of the vote if not the actual postponement of the November presidential election. This last subject, nightmare subject, is all over today's *New York Times*. It is the subject of the lead editorial, of a fine piece by Jon Meacham, on elections amid past crises, and of news coverage. I welcome this attention, but the law requiring the election and stipulating the expiration of any presidential term upon election day depends, finally, on respect for the law. A declaration of martial law—in effect, a coup d'état—could suspend enforcement of the election law, among others, while lulling fearful and powerless Americans into accepting perforce that this was, after all, only for their own good.

It may be interesting to hear a range of student responses to *The Plague*. The failure of imagination that Camus describes in the paragraph you quoted—people unable to imagine what by degrees they are actually seeing—makes the point that Amitav Ghosh makes in *The Great Derangement*, and that has always animated my own recoil from visions of a technological millennium, that "we" are ever on the verge of accomplishing. The coronavirus, in that sense, is a foretaste within a time frame that we are all experiencing of the disruption that global warming will deliver within a time frame too slow today for all but an informed minority to grasp not just notionally but also imaginatively. I've been there in my gut ever since I wrote "Global Requiem."

Your long reminiscence about your relationship with UNC, with the Tarheels basketball team, with Dean Smith, with the UNC president, is another example of your defeating boredom by recollection. This story is too much to share with your students, though you could lift your exciting description of that basketball game verbatim, and it would work in class. The longer recollection was interesting for me, however, because I was in and out of your life at the time and certainly remember how close you came to moving there. I seem to recall that one part of the decision was that there was nothing there for Dinny comparable to what she had at Williams.

As for the long haul you mention in your first paragraph, today's *New York Times* has an excellent piece by Nicholas Kristof sketching best and worst cases. What we can be sure about, I believe, is that even if the worst does not happen, even if we have a coronavirus lull in summer sufficient that the four of us are able to visit Ray Hart and Molly on the North Fork, even if the virus does not actually come back more lethal than ever in fall 2020, even if a vaccine is discovered in time for fall 2021, that fall will nonetheless be the first of the thereafter annual coronavirus seasons. This disease is going to be with us for the rest of our lives, and our lives will never be the same.

Jack


*March 24*

Dear Jack:

I once read that Hemingway ended each writing day mid-sentence so that he could pick up his train of thought quickly in morning. I don't know if that's true, but for years I have followed this practice and it has always served me well. I am convinced that many of my ideas emerge and come together while I am sleeping. My best writing time is from 6 to 10 a.m. When I pick up the pencil in the morning—yes, I write the first draft in longhand with a pencil—the words come faster than I can transcribe them. It is as if I am taking dictation from someone I've never met.

But all of that has changed since we have been writing to each other. Every morning I awaken with no idea what I might write until I read your response to yesterday's reflections. As with the comments of any good reader, your remarks always raise new questions and suggest ideas I had not considered. More important, you reveal to me things I had written that I had not realized I had written, and things I knew but did not know I knew.

Your message this morning raises so many issues and questions that I am not sure where to begin: love, the guilt or indebtedness (*Schuld*) that inevitably accompanies receiving a gift, your multiple near-death experiences, agnosticism creating an opening for belief in the afterlife, museums that have lost their way, growing hostility toward Asians, darkness, silence, the indifference of birds and animals to the human panic around them, and beauty, above all beauty. As I write these words three beautiful deer are loping across the field outside my window, oblivious to the growing dread I feel. Pondering all of this, my question is not only how we end, but where I should begin.

On Friday, I wrote to you about an unexpected breath of spring. The temperature soared and the last traces of snow and ice melted. I heard spring peepers for the first time, and in their staccato chirping I thought I heard notes of hope that the darkness eventually would lift. It was not until I received your response the next morning that I realized the day I wrote those words was the first day of spring. I sought solace by doing some work outside and even went so far as to put the snow shovels away in the other side of the barn. I have lived in this North Country long enough to know better, but this year more than most, I needed to believe that spring is arriving early.

That hope now has vanished and the revival spring promises seems distant dream. This morning I awoke to five or six inches of snow. I had to retrieve my snow shovel and begin my day with my familiar predawn ritual of clearing a path from the house to the barn. The snow was heavy; I'm getting too old for such routines. Pausing to catch my breath in the darkness I could see the wet snow clinging to bare branches and the needles of white pine, hemlock, and cedar trees. If it were January, the vista before me

would appear to be a winter wonderland that filled me with contentment, but today it leaves me restless. I recall my favorite poem—Wallace Stevens's "The Snowman." In his words I hear the "Nothing that is not there and the nothing that is." The plague reminds us of this "Nothing" that is always absent yet somehow forever present, reveals that in the end I am, you are, we are nothing but nothing nothing.

But what *is* nothing? The question, of course, erases itself in its very asking because nothing is precisely what *is not*. How can (k)not be undone, how can nothing be apprehended even if not comprehended?

Once again, Kierkegaard is my guide—he was the first philosopher to appreciate the inextricable relation between nothing and dread (*Angst*). In contrast to fear, which always has a determinate object, dread, he argues, is indeterminate; dread is not an object or a thing that can be seen, manipulated, controlled, or mastered. What we truly dread is no thing—no thing: "The nothing that is not there and the nothing that is." Nothing is unnamable; indeed, it is (impossibly) The Unnamable itself. To flee dread, we struggle to turn it into fear by transforming nothing into something—a determinate object we can manage. I fear a mighty foe, a hostile spouse, failure, rejection, loss of a loved one. I do not, however, fear death; rather, I dread the nothingness of death. The diseases I fear are treatable and can be cured; for these diseases diagnosis is a relief, but naming always harbors the unnamable. The diseases I dread are untreatable and incurable; for these diseases diagnosis brings despair. The search for a treatment is the struggle to transform dread into fear.

The plague is the current guise of the Unnamable. What makes the plague so dread-ful is that it is not only incurable, uncontrollable, unmanageable, unmasterable, but is unknowable. Its ways are not our ways, and it lives on our death. Every night on the news we see images of the enemy as a prickly sphere with protruding red triangular structures suggesting that if we can just crack the code or reprogram the cells, we will find a cure and all will be right with the world. However, no matter how accurate they are, these pictures are deceptive; rather than making the invisible visible, they are images of the unimaginable. There is neither treatment nor cure for nothing—even if symptoms are relieved and death is temporarily avoided, the plague does not disappear, but hides within, waiting to resurface another time. Even when it seems to be cured, this plague is only slumbering. Furthermore, in some distant forest, underground sewer, or melting permafrost, the next plague is brewing. Nothing wears infinite masks. The secret of our dread of the plague is its secrecy. Paradoxically, the very invisibility of the plague makes nothing visible. We can't be sure where the plague is or where it is not—it might be nowhere, it might be everywhere. We don't know who has the plague and who does not. My family, my friends, my neighbors, my coworkers might or might not have the plague. Indeed, I might already be sick—sick with a sickness unto death—or I might not, perhaps I have escaped the illness, perhaps I am immune, though this is unlikely for a person like me with a compromised immune system. Even if tests were available, they would not tell us enough; the moment after I am tested, I might suffer contamination without knowing it. The plague exposes the inescapability of our mortal condition: dis-ease, uncertainty, insecurity. That is why we dread it.

Dread is a mood, a disposition, an attunement that colors everything we experience. In the memorable words of Alexander Pope, "Everything is yellow to a jaundiced eye." Moods are not at our disposal; I can no more will myself to be happy than I can will myself out of dread. Moods settle like a mountain mist and lift for reasons we neither control nor understand. As long as the mood lingers, there is nothing we can do. Nothing but wait, wait not for something we can name, wait for something that remains unnamable.

Gazing out my window this morning, I no longer see the subtle green of the budding spring I thought I saw a few days ago; nor do I see the summer orange of your fruit trees with humming birds flitting around them. I see the empty whiteness of a winter that might have no end. All I can do is wait and wait and wait for what I do not know. How, then, can I be happy? Double-check with me tomorrow, but today, with every right, I think I am not.

Mark


*March 24*

Dear Mark:

*Ooomph!* Your final sentence is like a blow to the stomach: it takes my breath away. You are so powerfully engaged with your own thoughts and your own reading and, above all, with your decades-long engagement with the thinkers now memorialized in your sculpture garden that I sometimes wonder whether my lighter-weight thinking really gets through. For example, when you write ". . . in the end, I am, you are, we are nothing but nothing nothing," I know that you have, paradoxically, *something* in mind, and I know that I don't know what it is—or won't know until I spend a long time imagining what I *could* mean if *I* were to write a sentence like that. Still, this letter puts the lie to the thought that I rarely really get through to you. This last time, at least, it's clear that I did get through..

And how do I reply? A first, simple thought: my own long years in the Midwest and Northeast tell me that it is, yes, just around now that winter begins to seem a gray interminability, the perfect visual backdrop for the long wait now in progress for what manner of doom we cannot yet know. At Caltech, the joke was that they always sought to recruit star scientists from the East by inviting them in February or March. But as for what awaits, well, this morning, I received an email message from a friend in Fiesole, above Florence:

The latest news here is that contagions are diminishing and we *may* be past the peak. We will see. Meanwhile, we have to keep social distance when we go to the supermarket, so only a few are allowed in at a time; you have to stand in line for two hours outside, very eerie. You see long lines of people with masks, two meters from one another waiting silently. Also, you have to have a special certificate with you when you go out, detailing where you go and what you do, and you have to stay in your municipality. Reminds me of the military service.

When I was at the Gregorian in the sixties, I learned that Italian military service was universal. No one, even seminarians or priests, was exempt. So, Piero, my correspondent, though not in any case a Catholic, unless nominally, will have served in the military when he was younger. He knows whereof he speaks. Reading him and recalling my own thoughts/fears about imminent martial law in the United States, I wonder whether I should see a clue in his message to what awaits us here.

My poet friend Todd Boss, who has been living a barely believable vagabond life for almost two years now, going from one house-minding gig to another to another all over Europe and the Americas, is now back home in Minneapolis, in a small apartment that he shares with his son, who may now be eighteen or nineteen. Todd writes:

As you know, I've been living out of two suitcases for twenty-one months now. [He stayed briefly with us, and one of the suitcases is a cunningly stuffed backpack.] Sometimes I live artfully, but mostly I just live simply. The world is learning to work from home, but I've been doing that for most of my working life. It's a bit unsettling to watch the world catch on, but it's rewarding to know that once the world tastes freedom from workweek office hours and release from on-ramp-off-ramp hamster-wheeling, they're not going to want to go back. An age of nomadism, independence, and self-reliance waits around the corner from the coronavirus inoculation station, and it's going to mean big things for our creativity, our relationships, and our souls.

In his last sentence, he adds: "If the Great Sequester lasts much longer, I wouldn't be surprised to see sales of pianos on the uptick again."

Frankly, I *would* be surprised, and Todd seems to me to be whistling in the dark here. Yet a colleague of mine at UCI, an art historian, writes that he's delighted to stay home, deliver his lecture into the computer, and spend the rest of the day reading, exercising, and playing his viola. That's a kind of confirmation of Todd's vision. Todd also wrote: "Retirees know this, because the luxury of time is theirs. Now it is everyone's, and the awareness will spread quickly." I have indeed reveled in the luxury of time since my own retirement: the day still has twenty-four hours, but how I divide them is now up to me as never before. The coronavirus peril has, in an odd way, intensified this joy, because whether I write anything ever again seems so inconsequential against the enormity of the plague. Time as the greatest aphrodisiac also receives a fresh intensification as I find myself making love more than ever before in my life, and also loving love itself, loving to love, and this in all directions—love for you and Dinny, for other friends, for family, for new acquaintances like my Syrian savior and his daughter, and more than ever for Kitty.

But as our "check with me tomorrow" exchange underscores, moods are oh so fragile and mobile. My good friend Marilyn Sanders, an accomplished photographer whose work is in various museums, took a pair of pictures of me that I have dubbed *L'allegro* and *Il penseroso* after that famous pair of Milton poems. The first photo is jubilant, exuberant, the second severe, intense. In both, I am standing in front of a church, which is out of camera range, but what one does see is a pillar with, on several sides in several languages, the prayer or pious wish: "Let there be peace, and let it begin with me." During this plague period, however, neither of those extremes is too easily in reach. We live in a middling, cloudy, but nonstop malaise, don't we, punctuated by the drip-drip-drip of the latest notable American to test COVID-positive: again, that tightening of the noose. Senator Klobuchar's husband, President Bacow of Harvard and his wife, sports stars, others. I am braced for my brother Mike to be the first in our family because his life as a performer puts him at such risk, but there is going to be a first in millions of families. The mood may darken terrifyingly as in an eclipse of the sun for those with no knowledge of the solar system.

My copy of Robert Bellah's *Religion in Human Evolution* lies somewhere in a still-unpacked box from my Boston College office. At some early point in it, Bellah mentions the work of a scholar with a German name (Schaefer?), perhaps German American, on consensus-reality (as I'll call it). In effect, the argument advanced is that it is not only history that is the agreed-upon lie. No, reality itself—reality as socially or communally defined—is also an agreed-upon "lie," a shared working assumption. For Joyce, history was famously the nightmare from which he was trying to awake. But social reality is the dream from which, on the whole, no one wants to awake but into which something like climate change or plague can intrude with brutal violence. I've been braced for the climate change intrusion for long enough to have experienced over the years a great deal of our everyday American life as delusional, not excluding a great deal of our scientific life as I have been surrounded by it at an ever-more science-heavy institution like UCI. Bellah, building on the thinker just mentioned, wanted to speak of mysticism as thus a paradoxical awakening rather than a dreaming, as that moment when the steadying and socially necessary illusion drops away temporarily. Connections, surely, to Kierkegaard in that line of thought, not that Søren saw himself as a mystic. Not every religious radical is a mystic.

It's almost 11 p.m. as I write. I know that I, like you, write better in the morning, but my morning routine, set by years of living in California and collaborating with colleagues in New York, has begun with my reading email. Everything that comes to me, much of my daily work assignment, has been written three to nine hours earlier. I live at the western edge of my personal constituency. And I seem to have been conditioned as well by my years on the *Los Angeles Times* editorial board to swallow a large dose of news before beginning my work day. This was not the case before the invention of email, and you will recall how reluctant I was to adopt the once-new, now-antiquated technology. But it has shaped and continues to shape my daily routine start to finish.

Unless we watch *The Rachel Maddow Show*, which lately we have felt compelled to do, Kitty and I dine late and retire early: often before 9:30. On my last visit to you in Williamstown, I was hugely struck by how different a routine you and Dinny follow, repairing from your dining table to spend a couple hours in your den with that startlingly large television screen of yours, you surfing from one station to another, Dinny half-watching with you but also pursuing private agendas on her laptop. Here, we have a TV room with two comfortable swivel armchairs and a screen maybe half as large as yours but quite large enough for our simpler purposes. We are in those chairs only to watch 1) Rachel Maddow, 2) a rare sports event (Kitty easily tags along, to my slight surprise), or 3) a DVD, and of these we have many still unviewed. We stream nothing, though I'm sure we will begin doing so before long. In short, a daily rhythm sharply unlike yours, but as it affects this diary, one shaped also by my desire to see what the day has delivered before writing to you. I can, of course, write immediately on receipt of what you send, and once or twice I have done so: ideas do spring quickly to mind from what I have already on hand. But I want to be reasonably true to the empirical reality of a full day's experience, and so once in a while I find myself staying up late.

I don't follow Hemingway's rule, though it might be fun for me to try it. What I do do, however, not infrequently, is scribble a phrase or two, even a single word, on a blank page before retiring. Tonight, the words are "Grant Park" and "Census" and "Essential Infrastructure." Maybe you'll find out how those words connect tomorrow. Good night, my friend.

Jack

* * *

## MARCH 29–30: MARK BEGINS.

*The human mind: too large to cope with or too small to cope?. . . Augustine on memory . . . The Beatles' "Let It Be" . . . Buddha's detachment vs. Kierkegaard's resignation . . . COVID, Trump, and the decline of journalism . . . Ingmar Bergmann's Seventh Seal vs. Bach's love/death song "Bist du bei mir" . . . a one-time altar boy dreams of Satan celebrating Mass—and leering at him.*

---

*March 29*

Dear Jack:

It is a dark, gloomy day, in the forties, but feels colder, and it is raining hard—doesn't do much to lift one's spirits. Aaron emailed last night that terrible storms tore through Wisconsin and their garage and yard are underwater. I wrote back, Apocalypse Now: plague, flood, locusts are on the way.

I have more to say about the economy, but want to return to several of your comments from the day before yesterday. I did not respond immediately because I was planning to work outside on the lawn and in the gardens yesterday and my experience of physical labor is central to my answer to the questions you raised. I select two points from your characteristically thoughtful and provocative remarks.

What you call the inward turn of the mind is thus primeval, aboriginal. But turning inward, does the mind discover that it is too large to contain itself or, rather, too small to contain itself? Meditation, sleep, and sex are all alike in that somehow one must desire them but not desire them. Paul McCartney sang, "Let it be." One can set the stage, but then somehow, paradoxically, one must let it be and just wait for the show to begin on its own.

First point. No, the mind is not too small to contain itself, it is, I insist, too large to contain itself. Since the interplay between Buddhism and Christianity is so central to our conversation, I will explain my point with an example from each tradition. Keiji Nishitani's *Religion and Nothingness* is one of the most creative efforts to bring central tenets of Zen Buddhism together with the insights of Western philosophers like Hegel, Kierkeg-aard, Nietzsche, and Heidegger. I seem to recall that you were involved with the publication of this book when you were at the University of California Press. In his careful analysis of the structure of self-consciousness, he discovers a lacuna, gap, or blind spot. The mind, he suggests, cannot turn around fast enough to see itself seeing. In his book on the Kyoto school, Robert E. Carter offers a helpful explanation of Nishitani's point.

> To catch the self as objectified is easy, but to catch the self directly, as pure subjectivity, is impossible. Try this experiment: think of your self; now try to catch that which thinks of your self (now as an object of thought); now try to catch a glimpse of the self that just objectified the self. As soon as you try to do so, self becomes objectified—and so on to infinity . . . The self of pure subjectivity is known in a not-knowing: we know it is there, but we simply cannot capture it in ordinary consciousness whose only way of knowing is to objectify things with concepts. The self that we are searching for is not a self in the ordinary sense: it is a self that is not a self.

This gap is the opening through which the mind exceeds itself. Freud calls this opening the "navel" of the dream, which is the point of contact with "the unknowable." Not the unknown, which might yet be known, but the unknowable, which will never be known. Through this opening, the mind overflows and exceeds itself. Blindness always lies at the heart of insight, and, therefore, our self-awareness is forever incomplete. Only by knowing this impossibility of knowing can you enter what Western mystics call "the cloud of unknowing."

From East to West, Buddhism to Christianity. Recall for the moment our discussion of memory, the memory that is lost in the immediate present of dementia. When I suggest that the mind is too large to contain itself, I am thinking about Augustine's magnificent paean to memory in *The Confessions*. I have already discussed his interpretation of the three modalities of the present: the present of things present, the present of things past, and the present of things to come. In words I have never forgotten since I read *The Confession* in my freshman humanities course at Wesleyan, Augustine describes the memory as the "belly of the mind." Searching for God, he turns inward.

How great, my God, is this force of memory, how exceedingly great! It is like a vast and boundless subterranean shrine. Who has ever reached the bottom of it? Yet this is a faculty of my mind and belongs to my nature; nor can I myself grasp all that I am. Therefore, the mind is not large enough to contain itself. But where can that uncontained part of it be?

Memory reveals without revealing the self that is not a self, the self beyond the self, the self that is larger than the self, the self that can never be itself.

Second point. "Let it be." You are right when you point out that several of my previous messages develop insights I first presented in *The Moment of Complexity* and *Confidence Games*. The reason I have done this is that the plague presents a test for the fundamental belief that has always informed my teaching and writing. From my first class to the present day, I have told students and myself that the reason to study demanding writers is that their insights help us to negotiate the difficulties and complexities we inevitably encounter in life. If Hegel, Kierkegaard, Nietzsche, Heidegger, Derrida, and others cannot help now, they are not worth studying, and my life's work has been in vain.

I am not sure if you have read *Abiding Grace: Time, Modernity, Death*. If you have, you might recall that I end the book by rewriting McCarthy's lyrics that you cite.

Mazing Grace
Whisper words of wisdom
There will be no answer
Let it be
Let be, let it be
Let it be.

A little word—"no"—changes everything. You are right, "One can set the stage, but then, somehow, paradoxically, one must let it be and just wait for the show to begin on its own." This is the moment of grace, the moment when one sets aside the self-assertion of fulfilling the law, whatever that law might be, and lets go, lets go of everything. The Buddhists call this detachment, Kierkegaard calls it infinite resignation. Sometimes the only way to hold on is to let go. If you have the courage to let go, a miracle might occur, and you might receive everything back, though all is transformed. Being, you discover, is always being given, and life becomes a gift you have but never possess. In this instant, I do not lose self-consciousness in the immediacy of the present; rather, my self-consciousness expands in the infinity of a past that is never fully present and a future that never fully arrives.

This is the moment I experience as I create the art and tend the gardens here on Stone Hill. I am glad you have visited us here so you can picture where I am sitting as I write. Months ago, we began to plan how we might write to each other about what I am trying to experience and express through this labor. I still have a folder with notes from those conversations. Little did we expect that it would take the plague for us to discover how to proceed. You know that tending my garden is no small challenge. As the seasons change, four of our eight acres need constant attention. My labor becomes a daily ritual whose rhythm attunes me both to the world around and to underground currents within. Yesterday marked a pivotal moment in my personal seasonal calendar. The last ritual of winter and the first ritual of spring—cutting Russian sage and decorative grasses, some of which are 7–8 feet tall. It is a two-person job; Dinny wraps her arms around the grasses, and I use the gas-powered hedge trimmer to cut them. It would be easier to trim these back in the fall, but they are so beautiful when they die and dry that I always leave them standing through the winter. As you can see from the photographs below, yesterday they were more beautiful than ever as their subtle hues stood out against the deep blue sky.

Performing this annual ritual carries me back into the "cavern of my mind," where childhood memories are buried. As a boy growing up in suburban New Jersey, my father taught me the art of gardening, which he had learned from his father on the Gettysburg farm where he was raised. Living in a home without electricity or running water and plowing acres and acres of fields with no mechanized equipment, his labor was more arduous than mine. But he drove me hard and for that I am grateful. I used to cut twenty-five lawns a week with a push mower, and still have the ledger where I recorded every payment ranging from $1.50 to $2.25. In the days before everyone hired professional landscaping services, I

also took care of the gardens for the people whose lawns I mowed. What surprises me is that as I work my land today I repeatedly recall visual details from every single lawn I cut and garden I tended sixty years ago. Not just visual details, but also the smell, sound, and touch of specific shrubs, bushes, rocks. The particular obstacles to avoid in each lawn. There is a materiality, a tactility to memory that eludes yet shapes consciousness. One of my maxims in life is that I never fully trust a person who does not cut his or her own grass. When you do not have dirt under your fingernails, you lose touch with yourself. As I trim and rake, I stay in touch with myself by being transported beyond myself within myself. Once again recall Saint Augustine.

> Here are kept distinct and in their proper classifications all sensations which come to us, each its own route: for instance, light, color, and the shapes of bodies reach us through the eyes; all kinds of sound through the ears; and smells by the nostrils; all tastes by the mouth, and by the sensation of the whole body we derive our impression of what is hard or soft, hot or cold, rough or smooth, heavy or light, whether from outside or inside the body. And the great harbor of memory with its secret, numberless, and indefinable recesses, takes in all these things so that they may be reproduced and brought back again when the need arises. They all enter the memory by their various ways and are stored up in the memory. Or rather it is not the things themselves that enter; what happens is that the images of things perceived are there ready at hand for thought and recall.

The timing of this ritual of cutting the grasses is crucial; if you wait too long, new shoots will not be able to push their way through the dead stalks. This timing seems more important than ever this year.

Mark

*March 30*

Dear Mark:

Staggering to contemplate, as it must seem to us, the coronavirus seems to be redounding to the electoral advantage of President Trump. Among the reasons for this, I strongly suspect, is the collapse of American journalism because of the rise of the Internet. Craigslist deprived journalism of a crucial element in the business plan of every newspaper—namely, classified advertising. The fatal mistake that newspaper publishers made and then could not unmake—giving away digitally what they were still trying to sell physically—eroded circulation. The demand of investors for immediate and large (15 percent) return on investment from ownership of a mature product, at a time when they were willing to lose money for years on plausibly lucrative startups still in their youth or adolescence, cut further into economic viability. The result is that fewer than half as many reporters are gathering news as were a generation ago, thousands of papers have folded, and the information have-nots have become the core of the Trump constituency, not to gainsay the importance of fanatic Evangelicalism. Half of America simply does not realize and may never admit that the one or two hundred thousand American coronavirus dead—twice to four times the loss of life in the Vietnam War—that even the relatively cautious Anthony Fauci predicted today would be drastically fewer if Trump were not president now, and if Republicans had not been politically dominant and violently opposed to public health care. Perhaps, perhaps (but this will never happen) if Bernie Sanders were to close his campaign and call on the Democrats and, crucially, the media to give Biden, as the Democratic presidential nominee, the same daily platform that they give Trump, treating Trump's every statement as part of an election campaign and thus Biden's every statement as of equal interest to the public, then the election might become winnable again for the Democrats. For the moment, I am in a slough of despond. America as we have known it may simply be a casualty of this plague.

On our one acre, Kitty is the gardener, out there for most of most days. The weather has been only intermittently rainy, but the ground is still quite moist from earlier rain. It's a perfect time to plant and a perfect time to weed. She has planted potatoes, tomatoes, zucchini, eggplant, artichoke, and green beans. Because the garden is rather far from the house but near the street, she is also making the acquaintance of neighbors out strolling now more than ever, and it's been inspiriting. Since the plague has left me more heavily in charge of our provisioning than she, I am also now doing more cooking than she. She puts in time in the kitchen, but she has become a kind of sous-chef. Before we married but while I was already in part-time residence here in her house, it was a wonderful treat for me to have someone cooking for me, but I don't mind cooking at all, and I am getting especially good at coaxing as many meals as possible out of each preparation.

This afternoon, after launching a huge pot of hambone soup and with two hours of simmer to go, I went for a long up-and-downhill walk, meeting many, many more fellow walkers (and cyclists and skateboarders) than ever before. As I walked, I was thinking about your philosophy sculpture garden. You don't seem any longer to refer to it routinely by the title "Nexus"; do you still think of it under that name, or is it now more namelessly just *there*? In any case, as I walked, I thought how appropriate the German noun *Denkmal* might be for your ensemble. That German noun is a frozen imperative: "Think (for) once!" The suffix *-mal* means "once," as in *einmal, zweimal, dreimal, und so weiter*. Our *monument* carries some of the same connotation but only etymologically and so less audibly and more vaguely. The *mon-* morpheme at the beginning is "warn," so a monument is a warn-thing; cf. *admonitory* and such words. Thus was I musing as I walked along, and a further connection was to the thought of monuments to the anticipated American plague dead. Will there be any to these thousands of the fallen? As has lately been pointed out somewhere in the press, monuments to the World War I dead are everywhere in our country, yet the flu pandemic that followed the war and took many times more lives is nowhere memorialized except in history books.

As for the epistemology of self-knowledge, Mark, I rather think we are more in agreement than in disagreement. I say the mind is too small to contain itself. You disagree, but in support of your position you quote Augustine to me: "Therefore, the mind is not large enough to contain itself." Too small versus not large enough—there is something a little tail-chasing about this kind of discussion. The problem, I believe, is that we are speaking metaphorically of a universal experience, and size may not be the ideal metaphor. I have read Keiji Nishitani's *Religion and Nothingness*, and, yes, it was I who sponsored it for publication at the University of California Press, and for a reason I am about to explain I ended up reading it more closely than many a book that I saw into print at that press. In the passage you quote, Robert E. Carter captures just beautifully the thrust of the book. (You make me want to read *his* book.) And yet Nishitani would *never* write a paragraph as direct and clear as Carter's. Nothing could be less Japanese, at least less traditionally Japanese.

Jan van Bragt, who translated *Religion and Nothingness*, was a Catholic priest, brother, or seminarian (I cannot now remember which), a long-term missionary in the modern acculturating way, and it appeared to me that Nishitani's relationship to Western thinkers arrived, at least logistically or institutionally, in close company with the institutional presence of Christianity in Japan, perhaps especially in Nagoya. The translation itself, most unusually, arrived in California with an unusual young man as its escort. The fellow was very serious, very gifted linguistically, a native speaker of English but very Nipponized in manner who immediately began picking up local Mexican Spanish. As we were sending the work out to our never-skipped University of California Press step of copyediting, this very polite, very deferential young man alerted me earnestly that Nishitani had a circular mode of exposition that had to be respected. It was the Japanese way never to come directly to the point, he explained, but rather to circle around the point as if in a multisided conversation whose goal was to end with everyone in agreement without anyone's ever conceding a point to anyone else. Rather than give-and-take, this was a kind of patient, mutual give-and-give. Fascinating, but, to our copyeditor, utterly maddening. The marked-up manuscript was something to behold. You could see the copyeditor's blood gradually coming to a boil. First, his clarifications were quite modest, offered in the usual way with a marginal query like "Au. perhaps more clearly _____?" But they grew bolder and bolder: whole sentences appeared, then sentences with exclamation points, until in frustration the man was crossing out entire paragraphs, and at the very end he simply threw up his hands and quit! We paid him a kind of kill fee and started over with somebody else, though I don't really recall quite how the process ended.

In any case, Carter's way of employing the word "self" to illustrate the infinite recursion that is a part, potentially, of all human thought is graceful and effective. English, I'm told, is particularly explicit in its grammatical readiness to write, successively, *This is a sentence;* "*This is a sentence* is a sentence;" ' "*This is a sentence* is a sentence" IS A SENTENCE,' " ad infinitum. I never quite finished Michael Corballis's *The Recursive Mind: The Origins of Human Thought, Language, and Civilization*, but possibly I lost interest because the same point was being made with reference to one theater or period of human endeavor after another. Here, my point is that, as between you and me, I don't think there is any significant difference regarding the experience—only about the most apt language to characterize the experience.

Thanks for the photos. They have a bracing, Nordic look about them, a sense of snow only recently gone. But I wonder about that designation "Russian Sage." Is this grass-like plant an alien? Is it invasive? It looks, especially in that lovely photo from below, with the sky behind it, a bit like our lovely but horrendously invasive "Pampas Grass." Here's a link to Pampas Grass by its botanical name:

https://www.cal-ipc.org/plants/profile/cortaderia-selloana-profile/.

I planted some on a patch of ground near the trailer when I lived in Malibu and loved its ornamental effect. Later, I felt guilty because its lovely plume is just all seed, and those seeds blow far and wide. In University Hills, my University of California at Irvine residence was next door to a gay couple who had a stand of Pampas Grass, and they let me harvest a bouquet of the tall stalks for placement in a high narrow vase in my living room. They were pristine for the better part of a year and suited the room beautifully.

As you may recall, I was engaged by some parts of *Abiding Grace* but fought with other parts. I certainly do recall your concluding "correction" of Paul McCartney, though. Mother Mary did not come to you with the deleted *A-* or the inserted *no*, but these are certainly the words of your wisdom, your embrace of mortalism with the comfort it does provide of closure. Any claim that there is no answer is, of course, an answer, but such is the paradox. My friend Peter Heinegg, an atheist ex-Jesuit, calls mortalism the "open secret" of modern life. The anthology that expresses his faith-commitment is his *Mortalism: Readings on the Meaning of Life* (Prometheus Press). Peter was at Harvard when we were, just a bit ahead of us, and his field was comp lit. He is enormously, just *enormously* well read in the classics of French, German, Italian, Spanish, Russian, and to some degree Hebrew. In adulthood, he discovered that one of his grandfathers was Jewish. His wife, Rosie, is half-Jewish. She told me once that before teaching, e.g., *Faust* at Union College, from which he is now retired, Peter would always reread the work in its entirety in the original. His favorite philosopher, I

believe, is Schopenhauer, and he has assembled one enormous work—a
kind of anthology with commentary—called *Absurdism*. I'd like to help him
publish it, if possible. It would be his last work, for his health is failing. But
I'm not really sure that *Absurdism* is complete even now.

Time for me to get started on dinner. When I started my reply to you, a
phone call came from Hector Torres. Hector had already thanked me in a
very heartfelt voicemail message in Spanish for helping him and his family
out with my "relief" check. I didn't feel the need to call back, but that was a
very un-Mexican reaction. They find us cold, and I can see why. Hector's
way, and among Mexicans and other Latins he is not unique in this, is to
tell you that he loves you and then tell you again, and then, today, read me
two of his poems about love: one to his wife, about how he only loves her
the more as she ages; one to God, about how grateful he is to God for sending her to him. The poems, both of which speak of love too deep for words,
were delivered today as illustrations of how his love for me and Kitty is also
too deep for words. All this in Spanish, and I made my replies in Spanish,
but in the presence of such demonstrations, honestly, I would be tongue-
tied even in English—although, belatedly, not so much with Kitty. To gush
thus is just not our way, is it? A Cuban girlfriend, years ago in Chicago,
said to me once, "Te falta cariño." Which means "You lack affectionate-
ness," but their word *cariño* is really a word for something that doesn't quite
exist in our culture, and I wouldn't call this lack a hidden strength. Sweet,
though, even if awkward to be on the receiving end this afternoon of Hector's call, and I'd have been sending another check before too long in any
event.

Jack


*March 30*

Dear Jack:

As I watch videos of New York City, where I am supposed to be right
now, I am struck not only by the empty streets, but even more by the
silence. New York is always so busy, bustling, and noisy. Now there is only
silence, punctuated all too often by screeching ambulance sirens.

I have been thinking quite a bit about silence in the past few years. In our world of 24-7 news, iPhones, and earbuds, silence has become ever so rare. It often seems as if people are afraid of listening to the sounds of silence. Perhaps they dread hearing nothing. Silence, of course, is not one, but many; it can be social, political, psychological, and religious. Furthermore, it can be the mark of repression or resistance, bondage or freedom. Kierkegaard says silence can be either divine or demonic. The silence of the prison cell is not the same as the silence of the monk's cell. Never before have we heard the silence that is falling upon the streets where we have always roamed freely.

These are some of the thoughts I explore in *Seeing Silence*, which will be published soon. Last semester I taught a graduate seminar that grew out of that course entitled simply "Silence." I began the class with Ingmar Bergman's film *The Seventh Seal* (1957). Like everything else, Bergman's film looks different now than it did just a few months ago, and I would write that chapter and teach that class otherwise than I did. With the events cascading around us, words have failed me and I have found myself returning to the lessons *The Seventh Seal* teaches. No artist has developed a more extended and more profound meditation on silence than Bergman. The silence of the cosmos. The silence separating friends, family, and strangers. Above all, the silence of God. Other than Camus's *The Plague*, I know of no work of art that offers a more profound commentary on what we are going through than *The Seventh Seal*. It is worth rewatching the film and recalling its lessons.

As you know, the title of the film is from the eighth chapter of the Apocalypse of Saint John.

> Now when the Lamb broke the seventh seal, there was silence in heaven for what seemed like half an hour. Then I looked, and the seven angels that stand in the presence of God were given seven trumpets.
>
> Then another angel came and stood at the altar, holding a golden censer; and he was given a great quantity of incense to offer with the prayers of all God's people upon the golden altar in front of the throne. And from the angel's hand the smoke of the incense went up before God with the prayers of his people. Then the angel took the censer,

filled it from the altar fire, and threw it down upon the earth; and there wear peals of thunder, lightning, and an earthquake. (8:1–5)

The plague accompanied by thunderous silence is our earthquake.

Bergman's film was inspired by El Greco's painting "Vision of St. John" (1608–1614) and is set in Denmark during the Black Plague. His tale begins ominously with a raven, harbinger of death, soaring in an overcast sky. A knight, Antonius Block, and his squire, Jons, are resting on the beach, while returning to Denmark after spending ten years on a crusade to the Holy Land. The knight rises, washes his face in the sea, and turns to see what appears to be a monk dressed in a black cape, who claims to be death. When Death tells Antonius that he has come for him and grants no reprieves, the knight challenges him to a game of chess. The wager is that death will be delayed as long as the game continues—if the knight wins, he will be allowed to live. Predictably, Death draws black and the game begins.

El Greco, *The Vision of St. John*, CCØ

As the knight and his squire continue on their long journey home, they encounter countless "evil omens"—a corpse with no eyes, horses eating horses, open graves, an execution ground where mercenaries are burning alive a young girl accused of being a witch. The one ray of apparent hope is a family, Mia (Mary), Jof (Joseph), and their baby, Mikael, who are members of a traveling troupe heading to Elsinore, the home of Hamlet's castle, to perform on the church steps. Jof is something of a clown who has visions all the others ridicule. He wakens Mia to tell her he has seen the Virgin Mary and the baby Jesus. Jof is the only person who can see Death playing chess with Antonius; everyone else assumes he is playing against himself, which, in a certain sense, he is. Throughout the film, the troupe stages a farce revealing human folly against the tragic backdrop of the looming Apocalypse.

While the squire had given up faith long ago, the knight is a tormented soul suspended between belief and unbelief. Looking for a place to rest, they stumble upon a country church where an artist is painting an elaborate fresco of The Dance of Death. As the knight kneels before the altar, "pictures of the saints look down on him with stony eyes. Christ's face is turned upward, His mouth open in a cry of anguish." Bergman's Christ cannot move beyond the thirteenth station on the Via Dolorosa. Wracked by doubt and despair, Antonius turns to the confessional, where Death has secretly replaced the priest.

> Knight: Why can't I kill God within me? Why does He live on in this painful and humiliating way even though I curse Him and want to tear him out of my heart? Why, in spite of everything, is He a baffling reality that I cannot shake off?... No one can live in the face of death, knowing that all is nothingness.

The only relief from the darkness and gloom of the journey is when the knight and his squire meet the "holy family" and share a refreshing bowl of wild strawberries. But even in this moment of light, doubt clouds the knight's vision. He confesses to Mia, "Faith is a torment, did you know that? It is like loving someone who is out there in the darkness but never appears, no matter how loudly you call." Every call for help, or even for love, is met with silence.

Searching for protection from the dangers lurking in the dark forest ahead, Mia, Jof, and their baby join the motley crew the knight has gathered along the way. While pausing to rest, the knight and Death once again take up their game, and Death quickly checkmates the knight. After winning the bet, Death allows the knight and his companions to proceed to their destination, where they discover that everyone except Antonius's wife, Karin, has fled the castle.

After an awkward reunion Karin prepares the travelers' last supper. As they are breaking bread and drinking wine together, Karin reads from the Apocalypse.

> Karin: "And when the Lamb broke the seventh seal, there was silence in heaven for about the space of half an hour. And I saw seven angels which stood before God; and to them were given seven trumpets. And another . . ."

> Three mighty knocks sound on the large portal. Karin interrupts her reading and looks up from the book. Jons rises quickly and goes to open the door.

> Karin: "The first angel sounded, and there followed hail and fire mingled with blood, and they were cast upon the earth; and the third part of the trees was burnt up and all the green grass burnt away.

> Now the rain becomes quiet. There is suddenly an immense, frightening silence in the large, murky room where the burning torches throw uneasy shadows over the ceiling and the walls. Everyone listens tensely to the stillness.

Death enters and stares at the group until the knight breaks the silence. "From our darkness, we call out to Thee, Lord. Have mercy upon us because we are small, frightened and ignorant." But once again, there is no answer. Death, swinging his scythe, leads the pilgrims in his dance across the horizon and beyond into the gathering storm clouds in the sky.

Watching this film again today, it is hard not to think that, for us, this is the hour of God's silence. As corpses pile up in makeshift morgues and reporters on the nightly news issue the daily death count as they did when we first met each other in 1968, the earth is turning into a vast wasteland from which there is no exit. Our cries for help go unanswered. Will we or our loved ones join the Dance of Death? Is this brief interlude but a temporary reprieve? We know this ends with checkmate, and black always wins. The silence that surrounds us portends the silence that surely awaits us—perhaps now sooner rather than later. Once again and forever after Death whispers "I have nothing to tell."

Mark


*March 30*

Dear Mark:

Two plague-flavored incidents so far today.

First, we were visited by a masked and gloved technician from Valley Alarm to reassemble the security equipment damaged in our little household mishap last week and to reestablish electronic contact with the alarm center, the contact that, as we learned, was also somehow bollixed up by my attempt to put things back together. I wore a mask, too, but no gloves. We did not have to sign any bill or hand over a check. The bill will be handled electronically. Afterward, we disinfected the doorknobs, the alarm control box, the closet door knobs, etc. A very pleasant, thoughtful technician, who immediately noticed a couple Japanese works in our living room. (He is a collector, he says, having started with objects his father brought home after World War II.) It is as if the world around us, whatever its good intentions, has grown poisonous.

Second, I had my first medical consultation by Zoom. It was my annual appointment with my urologist. I have only moderate BPH but because of a history of prostatitis, I take Flomax. I also take Cialis, which he put me on when it became prescribable and affordable because its *other* effect is to retard BPH. And I've been on it long enough now that it does seem plausibly to have had that retarding effect, though you can't really measure what *hasn't* happened. So, I needed that prescription renewed, and now it will be renewed, but this was our annual appointment anyway, and he is quite responsible and reviewed my medical history in 2019 with me conscientiously. When we finished up, we spoke briefly about his situation. "I'm worried about making a living," he said. There are some things that can be handled by Zoom, but obviously all the more lucrative things cannot be. He mentioned postponing one prostate surgery. He mentioned payroll and "office assets," which besides rent surely must include the costly and probably rented equipment he has, testing equipment of a sort that I'm sure you have had direct experience of. My dentist, who is super high-tech and outstanding in every other way, is clearly in the same situation: his practice initially dropped 50 percent, he told me. He has a large clientele in upscale Newport Beach, and surely he can bear the loss for a while, but for how long a while?

In this latest letter, you embody your earlier point that when the future is closed off or radically foreshortened, the mind looks "forward" to the past. Before concluding, I will offer a comment or two on Bergman's *The Seventh Seal* and will share one remarkable related experience. But I do observe that you are looking backward to your first viewing of it, backward to your past teaching of it, and backward to your experience writing *Seeing Silence*, which, though the actual publication is current, is a part of your writing past—your memory of yourself as a writer.

Besides the questions that *The Seventh Seal* raises as a work of art, it raises for me the question of what work of art most commends itself in the thick of a plague. For me, it isn't a film but (no surprise, perhaps) a work of music or, more accurately, a work within a work. For Christmas one year, J. S. Bach gave his wife, Anna Magdalena, the gift of *A Little Musical Notebook*. One of the works in this not actually so little compilation is the aria, usually sung by a contralto, "*Bist du bei mir*":

> *Bist du bei mir,*
> *geh' ich mit Freude*
> *Zum Sterben und zu meiner Ruh,'*
> *Zum Sterben und zu meiner Ruh.'*
> *Ach, wie vergnügt,*
> *wär' so mein Ende,*
> *Es drückten deine lieben Hände*
> *Mir die getreuen Augen zu,*
> *Es drückten deine lieben Hände*
> *Mir die getreuen Augen zu.*

This short poem, in which God is not mentioned, is anonymous. Bach immortalized it by setting it to music, but he did not write it. For long, the assumption was that the reference in the opening line, "If you are with me," was to God. Later, the rather obvious countersuggestion was made that it could refer to the recipient, Anna Magdalena, younger than Johann Sebastian, and to his fond hope that she might be with him as he lay dying, and that hers would be the beloved hands that would close his faithful eyes for the last time.

I heard this aria for the first time, sung in German by Marilyn Horne, in March 1978, on Bach's birthday. I was living at the time in Philip Roth's Manhattan apartment, which had a minuscule galley kitchen; an ample study; a tiny, ascetic bedroom with only a double bed; and a lordly, salon-like living room with tall windows looking out on 83th Street between Madison and Fifth. The apartment was on a moderately high first floor, but still that salon had direct sunlight only for moments in each day. New York's classical music station chose to end the day's Bach programming with this aria at about 5:30 p.m. The day had been gray and drizzly, and the salon had never seemed more empty. The charms of New York are endless, as you know, but loneliness there is brutally intensified when the possibilities to escape it seem so endless but all also seem closed to oneself..

I love "Bist du bei mir" both as poetry and as music but somewhere down there in third or fourth place, I also love it for what it demonstrates about German as a language—namely, that German can be surpassingly tender and delicately simple, qualities that almost no one in Anglophonia ascribes to it. As you know, the German word for "enough" is *genug,* and the German prefix *ver-* is an intensifier, as in a word like *verloren* or Heidegger's famous *verworfen.* The same Germanic prefix lives in English in a word like "forlorn." These two linguistic components combine in the passive participle *vergnügt,* which is barely translatable into English and certainly not in just one word. The connotation is, "How it would be *enough and more than enough* if it should happen that yours were the hands," etc. In Germany, when you're going out for a night on the town, friends say to you, "Viel Vergnügen." Literally, this is something like, "Much satisfaction," but the context implies simply fun or delight. So can there be some semblance of delight in dying—spiritual delight, a last delight in love, even if there is pain as well. I am not so sanguine as to imagine that this is possible in every case, but one can wish for it, or pray for it. Kitty and I again attended the virtual service at Grace Episcopal Church in Newton last

Sunday, and the rector, Rev. Regina Walton, quoted what she said is venerable advice among spiritual directors: "Pray as you can, not as you can't." In the section "Secular Jews Confront the Tradition" within *The Norton Anthology of World Religions*, David Biale included Yehuda Amichai's "Gods Change, Prayers Are Here to Stay." It's quite a long poem, but the title stanza reads as follows (in translation):

> Tombstones crumble, they say, words tumble, words fade away,
> the tongues that spoke them turn to dust,
> the languages die as people do,
> some languages rise again,
> gods change up in heaven, gods get replaced,
> prayers are here to stay.

It is in that sense, at least, that Bach's "Bist du bei mir" is here to stay for me. It spoke to me one way as a lonely single man in New York yearning for love. And then along came Kitty. Though I had had "Bist du bei mir" played in an instrumental arrangement at my first wedding, I knew no one would remember that detail but me, and so I had it sung at my second wedding (this time by a soprano) with my translation added in the pew booklet:

> If thou art but with me,
> I go with joy
> to death and to my rest,
> to death and to my rest.
> Ah, how content,
> were so my ending,
> that thy dear hands
> should close my faithful eyes,
> that thy dear hands
> should close my faithful eyes.

The best I could do, but my own English certainly does not move me as the original German does. If she survives me, Kitty will be everything for me that Sebastian (as he was called) hoped Anna Magdalena, or God, would be for him. But as she and I approach the ninth anniversary of our romance, the fifth of our marriage, I now confront the faint possibility that, after all, I may survive her. Kurt Vonnegut, who might make good reading because he was always more wry than solemn, pops into my head, thanks to the memorable "So it goes" in his *Slaughterhouse-Five*. I wouldn't mind seeing a Vonnegut revival around now.

Two modest comments now about *The Seventh Seal*. It's been many years since I saw it, but your review of it and a little refresher I gave myself through Wikipedia made me think, first, that Bergman was drawing rather more on *Everyman* than on Revelations (Apocalypse). Like *Everyman*, *The Seventh Seal* is an allegory in which death is personified. Everyman bargains with Death in the morality play, and the bargain moves through a set of episodes that bear at least rough comparison to the episodic set in *The Seventh Seal*. Second, the knight and his sour but not unkind page or sidekick do put one in mind, don't they, of Don Quixote and Sancho Panza. Overall, and these easily conceded "inputs" aside, *The Seventh Seal* isn't *mainly* about silence: it's *mainly* about death. Surely that is what brought it into your mind, however apt you may find it for treatment under the "silence" heading.

To these two little observations, I might add one further. It's about our word *surd*, which most often has a mathematical reference—namely, an irrational number. But the word derives from the Latin *surdus, a, um* which means, alternately, either deaf or dumb. Death that can hear nothing from Antonius and tell us nothing at the end of Antonius's life is surd in that sense—deaf *and* dumb, taking nothing in, sending nothing out. Have you ever dealt with a highly educated person in humiliating physical distress, wired up in a hospital bed somewhere, catheterized, intubated, or whatever, and heard him say, "This is ridiculous"? A *ridiculum* is a small laughable thing, but in such a situation, such a person might also better cry, "This is absurd." It is indeed absurd. It tells you nothing, so, pal, take a hint: *infer nothing from it*. Something like that is what I say to myself, trying to be as blunt as I can be. If you say you know about death, Miles, and you know only what science knows, then you know it only as the deprivation of life, and, first, science on its own material terms has by no means achieved a satisfactory understanding of life—this must remain beyond reach until there is a satisfactory understanding of matter; and, second, science's own terms do not escape the limits of human intelligence, which terms do not escape the fact that the human being is an evolved animal, whose intelligence

has evolved, like that of all other animals, to a niche within which its intelligence works but beyond which it does not. Beyond that niche, who knows?
Humans certainly don't. How could they? They wouldn't then be human.
And you, Miles, in particular, don't know because you know even what science knows only via popularizations for the layman—a bare step beyond
hearsay. That's belief, Miles, not knowledge. So, face it: you know *nothing*
about death.

Finally, here comes my shocking little personal story, which is triggered
by the film's episode in which Death, as cunning and deceitful as Satan,
masquerades as a priest hearing the knight's confession. Mine is not a story
out of the Catholic confessional but rather a story out of the pre-Conciliar,
Tridentine Catholic Mass, the Mass of my long-lost altar boy years. Back
when Catholic priests celebrated Mass with their backs to the congregation,
they all had facing them at the center of the altar, at eye level above the altar
table, a small mirror that enabled them to look down the center aisle. This
little mirror was there to facilitate certain kinds of liturgical coordination,
coordination with processions up that center aisle, for example. Kneeling
on the bottom step of the altar podium, an altar boy could see the gleam of
that little mirror, but nothing reflected in it was directed at his eye: it was
directed at the priest's. Often, at an early weekday Mass in a winter month,
there would be no one or just a handful of people back in the pews. Then,
the mirror served no purpose at all; it was just inertly there.

Well, during the 1975-1976 academic year, when I was a fellow with the
University of Chicago's Committee on the Conceptual Foundations of Science, I lived in a Hyde Park boardinghouse with quite a cast of characters.
One was a slight, blonde, German American woman named Angela, as in
Angela Merkel. She pronounced her name *an-jell-uh* in the American way
rather than explain endlessly to people that the name was German and to
be pronounced with a hard *g*. Her family had immigrated early in the
twentieth century and preserved bitter memories of vilification during
World War I. Angela and I had a brief affair, and one night after we made
love and were asleep in my bed, she woke me up because, she said, I was
tossing and turning and moaning in so troubled a way. The cause was the
dream I was then having. In it, I was a drowsy altar boy on that bottom
step, paying little attention to the Latin drone coming from the priest,
until one moment when I chanced to look up, my eye caught that little

mirror, and I found the priest's gaze was turned directly and intensely upon me. But was he really a priest? The face that I actually saw, from the man fully robed for Mass, was the leering face of the devil—the crimson-and-black, maliciously smiling, cunningly omniscient face of evil personified, an evil demon apparently omniscient in particular about *me:* I myself had the demon's full, horrible attention.

What to make of this dream? Well, a thousand things could be made of it, and I'm not about to enumerate them. Suffice it to say that that night I was visited by a personification of every grievance I had ever had against the Roman Catholic Church, every darkest suspicion that I had ever entertained about it, every objection that I had been bold enough to raise against it, along perhaps with all that I had ever suppressed. I have had a good few intense dreams in my life, but this one was by far the most intense. I am grateful to Angela for waking me up. I wouldn't have wanted to miss it.

Jack

\* \* \*

## APRIL 3: MARK BEGINS.

*Losing touch . . . grandchildren lost in screens . . . disappearance of the real . . .
COVID cultivating suspicion and distrust . . . parents discovering unknown lives of
their children . . . hitting pause . . . distance creates closeness . . . Billy Joel, "Just the
Way You Are" . . . photographic memory archives . . . [anti-] social distancing . . .
existential trauma . . . whose modernity are we living?*

---

*April 3*

Dear Jack:

I was afraid I ran on too long and overburdened you yesterday. I'll be
briefer today, perhaps because I'm irritated and agitated. Every morning a
new concern—today I am worried that we, we in our family, are losing
touch.

Since Jackson and Taylor were born, every morning Kirsten has sent us
a photograph of them. Dinny has saved all of these images and is compiling
them to create what is, in effect, an open-ended "baby" book. It is fascinating to look back over the pictures and to see how they have developed;
daily images allow you to see subtle changes you would not otherwise
notice. While I usually enjoy the photographs and look forward to their
arrival, I have found the last two she sent disturbing.

Taylor, who is almost four, is absorbed in the computer screen with her
little finger above the mouse pad poised for action. Jackson is staring at the
computer screen, which displays a grid with the faces of all his classmates.
He is in kindergarten and this is his first day of online class. His teacher is
easing the kids into this new world by starting with a social hour like their
parents' burgeoning virtual cocktail parties.

Jackson and Taylor are accustomed to screens. Almost every evening
since they were infants, we have FaceTimed with them. They converse with
us easily, reporting on their day, showing us what they are reading or drawing, and sometimes even playing games with us. Since the quarantine, they
have not been able to play with their friends, not even the ones they know

best in the neighborhood. Desperate for human "contact" Kirsten and
other mothers have started scheduling virtual play dates. Scheduled play
dates have always seemed oxymoronic; they are symptomatic of lives that
are too busy and overstructured. When play is scheduled rather than spon-
taneous, it is no longer play.

I know Selma, Elsa, and millions of other kids spend hours staring into
screens on computers, iPads, and phones, but somehow I feel it's different
for Taylor and Jackson because they are so young. How many generations
have never known life without the Internet, or life without iPads and
iPhones? This is the first generation that has been completely cut off from
all *real* contact with anyone other than members of their immediate family. What will the long-term effect of this lack of physical contact be for
children who are so young? The other evening Taylor said, "We can't play
with our friends because of the virus?" What does she understand by that?
What is she thinking?

I remember an AT&T ad a few years ago before the arrival of the
iPhones. The tag line was "Reach out and touch someone." That's what
everyone is trying to do now, but, of course, virtual touching is not really
touching. In fact, we are all losing touch. We no longer shake hands or
embrace friends, we are afraid to tap someone gently on the shoulder,
sometimes we even hesitate to kiss those we love. Touch is even more
important for children than for adults. Physicians and child development

psychologists have been telling us for years how important physical contact is for infants and children. What had long been encouraged is now discouraged as everyone keeps his and her distance. There is a paradox here—social distancing is not social, but is actually is antisocial. What will be the long-term impact of what children are going through now? Will they lose touch not only with others, but even with themselves?

When I was writing *Speed Limits*, I read countless books on the negative impact of digital technologies on children and young people. Screens, we were told, create a sense of isolation that can warp the personality and lead to increased anxiety. Responsible parents were constantly warned to limit screen time. Now everything is reversed—what had long been discouraged is encouraged. When kids get bored or are driving their parents crazy, they are encouraged to get in touch with their friends—virtually, of course.

Losing touch, I suspect, is going to change social relations for children for a long time. The other day, Jackson asked me, "Morfar, why is sharing caring?" I asked him where he had heard that, and he responded that his teacher at school had taught it to them. Should I tell him that his teacher is wrong or at least that she is no longer right? In our post-plague world, sharing is no longer caring; to the contrary, caring is not sharing—not sharing your cup, your book, your bike, your toys—not sharing anything but, rather, keeping everything to yourself. Having learned that survival depends on standing apart, how will children ever learn to stand together?

Living under the rules of confinement is scrambling the interplay of closeness and distance. Kirsten is discovering that she had been losing touch with Taylor and Jackson. Dropping them off before 9 and picking them up after 5, they were in school more than at home, and were spending more time with their teachers than with her and Jonathan. Being out of touch with others is allowing her to get back in touch with her kids. In her diary, Kirsten confesses that she is discovering things about Taylor and Jackson that she had never known:

Stages of life are interesting as you think about when they develop traits that will make them who they are. Some, of course, will change. But some will be with them forever. What I knew about my daughter has been reinforced and amplified, while at the same time I feel I have discovered more. She is, first and foremost, silly, funny and perhaps even mischievous. I have heard her laugh in ways that our normal schedule didn't allow. She wants to have fun and to provoke, to laugh and be loved. It is driving me crazy a little bit because she keeps, for example, throwing anything she can get her hands on the floor. She looks you in the eye and drops whatever it is (a bag of markers, the TV remote, her water, her brother if she could) on the floor and dares you to respond. When I do, her dismissive nature of whatever the consequence is (no dessert! no TV! nothing!) is maddening. But I love her for it. She loves to sing, which I hadn't fully appreciated. And dance, which I knew, but not enough.

Sometimes you can only see what is closest to you from a distance. Kirsten continues,

> Last night a neighbor and I had a socially distanced happy hour. Lawn chairs out in our driveway, as kids popped in and out at different times. My neighbor knows my kids and sees them frequently. Taylor was asking and asking if her daughter Ellie, who is several years older, would come out to play. They hadn't yet, so Taylor ran off to do something. My neighbor noted how Taylor was a doer—she wanted something, she did it (at that moment she had gone to get a chair for herself), which reminded her of her own daughter. As Taylor came back, Ellie paused and looked at her in a new way. I don't know this to be true, but I think in that moment she noted something about Taylor's beauty. I saw it. I am her mom, so of course my eyes are only capable of seeing beauty. But I do believe Taylor to be beautiful. My neighbor looked at her, paused to consider her, and then made a comment that was to some effect— "Oh, this one is going to be interesting." I know why she said that; because she saw in Taylor both a beauty and a will that will make our lives complicated in years to come. But I appreciated it, and will always appreciate Taylor.

If they had not been sitting side by side talking to each other, would her neighbor have seen what Kirsten thought she saw, and would she have been able to see Taylor in a new way?

In the rush of our daily lives, I don't think Kirsten ever would have taken the time to tell me that story if we were sitting face-to-face. Indeed, she might not have realized what she was seeing in Taylor had she not written down her thoughts. I find that often the pace and distance of writing allow me to express thoughts and feelings that the presence of speech prohibits—like much of what I am writing to you. I miss Kirsten and Aaron and wish we could be near each other during this difficult time. But we remain close, and just as Kirsten is learning new things about Taylor and Jackson, so her writing is teaching me new things about her.

Sometimes distance unexpectedly creates closeness, and you have to lose touch to get in touch. Isn't it strange that living three thousand miles apart we are closer now than we were when you were living upstairs from Dinny and me on Gorham Street?

Mark

*April 3*

Dear Mark:

The saying that your letter first brings to mind is "Distance lends enchantment." But like all such sayings, it applies when it applies and doesn't when it doesn't. I'm sure that Kirsten is right about her neighbor's having *seen* Taylor as she would not have without the odd help of social distancing. But then Kirsten herself is seeing Taylor in new ways because of unwonted daily closeness. Closeness and intimacy are virtually synonymous, but closeness can either enable all kinds of wonderful unplanned noticing or induce a kind of invisibility. Billy Joel's wonderful song "Just the Way You Are" fondly chides his lover that she must not ever think that he "[doesn't] see [her] anymore."

Men can worry about their appearance just as women can, but our culture demands so much more in that regard from women, bases so much upon appearance, that it hurts a woman more than a man, I think, to sense that she is no longer seen, no longer really looked at. There's an old saying that a man should have his eyes wide open before marriage and half-shut afterward, but, hey, that's just another proverb that applies when it applies and doesn't when it doesn't.

About our own closeness and distance, it's certainly true that we've grown closer over the years. Our first friendship, on Gorham Street in Cambridge, was welcome and laid a kind of foundation, and we stayed pretty regularly in touch through your first years at Williams and mine at Loyola, then Montana, and then New York. After my move to California, though, my sense is that we drifted apart for some number of years. Still, there is one moment that stands out in my mind, though I can't pin it down chronologically. My sense is that for a few years I had stopped attending the annual meeting of the American Academy of Religion and the Society of Biblical Literature, regarding myself effectively as an ex-academic. But then one year I did show up. Somewhere in the meeting hotel, an escalator carried you up to the mezzanine level (let's say) just as I was about to head down. You were surprised—"Jack!"—and spontaneously wrapped me in a big hug right there at the exit point from the escalator: people had to walk around us for a few moments. We had hugged before at one point or another, I'm sure, but this seemed different. This hug seemed to say, "I've missed you." I was surprised but privately touched and quite pleased as well, and the moment has stayed with me.

So, perhaps there's something to be said for alternation, as in "Absence makes the heart grow fonder." Visiting an art gallery, don't you sometimes move in, then move back out, then further out maybe, then back in again. Or look away and then look back. Or even walk away and then walk back. When I was living in Philip's apartment, just a half block from the Met, I could view a painting of an afternoon, then go home, and go back the next day to view it again. I did this several times with works of medieval art that you never see in textbooks—below the masterpiece level but still good enough for display and for making some particular connection with me. When I wrote to you about your speaking at John Chandler's memorial service, I was noting the utility at a moment when many people will be speaking from the heart— speaking from close-up, so to speak— to have one speaker who speaks from further back and looks at the life-outline that can only really be seen from sufficiently far back.

Today, from inside your family, you are "irritated and agitated . . . worried that we are losing touch," but you are not worried that you personally are losing touch so much as that your grandchildren are. The daily photograph is actually a remarkable testimonial to your daughter's attachment to you and her mother, and the attachment that Dinny and you have to your grandchildren. But your own personality was shaped by plenty of physical contact in your early years, when it mattered so much. It's them that you're worried about. Today, David Brooks invites his readers to write to him about their mental health—the contact and support that they're enjoying or not—during this period of (as you call it and he is thinking about it) "antisocial distancing." I wrote him today about the enviable situation Kitty and I find ourselves in and how supported we have been by family and friends. I didn't want to write at too great length, but I could have said something about our plague diary, on the one hand, which is a big plus and about Kitty's continuing fear (mine, too) about the sanity and solvency of her son and daughter-in-law locked down as they are in their tiny apartment in Brooklyn, neither of them able to work from home: a big minus. Your irritation and agitation, as expressed in this letter, are vicarious for Taylor and Jackson but intensely personal where your diabetes support is concerned. Two distinct lines of concern, both worth sharing.

A retrospective comment, before I close, on your previous letter and specifically its reference to Hegel, a great German thinker—and indeed intensely, self-consciously German. Your reference to him makes me think of Germany itself and of my German editor there, Tobias Heyl. I've thought of writing Tobias just to see how he's doing, how this common threat may be differently experienced over there. What large lessons, if any, is a thoughtful German inclined to draw, there in a country which seems to have mounted against the coronavirus threat both an impressive degree of prosocial solidarity and an appropriate and timely application of large-scale medical science. Somewhere is there perhaps a pair of older Germans like you and me writing letters that link this crisis to modernity? And, by the way, how does China, how does Korea, define modernity, or does the word have much purchase there at all? My former student Tae-Kyung (Timothy Elijah) Sung has been leading the online learning division of California Baptist University since graduation—happy, of course, to have a steady job (he has a wife and two lively young sons plus an adopted daughter to support) but chagrined not to be in the live classroom, where he excels. Now, however, Tae must be the man of the hour at his university, his experience suddenly of life-saving importance. Tae was born in Seoul, brought to the United States at the age of three but still with many family contacts in Seoul. How does he contextualize and conceptualize this cultural moment? He and his family might be safer, might they not, if his parents had not sacrificed everything to come here? I wonder. . . .

Jack

\* \* \*

## APRIL 5: MARK BEGINS.

*Country music a possible bridge within the red/blue "partisan pandemic"?. . . Garth Brooks . . . Dolly Parton . . . the Enlightenment on trial . . . Trump and resentment of "elites" . . . red Okie vs. blue Okie (Merle Haggard from Muskogee vs. Woodie Guthrie from Okemah).*

---

*April 5*

Dear Jack:

This morning is the first time since we started writing that there is no message from you waiting for me. Needless to say, your silence fills me with foreboding. I've just emailed you to check if everything is OK. Add to this news of the first people I know personally who have contracted the virus (more about that tomorrow), and the furnace in the barn not working and my day is not off to a good start. Our rhythm has been interrupted and I really hope it's only temporary. I've been pondering what to do for a couple of hours, and decided that I will still write to you anyway. To cope with my worry, I'll send along some lighter reflections.

When it comes to music, you go high, I go low. As Garth Brooks croons, "I've got friends in low places." Where art is concerned, I see, but I cannot hear; it's always been that way. When in junior high school I joined the chorus and tried to play the trombone, but it just didn't take, so I retreated to the baseball diamond, basketball court, and football field, where I felt totally at home. During the sixties, it was folk music as much as rock and roll that captured my imagination. That was partly because of the close relationship between folk music and political causes like civil rights, and protest against the war in Vietnam. What would those protests have been without white guys and girls like Bob Dylan, Joan Baez, Judy Collins, Pete Seeger, Peter Paul and Mary, the Incredible String Band, and the Turtles, yes, the always-forgotten Turtles. Somewhere in the recesses of my memory, I seem to recall that you are one of the few who remembers and appreciates the Turtles. Listen to "Eve of Destruction" again; it could be an ode to our present moment.

When the folk wave faded, country music took its place, and with this development, the politics of protest music changed from left to right. Ken Burns's marvelous PBS series does a fine job of tracing the roots of country music. While many early country artists were influenced by blues and jazz, in its most recent incarnation, country music is almost exclusively white and, in many places, is undeniably redneck. While sensitive to these problems, I nonetheless must confess that something in that music resonates somewhere in my soul. Not quite Mozart, Brahms, or Bach, but it's about the best I can do.

A couple of nights ago, Garth Brooks and his wife, Trisha Yearwood, gave a free concert live on CBS. In class on Wednesday, I told the students to be sure not to miss the concert. Much to my surprise and dismay, not a single student had ever heard of Garth Brooks or Trisha Yearwood. Brooks is one of the most spectacular performers in any genre. If you've not seen his concert in the Notre Dame football stadium, find it on YouTube. It might even make a symphony-loving former Jesuit take country music seriously. Wednesday night's performance was totally different from stadium spectaculars. Garth and Trisha were alone in a tiny home studio playing acoustic guitars with no backup or amplification. They took live call-in requests and, as always, I was absolutely astonished by their ability to recall the lyrics of songs they had not sung for years, some of which had even been sung by other performers. Though all the songs were great, the most poignant for me at this moment in our personal and shared lives was "If Tomorrow Never Comes." How many survivors are asking with Garth, "Will she know how much I loved her?" Since death comes like a thief in the night even when it is expected, every word might be the last word, and every deed the last deed.

This morning Jon Meacham was on *Morning Joe*, where he is a regular contributor. Meacham is a distinguished historian and journalist who now lives in Nashville, where he is a presidential historian teaching at Vanderbilt University. While I was running the Institute for Religion, Culture, and Public Life at Columbia, I invited him to give a talk shortly after *Thomas Jefferson: The Art of Power* was published. I found him in person like I find him on TV—he is stuffy, but not arrogant, and rarely tells me something I didn't already know. A few years ago, he published a book with Tim McGraw—*Songs of America: Patriotism, Protest, and the Music That Made a*

*Nation.* McGraw, as you may know, is married to the country superstar Faith Hill; they are the first couple of Nashville. Like Garth and Trisha, Tim and Faith are trying to help people cope with the lockdown by tele-casting mini-concerts from their home. I have not read Meacham and McGraw's book because I assumed it would be more the chest-thumping, flag-waving patriotism of Toby Keith than the mournful ballads of Garth Brooks. After what Meacham had to say this morning, I might have to revise my thinking.

Conflicting responses to the coronavirus, Meacham claimed, have "put the Enlightenment on trial." This is a struggle between those who believe in reason and science and those who do not believe in them. This conflict represents a political divide between red and blue states. He proceeded to argue that this is a "partisan pandemic." He's right; when you look at the map of the spread of the virus it is surprising to see how the worst areas are currently in blue states, while in many red states there are many fewer cases so far. National polls consistently show that Trump supporters are much less likely to believe the pandemic is real, and are much more likely to agree with Fox News and right-wing talk radio that the threat is fake news or even a Democratic plot to overthrow Trump. But this is slowly, far too slowly, beginning to change as the plague inevitably spreads from the coasts to the heartland.

Meacham was not all doom and gloom this morning; he said that the best news he has heard in quite a while was Dolly Parton's recent announce-ment on NBC's Today Show that she is donating $1 million to Vanderbilt University to advance COVID-19 research. If Tim and Faith are the first couple of Music City, Dolly has long been the Queen of Nashville. Though I have never seen a poll on the political preference of country music fans, I am sure the vast majority of country people support Trump. I am also sure that Trump has never listened to country music, and couldn't find a coun-try station on the radio if his life depended on it. Dolly's generous gift is not only important for medical research, but is even more important for the way it might help to encourage people who have been believing in fake news to take the threat we all are facing seriously. For many of her devoted fans, if Dolly says it's true, it must be true.

The vote for Trump in 2016 was, in large part, a protest against coastal elites by people who felt their own interests and needs had been overlooked far too long. Though it's a caricature, caricatures often are partially true. Many of the people who support Trump drive pick-ups with gun racks and listen to country music on the radio. This music is their protest anthem. What if, through their music, Garth, Trisha, Tim, Faith, and Dolly can marshal a protest to this protest? While it's too much to dream of flipping right to left, maybe we can hope for a shift from far right to somewhere in between.

I am nervously awaiting your response.

Mark


*April 5*

Dear Mark:

I hope you get the heat back up. In early April in the Berkshires, you still need it. I mentioned that we have an exterminator coming the day after tomorrow. Actually, the complex set of systems that is an upper-middle-class American home calls for periodic maintenance and is prey to unpredictable breakdowns. I've been hoping hard that our place holds together while we're in the closest of seclusion through the next crucial weeks.

About Meacham's "partisan pandemic," in a way his using that phrase is a good example of his making a point that scarcely needed making—not for you, anyway. The *New York Times* has run several striking maps showing, along different parameters, how the blue and red states have adjusted, or not, to meet the galloping danger. On the one hand, the coastal areas, first, and the major urban areas, second, have had predictably heavier traffic from abroad and may, in the final tally, actually suffer a higher proportionate death toll than more inland or rural areas. But the opposite outcome seems just as likely or even likelier. Florida, in particular, may be on the eve of a real holocaust. But landlocked Wyoming, which has also been super-slow to acknowledge any threat or take any protective action, is interesting on those maps. Western Wyoming, full of tourist attractions along the Grand Tetons (think Jackson Hole), has as many cases proportionately as San Francisco. Eastern Wyoming, wide open country that few visit, has few cases. But the contagion can so easily spread through the whole state and across its borders either way. If states like Wyoming that have made minimal preparation suffer even heavier loss of life than Washington, New York, and California, will that bring some kind of change of heart? Will it work the way the Depression and World War II did to end the era of Harding, Coolidge, and Hoover and usher in the era of Roosevelt, Truman, Eisenhower, Kennedy, and Johnson?

If the pandemic has "put the Enlightenment on trial," it has only really done so in the reddest of red states, wouldn't you agree? Or would you? If catastrophic loss of life across the South and up through Mountain States to Idaho and Montana should incline the publics there to believe the scientists even if that means believing the despised liberals and trusting the scorned mainstream press, then the plague will have led the United States—set aside Gaia for the moment—to a crucially adaptive change. Kitty flagged a comment of Rush Limbaugh's for me recently. Limbaugh speaks of "four pillars of deception": science, academe, government, and the media. Will he and the rest of the right-wing apparatus of misinformation lose their credibility and their constituency in an agonizing reappraisal (to steal a phrase from decades ago) in the wake of a coronavirus massacre? The culture that now places hatred of liberals and intellectuals in a controlling position, a position that determines all other positions, will be very difficult to discharge, but mass agony could, I suppose, just possibly achieve the near-impossible. You've just had the first infection in your circle of acquaintances. I hung up the phone after a conversation with Pratap Pal earlier this week as he and I had both just agreed that we knew of no case so close. Within the next five minutes, Kitty told me that a case has turned up among the congregants at Messiah Church. Eventually, experiences like these, around the country, may become as common as, it seems, they already are in New York.

At that moment, could country music help? My son-in-law, Brian Formo, as Kitty and I learned on their last visit to the house, is both a fan and an admirer of Dolly Parton. After their visit, I bought a Parton greatest hits CD and the DVD of the comic classic *Nine to Five* with Dolly, Jane Fonda, and Lily Tomlin, which he warmly recommended. Dolly wrote a title song to accompany the film, in which, by the way, she shows herself quite a competent actress. The song was nominated for an Oscar but lost out to something not nearly as good. I've heard some other country music over the years, and it scores with me once in a great while, but, honestly, not often. I wouldn't be surprised, though, if a close look at Parton's entire output found nothing that could be called redneck in any political sense. Partly, I would guess, she has wanted to keep her brand above politics for sheer sales reasons, but if the full story could be known and she chose to speak her mind and damn the sales consequences, she might turn out to be a kind of East Tennessee-West Virginia Roosevelt Democrat. Her philanthropies are certainly compatible with that.

The one country song that really does reach me, every time, is Parton's "I Will Always Love You." I think I first knew it in Whitney Houston's soaring version—what a voice Houston had! She could almost have been an opera singer. Parton's is a much smaller voice, but in her original version (on my new CD) she used it well and did not allow it to be overwhelmed by orchestration. She kept everything simple, and the song works, if in another way.

I first began listening to country music during my year in Montana, where it was inescapable. Most of the time, I was eager to escape it, especially as it came nonstop through the wall of the duplex I was living in, but there were two or three times when it delighted me with its way of setting subjects to music that other kinds of popular music never touched. I recall one song, several stanzas long, with this as its refrain:

> If one woman could be both lover and wife,
> What a wonderful world this would be,
> And there could be love somewhere between lust
> And sittin' home watchin' TV.

How can you not chuckle at that? And the verses were similarly realistic and wry; in one, the man asks his wife, "Ain't I always nice to your kid sister? / Don't I take her dancin' ever' night?" There was another one in a similar sardonic vein, by a different singer, whose refrain was "I hope the man who has his finger on the button has a happy day." Same strength: a real subject but one that seems alive only in this corner of popular music, certainly only alive here in that sardonic vein.

The subject of nuclear destruction brings me to your including the Turtles on your short list of important protest singers. One thing about me and American popular music is that I heard almost none of it between the summer of 1960 and the summer of 1967. I've now checked, and the

Turtles' "Eve of Destruction" landed during this blackout period in my listening. During the first four of those years, I was immured in Milford Novitiate, where we seminarians had no access to radio or television. (The one exception made was allowing us to watch the Washington funeral procession for JFK.) During the last three years, I was in Europe and Israel, where American popular music did penetrate but only in unpredictable ways. In my room in Rome, I had a little transistor radio. It took forever to warm up, and one day it took so long that I had forgotten about it when suddenly it began playing, from the very first words, Bob Dylan's "Like a Rolling Stone." I was bowled over, riveted, deeply stirred. What was going on back home? Something was happening, and you didn't know what it was, did you, Signor Miles? My trip across the Atlantic had been on the *Queen Mary*, and there was a little lounge on the big liner for people in steerage where I heard the Beatles' "She Loves You" for the first time. It didn't make even a small fraction of the impact that Dylan's "Like a Rolling Stone" made, though later I came to love the Beatles, whose range certainly exceeds Dylan's, even if in certain of his grooves he is, as Jack Nicholson (of all people) once said in introducing him, "transcendent."

Could a wave of singers in the country idiom actually midwife a sea change in red-state popular opinion, building somehow on or through the coronavirus? If so, people like Garth Brooks will have to do more than take requests at a benefit for renditions of their repertory. They'll have to break new ground, won't they? Though I have now heard via YouTube the love song whose lyrics you quote, and though I have heard Brooks before and know that he is a country superstar, that song just doesn't speak my "language of love" the way that, say, Billy Joel does in his "Just the Way You Are." But as for a major social change springing from the coronavirus and country music in some kind of tandem, I do note in your closing line that your hopes are guarded—nothing big enough to be called a sea change: "While it's too much to dream of flipping right to left, maybe we can hope for a shift from far right to somewhere in between." Well, maybe. Merle Haggard was an "Okie from Muskogee," but you know who else was from Oklahoma? Woodie Guthrie! Woodie was about as far left as Bernie Sanders, and my brother sings his songs without bowdlerizing them of their radical stanzas.

So, again, maybe. This moment is surely likely to give birth to other surprises than the ghastly health surprise. You mention a couple singers below the Parton or Brooks level whom I've never heard of: Toby Keith, Tim McGraw. One of them? Or somebody now unknown and unimagined who can surprise and disturb the South the way Dylan surprised and disturbed me fifty years ago in my little garret room in Rome. An Italian word comes to mind: *Magari!* It's an expletive meaning something like "devoutly to be wished," but subtract the devotion first.

Jack

*  *  *

## APRIL 7: MARK BEGINS.

*The beauty of the Taconic Range at dawn . . . reading Williams's* This Is Happiness *aloud . . . teaching Kierkegaard's "The Unhappiest Man" . . . shared loneliness as a paradoxical bond: "dying alone together" . . . Church of the Holy Sepulchre closed for first time since the Black Death . . . New York's St. John the Divine turned into a* COVID *clinic . . . Reformation religious individualism vs. Catholic hierarchical communalism then and now . . . Berggruen Institute and "Letter to the Governments of the G20 Nations" . . .* COVID *crisis today, climate crisis tomorrow . . . ambition vs. realism in high school (music and sports) . . . envy and Shakespeare: "When in disgrace with fortune and men's eyes" . . . the saving kindness of a stranger.*

---

*April 7*

Dear Jack:

As I write this morning, it is not yet dawn. The large window I look through as I sit at my desk faces due west. On the evening of the summer solstice, the sun sets directly across the valley. As I begin my letter to you today, the dark sky is crystal clear and the moon is about to set behind the Taconic Range. As the moon descends, it gets larger and it is now huge. If you watch intently, you can actually see the moon appear to move as it slips out of vision. Just now there is a small cloud above the mountaintop, and the moon is shining through it to create the lavender color I so love and have only ever seen in the Renoir painting that hangs in the Clark Art Institute at the other end of Stone Hill.

I was interested to hear that you have talked with Georges Borchardt and shared your concerns about publishing. Indeed, I have three books at various stages of the publication process and have been dealing with and thinking about the implications of the plague for the publishing industry. I had thought of writing to you about these concerns this morning, but, after reading your letter yesterday, decided to defer those thoughts until tomorrow.

I was taken by your response, especially your continuing reflections on Williams's *This Is Happiness*. I am utterly delighted that you and Kitty are enjoying the book so much. Dinny and I have never read out loud to each other, and, in all honesty, I find it hard to imagine doing that with anyone. However, I understand why you do it—sharing thoughts about books creates the opportunity to talk about your personal concerns indirectly, through the words of others. I was drawn to the book for several reasons—my romanticized view of Ireland, my attraction to rural life, but most of all because of the question of happiness. Perhaps life's most profound question is: What is happiness? As I have told you more than once, I think what has drawn me to Kierkegaard from the first time I read his work is his exploration of the depths of what Hegel calls "unhappy consciousness." Last week I taught the first volume of *Either-Or*, which includes an essay entitled "The Unhappiest Man." What is happiness for the unhappiest man? I suspect the reason this question haunts me lies deeply buried in my past. Somewhere I have written, "The greatest gift and greatest curse my mother bequeathed me was her profound sense of melancholy." I wonder if my mother was ever truly happy.

My reason for suggesting that you read the book was rather simple—it is beautifully written and it is very Irish. You and Kitty are responding in ways I did not anticipate and I look forward to hearing more. As always, your letter goes straight to the essential point in what you are reading. You quote Noe at a turning point: "The only moment in my life so far when I was at one with other men, when the profound loneliness I lived in had been assuaged by the communal." How rare that moment is. How few times in life our profound loneliness is assuaged by the communal. The plague is now the gravity bearing down on us; can we lean to the pole together and defeat gravity? And might the dirt we find on our hands be as close to the real as we can come in this life?

As I ponder your reflections, a question that has long puzzled me returns in a new way. What is the relationship between profound loneliness and the experience of being truly at one with other people? This question quickly bleeds into another: Is profound loneliness the bond that joins us together? And what does this have to do with death? It is a cliché to say that we all die alone, but, as usual, what passes for common wisdom is too simple. A more faithful representation of our human condition would be to say that we all die alone *together*. The abiding question that today becomes urgent is whether confronting death—not just individual death, but mass death,

perhaps even human extinction—will drive us apart in separation and isolation, or bring us together in connection and solidarity. Whether or not the
human race has a future depends on how this question is answered.

Timely meditations for Holy Week in the era of the plague. Late last
night, I read in a release from the Catholic News Agency (surprised I stumbled on that, aren't you) that the Church of the Holy Sepulcher in Jerusalem
has been closed indefinitely. Unlike you, who have spent a considerable
amount of time in Israel, I've never been to Jerusalem. With Good Friday
and Easter later this week, this is a particularly difficult time for people to
be cut off from this church. While I have never believed that this is the site
of Golgotha or of the tomb where Jesus was supposedly buried and resur-
rected, I realize that it is a very important ritual site for millions of Christians from many traditions. It is also the location of the last four Stations of
the Cross. When you read *Seeing Silence*, you will see that I have structured
the fourteen chapters on the traditional Via Dolorosa.

The last time the Church of the Holy Sepulcher was closed because of
disease was during the outbreak of the Black Death in 1349. Then, as now,
the plague originated in Asia and spread along one of the major transportation routes at the time—the Silk Road. While the reports of deaths we
hear every day are difficult to comprehend—today 10,943 in the United
States, 1,349,904 worldwide—these numbers pale when compared to the
number of people who died during the Black Death. From 75 to 200 million people died in Eurasia; Europe's population declined between 30 and
60 percent. It took more than 200 years for the population of Europe to
return to its previous level. My mathematical ability is not up to calculating what the corresponding figures would be today, but you get the point.

Yesterday as I prepared to teach Kierkegaard's *Fear and Trembling*, I had
been thinking about the fourteenth-century plague before I heard of the
closing of the Church of the Holy Sepulcher. You, the erstwhile Catholic,
are teaching me, the erstwhile Protestant, something new about a book
I've studied and taught my entire adult life. Kierkegaard, more than anyone else in the Western tradition, is *the* philosopher of the singular individual. His vision is profoundly Protestant and his interpretation of the
individual can be traced directly to Martin Luther's reformation of
the Catholic Church. As you know better than I, during the High Middle
Ages, a person's salvation depended on his or her participation in the

Church universal through the sacraments. This doctrine of redemption was the source of the Church's religious authority, as well as its worldly economic and political power. As a result of his personal experience, Luther rejected this understanding of salvation and insisted that every person has an individual relationship to God. Salvation, in other words, is not mediated by a centralized and hierarchical church, but is a function of an individual's private relationship to a transcendent God. In today's economic and financial terms, Luther cut out the middlemen—pope, cardinals, and priests—and disintermediated the church, thereby privatizing, decentralizing and deregulating religion. For this reason, among others, I think modernity actually begins with Luther.

While we have discussed some of these issues over the years, suffering through the plague together casts them in a different light. Confined to our houses and separated by three thousand miles, you, Kitty, Dinny, and I are alone together. I have always thought that Luther's individualism is inseparable from the social, economic, and political changes brought by the Black Death. Now I am wondering if our plague will change the insidious individualism, selfishness, and narcissism that are destroying the earth and threatening mass death.

The centralized and hierarchical structure of the Catholic Church both mirrored and was mirrored by the centralized and hierarchical structure of feudalism. Serfs and their families were bound to manors, where they served their earthly lord as they served their heavenly lord in church. When the plague ravaged the population, the labor force was devastated, and the feudal structure broke down. Individuals were freed from lord and land and a competitive market for labor emerged. While multiple circumstances always play a role in historical events of this magnitude, the devastation of the northern European population by the plague was a major factor in the rise of Western individualism. Will history repeat itself?

Everywhere you turn today, people are, understandably, looking for a silver lining in this dark cloud. I have to confess that I am sick and tired of all the feel-good Hallmark moments of incessant newscasts reporting on people coming together in time of need—singing together from their balconies in Italy, pounding pots and pans together from their apartments in New York City, lining city streets nightly to cheer doctors, medical personnel, and first responders. I do not doubt the good intentions of desperate people or those reporting about them, but I do doubt specious optimism that diverts attention from the hard work that lies ahead. For every act of cooperation and support, there is an exploitative scheme or scam. Selling much-needed face masks for exorbitant prices on Amazon or on the black market, channeling medical supplies to more profitable markets in foreign countries, marketing drugs promising phony cures. The worst scam I've heard about is setting up fake testing sites and charging people for unauthorized and ineffective tests for the virus. Incomprehensible though it seems, the eighty-two-year-old secretary of commerce Wilbur Ross had the audacity to declare that history (as if he knew anything about history) is, in fact, repeating itself. Mass death in China, he suggested, might decimate their workforce, and thereby create a competitive advantage for U.S. companies. Where is the sense of the common good in all of this?

The most intriguing argument about impending mass death I've heard points in a very different direction by suggesting that more than anything else the plague might actually draw people together to confront the true existential crisis for the human race—climate change. You will recall that the other day I wrote to you proposing that the plague is nature's revenge for the devastation modern man has inflicted upon the environment. What if this mortal threat turned out to be an opportunity? This argument turns on the possibility of experiencing the confrontation with death completely differently from Kierkegaard and his existential follower Heidegger proposed. Pushing Kierkegaard's individualism to the breaking point, Heidegger insists that a person cannot become an authentic individual without facing death *alone*. Only by contemplating what will not be when you are not do you realize what you really now are as a unique individual.

Contrary to expectation, globalization has not only brought us together both as individuals and as societies, but has also driven us apart. Rather than Marshall McLuhan's global village, we find ourselves living in filter bubbles and silos unable to speak to each other or know ourselves. It is possible, if only faintly possible, that the plague will burst these bubbles, shatter these silos, and force people together at the precise moment everything and everybody seems to be flying apart. For this awareness to dawn, we must realize that while we are undeniably alone, we are alone *together*.

While the plague is disastrous, it is symptomatic of the even more deadly catastrophe of climate change. We now know or should know that it *can* happen here—mass death is *real*. Never before have so many people been facing the prospect of death together with the simultaneous awareness in real time that everyone around the world is in the same situation whether they admit or not. The two catastrophes—the plague and climate change—unfold at different rates, at least for now. The spread of the plague is explosive, and the emergence of environmental disaster is slow and incremental, until it reaches the tipping point. Once again we see that the plague and climate change are inseparably intertwined. Perhaps confronting the mass death nature is unleashing will bring us together to confront the mass death modern man has been unleashing on the earth for more than two hundred years. This would be a rare "moment in my life so far when I was at one with other men, when the profound loneliness I lived in had been assuaged by the communal."

A footnote about another report about another church I know much better than the Church of the Holy Sepulcher—the Cathedral of Saint John the Divine on Amsterdam Avenue between 110th and 113th Streets right next to St. Luke's Hospital, where I died without dying. This is the largest Gothic-style cathedral in the world. When I lived on the 13th floor (yes, it really was numbered the 13th floor) on 103rd Street, I looked north and had an unobstructed view of this magnificent cathedral. I also see it every day as I walk up Broadway to my office on 120th Street. There will be no services on Good Friday or Easter Sunday this week. This morning Episcopal authorities announced that the cathedral is being converted into an emergency hospital for two hundred patients suffering from the plague. This year the ritual of death and the hope for resurrection will play out in a different way.

Mark


*April 7*

Dear Mark:

The last time I was in the Cathedral of St. John the Divine, it was for the memorial service for the Russian poet Joseph Brodsky. That colossal structure is beautiful in its way, I suppose, though I find the National Cathedral—also Episcopal, of course—a much more successful venture in Gothic

Revival church architecture. John the Divine's cavernous immensity makes it just irredeemably gloomy, and its acoustics make it liturgically almost unusable—at least without much better sound engineering than the Episcopal Diocese of New York has ever managed to fund. At the Cathedral of Our Lady of the Angels, the new Catholic cathedral of Los Angeles, by the Spanish architect Rafael Moneo, the sides of the nave are covered with an immense tapestry representing the Communion of Saints. Behind the tapestry, however, are sound-absorbing panels that combined with the cloth itself give the edifice good acoustics for preaching. (For music, though, in my opinion, they stink. I attended a performance there of Mozart's *Requiem*, and from what would seem excellent seats, I was able to take in astonishingly little of the music.) Back to John the Divine, the scene of rows of beds of possibly dying patients lying beneath those funereally looming gothic arches—well, it's a cineast's dream, I suppose, but I should think that for a patient it would be depressing as well as, almost certainly in damp spring weather, bone-chilling.

The chief health officer of Los Angeles County urged Angelenos yesterday to abstain this week even from grocery shopping if they possibly can. We can certainly do that, thanks to our young friend's delivery yesterday, and the exterminator who was supposed to arrive today never came, so the rat(s) in the attic are spared to frolic longer. But Kitty's good friend Lorna dropped off a (sanitized) book today, and Kitty tells me that Lorna's son, daughter-in-law, and baby granddaughter (named Dancer) have all driven down from L.A. to celebrate Easter with Gramma. "Are they nuts?" I cried. I was genuinely dismayed. Was I overreacting? Lorna is an intelligent woman, with a doctorate in English, the widow of an aerospace engineer who moonlighted as an astronomy professor. She writes poetry and is the kind of friend who turns up organizing a discussion on one serious topic or another. Maybe people just have to create free zones for their families, but I worry that in spite of everything the message in its full gravity has just not gotten through to millions of our fellow Americans.

Different leadership could certainly make a difference. Your letter this morning, with its hope that the COVID pandemic could constitute a global teaching-and-learning moment, arrived just as I received through the Berggruen Institute a "Letter to Governments of the G20 Nations," signed by 165 leaders from 70 different countries. Many of the countries are small ones, many of the leaders are former heads of state or government ministers. There is a sprinkling of distinguished others, such as Joseph Stiglitz, Lawrence Summers, and Rowan Williams, but none of the world's real heavy political hitters. It is so painfully easy to imagine this letter, which proposes an expenditure of billions of dollars and is global enough to include billions for Africa in this time of plague, being ignored by the recipients just as the supposed commitments of the Paris Climate Accord are being ignored. And yet must it not be through the multiplication of such expressions of will and hope that the great shift in world public opinion about climate change that you dream of will come about? I mean, it's as easy to roll one's eyes at this letter as at the singing of the national anthem from Italian balconies or at this or that happy story closing a news report, but we must build on what we have to build on.

Receiving letters from you that leap so from one topic to another day by day opens the possibility of odd juxtapositions. You write this time of your mother's lifelong, perhaps truly unbroken melancholy, and your own preoccupation with happiness, your resulting response to a title like *This Is Happiness*. To this large and serious topic, I join your passing remark about trying the trombone, giving up, and settling for the consolation prize of being a triple-threat high school athlete. My association to this is my father, dapper in his St. Philip High School band uniform, holding his trombone. He had to give up the trombone, he told me, when he got false teeth and when, the first time he tried the trombone again, he blew his teeth out. Sometime, I mean to ask my very thoughtful dentist about the history of whole-mouth tooth extraction in our country. This was advised, it seems, more widely than now seems conceivable, and it happened to young men and women. Dad had a fuller upper and a full lower plate. But I still can't help chortling at him blowing his teeth out. What I think about happiness is that it happens when you are thinking about something else, something that really engrosses you, mentally or physically or emotionally, as in Mihaly Cziksentmihalyi's book *Flow*. Afterward, yes, as you look back at the end of fill-in-the-blank, you may consciously and retrospectively savor your happiness. And, when unhappy, you can sometimes witness and yearn for the genuine happiness you see in others. Call it envy if you like, and condemn it, but I find it forgivable.

> When in disgrace with fortune and men's eyes
> I all alone beweep my outcast state
> And trouble deaf heaven with my bootless cries
> And look upon myself and curse my fate,
> Wishing me like to one more rich in hope,
> Favored like him, like him with friends possess'd,
> Desiring this man's art and that man's scope,
> With what I most enjoy contented least,
> Then in these thoughts, myself almost despising,
> Haply I think on thee, and then my soul
> Like to the lark at heaven's gate arising...

Around the volta, my memory of Shakespeare's sonnet goes all wobbly, but it's the first two quatrains, anyway, that make my little point—namely, that happiness is something whose goodness we know and want even when we lack it, even perhaps when we have lacked it our whole life long. We are *made* for happiness, don't you sense that, too? When we are unhappy, we are not making a mistake when our reaction is *This is wrong, this shouldn't be.* Intellectually, statistically if you will, we can know that unhappiness is going to be our lot in life more often than not, but the irrepressible objection to unhappiness is still never truly unreasonable.

Today, I read chapter 31 of *This Is Happiness* to Kitty. This is the chapter in which Noe, gallantly but naïvely, calls on Annie Mooney to convey the message to her that Christy has come back to Faha in hopes of apologizing to her. I have enough experience with women I've left to know that they ain't that eager to hear your fine words, however heartfelt, however conscience-stricken. The gut reaction can be put in two words: "Spare me." And Kitty confirms this with reference to her second husband, who left her for a high school sweetheart (who subsequently dumped him, she reminded me). But Annie is a woman who has been deepened and in every way matured by her life's experience. No, she tells Noe, she does not wish to see Christy, but as she ushers him out, she adds, touching his arm gently, "But you may call again." How endearing, and it is a pleasure I yield to joyously to savor the admirable whenever I encounter it.

I close with my last exchange with Mo (no, his name is not Muhammad, but I am tired of little circumlocutions, so I am assigning him this pseudonym):

Dear Mo:

Our list is attached—not too long this time.

Also, I tallied up the accumulating receipts, and you have spent $398.12 on groceries for us. Since we really don't know how long this health crisis will last, could we set up a schedule of monthly payment? I could pay you now for what you bought mostly in March. Then early in May I could pay you for what you bought in April, and so forth. Would that be OK?

If we knew this would quickly be over, it would be one thing, but we don't, and Kitty and I don't want to abuse your kindness and generosity.

Peace,
Jack

Hi Jack,

In regards to the payment, I honestly do not mind waiting until this is over even if it takes a year, please tell Kitty that people like you guys who are filled with love and righteousness would not know how to abuse anyone's kindness or generosity even if they try very hard to do that.

Only if you guys feel better to pay now, I will accept it, otherwise I'm fine not collecting anything until I see both of you are comfortable leaving the house in God's will. If you and Kitty insist to pay every month then you can wright me a check or transfer the funds to my boa account, whatever works for you guys, but once again, I'm fine not collecting anything now.

I will work on this list and text you by tonight to tomorrow at the latest.

Thank you

Cheers,
[Mo]

What a dear, good man he is. The European Union may be coming apart. The United States may be coming disunited. Millions of us may die, and climate change may include our species in *The Sixth Extinction* that your friend Betsy Kolbert has written about so chillingly. But for the moments that remain, life is still sweetened by friends like this, and never mind his faulty English. I couldn't begin to reply to him in Arabic.

Jack

*Easter*

APRIL 11–12: MARK BEGINS.

*Drought and wildfires . . . playing* Caddyshack *. . . outsmarted by a ground-hog . . . guns and roses . . . nature out-thinking us . . . are we parasite or host? . . . viral intelligence . . . metaphors we live by . . . emergent creativity . . . plague everywhere and nowhere . . . virtual Easter service. . . .* Harold and Maude *. . . losing connections . . .* St. Matthew Passion *. . . impossibility of mourning . . .* Philip Roth's *The Plot Against America . . . reliving 9/11 . . . violence and the sacred . . . the sublime and the beautiful . . . agony of isolation . . . thinking the unthinkable . . . contemplating mass death.*

---

*April 11*

Dear Jack:

There seems to be strange weather everywhere. For you so much rain that you worry about your pool overflowing. Not long ago, months of drought left your garden parched and you feared approaching wildfires. Here it's cold, wind, and, yes, snow. Even Eliot's well-known "April is the cruelest month" can't express how terrible the weather was yesterday. The snow didn't stick in the valley, but this morning the mountaintops are white. Nonetheless, this morning when I came out to the barn, it seemed a bit lighter than it has been. I haven't heard the forecast for tomorrow. In the midst of this gloom and doom, a moment of comic relief that offers a lesson. I think we both need it!

One of my annual spring rituals has begun. You might recall that the barn where my study is located sits atop a small hill. Half the barn is my study and the other half is where I store my tractor and all the tools and equipment I need to maintain this place. There is no foundation and the equipment side has a dirt floor. Every spring I engage in combat with the local groundhog. The barn is usually absolutely quiet except for the occasional squirrel that gets into the loft. Yesterday I heard what I thought were faint noises from the equipment side of the barn and wondered if my annual battle were about to begin. Later in the day, I went into the other side of the barn to get my sledgehammer to reset one of my steel sculptures that had fallen over during the winter. And there it was, a pile of stones, dirt, and gravel from the groundhog extending his tunnel.

This struggle has been going on for years. I don't know if it's the same groundhog or one of its offspring. Even if I'd seen the critter, how do you tell groundhogs apart? When I first moved my study to the barn years ago, I had a groundhog problem, so I dug a trench one foot deep and one foot wide around the whole barn and put gridded wire fencing across the bottom, up the side of the trench, and a foot and a half up the side of the barn. That worked fine for years, until a groundhog decided to dig a tunnel on the side of the hill where the barn is perched. Then, last year, for reasons I cannot comprehend, he (if it is a he) decided to dig a tunnel under the barn that would surface through the dirt floor. From the outside opening of the tunnel to its inside opening is about twenty-five feet. You simply would not believe how large the piles of material he threw out are. Every day I fill in the holes, and every morning I find that he had dug out the openings again. Aaron and Kirsten are amused by all this and repeatedly tell me I am Bill Murray in *Caddyshack*. Needless to say, I'm considerably less amused.

While I have never seen the damn critter, I often hear him. I pound the floor with my baseball bat, and he goes silent for a few minutes. But as soon as I sit down at my desk to return to my reading or writing, he begins gnawing and clawing again. I have tried to get rid of him every way I can imagine but have failed. The local pest control guy who successfully traps squirrels, raccoons, and skunks for me says you cannot trap them because they are herbivorous and with grass and plants everywhere no bait attracts them. My neighbor is an accomplished hunter and shoots groundhogs on his property with his 22 rifle. He's offered it to me, but I've not yet taken him up on that.

An aside about guns. I don't know if I ever told you the story about taking the hunters' education course here in Williamstown. When I was a kid, I used to hunt with my father—pheasants and rabbits on the farm where he grew up, and grouse in the Pennsylvania mountains around the coal mining town where my mother grew up. One of my most vivid memories is hunting with my eighty-five-year-old grandfather, who was born just five years after the Civil War ended, on what had been his Gettysburg farm. When my father died, my brother took all the family guns—my grandfather's muzzle-loader and powder horn, my dad's double-barrel 12-gauge shotgun, my first single-barrel 12-gauge shotgun, the 22 rifle I learned to shoot with, my brother's 410 shotgun, and my dad's 30–30 deer rifle. I couldn't bear to let my brother get rid of them, so I agreed to take them. Massachusetts has strict gun laws, so I had to take the hunters' course to get my state firearms permit, which I still proudly carry in my wallet. The course was an education in more ways than one. Over half of those in the class were boys fourteen or younger. To pass the course, you had to pass a standardized multiple choice test and display the ability to handle a gun. I met a side of Williamstown I had never encountered, and they met a Williams professor in a place they had never seen one before. All six guns are hanging on the wall above where I am writing to you now.

Back to my groundhog problem. When everything I tried failed, I was expressing my frustration with the farmer who plows my drive during the winter. He said, "Why don't you use a smoke bomb?" I'd never heard of such a thing, but decided it was worth a try. The smoke bomb looks like a middle-sized firecracker with a long fuse. When lighting the fuse and placing the smoke bomb in the tunnel, it is important to be careful that the poison fumes do not get in my study. I probably shouldn't be admitting this but I've tried this method at least five or six times, but so far have had no success.

Having failed repeatedly, last fall I tried a different tactic. We had to have our deck repaired and there was some lumber left over. The boards were long, thick, and heavy. I decided I would use them to create a floor where the groundhog was digging through on the equipment side of the barn. The only place I could not fit a board was under a shelf on the outside wall of the barn that was about three inches from the ground. I was confident that the boards were heavy enough to keep the groundhog from breaking through. Yesterday when I checked to see if the noise I heard signaled that that the groundhog had awoken from his winter slumber, I discovered a big pile of dirt that had been dug out from under that shelf. "Thought that would work, did you? Not a chance. Your move. Try again."

Every spring I hope the groundhog will have moved on or, better yet, died over the winter. Now he's back and the game starts all over again. I hate to admit it, but the longer this struggle goes on, the more I am forced to respect this damn groundhog. I've never seen such persistence and determination. If only my students worked this hard. He digs the hole, I fill it, he digs it out again. He just doesn't give up, and gradually wears me down. "Busy as a beaver" is a tired cliché; I'd prefer to say "as determined as a groundhog." It's not just his determination that is impressive; this groundhog is smart, even sly and cunning. He knows enough to stay hidden—I hear him but do not see him. As I am writing now he is silent, but I know he's down there somewhere under the barn waiting for the right moment to start bugging me again. As I approach, he withdraws; I haven't figured out his daily and nightly rhythms yet, but I suspect he knows mine. It's painful to admit that the groundhog is outsmarting me.

I know you are always on my case about making connections between and among things that seem to be unrelated, but that's what I do—that's just the way my mind works. I have actually come to believe that the essence of creativity involves bringing together what is usually held apart. The more I think about my ongoing struggle with the groundhog, the more I think there is a lesson here about how to deal with the virus. Ever since Descartes split the world between smart minds and dumb bodies, people have underestimated nature. Intelligence is not limited to human beings, nor does cognition require consciousness and self-consciousness. Nature is intelligent and bodies are smart. The chemical processes carried out by the molecules in the cells of our bodies are really information processes. Always processing, calculating, and thinking, nature creates an environment of ambient intelligence to which humans must learn to adapt or else die.

Metaphors create the worlds in which we live by shaping the ways in which we think and how we act. Like cancer and other deadly diseases, the dominant metaphor people use when talking about the coronavirus is warfare. Doctors, nurses, and first responders are on the front lines, and the president declares himself a "wartime president." This is the wrong way to conceive this struggle; rather than war, it is better to think of the engagement with the plague as a game of intelligence and counterintelligence. Any leader who dismisses the advice of intelligence agencies will lose the war.

Like the groundhog, the coronavirus is smart, very smart—so smart that so far it's outsmarting the smartest human minds. To appreciate the stakes of this deadly game, it is important to understand the difference between bacteria and viruses. Both are pathogens that are invisible to the human eye and sometimes the human body, but are able to stealthily transfer from person to person. Bacteria are single-cell living organisms that create energy, produce food, and reproduce. They can live in many environments, including soil, water, and the human body, where they can be beneficial or detrimental. Indeed, we could not live without the multiple bacterial organisms in our bodies. Viruses, by contrast, are not living organisms and are only active when they are inside host cells. They invade a host cell and, as they rapidly multiply, move from cell to cell throughout the body, eventually spreading to other bodies. While bacterial infections are often localized, viral infections tend to become systemic, spreading throughout the whole body. When infected, the human body is the host for a deadly parasite.

Rather than thinking of a virus in terms of single cells, it is more productive to imagine the entire virus as something like a single organism that is intelligent. Just as the single trees in a forest communicate with each other and function as a collective organism, so the virus circulating through individual cells in separate bodies functions like a single intelligent organism that thrives by outsmarting its host. It's not nature that's dumb, it's man who is dumb, when he refuses to understand how smart his

foe is and lets down his guard before it's safe to do so. System against system, agent against counteragent, intelligence against counterintelligence. The human body is smart and its immune system is itself an information processing network whose counterintelligence activities involve cracking the code of the invader's messages. Smart bodies, however, don't have a chance when they are overridden by dumb minds.

The plague is not only smart, it is a master of disguise and deceit engaged in elaborate espionage activity. Its molecules have learned how to read their host well enough to conceal messages its host cannot detect. The coronavirus knows its host's cells better than the host itself. This knowledge enables it to find twists and folds in molecules where it can sink its teeth without being noticed. Its disguises are so effective that the virus remains invisible and often goes undetected. People who think they are healthy might actually carry the disease and serve as the most effective vehicles of transmission. What makes the plague so dreadful and difficult to manage is that it might be everywhere and might be nowhere. With such a crafty agent, direct assault is not just ineffective, but is actually impossible. You can't engage an opponent you cannot detect and don't even know if it's present or absent. To make progress, the intelligent activity of the aggressor must be met with a more effective counterintelligence response.

Just as I had long underestimated the intelligence of the groundhog, so many people are underestimating the intelligence of the plague. As it continues to outsmart us, we must confess that we still do not have any idea how this virus works or how to understand the language it is speaking. This parasite has learned how to adapt to its host, but we have not yet learned how to live with the intelligent agent consuming us from within. The best we can do for now is to try to avoid the plague's relentless seeking by locking ourselves up in our houses and hiding from it. But hiding is not understanding and, thus, can only be a short-term fix. When we become impatient and open our doors and windows, the virus will be there waiting for us. The plague, again like the groundhog, is relentless—its appetite is voracious, and its persistence and determination wear us down. As the coronavirus spreads, it is teaching us a painful lesson: we are not as smart as we think we are, and nature is not as dumb as we have long thought she is.

Mark

*April 12*

Dear Mark:

Kitty and I attended the virtual Easter Vigil service posted as a podcast last night by Grace Episcopal Church in Newton. Our own church was doing something live at 7 p.m., but they announced it late, and I had committed to pick up a big to-go Easter feast from our favorite local restaurant, a Greek restaurant, Christakis. The normal parking lot is three-quarters empty, but the six spaces in front of the restaurant now have chairs at the curb with RESERVED signs on them each with a roman numeral. So, you order by phone, show up at your appointed time, call the restaurant on your cellphone, tell them which space you're in, and they bring out your order. They allowed me, a regular, to pay by check, so I put the check under the windshield wiper and opened the trunk. A daughter of the proprietor's family, slender and with raven hair, very pretty even with her mask, smiled with her eyes and waved as I drove off.

So, we ate part of our feast last night (the larger part will be dinner tonight) and then "attended" church at our complete convenience. In talking about the collapse of journalism in Canada, the commission on democracy-after-journalism that Trudeau commissioned spoke of the way that the Internet has erased distance. Once, the local paper was truly local, and so were you, reading it. There was no digital subscribing from San Diego to a Washington or New York daily. We were all only somewhat milder versions of British colonials who read each day's news in the *Times* of London as it arrived weeks later by ship to Rangoon or wherever. Episcopalians around the country may often be "attending" virtual services through their local congregations, but all also have the option of "attending" the services at the National Cathedral. As you've noted, all these tendencies are now being built even more deeply into our way of life.

But as I learned from your email yesterday, reporting the strange fact that you have Internet connectivity in your barn office but have lost it in your house, and with it television and cell phone connectivity, we are all at the same time far more vulnerable now to isolation to real isolation than before the plague began. Imagine, though, that for most people through millennia of time, such isolation was normality itself. Think of Greek plays, or even Shakespearean plays, in which news is brought in breathlessly by a messenger, and an action that took place days ago or longer belatedly proceeds to transform the lives of the message's recipients.

Have you ever seen the movie *Harold and Maude*? It's about a hilariously depressed young man determined to commit suicide and the slightly loopy, indomitably cheerful old lady he lives with. Your technical ingenuity against the groundhog made me think of Harold's ingenuity in creating new gimmicks to do away with himself. I also remembered you in a similarly militant mode against gophers before Aaron's or Kirsten's marriages—Aaron's, I think. All was in readiness, and the grass was a lovely green carpet, perfect for a wedding until, ugh, a gopher mound would pop up. I thought of writing you "Dear Mr. Fudd" and signing "G. Hogg, Esq." but that moment has passed, now that it's the phone company you'd like to take after with a double-barreled shotgun.

We had gophers this spring, BTW, but poison chased them off, helped along, we were told, by noisy construction at the next house over. Gophers don't like noise, did you know? So, the beautiful silence around your place is gopher heaven. As for the rat in the attic, well, he's still there, but we have recovered the coordinates for the exterminator who did a good job last time, so there's hope. Under the plague, one hopes for the fewest visitors possible, so I was proud of myself yesterday that I got under the sink and unclogged the drain under Kitty's sink in our two-sink master bathroom. I was the despair of my father, an endlessly resourceful and skillful handyman, always singing as he fixed whatever was broken. It's not quite that I can't ever do such stuff, it's that I do it only under duress, don't enjoy it, and certainly don't excel at it. For breakfast this morning, Kitty put out lovely inherited china, which turns out to be Sears-Roebuck china from the teens of the previous century, thus ordinary in its day but extraordinary in ours. The cups are quite small, but I fancy that this is because the understanding is that a servant in livery is always ready with a piping hot refill. Big mugs? Tch, tch, those are for the help.

On Friday, as I was falling asleep after hearing the *St. Matthew Passion*, I had a further thought about "Mache dich mein Herze rein." It was that the sentiment it expresses is very close to the one you expressed to me when asked to speak at John Chandler's funeral—grieved to lose him but somehow ennobled by involvement in his last rites. A phrase very common in contemporary discussion of serious matters but never examined as such is "come to terms." I've thought about that phrase a fair bit, and I can only conclude that it means "find the language" to enable the doing of what at any given moment must be done. Asked once what my favorite text in the entire *Norton Anthology of World Religions* is, I chose, with some hesitation, this one:

> Seeking the builder of the house I sped along many paths in Samsara but to no avail; ill is birth again and again.

> O builder of the house, you are seen. Do not build the house again! All your beams are broken, and the ridgepole is shattered. The mind that has gone beyond things composite has attained the destruction of the cravings.

These terms are different terms from any Christian terms, or any postreligious ones, but they did for Siddartha Gautama the work that he needed them to do. Are they the *ipsissima verba*? We can easily doubt that, but they are an honest attempt to preserve and carry forward a cathartic, salvific moment in the life of an extraordinary man. More about this maybe later.

Because there is an element surely of surrender in them, they came to mind as you spoke of humankind's humbling at moments like this one when Mother Nature shows us who is in charge. I also thought of a line spoken by some famous biologist or other: "Evolution is smarter than you are." And of Einstein's wonderful line about his own death—not imminent at the time he spoke of it. He said that he regarded it as "an old debt coming due." His is a simple but for me enormously appealing way of admitting defeat. Time to pay up, no getting out of it, *c'est la vie, c'est la mort*. For the last two days, I have awakened in the morning with a slight wheeze. This is an asthmatic wheeze, but I thought I had had it adequately under control. I may have inadvertently missed a few doses of the inhaled steroid that I take to suppress the symptoms, but anything respiratory these days arrives as a memento mori. I feel mostly OK, but while living on happily for years to come, I try to be as ready as Einstein for my due date.

Final unrelated little item. You asked whether I had any input into Philip Roth's *The Plot Against America*. I did, actually, in one distinct but minor way. The strength of that novel is the verisimilitude of the American fascism that Roth imagines. That's what engaged him. The escape from fascism and restoration of democracy was just a wrap-up plot chore, and in his first draft I found the resolution implausible. One great public demonstration in New York led by Fiorello LaGuardia and Walter Winchell would not have sufficed to undo a regime as entrenched and omnipresent, down to humble Newark streets, as the one he had imagined. What he then did to soften this implausibility was insert a series of imagined, dated radio broadcasts over a series of some days as the Lindbergh regime crumbles. This slowed down the ending and made the climactic demonstration seem somewhat less a deus ex machina. That's my recollection of our interaction about the work, and you will note that everybody remembers and talks of the setup, the "it could happen here" verisimilitude, while nobody ever remembers or talks of the dénouement. I did point out to Philip—as if to insist that verisimilitude is not truth—that it was during this period that California nearly elected Upton Sinclair as governor, a socialist, and the Bernie Sanders of his day; that the 1930s were the high tide of American Communism; and that the headquarters of either the Socialist or the Communist Party of America in that era (I forget which) was, in fact, Newark. It may be that there is the same double potential again in the United States as we head for the 2020 election—if it does occur as we hope it will.

Jack

*April 12*

Dear Jack:

How should we celebrate Easter in the midst of the plague? Going through familiar rituals and listening to worn-out sermons online hardly suffices. The message must change because something new, something different, perhaps something "infinitely and qualitatively different," is being revealed to us. Pondering the horror raging around us this morning, I am transported back to an earlier moment of horror a few days after 9/11. For the entire month of August, Aaron attended classes preparing for his new job with Lehman Brothers on the top floor of the World Trade Center. The morning of September 11, he was in the American Express building across the street from the Twin Towers. After the plane crashed into the second tower, he and his colleagues left the building and waited on the street for the situation to clarify. While waiting, Aaron saw the people leaping to their death and was so upset that he left, heading west to the Hudson River, turning north and walking uptown. He was somewhere in the fifties when the second tower collapsed. Had Aaron stayed, he would have died; the people who had leaped to their death had saved his life. Death leading to life. Perhaps an Easter story.

At the time all of this was happening, I was reading in the barn, oblivious to the unfolding tragedy, until one of Aaron's friends called to ask me if he was OK. Somehow Nathan was able to get through to Aaron on his cell phone, and reported that he was making his way back to his apartment. Dinny had been in midtown attending a meeting with Williams trustees when all of this happened. As we talked after she returned, it became clear to me how traumatic this experience had been for Aaron. I decided I needed to go to New York and revisit the scene of the disaster with him. As the subway headed south, passengers got off at each stop, leaving us alone in the car. By the time we got off at Canal Street, it was late afternoon. The streets were completely deserted and utterly silent. When we approached the site, we heard the faint sound of the rhythmic beat of footsteps before seeing police and firemen solemnly attending to their duties. I will never forget turning a corner and seeing the damaged building Aaron had been in across the surprisingly small empty space where the Twin Towers had stood. More startling than the void was the twisted steel grid that was the last remains of the towers left standing. By now it was dusk and massive floodlights illuminated the twisted remains. I was overwhelmed not only by a sense of terror, but also most unexpectedly by an awareness of unspeakable beauty, no, that's not the right word, by an awareness of the inexpressible sublimity of the smoldering ruin. Here was a work of art made by no human hand that was more awe inspiring than anything Richard Serra or anybody else could create.

As we lingered, Aaron and I did not talk about what we were seeing; how could we? I wasn't able to process what I was experiencing at the time. In the following days, I gradually began to realize that what made that ruin so unsettling was the awareness that I was in the presence of overwhelming and incomprehensible power. What held me in its grip was not the thought of the terrorists, but the apprehension of the demonic power they deemed divine. As I struggled to find words to express what I knew words could not capture, my mind drifted back to a book I had studied while an undergraduate and I had taught from time to time—Rudolf Otto's *The Idea of the Holy.*

Otto, who was a Lutheran, published his book in 1923, shortly after Karl Barth discovered Kierkegaard's "infinitely and qualitatively different" God (*The Epistle to the Romans*, 1918), and a few years before Martin Heidegger appropriated Kierkegaard's concept of dread (*Being and Time*, 1927). I first encountered Otto's work indirectly in Mircea Eliade's *Sacred and Profane.* Eliade explains his idea of the sacred through Otto's notion of the holy. "Otto sets himself to discover the characteristics of this frightening and irrational experience. He finds *the feeling of terror* before the sacred, before the awe-inspiring mystery (*mysterium tremendum*), the majesty (*majestas*) that emanates an overwhelming superiority of power. . . . Otto characterizes all these experiences as numinous (from Latin *numen*, god), for they are induced by the revelation of an aspect of divine power. The numinous presents itself as something 'wholly other' (*ganz andere*), something basically and totally different." This was the power whose voice Luther heard in the thunderstorm that changed his life, this is the power Kierkegaard's Abraham heard on his four-day journey to Mount Moriah to sacrifice Isaac, and this is the power I now hear in death rattle of people dying from the plague.

Listen to the words Otto uses to describe the holy or sacred: "wholly other," "wild and demonic forms," "grisly horror and shuddering," "ineffable," "inexpressible," "tremor of fear," "uncanny," "verging on the bizarre and the abnormal," "demonic dread," "incalculable and arbitrary," "overpoweringness," "spectral," "absolute unapproachability," and "awe." Yes, "awe," "awe-ful." "Of modern languages." Otto writes, "English has the words 'awe,' 'aweful,' which in their deeper and most special sense approximate closely our meaning. The phrase, 'he stood aghast,' is also suggestive in this connection."

The subtitle of Otto's book is *An Inquiry into the Nonrational Factor in the Idea of the Divine and Its Relation to the Rational.* Since the original German title of the book was simply *Das Heilige*, the English translation *The Idea of the Holy* is misleading. Irreducibly nonrational, the holy or the sacred can never be conceptualized or rationalized; it always exceeds and surpasses human understanding. What Otto describes as the holy, and Eliade as the sacred, Kant, who was yet another Lutheran, described as the sublime. Eluding both theoretical and practical reason, Kant assigned the sublime to the realm of feeling and sensibility expressed in art. For Kant, and many moderns who came after him, art displaced religion as the locus of spiritual experience. Far from the beautiful art of Bach, this is another art, a more disturbing art, an art that allows the approach but never the arrival of something wholly other. Here is the terrifying art captured, though not contained, by a devastated Anslem Kiefer canvas, or of a twisted, smoking ruin of a once-proud iron-and-steel sculpture.

Kant distinguishes the sublime from the beautiful, which "is directly attended with a feeling of the furtherance of life, and is thus compatible with the charms of a playful imagination." The sublime, by contrast, is uncontrollable, unmasterable, overwhelming—it shatters every concept and all forms designed to contain it. Not limited to works of art, the sublime is powerfully present in the irresistible forces of nature. "In what we are wont to call sublime," Kant explains,

> in nature there is such an absence of anything leading to particular objective principles and corresponding forms of nature, that it is rather in its chaos, or in its wildest and most irregular disorder and desolation, provided it gives signs of magnitude and power, that nature chiefly excites the ideas of the sublime.

This is the chaos the sublime plague is revealing to us. Surely, it is giving signs, quantitative signs of magnitude and power. As the bodies pile up, the numbers add up: coffin after coffin with bodies transferred from refrigerated trucks to a mass grave on a distant island no one ever visits. No longer empty signs of other signs, these are signs of *real* bodies that "push to the point at which our faculty of imagination breaks down in presenting the concept of a magnitude, and proves unequal to the task." How can we imagine the unimaginable? How can we think the unthinkable? How can we name the unnameable? It is both awful and awe-ful.

Not so long ago, many people thought they had it all figured out—everything had been comprehended and history was over. They believed the real had been domesticated and nothing remained uncanny. They didn't understand what they were saying when they confidently declared,

"Nothing remains uncanny." Nothing *does* indeed remain uncanny. Over
the past few centuries, the world had become so disenchanted that we no
longer experienced the terror of the sublime. All the while the wholly
other did not disappear; rather, it slipped underground, lurking, waiting
subliminally (*sub*, under + *limen*, threshold) for the moment to break out
and attack humankind's "predatory hubris." There *is* a specter haunting the
world today. This strangely holy ghost is reenchanting the universe in ways
we never imagined, leaving people who thought they knew better to wonder how they missed it so long. If, as Aristotle insisted many centuries ago,
philosophy begins with wonder, perhaps by responding thoughtfully to
this mazing plague, philosophy can start anew.

One of the most important lessons that the plague seems to be teaching
us is that we are not the center of the universe, and nature's ways are not
always our ways. The overwhelming power of nature is sublime and will
forever exceed our grasp. There must be music that expresses the feeling of
the overwhelming power of the sublime, but I don't know what it is. We
failed to learn the lesson of 9/11. Will we learn the lesson of the plague
before it is too late to change our tune?

Happy Easter.

Mark

P.S. BTW, Miles, thanks to your brilliant plan of getting a humungous ham to
last through the plague, I'm going to be eating Easter ham until Christmas.


*April 12 (later on Easter Sunday)*

Dear Mark:

It keeps, ham does. It's cured. But I alert you: it does begin to dry out after
a while. Still, I made blueberry pancakes this morning for our Easter
breakfast, and with just ten seconds in the skillet, a couple slices that were
beginning to look a little dry came out delicious.

A few weeks after 9/11, I, too, had occasion to visit the World Trade Towers
site, and, yes, it was ghastly and perhaps awe- as well as horror-inspiring.
And I agree that religion or its unnamed or name-refusing equivalent
begins at the point where emotion no less than reason is overcome and

confronts its final inadequacy; such is essentially the point of my "Concluding Unscholarly Postscript." There, I engaged this moment under the heading of "invincible ignorance," thus under the "reason" heading rather than under the "emotion" heading, but I could have made the same point either way, or through the aesthetic mode as well: moments of artistic beauty that are just too much to bear and bring us to tears or some kind of inner exhaustion.

I may have told you this story once before. If so, I apologize. But years ago at Loyola, I was speaking in a class on religion and literature about death as, classically, that which has ever led the greatest minds—as they contemplated it—to the reflections that we now call religious. In this class, there was one boy who always sat at the back, just never ever spoke, but showed me in his written work that he was clearly the most thoughtful member of the class. After class on the day I am remembering, he came to me and said that death was not the only way to be led to the liminal moment I had spoken off. This boy had terrible acne, terrible oozing acne. His face was really painful to look at. And because of it, he confessed, he had never dated, could never imagine any girl wanting to date someone as ugly as him. But this had now changed. He was in love with her, and she with him, and the beauty and glory and relief of the experience so overwhelmed him, as it began, that he had to go to the chapel and just sit there for a while. Others have been comparably overwhelmed and never thought

White House photo/Alamy Stock Photo

to sit in a chapel, but our focus just now is on the enormous, unsought given, not on how one copes with or what one makes of it.

A moment of coronavirus horror reached me today as I read this story about what the virus did to the lungs of an otherwise healthy fifty-nine-year-old man (https://www.nytimes.com/video/health/100000007056651/covid-ards -acute-respiratory-distress-syndrome.html?searchResultPosition=1).

This is just much, much worse than the flu, and you don't need to be old and vulnerable for it to take you down in agony and isolation. I don't think it matters terribly whether we call the recoil, the experience of fear and wonder and one's own smallness, contemplating mass death, religious or transreligious or prereligious or something else. What strikes me is that there have been many moments in history, even fairly recent history, before this moment that have merited this reaction, received it, and then pro- voked philosophical reflection upon it. Remember Levinas, "No poetry after Auschwitz"? And for anyone worried about the perils of nuclear power run amok, Chernobyl and Fukushima are objectively more lethal by far than any demolished trio of skyscrapers. As much can be said alone of the many plagues that have come before this one and their cultural impacts—cf. William Hardy McNeill's *Plagues and Peoples*. Always, there are profiteers; always, there are saints; each sets an example; each example lasts. And this is just the beginning.

I certainly don't mean to minimize the scope and gravity of the plague that we're living through or to guess at just how its cultural impact will play out. But I do think that what will be different about this time will *not* be that as if for the first time the world will come face to face with the *mysterium tremendum et fascinans*. In regular synagogue prayers, YHWH is addressed as *adon venora*, which can literally be translated "master and hor- ror." That antinomy was the subject of my conference at Boston College almost exactly a year ago. So, the opportunity to take this point is always at hand and yet always avoidable. It's like Camus's saying that one is never without a reason to commit suicide. I don't wish it, but if Florida descends into a maelstrom worse than New York's, I don't expect Gov. Ron DeSantis to waver in his devotion to Trump and his conviction that he was right to proceed as he has proceeded. He won't be humbled or express wonderment at "how he had missed it for so long." He could have got "it" with much less than the coronavirus, and he may still miss it even in the wake of the coronavirus at its worst.

How I wish it were otherwise! And I imagine ordinary Floridians, too, not necessarily condemning him but just saying with that universal poor man's stoicism, "Hey, whaddaya gonna do? Shit happens," or the equivalent. I sound so cynical writing this way, and I do want to remain hopeful, but what am I gonna do?

Jack

\* \* \*

## APRIL 13: MARK BEGINS.

*Perils of connectivity . . . blackout . . . antisocial media . . . virus as an espionage game . . . agents political, economic, chemical . . . sleeper cells . . . country living—bear attack . . . the Singularity . . . vulnerability of workers . . . religions: comparing stories . . . other modernities and religious pluralism . . . finding truth and community in a diverse and divided America.*

---

*April 13*

Dear Jack:

Last night and this morning I've been more distressed by this situation than ever before, not because of the growing physical and biological threat, which I've been dealing with, but because of a technological threat I had not adequately considered. Dinny and I were watching a Netflix film when suddenly the cable to the house died. All the TVs went out, Internet down, WiFi gone, and no cell phone coverage. Spectrum is always trying to get us to give up our landline and use their phone service, but we have refused because of precisely this eventuality. How can you call the cable and Internet company when the cable and the Internet are not working? We are still in the dark about what happened and have no backup. For some equally unknown reason, the connection in the barn is still working for now. Last night it took forty-five minutes to get Spectrum on the phone; when we got through they insisted that there was an outage in the area. I said that's impossible because my barn computer still works. They weren't convinced and refused to schedule a technician. This morning, of course, there is still no cable. Another call, more pleas, and finally they agreed to send somebody today. If you think you are not addicted to email and texting, wait until they are both abruptly cut off.

I couldn't sleep last night because I kept thinking of so many things that had never before occurred to me. This experience takes isolation to another whole level, which is much more frightening. It really is possible to become totally cut off from the world and to have no idea what is going on. No newspapers, magazines, TV shows, news feeds because of the pandemic. I can't go to the neighbors for help, I can't go to the college or the coffee shop to connect. Our self-righteous NIMBY locals won't allow a cell tower to be built in South Williamstown, so we don't have cell phone coverage. I might be able to get in the car and drive toward town until I find a hot spot. Call me naïve, but until last night it had never occurred to me that I might not be able to teach my class because I had lost connectivity, and could not even contact the students to tell them what had happened. Physical isolation is hard enough, but total isolation is really, really hard. Even worse, consider being confined to your house or apartment for days, weeks, even months without being able to get news or communicate with others. Imagine not knowing whether the plague is spreading or receding, and not knowing who is sick, who is living and who is dead.

Tossing and turning last night, I thought back to my sophomore year in college in 1965, when the entire Northeast was simultaneously hit with a blackout, and to 2003, when most of the greater New York area went dark. While some people frolicked in candlelit bars and bedrooms, others were stuck in elevators or struggled to negotiate busy intersections without traffic lights. What if this were to happen again? The plague has made me more acutely aware than ever of our human vulnerability, but until the cable went dead, I did not fully comprehend the full extent of our technological vulnerability.

We keep forgetting how recent all this technology and the problems it brings are. It was not until 1991 that we could connect to the Williams network through a dial-up modem. Since Dinny was working in the College's Office of Information Technology, we were among the first cable Internet adopters in 1993 or 1994. During the early years, the connections were unreliable and slow. By the time she became the director, connectivity had improved, but was still unstable. Every time there was a thunderstorm she would stay awake because invariably the college network went down and she would have to get her guys to go in and restart the system. As the reliability of local, national, and international networks has improved, we have become less aware of how fragile all of these networks remain.

During the last presidential election, we became aware of the susceptibility of networks and social media to outside interference. For reasons of blatant self-interest, neither companies nor governments take these dangers seriously enough. Even before our blackout last night I had begun to worry about what the Russians, Chinese, and other public and private adversaries are doing online while we are scrambling to cope with the virus. Though messing with the elections is bad enough, they could be doing so much more to disrupt our lives. If someone really wants to hurt the United States, they should take down the Internet or crash the power grid now. Not only would we not have the resources to respond, but such a radical disruption would prevent us from dealing with the escalating health crisis we are facing.

All of this is a strange coincidence after having written to you just two days ago about reconceiving the struggle with the virus as an espionage game of intelligence and counterintelligence. The film we were watching last night, *Salt*, is a Cold War story starring Angelia Jolie as a superwoman CIA operative who is either a Russian mole or an American counteragent. Born in Russia and orphaned as a child, Evelyn Salt, along with other children, was trained to be a Russian agent, who was planted in a sleeper cell in the United States. After passing for a CIA agent for years, her Russian handler, who was part of a plot intended to overthrow their own government, activated her to kill the Russian president while he was attending a funeral in New York. Though I have my suspicions, I'm still not sure whose side Salt is on because we didn't get to see the end of the film. What is clear is that in the espionage game, coy deception and intelligence beat brute force every time.

As Putin and Xi Jinping know better than Trump, the intelligence game has changed. Not all agents are political, some are chemical, and not all viruses are biological; some are informational or disinformational. It is now possible to plant viruses in software programs and platforms that can remain dormant for years and be triggered remotely when the time is right. Worms are to computer programs what secret agents are to the KGB, CIA, and Mossad. The most notorious known worm is Stuxnet, which the CIA used in 2017 to attack Iran's nuclear program. I have read reports that some analysts are convinced there are hundreds if not thousands of worms embedded in programs running on the computers of the American government and businesses.

Our situation is even more precarious than I had realized. Suppose a foreign agent chose to activate a computer virus at the moment of our greatest vulnerability. What if a sleeper cell designed to pull the plug of the nation's Internet were switched on when hospitals are overflowing and cities are empty? What if worms slumbering in the programs responsible for operating the power grid were suddenly brought to life? What if the government, financial firms, hospitals, schools, prisons, factories, and businesses all went dead at the same time? Chaos . . . total chaos. That is the possibility I saw on the blank screen of our TV last night.

The effect of the plague will be long-lasting—indeed, the anxiety it provokes will never go away. Once you have been infected by invisible viruses or worms, you know they might be anywhere and strike at any time. I will never again sleep as soundly as I once did. For now, I am waiting, still waiting to be reconnected.

* * *

Mother Nature again. The Spectrum technician finally arrived. After surveying the situation, he discovered that the cable leading to the house had been disconnected on the phone pole across from my bone garden. He asked if we had had a bad windstorm recently, and I reported that the wind was unusually strong a couple of nights ago. He surmised that the

wind had broken the splice. Then he examined the cable more carefully and discovered that its orange plastic casing has a series of slash marks. He also noticed that the phone pole was damaged in the same area. He asked if anything had hit the pole. When I said, "No," he asked if there were any bears in the area, and I responded, "Sometimes, but I've not seen anything lately." He said, "Looks to me like a bear clawed this cable and the pole." Dinny agrees; I'm not so sure. As he was leaving, the cable guy, pointing to my bone garden, said, "Maybe it's revenge for that." We've reconnected now. I knew we were hanging by a thread, but I did not know that the thread that connects us to the world in this hour of need could be broken by wind or a curious bear.

Mark

*April 14*

Dear Mark:

Reading this unlikely tale from the life of an American driven into home retreat by the plague, I was prompted to circle back to an earlier point in our exchange when I spoke of my chronic skepticism vis-à-vis Kurzweil's Singularity and other extrapolations into the future from our contemporary digital technology. I couldn't find that prior reference, but it has been painfully clear to me from very early on that all these enterprises presuppose the unbroken continuity of a panoply of very earthy support systems to which almost no thought is given. An analogous older technology is that of nuclear power generation, which requires an unbroken provision of electricity *not generated by* the generating station itself as well as the undisrupted delivery—effectively, in perpetuity—of the large amounts of continuously changing water needed to cool the lethally toxic spent fuel. In a city like New York, the amount of manual labor required on a daily basis to keep indispensable infrastructure functional is on display nearly every day. You pass it on the sidewalk. Elsewhere, it's not quite as walk-past-it visible as in New York, but the same situation, beneath the surface, does obtain everywhere in our highly differentiated society. The systems we depend on, down to the humblest, are not under our individual control and very often are muscle dependent.

The young children and the aging parents of the upper and upper middle class in America are in the custody of the (muscles of the) least well-paid workers in our society. As much can be said of many lower-level workers in our hospitals. President Trump has lately lent his support to moves to *lower* the wages of agricultural workers so as to preserve what agribusiness requires as the minimum level of profit. My daughter once wrote for HuffPost a story about how the intake of new employees at Walmart commonly includes information on how to procure food stamps, the clear understanding being that Walmart's wages will not be enough to put food on an average new hire's table. Amazon has just fired three workers who dared to complain that their work put them in proximate danger of COVID-19 contagion. My point for the moment is not the social injustice of these arrangements but rather a warning, now perhaps coming home as never before, of how the most ontologically transformative technologies now in use or just over the horizon remain dependent on services like these. An old several-part proverb comes to mind:

> For the want of a nail the shoe was lost,
> For the want of a shoe the horse was lost,
> For the want of a horse the rider was lost,
> For the want of a rider the battle was lost,
> For the loss of a battle the kingdom was lost,
> All for the want of a horse shoe nail.

Today, I finished your roughly forty-year-old essay "Toward an Ontology of Relativism," and though it is certainly not light reading, I found it deeply engrossing. It might have been exceptionally interesting to read as I thought through how to stage *The Norton Anthology of World Religions*. Still, by and large I came away pleased or relieved that at certain key moments your essay seems consonant or compatible with what we do in the anthology. I quote in the preface, for example, Max Müller's dictum "He who knows one religion knows none." Or this, from the general introduction:

> In telling the life stories of six major, living, international religions through their respective primary texts, the editors of *The Norton Anthology of World Religions* have neither suppressed variability over time in service to any supposedly timeless essence of the thing nor, even when using the word *classical*, dignified any one age as truly golden. Each of the stories ends with modernity, but modernity in each case is neither the climax nor the denouement of the story. It is not the last chapter, only the latest.

It was an interesting surprise for me to discover that your mise en scène for this philosophical essay was the phenomenon of world religious pluralism as it impinged on constructive theology: "Not infrequently, the apprehension of the situational character of knowledge and truth stills the voice of constructive systematic theology and directs attention to the study of religion as an historical human phenomenon." And again, toward the end, "Not infrequently psycho-social pluralization brings an acute awareness of perspectival relativism that results in the stilling of the theological and metaphysical impulse." I couldn't agree more that not just in theology, but in all of the humanities, the methods of history have become the default methodology. But one might plausibly infer from sentences like those just quoted that the catalyst of the theoretical work done here would be a new departure in constructive systematic theology, this time taking its rise not just from Christianity but from the panoply of now-mingling world religions mutually constituting one another by simultaneous affirmation and negation. Francis X. Clooney, S.J.'s recent *His Hiding Place Is Darkness: A Hindu-Catholic Theopoetics of Absence* is conceivably the kind of work that could be catalyzed by the thinking you offer here. His methods are not those of history but of a theology in which the quest named in the classic phrase *fides quaerens intellectum* no longer proceeds from the writer's faith alone.

In fact, however, where your thoughts led you was not to that kind of engagement but to the "pluralism," thus intrusively to use the word, of humanity and divinity, human-ism and the-ism, athe-ology and the-ology. And once that turn was taken, investigation into the variety of world religious phenomena faded rapidly into the background in favor of investigation into the variety of extrareligious cultural phenomena. This movement from the still-religious to the postreligious seems a common enough one among those with a sufficiently wide acquaintance with religious variety, not that I am prepared to list here cases in point. As I see it, the variety of world religious assertions and assumptions—and we are not speaking here of variety in William James's sense of the word—has a mutually expulsive power. These colorful but wildly divergent variations cannot all be simultaneously true, but they can easily all be simultaneously false. Taking them thus brings a welcome closure and a simultaneous opening to a world of other subjects where God, religion, faith, etc., need never be mentioned. Obviously, this is not your story, because of your ongoing preoccupation with the roots of modernity in Lutheran Protestantism. But the other to *that* story would be neither the monothetic nor the polythetic other that you reject at the start of the essay but would rather be entirely other forms of synthesis than the Lutheran/Hegelian. Are there any such others? Do they grow from other roots than the Christian roots of Western modernity? Maybe the answer to that question is no. Maybe, in fact, a hunt for such an other would come up empty. Or maybe it is under way as we speak. The rather lame best I could do in the *NAWR* was this:

What is true of the six religions anthologized here may be true of religion in general. Just as there is no Hinduism as such but only a polythetic array of practices that may be differently combined, so there may be no religion as such but only a far greater array of practices that, again, may be differently combined, not just within recognized religious traditions but across them. Thus, Doniger lists "worship at shrines of Muslim saints" as a practice that "some Hindus" engage in without ceasing to be Hindu. Syncretism, the introduction of a feature from one religion into the life of another, is in itself an argument that the borrower and the lender are, or can be, related even when they are not, and never will be, identical. Multiple religious belonging—double or triple affiliation—sometimes takes syncretism a step further. And while borrowings across major borders are an additive process, adjustments within borders can often be a subtractive process, as seen in many statements that take the form of "I am a Buddhist, but . . .," "I am a Catholic, but . . ., "I am a Muslim, but . . .," and so forth. In such statements the speaker takes the broad term as a starting point and then qualifies it until it fits properly.

My work on the anthology is my first personal connection or application of this article, which as you say is a proem to all your later work. My second, more truly personal connection is to my 2002 essay—delivered once in public but never published (and I sent to you at some later point)—"Becoming Who I Am: Finding Truth and Community in a Diverse and Divided America." The point of connection was that my essay proceeded toward the formation of an American identity by way of a protracted series of negations, beginning with the infant's discovery that it (yes, *it*) is not its (m)other. After running through a series that included ethnic, sexual, economic, political, and religious negations in general, I turned to myself in particular and provided a relevant episode under each heading. Because the sexual entry involved bisexual orientation, you advised against my publishing it: "It will do you no good." And so I didn't publish it, and you were probably right, but I was even then, I suspect, rather less guarded on that subject than you are inclined to be.

To end on a light note, hoping I haven't already mentioned this on the phone, Kitty and I had a surprise Easter present on Sunday night. We were having a Zoom dinner with Kathleen, Brian, and Jennifer, Brian's mother, when Mo called, asking if he could make a delivery in fifteen minutes. What he brought was his Easter present: a box of six Krispy Kreme donuts. We were touched to the heart but also, me especially, repeatedly reduced to giggles. Krispy Kreme for Easter! Who'd a thunk?

Jack

* * *

## MAY 2–5: MARK BEGINS.

*Singularity, superintelligence, and posthumanism . . . evolution from carbon-based to silicon-based intelligence . . . Us (carbon) humans against Them (silicon)? . . .* COVID *as the disruption of this disruption . . ."compassion explosion" vs. "intelligence explosion" as marking the end of humanity as we have known it . . . Nagarjuna anticipating Kurzweil: who is essential to whom?*

*Fear of armed Trumpublicans carrying guns and waving Confederate flags . . . benevolent AI as the likelier "compassion explosion" . . . hug-hunger and home-schooling . . . humans as E. coli in the "gut" of a silicon future? . . . Hegel, Gregory Bateson ("mind as immanent in the total evolutionary structure"), and Jain* anekantavada, *or pluralism, as cognitively indispensable . . . species-specific intelligence analogous to discipline-specific methodology . . . childhood and second childhood struggling alike with life on Zoom.*

---

*May 2*

Dear Jack:

Your comments about discontent with screen life echo what Kirsten reported yesterday. She said that Jackson and Taylor are done with screens—they just don't want to communicate with anybody using Zoom or anything else. These remarks are related to some reflections on my classes that I've been intending to share with you.

Return of the repressed: in Sunday's *Boston Globe*, there were twenty-four pages of obituaries. *Twenty-four pages!* Even though Massachusetts has taken strict precautions, the plague has still hit the state very hard and the situation is not improving. There are 103 patients in a local nursing home; 45 have contracted the virus, and 17 have already died. This incredibly harsh reality stands in stark contrast to what I've been discussing with students. There is no way I could have anticipated how different the works appear from when I designed the course.

I am ending my Philosophy of Religion course by considering how new technologies are changing our understanding of what it means to be a human being. We began with Ray Kurzweil's *The Singularity Is Near* and then discussed Nick Bostrom's *Superintelligence*. Kurzweil is a fascinating person—long-time MIT professor, inventor, currently the director of research at Google, and recipient of the Presidential Medal of Honor. Bostrom is Swedish and currently is a professor of philosophy at Oxford and the founding director of the Future of Humanity Institute. If they were not such accomplished and respected scientists and philosophers, it would be hard to take many of their ideas seriously. Both are convinced that in the very near future there is going to be an "intelligence explosion" that not only will mark the end of humanity as we know it, but also will lead to the colonization of the universe by nonhuman forms of intelligence. Their ideas raise a host of issues that I want to discuss with you, but this morning will concentrate on a problem that is particularly relevant at this moment: the complex interplay between body and mind, and, by extension, of embodiment and disembodiment.

Online classes are in many ways experiments in disembodied education, so I decided to ask the students to reflect on their experience. Everyone agreed that they were surprised by how well the class was going. No one was dissatisfied and several students even said they preferred meeting online to "real" classes. I replied that I agreed with their assessment, but explained that there are some things I had not anticipated, and others that involve surprising paradoxes. Zoom is now so familiar that everyone knows how the faces of participants are displayed in a grid. Even though the resolution of the images is good, everyone appears to be strangely disembodied. I told students that this reminded me of the first virtual course I taught with Helsinki thirty years ago. Since the Internet was just emerging and the World Wide Web had not yet been created, we used teleconferencing technology in which there were two video feeds, one outgoing and one incoming. The image that appeared on a small TV screen was only the face of the person who was speaking. You could see neither the speaker's whole body nor the other people in the class. This was a totally new kind of talking head. It was not until I taught that course that I realized how much of my teaching depends on reading students' bodily responses and reactions. Furthermore, I had never realized how important ambient awareness is; while concentrating on a student who is speaking, I am simultaneously aware without necessarily being conscious of everyone else in the class. I know who is with me and who is not, who is engaged and whose mind is wandering. While I can see the faces of all the students on Zoom, I cannot read their body language and, thus, cannot engage them as fully as in a "real" classroom setting.

When placed in a broader context, the virtual classroom is an extension of the process of virtualization, dematerialization, and disembodiment that has been going on for several decades. The movement from modernism to postmodernism, and then to posthumanisim, can be understood in terms of the progressive virtualization of reality and, correlatively, the gradual disappearance of the body. This virtualization occurs in two interrelated stages: first, the transformation of the real into image in consumer capitalism; second, the digitization of the real in financial capitalism. By any traditional standard, the notion of virtual reality is an oxymoron—the real, however it is conceived, has long been regarded as the opposite of the virtual and vice versa. The collapse of this distinction, therefore, marks a significant change.

"Collapse" is not the right word; it's not so much that the real has collapsed into the virtual as that the real has been reduced to or consumed by the virtual. This reduction presupposes all forms chemical and biological to social and economic processes is encoded information. Digital information, in other words, is the *substance* of all reality. This development involves a change in the understanding of oppositions like mind/body, immateriality/materiality, and interiority/exteriority that have been the foundation of our understanding of ourselves and our world for centuries. If chemical and biological processes are information processes, bodies are smart and what had been regarded as material is really immaterial. Kurzweil makes this point as concisely as possible: "My body is temporary. Its particles turn over almost completely every month. Only the pattern of my body and brain have continuity." Here the process of dematerialization or virtualization is carried to its logical conclusion. Like the faces of students appearing in the grid on my computer, the body effectively vanishes in lines of digital code. By pushing these processes as far as possible, Kurzweil and his fellow believers become latter-day Gnostics whose project is to escape the temporal world, which is marred by decay. For such visionaries, death poses the ultimate engineering challenge. With the proliferation of transplants, natural and artificial implants, nanotechnology, neuroscience, genetic engineering,

CRISPR, and countless autonomous and semiautonomous medical devices, Kurzweil insists that within a few decades, people will be able to live for several hundred years and perhaps even forever.

This vision is even more grandiose than achieving immortality suggests. Some leading software engineers actually believe that with their codes and algorithms, they can conjure the next stage of evolution. If life is pattern rather than stuff, it is, in principle, possible for life to migrate from carbon to silicon. Nonbiological forms of intelligence are already many times faster and more powerful than human intelligence, and operate at speeds that preclude the possibility of human intervention. Furthermore, machines have become self-programming; algorithms can code programs too complex for human beings to understand or create. Bostrom as well as leading scientists and innovators like Stephen Hawking, Bill Joy, and Elon Musk warn that these software creations might get out of control and create "intelligent superorganisms" that are a greater threat to humanity than nuclear technology. To avoid this danger, some experts are calling for a ban, or at least the strict regulation of any research and development that might lead to superintelligence.

Is it possible or even desirable to prevent these developments? Might superintelligence create the next stage in the evolutionary process that would leave human nature behind? Far from an artificial intervention, might this development be a "natural" stage of evolution? If nature is intelligent and bodies are smart rather than dumb, and if humans are an integral part of nature and not separate from or opposed to it, then humankind's transformation of nature is nature's transformation of itself. Evolution is something like an intelligent self-creating and self-regulating network that is constantly evolving. But where is this process heading?

In his classic cyberpunk novel *Neuromancer*, William Gibson declares the human body merely "meat." Cyberspace, which is "a consensual illusion," holds the promise of escaping the prison house of the flesh. Is this where the disembodiment I see in the faces of my students on Zoom ends? Have leading computer scientists and engineers drunk the Kool Aid and succumbed to the "consensual illusion" of virtual reality?

All of this looks very different than it did three months ago. With death all around us, the plague exposes the vacuity of such cruel illusions by disclosing the deeper truth. At the very moment of the body's purported disappearance, it returns with a savage ferocity to reassert the inescapable mortality of our bodily being.

Mark


*May 2*

Dear Mark:

You leap in successive letters from a most intense preoccupation with your own body, your own kidney, to a meditation on disembodiment. I'm still recovering from the whiplash.

I infer, though with some hesitation, that the crisis of a day ago has eased, but do let me know. Today, the *New York Times* ran an agonizing account, agonizing in its detail, of how a COVID-19 patient who needed dialysis as well as COVID treatment failed to get it and died, despite repeated pleading from his family, who knew all too well what the relevant numbers (somehow these were shared with them) meant for their husband and father.

My friend Yonder Gillihan worries that without the structuring recurrence of his class in his students' lives, they will start falling to pieces. I overstate his concern, and you express no such concern, but I do suspect that your departing students will miss the venue your class has provided them for thinking past the echo chamber of the daily coronavirus news and into a deeper engagement with their own future. If I were a participant in the class discussion of Kurzweil and Bostrom, I would ask about the prospects for a "compassion explosion," for that explosion, no less than an "intelligence explosion," would also mark "the end of humanity as we have known it." I attended a conference once in Japan where a Buddhist thinker challenged Aristotle's identification of intelligence as the specific quality that makes the human species human. Closer observation would confirm that all animals think to some degree; ethology has come up with some astonishing examples in, e.g., the octopus. In any case, what to the speaker seemed truly unique about our species was our compassion. Other animals do not care for their sick, tend their wounded, feed or defend their aged, or bury their dead. We do. That would be a first classroom intervention. A second would be a simple question: "Whom does Kurzweil call when the toilet backs up?"

I am less dazzled than you are by "software engineers [who] actually believe that with their codes and algorithms, they can conjure the next stage of evolution." You conclude, "All this looks very different than it did three months ago." Not to me, it doesn't. To me, it looks just the same. Back in 1990, I read O. B. Hardison Jr.'s *Disappearing Through the Skylight: Culture and Technology in the Twentieth Century*, which won the *Los Angeles Times* Book Prize that year. Hardison, a professor of English, predicted that silicon-based intelligent life would succeed carbon-based human life. I was hugely skeptical then because I saw the entire research enterprise that was to reach this visionary goal as fiscally dependent on the status quo of massive government funding. I saw the researchers themselves as so fully in what you later call "the prison house of the flesh" that, rather than a vision, what they so confidently predict was an illusion—a conceptual possibility that was and would remain beyond physical realization. Just now, I retrieved the *New York Times* review of the book, by Michiko Kakutani, which nicely expresses the skepticism I shared at the promise of "a future in which computers will incorporate 'a great deal that is important to the spirit of carbon man—his soaring imagination, his brilliance, his creativity, his capacity for vision' while filtering out his 'undesirable self-defeating traits.'"

The coronavirus certainly does add a new layer of threat to the infrastructure that sustains the digital world that, because of the coronavirus, we now depend upon in major new ways. But preexisting layers of threat had long since struck me as so overpowering that I have not needed COVID-19 to teach me skepticism. In the dialogue you quote, Kurzweil's "Not yet, but there will be" reminds me of an old joke that has been circulating for decades—or maybe has stopped circulating because everyone has already heard it: "So, it seems they wired all the computers of the world into one giant computer, and then they asked it the great question, 'Is there a god?' And the answer came back quickly: 'Yes, there is. . . . *now!*'"

Kurzweil's vision seems to coincide pretty exactly with Yuval Hariri's in *Homo Deus*. And such supersessionist predictions that what God or the gods once did, Man or mankind or humankind shall now undertake have certainly been with us for a long long time. What else was there in Feuerbach's vision? Or in the Communist Internationale?

> *Es rettet uns kein höheres Wesen,*
> *Kein Gott, kein Engel, noch Tribun,*
> *Uns aus dem Elend zu erlösen*
> *Mussen wir schon selber tun.*

Which is not to say that there is nothing new here and certainly not to say that here is nothing dangerous: Gates and Joy and Musk are not worried about nothing, especially not when Kurzweil foresees carbon-based golems. I sent you Jerome Groopman's piece on the lax testing of medical implants and their sometimes lethal consequences, a kind of peril that you have experienced through having a beta version of an artificial pancreas installed in your body. Imagine—as colossal profit beckons for whoever first synthesizes a vaccine against COVID-19—that the synthesized vaccine turns out to be an even more catastrophic COVID-20 as it escapes from the laboratory. I believe in the risk far, far more readily than I believe in the promise, which, as the Hardison quote rather nicely illustrates, is a promise untouched by universal compassion, a promise for the (male) few at the expense of the many. The irony is that, for now and *now* has never been more crucial, the few remain hugely dependent on the many and can neither achieve immortality nor secure mere survival without them.

All this thus querulously asserted, I do find myself in rich sympathy with Kurzweil at one point in the passages you quote. I, too, see each human being, myself certainly included, as more like an event than like a thing—more like an endless performance in which the audience and the performers are identical and are replaced through iteration after iteration of a show that never closes than like a statue or a painting. But I have been enamored of this idea ever since first encountering the Buddhist notion of codependent origination, usually associated with the second-century philosopher Nagarjuna. Nothing is itself, everything is a coalescence of other things, and everything at every moment is passing away. *Sunnyata* is misleadingly translated "emptiness," I think; "evanescence" is much the better word. Of a piece with this, of course, is *anatman*, or nonself. Above, I deliberately write "*more* like an event than like a thing" because I am also to a degree quite like a thing—a living thing from moment to moment but still at each moment a thing, a self. This is why I am a Christian with Buddhist sympathies rather than a Buddhist. In any case, every American Buddhist I have ever come to know has always seemed to me a Buddhist with unacknowledged Christian tendencies. Similarly here, perhaps: you call these messiahs of digitized evolution "Gnostics whose project is to escape the temporal world, which is marred by decay." Gnostics if you prefer, but you could as easily call them cultural Christians.

Let me end with a fine, already quoted phrase in your penultimate paragraph that struck a spark of memory in me: "The prison house of the flesh." Our late friend John Maguire loved to quote W. H. Auden's elegy for W. B. Yeats. The last quatrain in that very great poem calls on the poet "in the prison of his days" to "teach the free man how to praise." The prison of his days is a prison because it is a house of flesh, is it not? The Academy of American Poets has a new coronavirus-linked program, "Shelter in Poems," on its website. Readers are invited not to write poems and send them in (God save us from that!) but to select poems from the academy's huge online archive and propose them for reading at this juncture in our common life. I might just suggest Auden's.

Jack

*May 3*

Dear Jack:

I understand your whiplash and should have explained where things stand. I have not yet made a decision about the blood test and CAT scan because I need more information. On Friday, I sent a list of questions to both my primary care physician here in Williamstown and my cardiologist in New York. I have not yet heard back from them. I should add that my immediate concern is not dialysis, though I've worried about that ever since I was diagnosed with diabetes over thirty years ago. The current issue is a problem I had not known about previously—diabetes can cause small blood vessels in the kidneys to constrict and this can raise blood pressure. Everything *is* interconnected. My cardiologist said this condition can be treated; I couldn't bring myself to ask him what kind of invasive procedure would be required.

Your letter raises a host of issues and questions, some of which I have been considering as I think about the best way to conclude my classes this week. You frame the questions Kurzweil and others raise in a particularly effective way, so effective that I am going to send two paragraphs of your letter to my Philosophy of Religion class and use them as the point of departure for our final discussion tomorrow. A couple of brief comments before I turn to more substantive issues. First, by using the phrase "prison house of the flesh," I was deliberately echoing Fredric Jameson's hugely influential book *The Prison House of Language*. Jameson, as you know, fashioned himself a Marxist and has had an inordinate impact on literary criticism and cultural studies for the past several decades. I've never found his work very helpful and have always attributed its impact to the eagerness of academic Marxists to find an intellectual justification for their preexisting political inclinations and uninformed criticisms of capitalism. Second, a strange coincidence. While looking for another book the other day, I noticed Hardison's *Disappearing Through the Skylight* on the shelf and made a mental note to take another look at it. I read it when it was published, probably at your suggestion. Third, animal intelligence. As my previous letter about my ongoing struggle with the groundhog made clear, I agree with you on this point. I thought I had outsmarted him, but, as the pictures I sent to you yesterday make clear, he's back and more determined than ever. So am I, of course: I refilled the hole he dug out, covered it with a couple of boards, and tomorrow I am going to the building supply store to get four cinderblocks to put on top of the boards. The groundhog reinforces my long-standing view of distributed understanding of intelligence, which extends both to nonanimal forms of life and macro and micro machines into which we are increasingly plugged. More about all of this below, but first a word about compassion.

You write, "If I were a participant in the class discussion of Kurzweil and Bostrom, I would ask about the prospects for a 'compassion explosion,' for that explosion, no less than an 'intelligence explosion' would also mark 'the end of humanity as we have known it." I would respond, "Seriously? A compassion explosion, are you kidding?" I do not deny that in the midst of this crisis there are many examples of genuine compassion, nowhere more so than among doctors, nurses, and other health care providers. TV is flooded with reports and advertisements promoting a feel-good optimism motivated by economic interest more than human concern. I am not convinced, because I think an explosion of violence is as likely as an explosion of compassion. The longer the shutdown continues, the more volatile the situation becomes. We have already discussed how Trump is using the health/wealth debate as a wedge issue to advance his political self-interest by further dividing red and blue states. Now we have images of protesters carrying all kinds of guns and waving the Confederate flag as well as a red flag with a swastika and the names of Trump and Pence taking over the Michigan state house. Legislators who are attempting to deal with the crisis have been forced to wear bulletproof vests. The president has tweeted that the people taking part in the "Operation Gridlock," like the participants in the Charlottesville parade, are "good people." So much for compassion.

The plague is creating deeper divisions not only within this country, but also between the United States and the rest of the world. Bill and Melinda Gates have stepped into the void created by the absence of responsible political leadership in this country. Right-wing agitators have predictably circulated all kinds of unsubstantiated conspiracy theories about Gates' intervention. Gates gave up on Trump and his Republican enablers a long time ago, and now is working closely with the European Commission. On Monday, the Gates Foundation announced a 7.5 million pound grant to finance tests, medicines, and vaccines to treat the coronavirus. A recent article on Politico reports that "Melinda Gates said the foundation views Europe as key to bringing international players to the table and preventing the wealthiest countries from putting their own needs first. 'That's why you see us focusing with Europe,' Gates said. 'It's the European leaders, quite honestly, who understand that we need global cooperation.'" She added: "I think they're doing the very best they can do in this situation.'" Hegel was wrong, World Spirit does not always move from Europe to America, but sometimes reverses itself and move from West to East.

The second substantive point you raise is somewhat more complicated. Sometimes you seem to confuse my discussion of the ideas of others with my own point of view. This seems to be the case with some of your comments about my take on Kurzweil and those who agree with him. I share many of your concerns about the denigration of the body and material process without which digital technologies are impossible. That is why I have been arguing that the plague represents the return of the repressed that makes our mortal bodily being undeniable. If, however, we take a longer evolutionary perspective, things become less clear.

To understand my position on this issue, it is necessary to stress that I have a more expansive view of technology and, by extension, of intelligence and cognition than you do. Ever since our distant ancestor first picked up a stick to use as a tool, our bodies and brains have been transformed by technology. One could argue that no technology has been more transformative for the human brain than writing. Digital technologies are an extension of writing, which rewires the brain faster than pens, typewriters, and books. If we look ahead a hundred, five hundred, even a thousand years, it seems undeniable that this interdependence will increase beyond anything we can now imagine. That is what I mean by "intervolution." When Bostrom describes self-programming algorithms creating a superintelligence that is beyond human control, he's not projecting a distant dystopian future, he's reporting what is already occurring. I have no doubt that the concerns of people like Musk and Joy are well founded; it is not only possible, but all too likely that this technology will be used for nefarious purposes, and it is not impossible that superintelligence will get out of control and turn against its creators.

> *Time out: I have to take a break. We are instituting a new tradition: A weekly family Zoom get-together at 10:30 Sunday morning. Years ago, my parents would call at 11 every Sunday for a chat. Now, thanks to technological progress, the four cousins can play together online.*

Where was I? Right: superintelligence run amok. My question is whether this result is inevitable. Let me toss your question back to you and ask whether there might be a compassionate AI explosion. An article in today's *New York Times*, "How A.I. Steered Doctors Toward a Possible Coronavirus Treatment," suggests this possibility. The author, Cade Metz, focuses on a company founded in London in 2013. I had never heard of BenevolentAI, so I checked out the website (https://benevolent.ai/). Their home page summarizes the company's mission:

> Our aim is to improve patients' lives. We create and use AI technologies to transform the way medicines are discovered, developed, tested and brought to market.

We have developed the Benevolent Platform™—a leading computational and experimental discovery platform that allows our scientists to find new ways to treat disease and personalise medicines to patients.

Metz reports that in late January, researchers at BenevolentAI turned their attention to finding a cure for the coronavirus. Within a few days, their machine learning system using the latest universal language tools had searched millions of scientific documents and compiled a huge interconnected database. Much to their surprise, they discovered that a drug called baricitinib, which had been designed to treat rheumatoid arthritis, might be used to treat the coronavirus. Since rheumatoid arthritis, like diabetes, results from a malfunction in the immune system, this possibility seemed worth testing. "Through their software, they found that baricitinib might also prevent the viral infection itself, blocking the way it enters cells." If successful, this drug would not merely reduce the immune response to the coronavirus, but would actually prevent the viral infection. With so many researchers everywhere in the world frantically competing to create an effective vaccine, many people were surprised that a recent start-up few people had ever heard of made such a promising discovery.

At Emory, the lab researchers were shocked that the paper had come from BenevolentAI. "It was crazy," said Christina Gavegnano, who took part in the work with H.I.V. "We kept asking: 'Who are these people? Does anyone know them?'"

A month later, Dr. Marconi proposed a clinical trial with baricitinib and another drug. As coronavirus cases mounted at his hospital, he and his *clinicians administered the pill as a compassionate measure to patients* [emphasis added], with encouraging results.

"We normally talk about 'bench to bedside,'" Dr. Stebbing said, referring to moving quickly from laboratory bench research into the treatment of patients. "This is about 'computer to bench to bedside.'"

While this development is potentially very important for the current crisis, it also has far-reaching implications that deserve serious consideration. Where you look for a "benevolence explosion" that depends on a rewiring of human affections, I hope for a benevolent AI explosion that depends on the impersonal calculation of self-generating algorithms. While these systems and networks might be semiautonomous for now, in the near future humans will drop out and the loop will be closed just like the artificial pancreas I wear on my belt.

*Clinicians administered the pill as a compassionate measure to patients.* Yes, superintelligence might get out of control and declare war on the human race. However, what if it led to a benevolent AI explosion that would enable scientists and physicians to wage a different war—a war on cancer, diabetes, and the plague?

Mark

*May 3*

Dear Mark:

I have made friends twice with Africans, and both times were both enjoyable and educational. I've mentioned already sharing my apartment at Harvard with the late Dr. Anthony Akingbade. Earlier, in Israel, I was briefly close to a priest from the country then called Upper Volta. I can no longer remember his name, but having been in Israel much longer than he and being at the time pretty fluent in Hebrew, I was able to help him across a couple of customs or immigration hurdles, and somehow at another point in that year he and I ended up seated next to each other on a long, hot, seemingly endless bus trip into the Negev. His father was a riverboat trader on the Volta River, and a skillful navigator of the river, proud of his prosperity and his skill. In the life of their village, my friend told me, the arrival of television was not culturally very disruptive at all. People simply gathered around the set the way they would gather around to hear stories or news from a visitor or "professional" storyteller. What *was* disruptive was writing, and he described to me how humiliating it was for his father when he was shown the Volta on a map and the route that he traversed was pointed out to him. For him, that stretch was a dauntingly long distance, traversing it a real achievement, but on the map it seemed so small as to almost disappear. He was crestfallen, almost crushed. A painful moment in memory for the man's son, who was telling me the story.

Why do I find this story coming to mind? Because, in an earlier message, you said that Jackson and Taylor were completely fed up with Zoom. No more Zoom for them. Been there, done that. But in this letter, you describe the four cousins getting together and *playing* via Zoom. My suspicion is that it is not just the getting together of the four cousins but also of their six elders, counting you two, their grandparents. Even in their separate locations under your roof, there is just enough touch, enough of the human warmth and closeness that made television welcome in an Upper Volta village because it did not shrink and divide the world the way writing does—or, I might add, texting does. In the *New York Times* today, Frank Bruni writes about the brilliant Laurie Garrett, alone now in her Brooklyn Heights apartment, though in demand for her expertise all around the world. "If I don't get hugged soon," she told Bruni, "I'm going to go bananas. I'm desperate to be hugged." As of this moment, all of the Taylors are getting regularly hugged, and nobody is going bananas. It's different for those Zooming from one solitary isolation to another. Zoom helps a lot to ease the isolation, and yet it does not help enough.

You didn't tell me just what part of my letter is going to make it into your class, but I'll be interested to hear how it goes. I stand by my "explosion of compassion" claim, and everything you write after "I would respond, 'Seriously?'" only makes my point. Take the casual heartlessness that you notice (I do too) around us to be "humanity as we know it." An explosion of compassion that could end *that* humanity would be as transformative as the explosion of intelligence of which Kurzweil and Bostrom dream. That compassion explosion ain't gonna happen, you clearly believe. I'm just as pessimistic. I simply happen to be equally pessimistic about the other explosion.

When I read the Cade Metz article this morning, my mind jumped immediately to your wonderful description in the third chapter of *Intervolution* of how AlphaGo was prepared for its match against the Korean Go champion Sedol:

> In preparation for the match, AlphaGo first played 100,000 games of Go, which were on the Internet, and then over the course of several months played 30 million games against itself. The result was that AlphaGo defeated Fan Hui 5-0. This was the first time a machine had

beaten a human playing Go. But the DeepMind team was not satisfied
with this victory—they wanted was to defeat the best Go player in the
world just as IBM wanted to beat the best chess player in the world. To
achieve this goal, the engineers upgraded AlphaGo to AlphaGo Zero.
In contrast to AlphaGo, which began its training by replaying games
people had played, AlphaGo Zero did not use any data from human
games, but played millions of games against itself. The word "Zero" was
added to underscore the fact that the neural network trained itself
without any human assistance. The designers explain, "We subsequently applied our reinforcement learning pipeline to a second
instance of AlphaGo Zero using a larger network and over a longer
duration. Training again started from completely random behavior
and continued for approximately 40 days. Over the course of training,
29 million games of self-play were generated. Parameters were updated
from 3.1 million mini-batches of 2,048 positions each."

I had to read your second chapter very slowly, as you know, but I just raced
through the third. You were writing there about just the AI technology
that BenevolentAI is employing in the search for a COVID-19 vaccine,
right? How exciting! Godspeed to them, and may they remain benevolent
and philanthropic if they succeed! Some time ago, Kathleen interviewed
Patrick Soon-Shiong, the billionaire medical inventor who now owns the
*Los Angeles Times*. His dream in the interview seemed to be that of enabling
physicians armed with a portable device to combine a quick read of a
patient's genome with this kind of blazing search of the Internet of medical
knowledge. In other words, the dream was of a diagnostic tool so intelligent that no mere human physician's mind could match it. There's no reason why a compassion explosion, should such an explosion occur, should be
merely a "rewiring of human affections." That's your phrase, not mine; a
compassion explosion could also include an executive function organizing
other human capacities or transhuman capacities. The sad fact is, however,
that every technical breakthrough ever achieved has been exploited to benefit some at the expense of others. Jeff Bezos achieved such a breakthrough
with Amazon, and I am from seclusion a more active Amazon customer
than ever. But he has also sowed financial ruin around the American economy. But enough: I need not belabor this point—you're already there.

To end with a narrower and admittedly speculative point, what I continue to doubt is that humans can ever, even through self-programming computers, build themselves out of any technology that originated with them. An image I have entertained is that of the future of the human species in the new world of AI androids as analogous to the future of E. coli in the human digestive system. E. coli has certain benevolent, indeed indispensable functions in our digestive biota. It can also turn lethal and poison us when it escapes. My point is that we will never be done with it. Even a patient without intestines, if being kept alive by some sort of life-support intestine-equivalent, will depend on the E.coli in other people's intestines. We will remain as indispensable and inescapable for all we create as we are indispensable and inescapable for ourselves. Maybe we do need *ein höheres Wesen* to rescue us.

Jack


*May 4*

Dear Jack:

Your letter this morning reminded me of another point I intended to make in response to your comments on Kurzweil and Bostrom. These thoughts take me back to our earlier discussion of emergent complex adaptive systems and are related to the issues I hope to raise in the last class for my Philosophy of Religion course later this morning. After reflecting on our latest exchange, I've decided to recast the question of the relation between religion and technology in a way that raises the possibility of overturning the deleterious effects of the Anthropocene by subverting the divisive oppositions upon which it is grounded. The seeds for this alternative vision were already present in the article I wrote nearly forty years ago that I called to your attention not long ago—"Toward an Ontology of Relativism." In a recent letter, you mentioned that you had read this essay and called it to the attention of a former colleague at Boston College. The gist of my argument in that article was that truth is relative because being is relational. I still hold that position, and much, if not all, of what I have written since then is an elaboration of that insight. Relativism, or, in Nietzsche's terms, perspectivism, is usually seen to lead to solipsism in which each individual is trapped in his or her private subjectivity and is unable to understand or even communicate with anyone else. The silos today's anti-social media create are examples of such solipsistic subjectivity. Such solipsism is self-contradictory and self-destructive because everything and everybody is inextricably interrelated. In other words, being is relational; to be is to be related. Nothing is itself by itself, and, therefore, I become myself in and through my relationship with other people, and, in the final analysis, everything else in the entire cosmos.

This is the vision I first glimpsed in Hegel's *Science of Logic* and *Phenomenology of Spirit*. By another of those coincidences that keep occurring, I was rereading Gregory Bateson's *Steps to an Ecology of Mind* when your letter arrived yesterday. This book was published in 1972 and quickly became one of the urtexts of the counterculture. Stewart Brand, who, as I've mentioned before, was one of Ken Kesey's Merry Pranksters and the founding editor of the *Whole Earth Catalog*, became a Bateson devotee. Bateson (1904–1980) lived the final years of his life in a small cottage on the grounds of the Esalen Institute in Big Sur. The pop version of Bateson's work has tended to obscure its serious intent as well as the rigor of his argument.

Bateson was one of the first to recognize the far-reaching philosophical and spiritual implications of information theory and cybernetics. When I finally read the book a few years ago, it was a revelation. His interpretation of information theory and cybernetics is completely consistent with the principles grounding Hegel's system. My later effort to establish a connection among Hegel's system, information theory, and emergent complex adaptive systems reinforces the relevance of Bateson's insights. More important in the context of our discussion the last few days, bringing together Bateson and Hegel creates the possibility of refiguring the relationship between religion and technology in a way quite different from Kurzweil and his epigones. To understand this argument, it is necessary to give up the traditional theistic image of a personal God. In his mature *philosophical* writings, Hegel replaces the word "God" with his preferred terms of "Absolute" or "Absolute Spirit"; I would add the "Infinite" or "Real."

While this is not the place to develop this argument in any detail, a few quotations from Bateson will suffice to clarify my point. Bateson's argument depends on an interpretation of the mind as a cybernetic system consisting of multiple layers of subsystems joined in recursive feedback loops that extend first to the body, and then beyond the body to the surrounding environment. Mind, body, and environment form a complex network in which being is relational.

> We get a picture, then, of mind as synonymous with cybernetic system—the relevant total-information processing, trial-and error completing unit. And we know that within Mind in the widest sense there will be a hierarchy of subsystems, any one of which we can call an individual mind. . . .

> It means, you see, that I now localize something which I am calling "mind" immanent in the large biological system—the ecosystem. Or, if I draw the system boundaries at a different level, then the mind is immanent in the total evolutionary structure. If this identity between mental and evolutionary units is broadly right, then we face a number of shifts in our thinking.

This is very close to what I mean by "intervolution."

Where I disagree with Bateson, and this is an important point, is that I do not think this ecological/evolutionary system is governed by the principle of equilibrium. Here the cybernetic model of negative feedback is misleading. Rather than closed and tending toward homeostasis, emergent complex adaptive systems are open and operate according to the principle of positive feedback. They drift far from equilibrium, thereby creating periodic unpredictable disruptions. This points toward my Kierkegaardian/Derridean corrective to Hegel's systematic system. Instead of simple opposites, structure and event, order and disruption, and reason and unreason are intertwined in such a way that each is a condition of the other. This quasi-dialectical interplay can be observed in machine learning operating through neural networks, which I have previously described to you. What I did not sufficiently stress is that every neural network is a black box, because nobody really understands how they work. This means that the heart of artificial intelligence, which increasingly forms the operating system of our world, is, like the human brain itself, at least for now, unfathomable. The unknowability of the mind in itself, the body in itself, the thing in itself, and the world in itself is the origin of both terror and hope.

And now, the final piece of this puzzle. When these two sides of emergent complex adaptive networks—the constructive and the deconstructive—are taken together, they form a reality that structurally and functionally resembles what once was known as God. Bateson points to this similarity when he writes,

> The cybernetic epistemology which I have offered you would suggest a new approach. The individual mind is immanent but not only in the body. It is immanent also in pathways and messages outside the body; and there is a larger Mind of which the individual mind is only a subsystem. This larger Mind is comparable to God and is perhaps what some people mean by "God," but it is still immanent in the total interconnected social system and planetary ecology.

Here is a spiritual vision that makes sense of our current condition without falling prey to the dangers of anthropocentrism. Rather than human intelligence seeding first the planet and then the universe, our minds and bodies are incarnations of an infinite process that simultaneously includes and surpasses them. To be *is* to be related, and this reality is affirmed even in the effort to negate. Everything *is* "entwined, enmeshed, enamored," and, hence (the) All intervolves. This is the lesson the plague is teaching us, and if we do not understand it, what is now known as humanity has no future.

Mark


*May 5*

Dear Mark:

I heard the claim made years ago that for every philosophical term in English, there are ten in Greek, and one hundred in Sanskrit. That saying came to mind as I read your letter today about your view, with Bateson, of "mind as immanent in the total evolutionary structure." I understand that because you want to stress positive feedback loops, you understand yourself to revise or at least refine Bateson by underscoring that the total evolutionary structure is indeed a total *evolutionary* structure: equilbrium, then disequilibrium, then sublation to a new equilibrium, *ad infinitum*.

You assert the relationality of being. From this it would seem to follow that a being seeking to know being must know it relationally—that is, with other beings. A core principle of Jainism, as expounded first by Mahavira, a contemporary of Buddha, is, in Sanskrit, *anekantavada*, literally "not-one-side-ness." The plurality of perspectives—knowledge in and by group(s) rather than in or by the singular mind—is not optional to knowledge, not an addition of your knowledge to my knowledge, not some kind of mutual tolerance. For there to be knowledge *at all,* knowledge in the first place, anywhere by anyone, there *must* be this plurality. It is conditio sine qua non. And what each says to the others in such groups, or by such process, is *syadvada,* which I believe can be translated "Yes, but. . . ." All assertions of knowledge are conditional, and once their conditions are reckoned with, all are true, but ever and only with their conditions attached.

By a crazily roundabout path, UCI received millions of endowment dollars for chairs in Hinduism but then gave the money back because the donors were judged tainted by the Hindu chauvinism now so fiercely dominant in Narendra Modi's India. I say "crazily roundabout" because, when the dust settled, UCI did end up with chairs in Sikhism and Jainism as well as, in addition, a Buddhism chair on the way—but still no chair in Hinduism. And since UCI has no department of religious studies, in what department did the Jain chair end up? In the philosophy department! Read the Wikipedia article on syadvada with its intricate typology of assertions, negations, simultaneous assertions and negations, and complications running on from there, and you might not be surprised that a crew trained in logical analysis might be intrigued. Jainism believes that, yes, there is truth, and, yes, there is language, but the latter never quite reaches the former. The process of human learning is endless if also asymptotic.

If we add a naturalistic, ecological dimension to this vision, then would it not follow that the knowledge possessed by each species is knowledge conditioned by its ecological/evolutionary niche: valid there, invalid elsewhere. By an only modest extrapolation, the pseudospeciation of spheres of human expertise are analogously valid and analogously circumscribed. Ignorance results in principle, and wreckage in practice, when "we" extrapolate from "our" sphere to others or, worse, succeed in expanding our extrapolation materially beyond "our" niche. Success in extending "our" knowledge until, in the words of Kurzweil's that you quote, "the entire universe will be

saturated with *our* intelligence" is the most radical negation possible of the
relationality of either being or inclusive knowing. As so very often in these
grand visions, the most important and least examined word is the first-
person plural pronoun.

Dave Eggers has just published an acerbic self-interrogation in the *New
York Times* entitled "Flattening the Truth on Coronavirus." The dialogue is
playful at times but in a very bitter way. One Blanchot-esque reference
point, with hyperlink provided, anchors his claim that the shortest path
ever recorded to a vaccine took four years. Four years! The way we are living now may well be the way we will be living for years to come, but is such
a life—are such lives—sustainable over years of time, even the optimistic
four? Can life, our lives as we are now living them, be sustained long
enough for us to live out a life sentence?

Claims now being made that Zoom produces autonomic and quite disruptive effects in our brains (see "Why Zoom Is Terrible" in today's *New
York Times*) received an unwelcome confirmation in the sleep-disruption
and weird oneiric experiences I lived through last night. I am lactose intol-
erant but can handle milk nicely in smaller doses. I fear I may have to use
Zoom the same way. Putting just that much in writing here, I immediately
feel a small rush of relief at the prospect. Maybe this gut feeling is one I
have in common with your younger grandchildren. But as so often, the
very young and the very old are verily the most at risk. They don't call it
second childhood for nothin.'

Jack

* * *

## MAY 5: MARK BEGINS.

*Beauty and death . . . Norman Maclean's* A River Runs Through It *. . . rhythm and grace . . . lines written in water . . . Montana beauty . . . seeing the invisible . . . emptiness and fullness . . . creation: Tiamat and Marduk, Dionysus and Apollo . . . the dance of death . . . haunted by waters . . . Brad Pitt and Robert Redford . . . John Steinbeck's* East of Eden *. . . creatio ex nihilo . . . fisher of men . . . fishing and hunting . . ."Ashes! Ashes! We all fall down."*

---

*May 5*

Dear Jack:

Today I want to share with you some thoughts on beauty—more precisely, on beauty and death. We have already discussed the sublime and death, but now I am thinking about beauty and mortality.

A couple of days ago, Robert Redford's film adaptation of Norman Maclean's classic *A River Runs Through It* was on TV while I was exercising. Dinny had recorded it for me knowing how much I like it. It is a beautiful film of a book that gets better with time. Having been reminded how much I appreciated the film, I decided to reread the book. Though I never met Maclean, I felt I almost knew him because Alan Thomas worked with him, and after his death edited his unfinished manuscript into what became the wonderful book *Young Men and Fire*. By a coincidence too weird to be a matter of chance, the day after I saw the film, an op-ed by Anthony Tommasini entitled "A Father's Love, Whether He Says Too Much or Not Enough" was published in the *New York Times*. It is not a very good article by a voluble Italian who does not understand the virtue of Scottish Presbyterians' reticence, and misses Maclean's most enduring insights.

The opening and the closing lines of the film and the book remain unforgettable—respectively, "In our family, there was no clear line between religion and fly fishing" and "I am haunted by water." In between Maclean tells the story of love between brothers and their relation to a Calvinist father who might well have been my own. What the river was to Maclean, the mountains are to me, and what fishing was to his father, hunting was to my father. I have known this for a long time, and in *Field Notes from Elsewhere*, I actually rewrote this sentence to read, "In our family there was no clear line between religion and hunting." Alongside that sentence I included a photograph of my grandfather, with whom I hunted. He is kneeling beside his hound dog, wearing a fedora precisely like the one Norman and Paul wore while fishing, and holding his muzzle-loader, which now hangs in the barn where I am writing. I have never understood why people don't realize that fishing is as violent for the fish as hunting is for the pheasant or grouse. For my father as for Maclean's father, hunting was no more about hunting than fishing was about fishing. They were about beauty and, by extension, art. What I know now that I could not have known then is that it takes a lifetime to learn that lesson.

From his earliest instruction, John taught his sons Norman and Paul that fly fishing is an art that cultivates an appreciation for the glory of God's creation.

> . . . Power comes not from power everywhere but from knowing where to put it on. "Remember," as my father kept saying, "it is an art that is performed on a four-count rhythm between ten and two o'clock."
>
> My father was very sure about certain matters pertaining to the universe. To him, all good things—trout as well as eternal salvation—come by art and art does not come easy.
>
> So my brother and I learned to cast Presbyterian-style, on a metronome.

While Norman, the older, and Paul were both writers, Norman wrote prose and Paul wrote poetry. This is not completely fair because, as Norman's novella shows, his prose is poetic, and Paul, after all, was a newspaper reporter whose stories were narratives often bordering on fiction. Though I did not realize it at the time, when I made Aaron and Kirsten write essays every week for the summers between elementary school and college, I was repeating the pedagogy Pastor Maclean developed for his children. When it came to fishing, Norman agreed with his father without a hint of envy or jealousy. "He is my brother and an artist and when a four-and-a-half-ounce rod is in his hand he is a major artist."

Rhythm, it's all about rhythm: not only the rhythm of rod and line, but the rhythm of fish and river, and, more important, the synchronization of the rhythms of river, fish, and fishermen. Paul read the Big Blackfoot River as creatively as my father read Gettysburg cornfields and Williamstown mountains. Paul saw what others overlooked. "All there is to thinking . . . is seeing something noticeable which makes you see something you weren't noticing which makes you see something that isn't even visible." Fishing, the art of fly fishing, teaches you, impossibly, to see the invisible, and thereby to think the unthinkable. To see the invisible within, not beyond the visible, is to read the word in water. Water and word, the eternal struggle reenacted every dawn and dusk. This is what Norman saw in the river every morning. "At sunrise everything is luminous but not clear." What is luminous but not clear is obscure; once you've seen this obscurity nothing is ever clear again. Nothing.

The latent fullness of this manifest emptiness is what I see every morning on the mountain.

The world, ancient myths teach is, did not originate once and for all at a moment in the distant past but is created anew every time dawning light reveals changing patterns. This endlessly recurrent event almost makes it possible to believe that rumors of death are nothing but idle gossip. Eternity is neither the infinite extension of time nor its negation; rather, eternity and time meet in the paradoxical moment when creation repeatedly emerges as if from nothing. As I write these words, dawn is slowly breaking on the Berkshire Mountains. For almost three decades, I have begun each day in silence, watching first light gradually dispel lingering darkness. The most fascinating moment in this ritual process is not when the sun's rays first touch the mountain, but the instant just before dawn when all of what will be creation hovers on the edge of emergence. I am never sure whether light makes the mountains appear or the mountains make light visible. In the twinkling of an eye, betwixt and between not appearing and appearing, reality remains virtual and all things seem possible.

Water and Word. Tiamat and Marduk. Dionysus and Apollo. "In the beginning was the Word." Before the beginning was Water.

In the beginning, God created the heaven and the earth.

And the earth was without form and void; and darkness was upon the face of the deep. And the spirit of God moved upon the face of the waters.

And God said, Let there be light: and there was light.

As Norman's tale nears its end, he climbs up the bank of the river and sits beside his father who had been reading the Good Book. The shadow cast by the mountain creeping up the hillside casts a melancholy hue over father and son.

    "What have you been reading?" I asked. "A book," he said. It was on the ground on the other side of him. So I would not have to bother to look over his knees to see it, he said, "a good book."

    Then he told me, "In the part I was reading it says the Word was in the beginning, and that's right. I used to think the water was first, but if you listen carefully you will hear that the words are underneath the water."

    "That's because you are a preacher first and then you are a fisherman," I told him. "If you ask Paul, he will tell you that the words are formed out of water."

The lines of poets, like the lines of the fly fishermen, are written with water.

    As they talk together, John and Norman are watching Paul fish the river beneath them. As his wrist moves to the beat of his mother's metronome, the fishing rod becomes a wand that "makes contact with the magic current of the world." He hooks a fish as big as the one he promised to catch for what they all suspected would be his last fish on their last fishing trip together. Paul had led a joyful but reckless life, and his death was near, though no one spoke a word about it. The giant fish struggled valiantly but to no avail and eventually succumbed in the "Dance of Death" with the artist. When Paul smiled as only he could smile and stood triumphant with his trophy, his father snapped a photograph, which soon would become his most valuable memento. In this moment of time outside of time, death and art come together in exquisite beauty. Not only the death of the fish, but also the death of Paul, and not only the beauty of the fish, but also the beauty of Paul. This beauty was all the more beautiful because death was so near.

"That's his limit," I said to my father.

"He is beautiful," my father said, although my brother had just finished catching his limit in the hole where my father had already fished.

This was the last fish we were ever to see Paul catch. My father and I talked about this moment several times later, and whatever our other feelings, we always felt it was fitting that, when we saw him catch his last fish, we never saw the fish but only the artistry of the fisherman.

As the sun begins to set and the light grows dim, we must learn see beauty even in death or we will not see it at all.

> Eventually, all things merge into one, and a river runs through it. The river was cut by the world's great flood and runs over rocks from the basement of time. On some of the rocks are timeless raindrops. Under the rocks there are the words, and some of the words are theirs.
> I am haunted by waters.

Before the beginning and after the end there is water—flowing water.

Mark

*May 5*

Dear Mark:

I have read both *Young Men and Fire* and *A River Runs Through It,* though it's been years now. I found the former engrossing, though "engulfing" might be a better word: Maclean seemed somehow overcome by his own material. As for the latter book, so much better known and more widely celebrated, it has been just a bit too portentous for me to quite yield to it. And though my father was not much like Tommasini's, I did like Tommasini's column for the frank honor it paid to a kind of filial relationship alien to his own and remote otherwise from his sensibility.

As for the movie, which I also saw when it was first released, two comments:

First, I was dazzled by the beauty of Brad Pitt at that age and in that film. He's been in countless films since, most of which, when I saw them at all, meant little to me. And his face with whoever was at the moment the woman in his life has been staring out at me from supermarket checkout lines from that moment on, possibly the most overexposed male face in America. I've long since grown rather tired of it, though he did a wonderful job on *Saturday Night Live* presenting the now-banished Anthony Fauci. But that film, which I gather we both liked more than the critics did, could put me in mind of Hopkins's poem "The Leaden Echo and the Golden Echo," in which heaven is the gathering up and capturing, for all time, of the fleeting moments of beauty and perfection that grace any good life—moments like the one captured in the photo of Paul with his the last trout. (The film lingered effectively over this moment.) Film actors of great natural beauty are blessed and cursed by the way their moments of "glad grace," to use Yeats's phrase, can be fixed forever by eyes and instruments that know how to capture them best in motion. This, I believe, was the blessing/curse visited upon Claire Bloom after her sensational debut beside Charlie Chaplin (who became a lifelong friend) in *Limelight*. Robert Redford, who directed *A River Runs Through It,* reportedly cast Pitt as Paul because Pitt reminded Redford of himself at the same age. When I first read that, I didn't think of Redford in *Butch Cassidy and the Sundance Kid* but of him in *The Natural*. On-screen, however, especially in that film, he struck me as a wooden actor with little going for him but a pretty face. Shirley Temple's mother would sometimes call out to her on the set, "Sparkle, Shirley! Sparkle!" She knew whereof she spoke, that lady did, and there are ways for a man with Pitt's star quality and sex appeal to just, wow, turn it on, just dazzle you with a look as Pitt certainly could and does in that film. With his beauty, he was perfectly cast.

Second, the film, though it certainly included fly fishing in some wonderful footage of Montana beauty, brought more powerfully to the fore than in the book the tortured relationship between the two brothers—the good, prosaic brother and the bad, poetic brother; the classic saint and the romantic sinner. The two are much like Aaron and Caleb, the twin brothers in John Steinbeck's *East of Eden*, who are more central to the film

version than they are in the novel. I can easily imagine that Redford, probably a much better director than actor, had that classic film in mind. James
Dean, just as irresistible in his day as Brad Pitt in ours, plays Caleb—the
beautiful bad (or good/bad) boy with his dangerous liaisons and incipient
addictions. There is a heart-stoppingly romantic moment in the film when
Caleb and Aaron's girlfriend, attending a local carnival, take a ride on the
Ferris wheel. It breaks down with them alone in their swinging seat up at
the very top of the carousel, surrounded by the night sky and the stars, as
it were, with the sad, crazy world far below. As a teenager, I dissolved into
that scene when I first saw it! *She is too good for him, too pure, but, oh, how he
loves her!*

A word now about water and Genesis 1:1. I have always been surprised
that this verse has not regularly been seen even in the most traditional and
literalist exegesis as the prime refutation of the notion of *creatio ex nihilo.*
What is there at the beginning, not before God but definitely before God's
first creative word, is indeed the deep, the abyss, the watery chaos, *tehom* in
Hebrew. Elohim does not create tehom. He merely dominates it, sets limits
to it, and brings his order into its chaos. First, he opens a large bubble within
it—water above the bubble and water below. Then, from within the water
below, he makes the dry land appear. Rain is the water above the dome-
shaped firmament (bubble) that he allows to fall down to fertilize the land
below; rivers are the water below the land bubbling up. So, the water is

primeval, uncreated, but so is the uncreated Word of God, the Word not yet spoken but only thought, the Word as the logos still in the mind of God, the divine capacity to create before the first act of creation. In the Gospels, including the Gospel of Mark, when Jesus stills the storm on the (note well) *sea* of Galilee and when he walks on the water, he signals his identity with Yahweh as clearly as when in the Gospel of John he says, "Before Abraham was, I AM." Power to rule the waters by saying, "Thus far and no farther" or "Be still" is the signature divine power. And, necessarily, the capacity to create includes the capacity to refrain from creating; it is that capacity, along with—and this will appear spectacularly as early as Genesis 6—the capacity to destroy and/or to start over. As there was an initial creation, so there can be (but will there be?) a *final* destruction. After which, nothing, or just a return to tehom in an eternal recurrence? The question clearly occurred to the author of Revelation in whose vision of the end of time, darkness turns to light, and the sea—even the sea!—dries up. For all the madness in that work, which could so easily have been excluded from the New Testament, there is also serious thought.

Guns in my boyhood stood for the killing of people, not of animals, and fishing, what little of it we ever did, was the very worm-on-hook fishing that the proudly artistic fly fishermen of *A River Runs Through It* most disdain. Water was Lake Michigan, whose far side you could not see; water in a more likable, swimmable, boatable form came with vacation lakes in Wisconsin; water was also, often enough, the Chicago River—tamed, controlled by locks, greenish, and uninviting— when you were downtown; and, once or twice a year, water was the mighty Mississippi, which we crossed on a long, long bridge en route to visit my father's older sister, Aunt Marge, Sister Mary Carolanne, BVM at Clarke College in Dubuque, Iowa. It's an odd fact but true that Catholic nuns were among the earliest American women to pursue advanced degrees in the sciences. (I suspect they were allowed this privilege because the male chemists, usually Protestant, didn't see them quite as real women.) Aunt Marge was the chairman of the Clarke College chemistry department.

In any case, water for me was not the ocean until I set sail for England on the *Queen Elizabeth* at the age of twenty-two. Until then, but never thereafter, the ocean was just those large blue spaces on wall maps. Before then, I had never laid eyes on its astonishing, frightening, mysterious, gorgeous, and heaving vastness. It's a white man's fantasy, I think, that the Indians referred to the Mississippi as "the Father of Waters." No, even that majestic stream is a child, not the father, of the true Father of Waters, which is the world-encircling ocean flowing between and around but also under the continents, at least if we take the source of the world's ground-water to be downward seepage from the rain that first rises as evaporation from the oceans and then falls as condensation upon the land. Finally, though, what's in a word? Call the whole global watery reality "river" if you prefer or call it "ocean" or "wellspring" or the lovely plural "seas"—all these are just different names for aspects, manifestations, of the same one wet destructive and creative reality. Each of us, I've been told, has in him molecules of water that are as old as the Big Bang. Ashes to ashes and dust to dust? As lief write, ashes to rivers and dust to seas.

Final association: Keats's epitaph, "Here lies one whose name was writ in water." Did you mean to allude to that when you wrote, "The lines of poets, like the lines of the fly fishermen, are written in water"? As I made that association, I thought to myself that in assertions such as "no clear line between religion and fly fishing" or "between religion and hunting," the latter terms may be metonymy not for nature but for art. If so, then these discussions can be subsumed into the perhaps larger conjunction of religion and art, or the perhaps still larger one of religion and play. This particular kind of bloody play includes the real, the cruel, the agonizing, and the entirely gratuitous killing of the fish or the beast, but such death scarcely removes the activity itself from the category of play. Death, however symbolic, figures in the commonest children's games. "You're out!" "All fall down." "Sudden-death overtime." And a thousand comparables (think, "killer app"). Or take the famous short story "The Most Dangerous Game," in which the prey is a human being, armed by a Russian hunter for the sport of it, and turned loose on the hunter's private island because he finds it a richer challenge to hunt down and kill shipwrecked humans than to stalk and kill mere dumb animals. Or "The Great Game" as played by the Russian Empire against the British Empire for control of the realm from India through Afghanistan to Persia; it is from within that game that we have the bloody couplet "Ours was not to reason why / Ours was but to do or die." Or of bitter veterans, some of them poets, who wrote of war as a giant ghastly game of charades, *La grande illusion*. Maybe the meanings of guns as in my boyhood and in yours are not finally so very divergent after all. And now, of course, enter Donald J. Trump, ever the winner, boasting of his skill in keeping the COVID-19 death toll in our country down to, hey, just sixty, seventy, eighty thousand. Not bad, Donald! Pretty low! A bit like your golf score.

Jack

* * *

## MAY 9–13: MARK BEGINS.

*Spring snow . . . first mowing . . . gardening rituals . . . resisting the instrumental and utilitarian . . . therapeutic obsessions . . . fragile earth . . . keeping the Sabbath . . . work and play . . . sharing the wealth . . . SoCal warmth . . . Jesuit training . . . housecleaning . . . secrets of a hairdresser . . . Richard Prum's* The Evolution of Beauty *. . . touching intimacy . . . Bygone dinner parties . . . Edward Albee's* Who's Afraid of Virginia Woolf?*. . . Lutheranism, Calvinism, Catholicism . . . rarity of reciprocation . . . Noam Chomsky's generative grammar . . . prescriptions from Daniel Defoe's* A Journal from the Plague Year *(1722) . . . tenure inflation . . . muzzling Anthony Fauci . . . Watching* The Crown.

---

*May 9*

Dear Jack:

It's a very depressing morning—not only the further spread of the virus and the ominous political and judicial developments you mention, but the weather. It's snowing! Twenty degrees, the wind howling, several of inches on the ground, and the snow still falling! Since I am sure it's hard to imagine as you drink your morning coffee beside a window open to your blossoming orange and lemon trees, I just sent you a picture. To make matters even worse, the groundhog outsmarted our new trap last night. I will spare you the details of how this trap works; suffice it to say, this trap does not have a heart.

Spring in a literal and a figurative sense has been very late this year. The forsythia and daffodils recently bloomed, but there are only the faintest signs of buds on the apple, crabapple, and redbud trees. Usually by early May green appears at the foot of the mountain and slowly creeps upward until it reaches the top at the end of the month. Not this year—everything is out of whack; everywhere you turn, rhythms upon which we have relied for all our lives have been disrupted. It is no consolation that the cold and snow are not limited to the Berkshires, as it often is.

This unusual arctic cold had been predicted so was not a surprise. Having heard the forecast, on Thursday Dinny and I decided to mow the grass for the first time this year. This will now be our weekly ritual until around the first of November. As you now, mowing our lawn is no small undertaking. It takes Dinny three hours on the tractor, while I mow two miles of edges with the hand mower and finish up with the weed whacker. Sometimes I even use a propane blowtorch to kill weeds along the edge of the gardens and around the sculptures. Maintaining the more than three acres of lawn and garden requires many hours of hard work, but it is very important for me and I actually enjoy it. Working outside reminds me of the lessons my father taught me when I was young. In recent years, each spring I wonder if I will be able to continue taking care of the grounds. After Thursday, I know I'm good for another season, unless, of course, the plague strikes me down.

Mowing lawns and caring for gardens raise questions that are related to yesterday's discussion of leisure. As I have mentioned before, few people cut their own grass these days. Landscaping services with large crews often of Hispanic workers sweep in with big mowers and noisy leaf blowers and are done in half an hour or less. Lawn care has become a huge business. I recently read that Americans spend $29 billion annually on their lawns. Gardens are more complicated than lawns. While there are many different kinds of gardens, they can be divided into two basic types—productive and nonproductive, which roughly corresponds to the difference between utilitarian vegetable and flower or ornamental gardens. This distinction tends to be gendered—productive gardens are the domain of men, ornamental flower gardens are the concern of women. With this insight, we return to the question of leisure. While productive gardens and, by extension, farms require work, which can often be mechanized, nonproductive gardens allow leisure and usually require working with your hands.

You correctly pointed out that in previous times, leisure was an aristocratic luxury. In recent years, however, this has changed. Social status is no longer measured by how little you work, but by how much you work. If you are not working, you are not in play, and if you are not in play, you are not really important. I saw this again and again during the years I attended the Sun Valley Conference. Multibillionaires like Warren Buffet (ninety-one), Rupert Murdoch (ninety), and Sumner Redstone (ninety-seven, died 2020) cannot stop working long after there is any practical reason to do so. I'm not sure why, but I think it's because they fear not being in play more than they fear death.

The longer I've thought about the relation between work and play, the more complicated it's become. Paradoxically, being in play is not the same as playing, and what others regard as work can sometimes be play. Taking care of our lawn and gardens requires many hours of demanding physical labor, and yet, for me, this is more like play than work. My lawn and gardens are not functional; indeed, they serve no practical purpose. Rather than productive, the labor required to maintain them is its own reward. Mowing, trimming, digging, edging, raking—all by hand—attune mind and body to rhythms that both transcend and include our individual lives.

I have long been obsessive about my lawn and gardens—I know exactly how I want the grass cut, the bark spread, the bushes trimmed, the gardens to be cultivated and edged. Nobody else can do it to my satisfaction. I realize my efforts are futile because nature undoes my work almost as fast as I complete my labor. In the long run, the weeds always win. I also admit a further paradox: after all this work, almost nobody ever sees our lawn and gardens. I often say that spending hours and hours cultivating gardens no one ever sees is like writing a book nobody ever reads. Perhaps this is where my gardens and our letters intersect.

It is not too much to say that my gardens are sacred to me, and tending them comes as close to religion as I ever get. While Georges Bataille, whose most important insights come from Hegel, never wrote about gardens, his interpretation of the religion suggests why I regard my gardens as sacred. Religion, like art, he argues, involves an expenditure without any expectation of return. This nonproductive activity interrupts economic circuits of exchange. Far from utilitarian or instrumental, the value of whatever is deemed sacred is intrinsic. In contrast to the machinations of rational economics, the value of what is sacred is incalculable. I fully realize that my obsession with having my gardens just right makes no sense. Why work so hard and spend so much money on what nobody ever sees? I know all of this, yet I do it again, and again, and again. Strangely, this eternal repetition of the same lifts me out of time. Time is the domain of work, play is the realm of eternity. When God threw Adam out of the Garden, he was

condemned to work, and thereby fell into time. Always purposeful, work binds the present to the future; ever purposeless, play frees one from the future for the present.

The first mowing of spring is always the most glorious. Week after week, the brown grass of winter gradually turns greener and greener until its emerald hue is worthy of Ireland and it is finally long enough to mow. Early season moisture turns the humus whence we come a deep rich brown. Dinny and I both know this will have to be done all over again in a few days, but on Thursday with our labor complete, we paused for our weekly ritual—a gin and tonic while sitting on the deck admiring not so much the work we had done but marveling at what we had been allowed to do. This is as close to Eden as I will ever get.

It has stopped snowing now and the sun has appeared from behind the clouds. The wind still roars and what had been such a verdant green is now covered with a blanket of white. A thin skin of ice covers the pond. Twenty degrees feels much colder in May than it is in December.

Mark

*May 9*

Dear Mark:

In discussions of ecology and the Bible, attention is often paid to the difference between the first account of creation, Genesis 1, and the second, Genesis 2 and following.

In the first account, God creates a human couple and tells them to be fruitful and multiply and have dominion over the whole world. (The Hebrew root is the one that would also refer to a conqueror placing his foot on the neck of a defeated foe.)

In the second, which if we read consecutively is only necessary because the first creation proved a failure, we are back, in effect, to the third day or so of the earlier six-day attempt: sky, ocean, and the dry land gathered together are in place, but nothing living, not even a plant, has appeared. God then creates the man, creates him first rather than last, as in the earlier account; then creates the animals with his cooperation; then puts him to sleep and creates the woman to keep him company. Then places them in a garden where all their needs are met, *but* he instructs the man to "tend" or "keep" (the root is the same as will be used in "keeping" the Sabbath) this garden. Work of this sort is not a punishment. It might seem rather like the work involved in your tending your "garden." And sexual joy is explicitly a part of paradise in this second creation ("bone of my bone, and flesh of my flesh" and "the two become one") as it was not in the first account. Only after their disobedience is the man cursed with thankless agricultural labor and the woman with agonizing parturitional labor, and only then are both cursed with mortality: in Eden, they were immortals.

In the Episcopal Eucharist liturgy, we pray each week for "this fragile Earth, our island home." Eden, in Genesis, is like an island on the land, very much indeed like an oasis. Expulsion from it is expulsion into the desert, the wilderness. We may only find our way to species survival if somehow the work of tending our "island home" can come to seem like a blessing rather than a curse, a reward rather than a punishment. Does the present moment have any potential at all to lead in that direction? I myself think that the address must somehow be first to the economy.

You're on the subscription list for the WorldPost, and you saw, on April 17, Nicolas Berggruen's piece "Sharing the Wealth as We Recover

Health." His proposal, stated with remarkable concision, is capitalist
enough to be thinkable and yet radical enough in its scope and in its core
idea of "pre-distribution" to promise a recovery that could include the millions of people excluded from recovery in the form of trillions of dollars
already recklessly expended. I've grown up hearing conservatives mock
government programs as "throwing money" at problems that money can't
solve. But have we ever, *ever* before seen our government throw so much
money so wildly, with so little forethought or accountability, as in these
past weeks? The same seems to me to be happening at the California state
level, and I wonder how much of the appropriated money is making it all
the way through the bureaucratic obstacle course. Haste of this sort is an
open invitation to the thieves ever ready to prey on public programs
intended for the needy. What have the taxpayers acquired for all that we
have just spent? Berggruen's idea, had it been adopted, would definitely
have left us the people with something more to show for our money than
we are receiving. And, to close the circle, it would in time restore millions
to the work that, quite often, they truly do love.

The weather is warm but not at all too warm here in SoCal, yet the work
that Kitty and I have to do we will hire done—to ready this property for the
coming fire season. I cringe at the thought that the season might come and
throw hundreds of people, maybe thousands, together with no hope of
maintaining social distance or disinfection. I'm sure you've read about the
studies predicting that global warming might mean much more snow in the
Northeast. Your May (May!) inches (looked like as many as three in the photos you sent) would seem to be a part of that. The "new normal" of year-
round fire danger in SoCal is a part of it, too. But Trump's new campaign
strategy, apparently, is to tar the Democrats with leading the country via
the "Green New Deal" into a second economic disaster equaling the current
one rather than following him into an economic recovery pursued without
regard for the tens of thousands of lives that will be lost. His leadership, and
he has tens of millions of followers, is a disaster within our disaster. COVID-
19 has now penetrated the White House itself, and there is little reason to
expect the two cases just reported to be the last.

I do work hard, I think, but have always envied people able to work on
a regular schedule. I just can never quite manage to do that. I was employed
from the age of ten onward in work for pay but never entrepreneurially,

never for myself, as with a lawn-mowing business or a paper route. I worked
in grocery stores, then for a local newspaper, then as a soda jerk, but always
with a boss, never on my own. For the bosses, I could show up on time and
stick to the schedule. On my own, I just never could and still never can. I
go in fits and starts, plunges and then evasions, surrenders to sudden interests, and late immersions in what finally cannot be postponed any longer.
Just now, after weeks of letting our housecleaning just slide past, Kitty and
I, well matched perhaps in this very regard, are getting down to business,
and the house will get cleaned in due course but in only a semiorganized
way. Meanwhile, in a somewhat similar pattern, she has her garden coming
along well enough that we're already eating the lettuce, but today at dinner
I chose to inform her that she had forgotten to put a full dozen seedlings in
the ground. She was on the point of reaching then and there for her trowel.
But no: tomorrow is Mother's Day, I'm planning a champagne breakfast,
and if the seedlings survive, it may be because I plant them tomorrow
afternoon myself.

As I write, I'm feeling pretty good, physically, but this morning I woke
with a slight wheeze, with chest congestion, and with unwelcome fatigue
and malaise. I just took it easy through much of the day, read, napped, did
a few minor chores, took a decongestant pill, went through my sinus irriga-
tion drill, and cooked our dinner. But I was adamant that even if and when
our now-ailing housekeeper is able to work for us again (she's lamed now
with a strained back), we will vacate the house while she is here, and do a
little disinfecting of the bathrooms and kitchen after she departs and
before resuming normal routines. I'd actually rather clean the damned
house myself, but, to quote a line that Jackie never tired of using against
me, "there are two of us here."

I've read Bataille on sacrifice, and found myself easily in agreement, but
haven't such ideas been around for a long, long time—well before even
Hegel? Our word "liturgy" comes from the Greek for "public work," like a
festival, like the Olympics, like an expense undertaken for the public good
but not good of a merely utilitarian sort—public service in just the way that
nonsensical religious ceremonies are properly referred to as religious "services." The Hebrew word for worship is *avodah*, which is also the Hebrew
word for "work." But when the avodah consisted of *holah,* the holocaust or
whole-incineration of an animal so that there was nothing left to eat, what

was the point? Wherein lay the service? To God, of course; if it were for him, it couldn't be for us. Its point was the same as the point of a libation, when wine is deliberately spilled on the ground. What is waste in the immanent world signals that the immanent world, where such an act makes no sense, is not the whole world. There is a world beyond common sense, beyond business, beyond even sanity, where such waste does make sense.

Art is lavishly wasteful, or can be, in just the same way. And Richard Prum demonstrates wonderfully well in *The Evolution of Beauty* that the capacity to do this—to engage in expenditures that do *not* actually come down to pragmatic strategies for enhanced reproductive success, so long as they stop short of extinction—is as old as sexual reproduction itself. And, so, in us, this capacity becomes the endless and glorious parade of extravagances in the service of love. Champagne on Mother's Day has a smidgen of such extravagance. We can't regret what we did for love, can we—whether for the love of God, or the love of art, or the love of our lovers. Edith Piaf: *Non, rien de rien, non, je ne regrette rien!*

Jack


*May 12*

Dear Mark:

Kathleen and Brian formerly had a housekeeper. (We used to say "cleaning lady," and my grandmother was a cleaning lady, but the phrase is now thought disparaging.) Though they live in an apartment so small that I myself can scarcely imagine hiring someone to clean it for me, Kathleen lately asked me if Kitty and I were spending much time cleaning our much larger house. She asked because she and Brian were spending quite a bit of time as their own cleaning people, their person having been furloughed with pay. I answered that, really, we weren't spending much time, just a lick here and there where necessary. The truth is, I suspect, that we were unconsciously waiting for Mary Lou, our own furloughed housekeeper, to start cleaning for us again. Kitty had been paying her, since we didn't want her to intrude on our quarantine. Then, after a while, we thought to ourselves, well, we could leave the house while she works (she has a key) and move back in after she finishes, couldn't we? But she is no longer young and often ailing, it seems, and just now her back is out. So, today, we bit the bullet and dove into a major spring cleaning.

(Do you consider "dove" ungrammatical? I grew up using the strong past form of the verb "to dive," but I gather "dived" is now thought proper, and exclusively so. I once dated a woman who used "drug" as the past tense of "drag," and I loved it, loved how quaint and countrified and just *American* it sounded.)

So, I've been vacuuming all day, doing the part of housecleaning that Kitty likes least. And I've still got one room to go of our eight. Granted, I am doing in some ways a far more thorough job (moving furniture, vacuuming inside closets, etc.) than Mary Lou ever did, but I still come away appreciative of the real work involved. As a Jesuit novice, one does at some point every available bit of menial labor involved in keeping an institution clean (and its inmates fed and clothed). And every Jesuit novice, at least in my day, also spent six weeks working as a hospital orderly. Some of the early Jesuits, including one who died in the process, worked caring for plague victims. My reward for today's menial work, happily, was that Kitty planned and cooked dinner, and it was just delicious: a tomato, apple, onion, and charred ground beef dish from the Trent area in Alto-Adige in Northeastern Italy, from a special cookbook she has.

This is a guess on my part, but I suspect the Council of Trent took place up there at the border between Italy and Austria as a way of cultivating the Habsburg emperor and, in the process, emphasizing the international, small-c catholic character of what the Reformation wanted to call the "Roman" church. Rome returned the favor in spades, scoring Lutheranism as a parochially German movement, Calvinism a narrowly Swiss movement, and Anglicanism a marginal English movement. The Western or Latin Catholic Church really only shrank to "Roman" Catholic with the Reformation, and to this day it's a rare Catholic who calls him- or herself a "Roman" Catholic. That phrase betrays Protestant origins. History certainly would have been different if Luther's grand dream had come true and the emperor had converted to Lutheranism. Your writing about Vasso, your hairdresser, brings to mind Andy Tristen, Kitty's and my hairdresser, but first two other comments: first about hairdressers and intimacy, second about dinner parties.

Does intimacy precede and lead to touch, or does touch precede and lead to intimacy? The process can go forward in either way, I believe, and can also stop short in either way. The barbering/hairdressing situation is one in which touch occurs but both parties are also at every moment in full view of one another and able to speak easily. In that setting, I think the modest amount of touch, joined to the relative privacy, invites confidence, as if to say, "I *must* find this man trustworthy. If I didn't, how could I possibly allow him to take these liberties with my head and my hair." But for this to happen, there does have to be a modicum of *interest* or *curiosity* for the conversational flow to begin. I say this because I have received any number of haircuts or hair stylings in near silence, and also received conversational overtures that I just didn't want to accept. And I enjoy massage as well, but with my face down in a face rest, I have no desire to talk at all or, particularly, to be talked to: massage is a kind of return to speechless infancy.

Your story of Vasso at your dinner table is partly a story about you and Dinny as independent spirits and partly a story about the fact that the Williamstown gentry are not inviting their nearest and colleagues to dinner the way they used to, let alone their hairdressers or other service providers. Do you have any hunch about why this is? Both sides of your Vasso story do matter. I was once eating in a fast food restaurant with Hector Torres, whom I think I've mentioned more than once before, and Hector said to me that in Mexico "Someone like you, Mr. Jack [that's the family's nickname for me], would never be seen in public dining with someone like me." That's one side of your story. The other side is that in ten years in the UCI English Department, I received dinner invitations only from two "classmates" (new hires in my year) and from two colleagues whom I had known for years before being hired. I invited a number of other colleagues to lunch or dinner, usually lunch, and they would accept. But when I attended my first faculty meeting and was introduced (mind you, I had not gone through the usual rigmarole of campus visits before being hired), the meeting ended, everyone left, some of them chatting among themselves, and no one said a word to me. So, that's the other side, and you've observed the like as a change occurring over the years at Williamstown.

I wonder sometimes whether there may not be some deterrent feature or other of my manner or personality that makes me seem, as it were, not inviting or invite-able company. Over the years, the ratio of invitations that I have made as against those that I have received is easily 8–1. People do accept my invitations cordially, but reciprocation is exceedingly rare. At this late point on my life-trajectory, I'm only mildly wistful about that, but at certain past points, the whole matter was a much deeper sorrow. Talking to Kitty about this just recently, as it happens, I remembered a funny comment made to me way back at Loyola by a Black student, Gloria Miles, a freshman, who was in my office for some routine reason. We chatted a bit, she may have said something complimentary. What I recall clearly is that I said, yes, I was enjoying college teaching but I didn't think I could handle high school teaching because I doubted that I could maintain discipline. She answered, "Oh, Dr. Miles, you would have no trouble at all. You're naturally scary."

So, maybe something like that has been operative and has been the deterrent. Kitty said that a professionally successful and wonderfully generous member of our church told her that he didn't talk to me because "I wouldn't know what to say." We do talk now, but I gather he felt this quite early, well before he learned even all those things (books, awards, etc.) that, you might say, could induce hesitation.

So, as always, there is a sociological dimension to one's interactions and a psychological one, and one is never the best judge of just how they intertwine in one's own case. It's an African proverb, I think, that the monkey never sees his own behind, only the other monkey's.

Back to Andy Tristen: from earliest days, back when he was just a shampoo boy in Kitty's earlier beauty shop and well before he set up on his own, Andy was prized for his great scalp massages, sliding over into neck massages. He has very strong hands, and this is still a bonus feature of getting your hair done by Andy. And if I'm even half-right about what I say above, his mini-massage builds a trust that doesn't only relax the neck muscles but over time also loosens the tongue. COVID-19 has been devastating for people in Andy's line of work, but if a vaccine is found and normal life can resume, what a boom time it will be for all those providing the touch-starved with the simple, elemental kind of attention one receives in a scalp massage .

Jack

*May 13*

Dear Jack:

With the interruption drawing near, there is something else I want to write to you about this morning, but there are several points in your letter to which I need to respond. First, yes, always "dove," never "dived." I've long been fascinated by the way young children still learning language use the past tense of verbs by following the rules of whose exceptions they are unaware. Doved, runned, swimmed, stoled, etc. It's almost enough to make you believe in Noam Chomsky's generative grammar.

Second, dinner parties. I have often thought about the reasons they have all but disappeared and agree with what you say. One of our most memorable experiences when we first came to Williamstown was going out to dinner with the most famous Williams faculty member: James McGregor Burns, who was one of your fellow Pulitzer Prize winners. His wife, Joan, would sit in on my courses, and as a gesture of gratitude they would ask us out to dinner at the end of the semester. Always a restaurant, never their home. Before we arrived in town, I had heard that Edward Albee had spent several summers at Williamstown's renowned summer theater, and that the inspiration for *Who's Afraid of Virginia Wolf* was what he observed while here. There are probably many small liberal arts colleges where people think the play is about their faculty. When Joan first invited Dinny and me out to dinner, I asked a colleague if the story about Albee was true. He responded, "Oh, yeah, it's true. It's modeled on Jim Burns and his first wife. That marriage was pretty spectacular." I went to our first dinner eager to talk to Jim about his work and the state of the world, but he was not interested in that. All he wanted to talk about was who was sleeping with whom in the junior faculty. He clearly felt the sexual prowess of his generation far exceeded what I reported about my colleagues. Jim was relentless, and the more the conversation degenerated, the more I realized we were living the play and the movie. Jim and Joan were George (Richard Burton) and Martha (Elizabeth Taylor) and Dinny and I were Nick (George Segal) and Honey (Sandy Dennis). Early lesson learned: life really does imitate art.

I am actually reassured by your report that your experience is also that your dinner invitations are not reciprocated. I thought it was just us! I had the same experience that you had at UCI when I was a visiting professor at the University of North Carolina. Not until the last week I was there did I receive a dinner invitation. The legendary African American journalist Chuck Stone invited me to what turned out to be a very enjoyable dinner. And then, just before I left, Dean Smith and his wife invited Dinny and me to join them for dinner. Hard to top that.

The question of why the custom has vanished is not easy to answer. In addition to your observations, I would add two points. First, with both partners working, there is less time to prepare for such gatherings. True, but not convincing; you can always make time for what is important. There is another factor that I think is more important. When we first came, dinner parties were one of the primary settings where junior and senior faculty members would mix. I always valued the opportunity to get to know people who had taught at the college for many years, and I think such gatherings improved our professional relationships. Somewhere along the way all of this changed and junior faculty began to resent dinner invitations. They claimed that, far from cultivating an atmosphere of collegiality, they felt they and their spouses or partners were being put on display so they could be judged and they feared their performance could have a negative effect on their tenure prospects. While I have heard this complaint repeatedly, it makes no sense because almost everybody gets tenure now and when I came to Williams the chances of tenure were less than 50 percent. I do, however, think this attitude is a symptom of the deleterious effect of the increasingly judgmental attitude on college campuses today.

Now for what I really want to write to you about today. *Plus ça change, plus c'est la même chose.* Having considered the plague from so many different angles, I figured I needed a bit more historical perspective. We constantly hear about the marvels of modern medicine. There is no doubt that remarkable progress in treating diseases has been made, and no one has benefited from these advances more than I. However, with the plague still spreading, starry-eyed technologists' predictions of miraculous cures and even the imminent mastery of death seem cruel and deluded. To get a better sense of whether things have changed that much, I recently read Daniel Defoe's *A Journal of the Plague Year* (1722). Defoe (1659–1731) was an interesting character who is best known for his novels *Robinson Crusoe* (1719) and

A

# JOURNAL

OF THE

## 𝕻lague 𝕰ear:

BEING

Obſervations or Memorials,

Of the moſt Remarkable

## OCCURRENCES,

As well

## PUBLICK *as* PRIVATE,

Which happened in

## L O N D O N

During the laſt

## GREAT VISITATION
In 1665.

Written by a CITIZEN who continued all the
while in *London.* Never made publick before

L O N D O N :
Printed for E. *Nutt* at the *Royal-Exchange;* *J. Roberts*
in *Warwick-Lane* ; *A. D·dd* without *Temple-Bar* ;
and *J. Graves* in St. *James's-ſtreet.* 1722.

*Moll Flanders* (1722). He was also a secret agent for William III, and an unsuccessful merchant who spent many years in debtors' prison. *A Journal of the Plague Year* is a cross between fiction and nonfiction that tells the story of the Great Plague of London in 1665-1666.

While filled with lively accounts of the shady schemes of colorful characters in an impossible situation, what is most intriguing about the book at this particular moment is how little responses to and strategies for coping with the plague have changed in three and a half centuries. Historians think the plague was brought to London by rats on trading ships from the Netherlands. Eventually one quarter of the city's population died (two hundred thousand people). The first thing Defoe discusses is the way the plague exposed the wealth gap in London at that time. At the far end of the town from where he lived, "the richer sort of people, especially the nobility and gentry from the west part of the city, thronged out of town with their families and servants in an unusual manner then empty wagons and carts appeared, and spare horses with servants, who, it was apparent, were returning or sent from the countries to fetch more people." The poor and less wealthy with no country retreat were forced to stay in the city. Defoe reports that, as people fled,

> the face of London was—now indeed strangely altered. . . . Business led me out sometimes to the other end of town, even when the sickness was chiefly there; and as the thing was new to me, as well as to everybody else, it was a most surprising thing to see those streets which were usually so thronged now grown desolate, and so few people to be seen in them.

Much to my surprise, those who had to remain in London during the plague already knew enough to practice social distancing. The remaining people Defoe saw "walked in the middle of the great street, neither on one side or the other, because, as I suppose, they would not mingle with anybody that came out of houses, or meet with smells and scent from houses that might be infected."

Then as now, people suffered delusions, and there were crooks and charlatans eager to take advantage of them. For tricksters, it was, in the fine phrase of Joan Didion, "a year of magical thinking." Quacks parading as real doctors prescribed

> infallible preventive pills against the plague. Never-failing preservatives against the infection. Sovereign cordials against the corruption of the air. Exact regulations for the conduct of the body in case of an infection. Anti-pestilential pills. Incomparable drink against the plague never found out before. A universal remedy for the plague. The only true plague water. The royal antidote against all kinds of infection;—and such number that I cannot reckon up, and if I could, would fill a book of themselves to set down."

In the midst of all of these shenanigans, committed doctors and health care workers risked their lives to serve the sick and suffering. "They ventured their lives so far as even to lose them in the service of mankind. They endeavored to do good, and to save the lives of others."

Even more unexpected, the recommendations and regulations issued by the Center for Disease Control were anticipated by London's civil magistrates 355 years ago.

ORDERS CONCERNING INFECTED HOUSES AND PERSONS SICK
OF THE PLAGUE

Notice be given of the Sickness.

Sequestration of the Sick.

Airing of stuff.

Shutting up of the House.

None to be removed out of infected houses.

Burial of the Dead.

Every visited House to be marked.

Every visited House to be watched.

Inmates.

Where several inmates are in one and the same house, and any person becomes infected, none of the others can be removed.

Hackney-Coaches [Taxis]

Care be taken of hackney-coachmen that they have stood unemployed by the space of five or six days after carrying an infected person.

ORDERS CONCERNING LOOSE PERSONS AND IDLE ASSEMBLIES

Beggars [and homeless]

It is now ordered that such constables, and others whom this matter may any concern, take special care that no wandering beggars be suffered in the streets of this city in any matter or fashion whatsoever, upon the penalty provided by the law.

Plays [theaters and sporting events]

That all plays, bear-baiting games, singing of ballads, or such like assemblies of people be utterly prohibited.

Feasting prohibited [restaurants]

All public feasting…and dinners at taverns, ale-houses, and other places of common entertainment be foreborne till further order and allowance.

Tippling-houses [bars]

Disorderly tippling in taverns, ale-houses, coffee-houses, and cellars be severely looked into, as the common sin of this time and greatest occasion of dispersing the plague.

London city officials and police took these rules and regulations much more seriously than Trump and many of the governors who have drunk his Kool Aid. When people were quarantined, two wardens were posted at the house twenty-four hours a day to be sure the infected did not try to escape. Much of Defoe's narrative consists of comical stories of efforts of the sequestered to elude the guards and get out of their houses. Tragically, it took a disaster to end this disaster. On September 2, 1666, the Great Fire of London broke out and killed many of the rats carrying the fleas that spread the plague. By the time the plague ended, 2.5 percent of England's entire population had died, compared to 2 percent (including both civilians and soldiers) who died in World War I.

Three and a half centuries later, we still don't have a cure or vaccine for the plague. All we can do is to try to manage the disease in a way that will minimize its spread. As Trump's failure to heed multiple warnings from his advisors has become undeniable, officials from the Obama administration have become increasingly outspoken about the current administration's failures. Not only did Trump close down the division of the National Institute of Health responsible for developing a response to a possible pandemic, his team also ignored the detailed playbook for dealing with the plague the Obama administration left for them. The authors of that report could have saved themselves the trouble of writing such a hefty volume, and recommended that their successors read Daniel Defoe's *A Journal of the Plague Year*, which presents a plan there that requires only minimal updating. It is, of course, hard to imagine that Trump or any of his cronies has ever heard of Daniel Defoe, or has any idea that there was a similar plague in London three and a half centuries ago.

Mark

*May 13*

Dear Mark:

A final brief comment on our little dinner party question, and I'm done. You may be right (and you would be in a position to know) that untenured faculty in recent years have taken no pleasure in attending dinner parties hosted by senior faculty who hold their fates in hand. I was struck, though, by something you said almost in passing—namely, that in the days of dinner parties, only 50 percent of tenure candidates were tenured. Now, by a kind of tenure inflation that seems to parallel grade inflation, you say that nearly every candidate for tenure gets it. This would seem to argue for a more relaxed intergenerational social scene. And in any case, your view would seem to leave the doors open for dinner parties either among junior or among senior faculty. But if less such social entertaining now takes place, it may be because the old system of "faculty wives" is long gone—gone by now even for senior faculty. Kitty's first husband was a postdoc in neurology at Harvard, which was enough to qualify her for "faculty wives" luncheons hosted by Mrs. Nathan Pusey. Conceivably, "faculty husbands" could now be assuming the role that faculty wives once played, but the truth is that female faculty seem never to marry such men. Instead, whatever the gender, you have, in effect, two faculty husbands and no wife, which means no time for entertaining except in a few heroically happy cases.

As we began our diary, I too immediately thought of Defoe's diary, but I don't own a copy and until further notice, the UCI library is closed and not lending. One may return books by dropping them in the after-hours box but not borrow any. Do you own a copy? Or did you read the whole thing online?

The parallels you point out are interesting, but there is one utterly crucial regard in which our plague differs from London's in 1665-1666. And that is that there was no effort on the part of Charles II or the Tories supporting him to deny the seriousness of the plague or argue against any of the efforts being made to stop it. Though, yes, there was a rich/poor divide, with the rich mainly escaping the city, all of London was ideologically and practically on the same side. How insanely different our American plight! The Republican-dominated Supreme Court of Wisconsin has just declared the social distancing and related closures mandated by the Democratic governor to be against the state's constitution. Against the constitution! It's now every Wisconsinite for him/herself, and a plague simply cannot be fought that way. The CDC has prepared detailed, sane, step-by-step guidelines for how different sectors of American society can safely return to activity, but the president has suppressed these guidelines! He has also flatly denied the qualified opinion of Anthony Fauci, MD, the government's leading epidemiologist, that COVID-19 will surge in Fall.

Remember the enormous digital clock above Times Square that used to report the population of the world? What we could use now is a prominently positioned clock like that reporting the COVID-19 death toll in the United States. It will probably top 85,000 tomorrow, and we're only in mid-May. Imagine when the toll tops 100,000, or 150,000! When and if the toll reaches these terrifying numbers and escapes its current hot spots, people can have all the "freedom" the Republicans defend for them, but don't count on them thronging any longer to restaurants or bars, or showing up for work rather than lining up, six feet apart and masked, for welfare. And what happens when the virus takes down the delivery drivers? Fire season approaches, and 43 percent (I read in the *LA Times* this morning) of the wildfire-fighting force are prisoners—prisoners locked in where the virus is raging. How many firefighters will we lose?

Kitty and I are continuing to watch *The Crown*, and a big surprise in it is the enormous attention paid to Edward VIII, who abdicated and lived thereafter in arch luxury as the Duke of Windsor with Wallis Simpson, his previously married and twice divorced American wife. I presume that before the series ends, as we pass through World War II, Edward's Nazi sympathies will come to the fore, but perhaps not. In any case, in these earlier episodes, it's all about the Church of England and its prohibition of divorce. It's astonishing how decisive a role religion has played in shaping the English monarchy. Charles II favored religious toleration, but because behind this there stood his Catholic sympathies, he had to be deposed in favor of an imported Dutch Calvinist, William of Orange. In our day, it was Princess Margaret's position as in succession to the throne, which meant also the monarch's role as pope of England, that forced her (or forced others to force her) to terminate her engagement to the English war hero and flying ace, Captain Peter Townsend, who was en route to a divorce when she and he first met.

This TV series is separated from the events it portrays by about the same length of time that separated Defoe from the Plague whose "diary" he was bold to create and that separated Tolstoy from Napoleon's Russian campaigns, the wars of *War and Peace*. The last battle in that war is the Russian victory celebrated in the *1812 Overture* by Peter Tschaikowski, Tolstoy's younger contemporary. If any major Western writer or composer has taken on the flu epidemic of 1918–1919 as a subject, I am unaware of it. If the death toll of the current plague equals or surpasses that of a century ago, I wonder whether, sixty or so years from now, there will still even be novelists and novel-readers or television audiences and historical dramas on television to divert them. The death toll from COVID-19 will be much more than a mere body count, but what may come to light as the world we have known dies is one not to be read out of today's technological extrapolations. A major new variable is changing all calculations, and all prior bets are off.

Jack

Memorial Day

## JUNE 21–26: MARK BEGINS.

*Different upbringings a key to clashing reactions to French thought? . . . Complexity theory: Hegel and host/parasite, Serres's* The Parasite, *Miller's "The Critic as Host" . . . endless, exhausting challenges for (grand)parents and kids homebound and Zoom-fatigued or Zoom-resistant . . . arithmetic builds a "fort" . . . can online education be as much fun as a video game? . . . distancing, masking, and generalized suspicion and fear in children . . . a tale from Hollywood: how not to cooperate with a filmmaker . . . writers who come to you vs. writers who force you to go to them . . . cancel culture and the case of a canceled friend . . . George Floyd, Black Lives Matter, and police violence against whites . . . police, family, and "The Badge" . . . our second plague: contagious, undirected, directionless anger—where will it end, how far will it go?*

---

*June 21*

Dear Jack:

Whew! After the week you had and everything going on in the world, it was Michel Serres who hit a raw nerve. I have much else on my mind, and realize it is futile to try to change your view of his work, which is not really the issue. Before proceeding to other matters, I want to offer a few thoughts that seem to me to be relevant to our contrasting perspectives. In fact, I did find your comments "pissy" and, in all honesty, largely beside the point, or beside the point for which I was using Serres's argument. After reading your letter, my question was, "Why does Serres irritate Jack so much?" Or, in my more usual idiom, "Of what is his excessive irritation a symptom?"

As always, there are no easy answers. As you freely admit, you have never been all that interested in postmodernism or as captivated by French theory as I have been. In part, this is a function of the differences between our personal and educational backgrounds. Catholic schools and Jesuit training have left their mark on you, as a mother literature teacher and father science teacher, public education (more on this later), and early exposure to continental philosophy have left their mark on me. As our exchange has amply indicated, my intellectual position fluctuates between Hegel and Kierkegaard. In Derrida's work, I found something like a position that falls in between the two. Over the years, as Derrida drifted further and further toward the Kierkegaard pole of that relationship, I became convinced that while his basic argument is important, it nevertheless needs a corrective. Derrida endlessly repeats that systems and structures are inevitably hegemonic; in other words, they constitute themselves through a process of totalization that excludes difference and represses otherness. Though this obviously is true for some systems and structures, it is not necessarily true for all of them. During the late 1990s, my uneasiness with Derrida's totalizing view of structures and systems increased as I became convinced that to address the two most critical issues of the time—first, the rise of the Internet and the World Wide Web and, second, the emerging climate crisis—required some kind of notion of an integral whole. At this juncture, my question became, "Is it possible to imagine a nontotalizing system or structure that still acts as a whole?" I found a way to answer this question positively in complexity theory.

As I turned to complexity theory, I found myself immersed in cybernetics and information theory, and this is where Serres became helpful. For reasons I have never understood, Serres was always excluded from debates surrounding deconstruction and postmodernism, and yet it has always been clear to me that his thinking has much to add to these discussions. I suspect his marginalization was the result of some Left Bank pettiness, though I have no evidence to support this thought. As I noted in my previous letter, one of the reasons his work is interesting is because he understands the biological and natural sciences. Nowhere is this more evident than in the book to which you refer—*Hermès*. His argument in *The Parasite* is the most imaginative integration of literary theory and information theory I know. You pick apart his argument for mistranslations, differing points of evidence, etc., etc.; however, I think such comments are more or less beside the point in this context. Surely Serres knows the difference between mice and rats in *Aesop's Fables*. The different associations provoked by the different animals establish multiple vectors he traces in the following pages.

Rather than an analytic work of literary scholarship, think of the book as something like a David Salle layered painting or a Robert Venturi pastiche. Words and images are appropriated and reassembled to create a work that is related to, but different from, the fragments from which it is assembled—and "assemblage," as Deleuze insists, is the operative word here. As the mind jumps from fables to biblical stories, literary theory, information theory, cybernetics, and thermodynamics, new insights emerge like the self-organization of a Chuck Close painting. If you know the field on which Serres is playing, he does not have to mention Hegel's master/slave dialectic explicitly for it to be operative in his text.

I know this goes against the grain of more than your thinking, but I want to encourage you to reconsider Serres's vision. In previous letters, you have expressed appreciation for my early essay on relativity as an index of the relationality of being. This insight is also at work in my argument about intervolution. Serres's rich account of the parasite/host relation affords another angle from which to approach my basic insight. Yes, of course, there is no parasite without a host and no host without a parasite. In the book that launched deconstruction in the United States, *Deconstruction and Criticism*, your erstwhile colleague at UCI, J. Hillis Miller, develops this insight in an essay entitled "The Critic as Host." Miller's range is much more limited than that of Serres; moreover, he is completely ignorant of information theory and, therefore, cannot see the broader implications of his own argument. No one, to my knowledge, has drawn a connection between the arguments of Serres and Miller. In previous letters, I have discussed how the parasite/host relationship illuminates similarities among the plague, financial capitalism, and climate change. COVID-19/human cells, 00.1 percent/99.999 percent, bacteria/intestine, humans/earth, parasite/host, and vice versa. Always vice versa.

Since I last wrote, the world has continued to spin out of control—with the plague raging, cities and states are reopening and the federal government has abdicated responsibility for addressing the catastrophe; with peaceful demonstrations punctuated by violence, the political fabric of the country is unraveling; contrary to all economic theory, meanwhile, the stock market keeps climbing with the rise in unemployment. Secluded in the mountains of Massachusetts, I have felt increasingly isolated from the turmoil engulfing the lives of so many people. All of this changed on

Saturday when this solitude and silence were shattered by the arrival of Kirsten, Jackson, and Taylor. Though it's been less than a week so far, I have already come to see much more clearly how profound the challenges are for families struggling to work from home, while at the same time caring for children and providing home schooling. Dinny and I are going to take care of the kids for several weeks to give Kirsten and Jonathan a chance to catch up with their work. Let's just say that in the past few days, my appreciation for pre-K and kindergarten teachers has skyrocketed.

While the media are preoccupied with the problems colleges and universities will face this fall, far too little attention is being paid to the difficulties the plague is creating for the country's vast network of public schools. Kirsten works for the Council of Chief State School Officers (CCSSO), which is a nonprofit that assists leaders in public education from each state as well as the Department of Education. During the Obama administration, her organization worked very effectively with Arne Duncan, but Betsy DeVos is another story altogether. Her religious ideology influences every decision she makes. As I have watched Kirsten trying to support public schools across the country and have watched Aaron and Frida trying to help Selma negotiate the transition from middle school to high school in Chicago, I've begun to understand the magnitude of these problems. Selma's high school has two thousand students, which is the same size as Williams College; some schools in Chicago have four thousand students, which is the same size as Columbia College. Having registered these numbers, I did a little research on national numbers.

|               | Public Schools | Students    |
|---------------|----------------|-------------|
| Chicago       | 642            | 355,000     |
| New York City | 1,700          | 1.1 million |
| United States | 95,000         | 50.8 million |

In most cases, these schools are underfunded and have inadequate facilities and an insufficient number of teachers and administrators. In addition to this, most of these schools have neither the technology nor the instructional technology staff to deliver high-quality online education. The policies of the Trump administration are compounding problems by diverting funds from public to private schools. While responsibility for school funding and education lies at the local and state levels, it is impossible to meet the unprecedented challenges resulting from the pandemic without support and guidance from the federal government. In the absence of adequate governmental leadership, schools are turning to organizations like Kirsten's for guidance, but their resources are now stretched to the breaking point. Until last year, CCSSO received generous support from the Gates Foundation. However, with the arrival of the Trump administration, Gates has become disillusioned with Washington and has been redirecting his resources elsewhere. At the same time that Kirsten and her colleagues are struggling to meet escalating demands, they must also seek new funding to meet operating expenses.

As you know, I have spent my entire career teaching the best undergraduates at one of the nation's top liberal arts colleges and graduate students at a leading research university. While higher education is crucial for personal and social development, early childhood education is arguably even more important. As I watch Jackson (six) and Taylor (four) use computers, iPads, and iPhones, I am astonished by their knowledge of and ability to use these devices. Taylor can turn on Kirsten's computer, log on to email, play games, and even access Zoom, where she knows how to activate audio and video. Jackson also knows how to find online workbooks for math and language, as well as a library of books for different reading levels. I have also been impressed by the ability of their schools to launch online courses and programs very quickly and effectively. Since March, Jackson has had daily online classes and Taylor has met with her teachers and classmates several days a week. And yet these programs don't work for kids who are so young. While they are mesmerized by screens and nag to use them for games and videos from the time they wake up until they go to bed, they resist online classes. When I ask Jackson why he doesn't like classes on the computer, he says, "I hate Zoom. It's so boring, nobody does anything, everybody just sits there." Some parents have tried to have Zoom playdates but neither Jackson nor Taylor will have anything to do with it. They would prefer not to see their friends than to see them on Zoom.

This resistance, which I gather is not unusual, has enormous educational and social implications. I never attended what was then called "nursery school" and did not begin to learn to read until first grade. In the world of helicopter parents, everything starts earlier and moves faster. Reading and arithmetic begin in pre-K and move into high gear in kindergarten. Needless to say, these basic skills are the foundation of everything that follows. Online instruction is not only ineffective for children, but also actually discourages interest in reading. There are endless paradoxes in all of this. For years, high-tech companies have hawked their wares with the promise of mass personalization and customization, which have been used for everything from marketing and investment to political promotions and medical applications. Financially strapped school districts, however, cannot afford to produce or purchase such specialized programs. Kirsten lives in Montgomery County in Maryland, which has a reputation for having an outstanding school system. Nevertheless, the instruction Jackson has received is a district-wide curriculum, which is geared considerably lower than the level at which his class had been working. This is one reason he finds his classes so boring. It is an inconvenient truth that when the principle of equality is carried too far, it creates inequalities. Some kids are simply smarter than others, and if early education does not take this into account, not only individuals suffer, but the entire society suffers.

These disparities lead to additional problems. As I have noted, Kirsten is responsible for working with state officials to develop effective methods for assessing not only teacher effectiveness, but also student performance. This information is crucial for making promotion and placement decisions as well as curricular planning. With the arrival of the virus, students lost one-quarter of the school year. Just as colleges switched from grading to pass/fail, so primary, secondary, and tertiary schools suspended traditional performance assessments. For young children the issue is not simply a matter of content but, more important, the mastery of basic skills necessary for further work. With limited time and resources, how can each individual student be evaluated and how can curricula be modified to meet students' needs?

Over the past several decades, there have been countless books warning of the way digital media shorten kids' attention spans and create terminal distraction. I have always found these arguments misguided. As I watch Jackson and Taylor surfing apps and playing games, I am impressed by their intense concentration for long periods of time. They are interested, patient, and totally engaged. The contrast with school screen time could not be more obvious. As I discovered when working with the Global

Education Network, online education does not involve doing the same thing differently, but doing something different. We started by attempting to replicate traditional classrooms—large lectures, medium lectures/ discussions, and small seminars—but eventually realized this would not work. We had to find a way to create a new form of education that takes advantage of digital multimedia. This proved to be technically difficult, educationally challenging, and financially expensive. Twenty years ago, we were spending between $750,000 and $1.2 million per course. The result was fabulous courses that held the attention of young people. But, alas, no one was buying what we were selling. The issue of creative course content and imaginative interactive engagement is even more important for young children. To transform education into something like a video game, Dungeons and Dragons, or a Harry Potter story is not necessarily to water it down.

The second area for concern created by the lockdown is the social impact of isolation on young children. Jackson and Taylor have not even seen, let alone interacted with their friends, for almost one hundred days. They are fortunate to be close enough in age to be able to play together. Nonetheless, this is not the same as being in regular contact with other kids in and out of school as well in the countless activities that are so important for young kids. When this social separation is compounded by immersion in screens for hours every day, we run the danger of producing a generation of social misfits at precisely the time we most need people who know how to communicate and cooperate in ways that will help to solve the monumental problems we face.

This difficulty is compounded by the broader inculcation of suspicion that is occurring. The invisibility and unpredictability of the virus make every other person a potential threat. Though neither Jackson nor Taylor really understands the virus, they clearly realize that they must be suspicious of anyone outside of their immediate family. Unlike leprosy, for example, there are no marks by which victims can be identified and locked up in asylums or confined to ghettos. Since the outer is not the inner, you must constantly be on your guard. You can't trust anyone because this invisible threat is everywhere and even those you once thought were your closest friends might infect you. The best that can be done is to keep your distance. When trust gives way to suspicion, the social fabric frays.

Having realized that for a six-year-old, sitting in front of an iPad solving addition, subtraction, multiplication, and division problems is not an effective way to learn, I decided to try an alternative strategy for teaching Jackson arithmetic and measurements. We have designed and built a house—or, in Jackson's terms, a fort—in the woods at the edge of my sculpture park. This is about as far from my usual pedagogy as it is possible to imagine. He started by learning inches, feet, and yards, and then mastered how to add, subtract, and measure. After this we went into the woods and found four trees we could use as the frame for the fort. We cleared the underbrush and prepared the site. Then we measured the distance between the trees and created a scale drawing that we used as a blueprint. We figured out the width, length, and number of the boards we needed and went to the lumberyard to get the wood. Jackson helped the man measure and cut the boards to the required length. We then brought the boards home and followed our drawing to create the structure. I was totally surprised by how well Jackson was able to drive the nails. For the past several months, he, like his uncle Aaron, has been obsessed with *Star Wars*. When he arrived, the first thing he did was to get Aaron's *Star Wars* figures to use with his countless *Star Wars* Lego constructions in endless battles. The fort is home base for the Empire. When all the boards were nailed to the trees, he asked me to build a ladder so he would have a lookout from which he could watch for Darth Vader and his troops. I found an old wooden stepladder that I leaned against one of the trees, and that seemed to do the trick. The fort, Jackson declared, was finished. Though I don't know how much he learned or how much he will remember, I am sure it was more than he would have learned sitting in front of a screen.

I have many more thoughts about what I am learning from Jackson and Taylor, but two final things to report. The kids have closely followed my adventure with the groundhog and have desperately hoped I would not shoot him before they arrived. I have not, and the critter has become more elusive than ever. In lieu of catching or killing the damn groundhog, we watched *Caddyshack* last night. I have always associated that film with Bill Murray, and had forgotten Chevy Chase and Rodney Dangerfield, who played their favorite character. It is impossible to convey a sense of their

euphoric laughter. When the film ended long after their bedtime, Taylor announced she was going out on the deck to look at the stars, only to return a few minutes later screaming, "There are lightning bugs outside." Obviously, that was too much to resist, so we had another half hour of frenzied delight chasing and, much to my surprise, catching lightning bugs. And then this morning, as if rubbing in my failures, Mama Groundhog and her new baby greeted me by strolling across the lawn.

Remember Dinny taught elementary school for three years

right after we were married. Last night she said, "I sure am glad we had kids before iPhones and iPads." While school might be out for the kids, Dinny and I are getting an education neither of us ever could have. If colleges and universities don't realize what is happening at the earliest stage of the educational process, their failure will be even greater.

Mark

P.S. You might remember that the intersecting incomplete figure eights surrounding the firepit are oriented on the lines of the summer and winter solstice. As we do for every solstice, tonight we will have a fire to honor the gods. The summer solstice is always bittersweet because, just as summer begins, the days start getting shorter and everything begins heading toward winter's darkness and cold.

P.P.S. It was with considerable sadness that we canceled our reservations to fly to Montana for our visit with Ray and Molly. I had really been looking forward to the six of us getting together on the North Fork. I think it is fair to say that our three careers taken together tell a significant part of the story of the study of religion during the last half century. While we tried to ease the disappointment by promising to make the trip next year, we know, with our precarious health and Ray's age (to say nothing of our own), that that is uncertain.


*June 26*

Dear Mark:

Before turning to the week that was, let me risk one slight further comment about Michel Serres and my antipathy toward the style that you find so sympathetic. I use the word "style" deliberately. Some would say that style and substance are inseparable, but for the moment let's regard them as separable. In that case, one may be put off by an antipathetic style even when one might be nourished by the substance behind it. Let me illustrate with a story—colorful enough whether or not you will agree with the moral I draw.

Dan Brown's sensational *The Da Vinci Code* came out in 2003, and I was persuaded by the director of public programming at the Getty Museum to give a talk about/against/around it. Some time after that talk, the assistant to a powerful movie producer phoned me at the Getty and, after slathering on the most incredible flattery about my brilliance blah blah and how his boss loved to invite brilliant people over—no agenda, just to talk, etc., he invited me to come to lunch in the gentleman's office. I replied that I would be happy to entertain him any time for lunch at the Getty. I had immediately guessed that this had to be about a film version of *The Da Vinci Code,* and I was right, but it was he who wanted to speak to me, and I was disinclined to serve in any slightest way as a consultant on that of all films. On the spot, I decided that he would come to me, or the meeting would not happen. The assistant was stunned; in this town, his boss's invitations were not declined. In repeated calls, the flunky kept repeating the invitation, each time with some further incentive and a touch of anxiety, as if he were failing in his assignment. At length, I was invited to an unheard-of private dinner with the boss's boss in her sumptuous home. Besides the two of them, the studio chief and the designated screenwriter would all be in attendance. I had to smile: all this because it just would not *do* for me, a commoner, not to go to them, the aristocrats of entertainment. It would not *do* for me to require them to come to me. But at the eleventh hour, what the hell, I did go (I had begun to worry about getting the poor assistant into some kind of trouble), and it was about as bad as I thought it would be (the film was rather a flop), but I'll leave my recollections of table talk that night for another time.

My point—the moral of this little story—is that there are writers, Serres certainly among them, who, like film moguls, require that you come to where they are, and then there are writers like William H. McNeill (and, to the best of my ability, like me) who labor patiently to go to where you are—and then go on. Serres's may well only be a style, but it's a style that I resist on the page as I did on that occasion in person. I conceded at the start of this riff that, put off by an antipathetic style, one may risk losing some nourishing substance. In the producer's case, I was told by one Hollywood maven that I could have demanded up front a substantial fee for my time. Substance indeed, but I wanted no part of that silly film. In Serres's case, well, you know quite well all the substance that I am missing out on because of my recalcitrance.

Anyway, if and when UCI's library starts lending again, I'll borrow *The Parasite,* which they do have; they also have quite a few of his other titles all in French. I've read Hillis Miller's "The Critic as Host," by the way, and actually alluded to it in the first talk I ever gave at UCI, when, unbeknownst to me, they were looking me over. When days before my retirement I won the Distinguished Faculty Research Award, I was told that I was the first humanist winner in twenty-five years, the previous winner being, yes, Hillis Miller.

Your remarks on elementary education through the continuing COVID-19 pandemic are very thoughtful. It's been noted that economic recovery depends on childcare being somehow provided for the workers expected to return now to prior employment. The custodial component in elementary education, public or private, is economically crucial in the short run; in the long run, of course, it's the core educational component that will matter. The description you provide of your grandchildren's online schooling surely must be considered an optimal version of what is available nationwide, and yet the picture you draw strikes me as severely mixed. On the one hand, Taylor and Jackson seem little virtuosos in their handling of the components of online education. On the other hand, you report that they hate Zoom classes and, actually, hate Zoom in general. I believe I sent you earlier a link to a striking *New York Times* op-ed entitled "Why Zoom Is Terrible" on the kinds of brain stress that Zoom imposes, rarely noted at the time but experienced afterward as fatigue and irritation. That may be a part of their reaction, but your GEN experience is that effective digital instruction is a fabulously costly, top-to-bottom reconceptualization and reconstruction of every aspect of instruction. This ain't gonna happen in a hurry even at the university level,* and the obstacles to even rudimentary online instruction at the elementary level—much less online provision of the many latent functions of ordinary elementary instruction —seem insuperable in the short run.

All of which makes me see the education/childcare crisis as something close to a fourth crisis about to become acute around August 2020. The first crisis looming around then will be skyrocketing COVID-19 deaths. The second will be looming economic catastrophe when the federal government stops subsidizing the unemployed and they are forced out into the streets as the newly homeless, when consumption collapses in consequence, when mega bankruptcies multiply, and finally, as the last domino, when the stock market is finally affected and all portfolios shrink in value because the United States itself has shrunk in value. The third crisis could be a governmental crisis first as the Trump Justice Department's manipulation of the courts and of federal prosecutors for private interests (Trump and his henchmen) undermines faith in the judiciary and, second, as a combination of Republican vote suppression at the state level plus COVID complications in conventional polling brings about a crisis in the executive. The supreme boast of the American governmental system has been the peaceful transition from one presidency to the next through 250 years; that core strength is now in patent jeopardy. Add now to these three what I just called an "education/childcare crisis," the fourth crisis which could also be called, wouldn't you agree, simply the "home crisis" or the "home life crisis." You've been candid about the stresses of Kirsten and Jonathan's home life crisis, which has now become your own, with five, and now six, people under your roof instead of the usual two.

That said, and all appropriate space allotted to gloom and apprehension, you are responding with wonderful creativity to this challenge. I loved the story of Jackson's fort, and I am confident that he will retain plenty of what he learned. (Make a second fort, and set up a tin-can telephone between them?) Why does online instruction kill children's appetite for reading? You mentioned that it does in passing but not why it does. Do you know? I'm sure you have heard how the lords of Silicon Valley severely restrict their children's access to online media. How much reading are you all doing? Any reading together? Or aloud? Any memorization of nursery rhymes or children's rhyming poetry like that of Shel Silverstein? Kathleen liked his poetry so much that she announced one day that she was changing her name from Kathleen Miles to Kathleen Silverstein. With a little effort, Dinny ("I'm sure glad we had kids before iPhone and iPad") can roll the clock back and get everybody unplugged for a while.

Out-of-step education can be superior education, and maybe the key—which you've already found with Jackson—is fun. I've read that at the end of their careers, college professors have fewer regrets and more sense of satisfaction than those in any other profession. A nickel dropped for me when my dear friend Boyd Groth, MD, told me, while still in med school, "You know what? Sick people are no fun to be with." Well, who is more fun to be with than somebody who understands something for the first time and does so in your close company? You get to share in the delight of that

"Aha!" moment. I think of Mary Martin swinging across a Broadway stage as Peter Pan on Broadway and singing "Look at me . . . I'm *fly*-ing."

As a schoolteacher, you're there on the ground looking up and laughing with pleasure as your student takes flight. As a college professor, you participate in a rich but quieter and mediated way in such moments, but with little kids the special kick is that you can be right there on the very spot. My brother Mike is gifted in teaching music to small children, even *very* small ones. At the Old Town School of Folk Music, years ago, he introduced a Saturday morning program called Wiggle Worms for the littlest kids. The program caught on right away, and it was amazing how far he could bring them along. The thing I noticed, though, in a video of him in action was how often he was simply laughing with joy, how he was just having a *ball* doing this. At least for the summer ahead, that's my hope for you. Oh, and in that vein, I'm now going to have Kitty and me watch *Caddyshack*. I'd never heard of it but always found Chevy Chase somebody who could just walk on stage and leave me with a chuckle bubbling up. I still laugh every single time I remember his line on *SNL*, imitating the standard signoff of a TV news reporter: "From Washington, for NBC, I'm Chevy Chase . . . and *you're not*." Did I say chuckle? Giggle is more like it.

On to the week that was. On Saturday, Kathleen, and Brian came here for the second of our outdoor, socially distanced dinners. They brought not just their own food but also all their own dishes and tableware. (If our country has a stricter COVID safety enforcer than Kathleen, I haven't met him/her.) I had said that for Father's Day I wanted something like a paint set, something to take me away from the computer and involve me visually rather than aurally. I think they'll come up with something like that for my birthday, but for Father's Day they gave me a picture puzzle. For their first (paper) anniversary, I played "It's Only a Paper Moon" for them on the piano, and they halfway sang along. A good time was had by all, BUT . . .

. . . needless to say, talk turned after a while to the George Floyd demonstrations and all that has ensued/is still ensuing. Kathleen had asked me to listen to a two-hour podcast by Sam Harris and share my reactions with her. I hadn't then got round to that but a day later, I did. Harris, after protesting ad nauseam that he knows racism is a problem, that George Floyd's death in custody was an atrocity, that the police need reforming, and so forth and so on, and this after preaching ad majorem nauseam that he himself stands only for reason over sensation, for respect for facts, for the priority of reasonable conversation—after all that, he comes round to what he really wants to talk about, which is police violence toward white people, the collective madness of the defund-the-police Left, and the inherent difficulty of policing. He includes a whole riff on how to conduct oneself when being arrested and on why, because any encounter with a resisting arrestee puts the policeman's gun in play, the policeman's life is necessarily also in play and so a policeman who kills is often plausibly killing in self-defense against someone who is after his gun.

Kathleen was impressed by Harris's contrarian boldness in raising such subjects at just this time. I conceded that point and was genuinely instructed by two sources he cited, both by Black writers—one a column in *Time Magazine* by John McWhorter; the other an article for the National Bureau of Economic Research by Harvard economist Roland G. Fryer Jr. However, Harris's studied reasonability—already somewhat tainted for me by his preachy but finally preening rationalism, his professed devotion to factuality—seemed to me to desert him as he omitted the PC excesses of the Right and lingered only over those of the Left. Full disclosure: I began prejudicially prepared to hear again the de haut en bas tone that I remembered too well from his *Letter to a Christian Nation*. And hear it I certainly did.

In the discussion about Harris and the Savonarola censoriousness of the aroused Left, Kathleen insisted that I, not being on social media, had "no idea what it's like out there"—by which she meant how extreme the left-liberal trashing can be of anyone judged to have stepped out of line. Brian at one point used the current phrase "cancel culture." On other occasions, I note, Kathleen has commended me for not bothering with social media, but I claimed for myself that I do at least have a mediated knowledge of the world of dueling trolls. I experience it, for example, through my friend Larry Christon, who lately did a piece of what I would call service journalism on "literary Orange County." Practiced reporter that he is, he did his homework and uncovered all kinds of stuff going on, much more than an outsider might ever guess, and he provided a plethora of links along the way for those interested in taking part. Only at the very end did he risk the following long view:

Great writers usually work out of the conditions of place, like James
Joyce's Dublin or Philip Roth's Newark. Orange County lacks a deep
history, and it hasn't experienced violent social upheaval and the kind
of suffering that leads to a hard, basic assessment of being alive. It
really is largely a happy place, a lot of it glowingly beautiful, and still in
cheerful thrall to America's unbounded faith in capitalism and technology. But how is that faith expressed in the admiration of political
justice, in the treatment of the natural landscape, in the arts, in the
life of the soul as people try to get through the day with a sense of
purpose and meaning?

There are a lot of stories in these questions. Orange county's coming
of age as a place of regional literary identity gone wide, like Faulkner's
Mississippi or Willa Cather's Great Plains, still waits to be written.

Well, largely it seems for the words just quoted, he brought a hailstorm of
vitriolic, even vicious criticism down on his head—most but not quite all of
it from Orange County Hispanics. He was stunned by the intensity of the
reaction to so slight a provocation. He had envisioned, may still envision, a
short series on literary OC. I've urged him to build some of this response
into a future piece. Strikingly, he reached out to those who wrote in inviting them into conversation with him, and every last one declined. I take it
that the implied message to him was "You are beneath contempt and not
worth even talking to."

So, yeah, such stuff happens, but open-minded, well-intentioned people
who live their media lives more or less on the left have rich occasion to
experience the extremes that thrive there. They have less occasion, down to
almost none, to experience the extremes that thrive on the right. This was
my opening point when I wrote Kathleen the following long response to
Harris—more than she expected, I warrant, but I got caught up in the task.
I know that you have been a fairly regular reader of the WorldPost weekly
roundup. These are morphing now into a weekly Noēma roundup. Do read
Nathan Gardels's most recent effort as background for what follows here.
Also, a local detail: angry protesters have just torn down and trashed a
statue of the Franciscan missionary Father Junipero Serra, of the Califor-
nia Missions, that stood for many years in a small shady plaza just south of
Olvera Street. The Olvera Street ensemble, often called in LA "the Pueblo,"

is a kind of latter-day, touristy but beloved re-creation of the original Mexican settlement here, El Pueblo de Nuestra Señora la Reina de los Angeles,
which historically did begin in roughly this spot. Anyway, here's what I
wrote to Kathleen about Harris:

6/22/20
(your first wedding anniversary!)

Dear Kathleen:

As promised, I am writing with comments about Nathan's WorldPost/
Noēma roundup and Sam Harris's lengthy podcast.

First Nathan.

I warmly agree with the thrust of his piece, and his quotes, especially
from Fuentes and Paz, are beautifully apposite—perhaps particularly so
in view of the trashing (after he wrote) of a statue of Father Junipero
Serra that has stood for years in the little plaza south of Olvera Street in
downtown LA. The piece does not end quite as well as it begins. The
strongest defense of the approach to the Latin American past urged by
Fuentes and Paz is that if the great sinners of the past are erased from
public remembrance, then forgotten as well will be their sins. But to
remember those sins effectively, we must also remember those who committed them. If they have been honored for their achievements so much
that their crimes have been forgotten, then the solution must be simply
to add remembrance of the crimes to the storybook of public remembrance and, if statues happen to be involved, add compensatory statues
to those already in place. Thus, on the plaza below Olvera Street, a statue
of Moctezuma could look across at the statue of Serra. Both, as the two
great Mexican writers knew, played a large part in making Mexico (and
Mexican California) what they are. In short, the solution must be both-
and rather than either-or. I wish that this was the point that Nathan had
come round to in his conclusion, but the piece is still timely and strong.

About Sam Harris, let me begin with two global observations about
his long talk and then perhaps descend to a few selected particulars.
    First, you and I (and various others whom we know and respect)
all agree that road rage is rampant on (to use a dated phrase) the

information superhighway. Cancel culture has escalated into something close to cancel culture war, and on either side there are wars within wars. But you may have and Harris certainly does have the road rage rampant on the left far more vividly in mind than the road rage on the right. My situation is a bit different. I receive occasional deliveries of humor or inspiration from, e.g., my conservative Catholic first cousin Kathleen, my favorite cousin, for whom you are named; and what she sends usually comes from the right. From childhood on through my heavily Catholic education, I have lived within easier reach of the Right than I suspect is true for either you or Harris. His declared fear is that extremism of the Left will provoke extremism of the Right and carry Donald Trump to a second term, but if so, then why not spend at least a *little* time talking about extremism on the right? Harris spends none.

Parenthetically, I think there is quite strong reason to guess that the "silent majority" white backlash that carried Richard Nixon to power in 1968 will not be there this time for Donald J. Trump, at least not at the polls. Nixon and the Republicans followed a notorious "southern strategy" of appealing in code to white southern racism, and Trump has clearly been doing that as well, but, once again, it just may not work this time. Harris seemed to me to come close to taking his allegation of this proximate danger as self-evident and in no need of demonstration. But I beg to differ: the backlash case does not quite make itself.

My second broad point touches what impresses most in his long talk—namely, the statistics about police violence across race. Here, I quite agree, he pulled together some fully relevant facts, though I will have something to say about them below. And I agree with you as well that it took some courage to make these points against the headwind of the national Black Lives Matter demonstrations for racial justice and police reform. That much duly granted, however, his endlessly preached devotion to facts, reason, and patient attention to relevant detail deserts him when he touches on the matter of "defunding" the police. Vice President Biden has quite explicitly opposed any such call to disband police departments and leave policing somehow up to the people. He never mentions Biden, nor does he take any kind of close look at even the strongest possible actual moves in that direction—the one already behind us in Camden and the one pending in Minneapolis. He never mentions by name a single thinker or writer or other leader with a worked out proposal to radically defund a police department or all police departments. At one point, he summarizes his alleged consensus: "Any desire for law enforcement equals a form of racism." To put no finer point on the matter, *no such consensus exists.* In short, then, by his offering specifics on one side only, I don't think he lives up to his own proclaimed ideals of rational conversation and even-handedness.

Decades ago, Tom Wolfe, the late conservative novelist and practitioner of the "new journalism" of the 1970s, wrote a famous essay entitled "Radical Chic and Mao-Maoing the Flak-Catchers." Part of it was set in the sumptuous salon of Leonard Bernstein, who was satirically quoted as saying, probably to a Black Panther, "I dig. I dig utterly." All this came back to me when Harris began speaking about rich people affecting "woke" attitudes to expiate their sense of guilt. He seemed to me to be reinventing radical chic with a new play on "woke." But honestly, Kathleen, and you know this as well as I do, for every plutocrat yearning to expiate his guilt, there are a thousand or more who don't give a shit. Here, again, I saw Harris creating a kind of castle in the air with some limousine liberals up at the top and the foolish demonstrators at the bottom surrendering surrendering to a mass call to abandon all policing and in the process reelecting DJT. I just don't quite see it, and I wouldn't flinch from it if I did see it.

There is surely more to say, and even I probably have some more to say, but it's now past my bedtime, so this will have to do.

Happy anniversary to you both!

It was only after I sent this that I got around to reading John McWhorter and Roland G. Fryer, Jr. The *New York Times* quotes Fryer as saying that his finding that police kill white suspects as often as Black was "the most surprising find of his career." Harris, as I recall his podcast, went a step further and said that they kill white suspects *more often* than Black suspects. In any case, Fry makes the further and quite plausible and relevant interpretive comment, omitted by Harris, that racial bias disappears when a life is about to be taken because the potential consequences for the police involved are so grave. If they were graver a bit further down on the scale of excessively violent police action toward suspects, he suggests, the racial bias might disappear there as well. Because Harris made so much of the slaying of Tony Timpa, a white man, by the Dallas police, I found that video on YouTube and viewed it as well. Interestingly, it was preceded by a very long commercial for the conservative paper *Epoch Times*. As you know, Trump has retweeted videos of Black crime on white victims—ordinary crime, not cop crime—and added his gloss: "Where's the outrage?" So, whether he quite wishes it or not, Harris's subject seems to be growing as a propaganda theme on the right.

To the point that I make in the letter about my right-wing channels, so to call them, I later shared with Kathleen the following little text, sent me by Cousin Kathleen, her namesake:

### "The Badge

"Yes . . . let's all join in the hatred of all police for the sins of a few. Let's defund one of the most important public institutions in our country's history. Let's have all badges removed and allow people to tend to their own safety and security.

"But before you do so, let me tell you about the badge and the thousands of good men and women it represents.

"This badge ran towards certain death as the Towers collapsed on 9/11.

- This badge ran into the line of fire to save the people in the Pulse Night Club.
- This badge sheltered thousands as bullets rained down from the Mandalay Hotel in Las Vegas.
- This badge protected a BLM rally that left five officers dead in Dallas.
- This badge ran into the Sandy Hook School to stop a school shooter.
- This badge killed the Oregon District mass shooter in seconds.
- This badge has done CPR on your drowned child.
- This badge has fist fought the wife beater who left his spouse in a coma.
- This badge has run into burning buildings to save the occupants.

- This badge has been shot for simply existing.
- This badge has waded through flood waters to rescue the elderly trapped on the roof.
- This badge has intentionally crashed into the wrong way driver to protect innocent motorists.
- This badge has helped find the lost child so his mother would stop crying hysterically.
- This badge has helped the injured dog off the road and rushed it to the vet.
- This badge has escorted the elderly woman across the street because she couldn't see well and was afraid to cross.
- This badge has bought food for hungry kids because they had been abandoned.
- This badge has been soaked in blood and tears.
- This badge has been covered by a mourning band to honor those who have sacrificed everything in service by giving their lives for you and your families.

"You may hate me because I wear it. But I wear it with pride. Despite your hate and your anger, I will await the next call for help. And, I will come running without hesitation. Just like the thousands of men and women across this great nation.

This badge. ~Unknown"

This text was followed, when I received it from my cousin, by words added, I think, by whoever had forwarded it to her: "Every cop, cop friend, cop relative, and supporter should copy and paste!!! Don't break the law and you won't have a problem."

Two details since all these exchanges and then I'm almost done for this week.

One. The "live mic" capture of grossly, hideously racist conversation among New Jersey cops, though it may only count as anecdotal evidence, confirms what the head of the Black policeman's league said on camera recently to Rachel Maddow. He said that hiring more Black cops was not the answer because they too can be poisoned by a poisonous cop culture. It's the culture that has to be corrected.

Two. In Madison, Wisconsin, a state legislator was beaten up by demonstrators (against what?) for the offense of taking a cell phone picture. In the same state capitol, protesters (against what?) have just torn down and beheaded a statue of Hans Christian Beg, a Norwegian immigrant who was an abolitionist and fought for the Union in the Civil War. It's unclear to me whether either of these actions were done by Black demonstrators; I certainly doubt that they were done by Blacks alone. We seem to be witnessing the upwelling of a diffuse, undirected and directionless rage, emphatically including but not confined to whites—a thirst for revenge against whoever and whatever has taken away our country and everything that whites (or Asians or Hispanics or Millennials or Christians or . . . or . . .) have counted on. The trashing of the Junipero Serra statue and of that of a conquistador somewhere in Northern California bespeak rage among Latinos. Asians are furious over being blamed for the "Kung Flu."

Two days ago, Viet Thanh Nguyen, a brilliant novelist (his *The Sympathizer* is a triumph), published a wonderful review of Spike Lee's *Da Five Bloods* in the *New York Times*. Thanh Nguyen admires Lee's work and yet sees with wonderful clarity how, like all American war movies, it locates all subjectivity within the American participants, none in their screen enemies. Brian, who sees just about everything that comes out, seemed underwhelmed by *Da Five Bloods*, which I am still curious to view, but he did lead me to hope that Lee might have escaped what, most spectacularly and horribly, Francis Ford Coppola failed to escape in *Apocalypse Now*. I just loathed that movie and recoiled from so much celebration of it at the time and, worse, even humor about some of its special effects (especially the use of Wagner's "The Ride of the Valkyries" as background music for American attack helicopters). For me, the Vietnamese in that movie were just like the Mexicans or Indians being mowed down in so many old Western movies. Coppola's treatment of them was a kind of racism —juvenile perhaps rather than consciously prejudiced, but, like Donald Trump's juvenile racism, not excusable for that reason.

Sorry, I'm digressing. My point is simply that there is so much diffuse, unfocused, undischarged and, alas, sometimes well-grounded anger loose in our land that it has to constitute a peril in itself. David Ignatius (whom you know from Sun Valley?) penned a very sobering piece yesterday in the *Post* entitled "America's pandemic response doesn't bode well for a potential cyberattack." Sen. Angus King (I-Maine) and Rep. Mike Galla-gher (R-Wis) cochaired a report, "Cybersecurity Lessons from the Pan-demic," that says that not just because of Trump but also for other, more structural reasons, our country is ill prepared for a coordinated response to a coordinated attack against our digital infrastructure. The anger(s) I mention are grounded: I just conceded that. And yet they weaken us. They do, and so much else lies just ahead that will weaken us much further.

Jack

*Coursera—I see their ads in prime time, touting all kinds of big-name academic collaborators. Have you ever looked at their products? The skinny on MOOGs for a while has been that no teaching tool with an 80 percent dropout rate could be much good. Have they solved any of the production-cost problems that sank GEN?

Independence Day

## JULY 5-7: MARK BEGINS.

*Parenthood, grandparenthood, and the pandemic . . . when "You can have it all" becomes "You must do it all" . . . leaving for the city vs. leaving the city . . . Nietzsche, the world as "real fake," and Trump at Mount Rushmore . . . why houses now cost so much . . . housing, homelessness, Blacks, Hispanics, and the pandemic . . . the forgotten power of truly local networks . . . the moral complexity of gift-giving . . . monuments and Black Lives Matter . . . Thoreau,* A Week on the Concord and Merrimack Rivers *. . . two Mount Greylock epiphanies.*

---

*July 5*

Dear Jack:

Three weeks ago today Kirsten, Jonathan, Jackson, and Taylor arrived; one week ago today Aaron, Frida, Selma, and Elsa arrived. This morning both families left to drive back to Potomac (seven hours) and Chicago (fourteen hours). I wonder when, if ever, they will feel that it is safe enough to fly. With childcare responsibilities and Kirsten working in the barn, this is the longest time I've been away from my desk in years. While trying to remain attentive to world events as they rage out of control and clipping articles as well as jotting notes to try to keep track of what's going on, keeping up with Jackson and Taylor has been more than a full-time job. No, that's not right—it was not a job, it was a delight. The opportunity to spend three weeks with Jackson and Taylor and a week with Selma and Elsa was an unexpected gift of the pandemic. I doubt it will happen ever again. After we visited my parents with Aaron and Kirsten, my mother always would write how unbearably silent the house was without us. This afternoon, I hear that deafening silence.

   Play and work combined to transform the past three weeks into something like fieldwork in the world now aborning. During the entire time they were here, Kirsten, Jonathan, Aaron, and Frida all retreated to a different room where they worked all day. They all have very high-powered jobs, which have become even more demanding since the pandemic broke out. Most days they were on their phones or Zoom 75 percent of the time or more. Dinny and I were responsible for entertaining the kids and preventing them from bothering their parents. Dinner table conversation consisted of reports on their work that day and reflections on the deteriorating situation in the country. As you can imagine, between Alabama and Sweden, there was a broad range of opinions.

One of the things I found most surprising is that all four of them said that working remotely is going to be the new normal for them. They do not expect to have to be physically present ever again for more than one or at most two days a week. Even before the pandemic broke out, Kirsten's organization and Frida's company had already moved into smaller quarters and had eliminated personal offices and desks. If this represents a general trend, I think it would be a massive transformation with radical social, economic, and political implications. Since we talked about both the personal impact and broader significance of this change, I thought quite a bit about my last letter, in which I tried to think through the implications of this trend for the analysis Sonia Shah develops in *The Next Great Migration*. You will recall that I noted that my parents were the first generation to leave the valley by moving away from the areas of Pennsylvania where the Coopers and Taylors had originally settled. I also argued that modernity and mobility are inseparable. This mobility has been both geographical and social. While countless immigrants left the Old World behind and moved to the United States, others who were already here left the country to move to the city. For both immigrants and emigrants, to be on the make was to be on the move. After the past three weeks, I am beginning to suspect that that important trend is going to change.

My reflections on this issue took an unexpected turn a few days ago when I received an email from a young South Korean researcher asking to interview me about a brief essay entitled "How the World Became a Real Fake," which I published in 2003. In all honesty, I had forgotten about this essay and had to do a Google search to find it. When I reread it, I was struck by its relevance not only for our discussion of migration and much else, but also for our dinner table conversations about how work and family life are changing. The title of the essay was inspired by a brief chapter in Nietzsche's *Twilight of the Idols*: "How the 'True World' Finally Became a Fable: The History of an Error." In the last aphorism of this parable, Nietzsche writes, "The true world—we have abolished. What world has remained? The apparent one perhaps? But no! *With the true world we have also abolished the apparent one.*" I have already argued that Trump's fake news, alternative realities, and reality TV are quintessentially postmodern, symptoms of a new cultural disease that Nietzsche presciently diagnosed as nihilism. He offers his most concise and explicit formulation of this condition in his posthumously published *The Will to Power*. The title of this aphorism is "Belief in the Ego." If Trump and his Republican enablers read or knew anything about the history of philosophy, they could appropriate these lines as their governing manifesto.

> Against positivism, which halts at phenomena—"There are only *facts*—I would say: No, facts is precisely what is not, only interpretations. We cannot establish any fact "in itself": perhaps it is folly to want to do such a thing. . . .
>
> In so far as the word "knowledge" has any meaning, the world is knowable; but it is *interpretable* otherwise, it has no meaning behind it, but countless meanings.—"Perspectivism."
>
> It is our needs that interpret the world; our drives and their For and Against. Every drive is a kind of lust to rule; each one has its perspective that it would like to compel all the other drives to accept as a norm.

When it's turtles all the way down and all the way in, nothing remains to check the ego's voracious desires. But what, you might ask, does all of this have to do with working at home and the next great migration? Well, it turns out, quite a bit, I think.

Through his creative misprision of Nietzsche, Foucault fashioned a genealogical method that is quite useful. Without mentioning Nietzsche's name, the parable I fashioned offers a variation of his genealogy of his diagnosis of what helps to clarify our current crisis. I am including my account in its entirety because it concisely summarizes some of the points I've been trying to make, and I cannot say it any better now than I did seventeen years ago. I will conclude today's letter by explaining how it helps me understand what I observed during the past three weeks.

In the beginning, small bands of our ancestors lived in valleys often separated by great distances from other tribes. Since there were no transportation routes or lines of communication among these valleys, the villagers did not know what was on the other side of the mountain. In the earliest years, they lived off the bounty of the land, gathering abundant plants, fruits, and game. Gradually, the tribesmen created primitive technologies to help them satisfy their daily needs. They also developed routines intended to organize their day-to-day affairs. With limited resources to defend themselves against the unpredictable and sometimes violent forces of nature, tribes fabricated myths to explain what otherwise remained mysterious. If nature could not be controlled, perhaps the gods could be; rituals were extensions of primitive technologies designed to manage the world. Since they never left the valley, it never occurred to the villagers that there were other tribes with other gods. They did not doubt that their world and its gods were real.

But, one day, the fruit grew scarce and game was harder to find. While women remained in the valley to tend the home fires, men ventured over the mountain in search of food. As they wandered farther and farther, they eventually discovered other villages. Though the inhabitants looked like them, they did not talk like them. Startled and afraid, the tribesmen fled back to the safety and security of their own valley. But they could not remain at home because they needed food to survive. So they returned to the neighboring valleys armed to defend themselves against strangers who seemed to be hostile. As different tribes competed for limited resources, wars inevitably broke out. Though these battles were often costly for everyone involved, they appeared inevitable. The more new valleys tribesmen entered, the more conflicts broke out and the more people were killed. Eventually, it became clear to the villagers that more than food was at stake. The other tribes fought so hard because they believed in other gods as firmly as the tribesmen believed in theirs. With the dawning of this awareness, reality would never again be quite the same—or so it seemed.

Confronted by gods they had never imagined, different tribes began to suspect that there might be a God above the gods—a God more distant and more powerful than the gods of different tribes. This

God was never present but always remained distant. What communication there was with this absent God was through His delegated subordinates and messengers. Unlike the years in the peaceful valley, the real no longer was present but now appeared to be elsewhere. The gap that opened between believers and their god did not pose an insurmountable problem because God could bridge it. Though many different people conceived an omnipotent deity, every tribe was convinced that its god was the special emissary of the One True God. Their god was real and all others were fake. Since different tribes believed their god was the true God, wars became even more violent. Because wars were religious, compromise was out of the question.

Century after century, the death toll mounted; hundreds, thousands, millions, millions of millions died defending the true God and just cause against the forces of evil. As transportation routes and communication lines steadily expanded, the world became more interconnected and, thus, more complicated. With the increasing mobility of bodies and minds, gods encountered more and more gods in a virtual pantheon where there seemed to be neither order nor reason. Eventually, some thoughtful people began to question the gods as well as God. What if all gods—even the highest God—were fake? What if we were not the gods' creation but the gods were our invention? What if the gods were not real but expressions of human passions, desires, and interests? What if the gods reflect our conflicts with each other and within ourselves? What if the gods bring war and not peace? Some doubters began to wonder whether they should join in a common struggle against the gods instead of warring with each other.

When people drifted from their tribes, they discovered that a world without gods is both terrifying and liberating. In the absence of gods, nothing was certain, nothing secure. Meaning and purpose had to be invented instead of discovered. But is it really possible, many wondered, to affirm the meaning and purpose of life without a firm foundation for belief? With no trustworthy anchors to ground life, people felt abandoned; they were left to wander in a desert where nothing any longer seemed real. As the years passed, the security of the verdant valley became a distant memory. The gods took flight and the specter of an unfathomable abyss open in their midst. The twilight of the gods marked the dawn of a new age. Faced with this void, people responded in different ways: exiles somberly despaired over what they had lost and nomads joyfully affirmed what they now were free to find.

Confronted with the harsh reality of the absence of the gods, many people were devastated by despair and lost hope. For exiles suspended between a past that was unrecoverable and a future that remained closed, the present seemed empty. Exile was bearable only as long as hope remained possible. If the real however imagined were *never* present, the nothingness of reality or the reality of nothingness would become overwhelming. Slipping into an unhappy consciousness for which there is no cure, exiles suffered life as a process of interminable mourning.

For nomads, the recognition that ancient gods were fake did not mean that nothing is real but opened the possibility of believing in the multiple worlds inhabited by different people. They lived in neither valleys nor deserts but dwelled on an endless plateau where new realities repeatedly emerged in unexpected ways. On this plane without horizon, heaven and earth were indistinguishable. Rather than mourn a past that could never return or await a future that never arrived, joyful nomads affirmed the here-and-now in all its difference, diversity and complexity as the only reality there was. Their beliefs were never secure because they believed that foundations were always lacking. Far from a threat to be avoided, they welcomed the lack of certainty and security as the trace of an unknowable future fraught with possibility. For believing nonbelievers, life, like art, was purposeless or, more precisely, life had no purpose beyond itself. Having recognized a confidence game when they saw it, these savvy players discovered that artifice is a fake that knows it's a fake. These fakes were not real and true nonbelievers knew it.

Not everyone, however, was able or willing to play such dicey confidence games. Uncertainty and insecurity became so unsettling that many people panicked and fled into the arms of gods who seemed to have vanished. Having strayed from the beliefs and traditions that gave meaning and purpose to life, latter-day believers raised their voices to insist that it was necessary to recover the abiding foundations without which life is impossible. In a world that had become incomprehensibly complex, the return to simple realities and verities, which promised moral clarity and absolute certainty, appeared to be salutary.

But things were not quite so simple. As new worlds continued to emerge, valleys, which once were protective, became fragile bubbles, which exposed everyone to real dangers. True believers, like their ancient ancestors, did not venture outside and, thus, did not doubt that their reality was Reality. While claiming to be realists, bubble people failed to understand the world they presumed to manage. Fundamentalists of every stripe—religious as well as political—believed theirs was the only bubble and that it never would burst.

The world of religious bubbles was the world of real fakes. In contrast to artifice, which was a fake recognized as a fake, the real fake was the fake not acknowledged to be a fake and hence taken to be the real thing. Though the possibility that their real was a fake never occurred to bubble people, others began suspect—albeit quietly—that their real was truly a fake but chose to forget this prospect so they could go on believing awhile longer. This faithful forgetting, however, was strange; for the fake to continue to appear real, believers not only had to forget that it was a fake but also had to forget that they had forgotten their suspicions of fakery. This will to forget is what made true belief, moral clarity, and absolute certainty once again seem to be possible.

What drew people to religious bubbles was also what eventually caused those bubbles to burst. The search for security led to the very insecurity believers sought to avoid. When bubbles inevitably collided, the result was often bloody. Having brought the world to the brink of disaster old orthodoxies collapsed, leaving nothing the same. Some who survived realized that true belief rather than unbelief posed the greatest danger to human survival. The challenge, they concluded, was not to find redemption from a world that often seems dark but to learn to live without redemption in a world where the interplay of light and darkness creates infinite shades of difference, which are inescapably disruptive, overwhelmingly beautiful and infinitely complex.

I am writing to you on July 5. Yesterday Trump ignored the advice of medical experts and defied the prescribed policies of his own agencies by holding large rallies on the sacred land of Native Americans in the Black Hills of South Dakota and on the lawn of the people's house he thinks he owns. Ignorance, incompetence, and defiance have created a toxic mixture that is disrupting every aspect of life. The raging pandemic is reversing the population flow from country to city that created modernity. According to real estate agents, people are fleeing cities for the suburbs and beyond, to small towns generations of young people have been desperate to escape. As cities become ghost towns, wildlife returns to reclaim territory that had been overtaken by an invasive species. A recent article in the *Guardian* reports jackals in Tel Aviv, mountain goats in Llandudno (Wales), sheep in Istanbul, deer in Nara (Japan), wild boar in Ajaccio (Corsica), horses in Kashmir, and buffalo in New Delhi. What if the next great migration reverses the centuries-long migration of people from the country to the city? What if the pandemic draws people back to the valleys where their ancestors landed and their parents still live? What if the pandemic revealed a silent disease that has been eroding the soul since the dawn of modernity?

Last week foodie author Deb Perelman published a provocative cri de coeur, "In the COVID-19 Economy, You can Have a Kid or a Job. You Can't Have Both." She expresses a growing concern that deserves more attention and effectively captures much of what I have observed during the past three weeks.

> Let me say the quiet part out loud: In the COVID-19 economy, you're allowed a kid *or* a job. Why isn't anyone talking about this? Why are we not hearing a primal scream so deafening that no plodding policy can be implemented without addressing the people buried by it?... I think it's because when you're home schooling all day, and not performing the work you were hired to do until the wee hours of the morning, and do it on repeat for 106 days (not that anyone is counting), you might be a bit too fried to funnel your rage effectively.

This is precisely the problem Kirsten has been working on late into the night for more than three weeks. Her three-hundred-page guide for school systems in all fifty states will be issued tomorrow.

Perelman states explicitly what most people know but no one wants to admit—school and childcare are inseparable. While advanced countries like Sweden, Denmark, and Finland have state-funded childcare beginning with infancy, a half-century since the beginning of the feminist movement began, the United States still refuses to provide adequate support for children and their parents. With the pandemic, the consequences of this failure are pushing working parents to the breaking point. When young kids are not in school, someone has to take care of them and now must also teach them what they should be learning in school. After the past three weeks, I can personally testify to how demanding this is. Perelman also gives voice to another unspoken assumption: several generations raised to believe that women do not need to sacrifice having a family to have a career are learning the hard lesson that when push comes to shove, Mom is expected to take care of the kids while Dad is working. The promise of "You can have it all" has become "You must do it all," and it's not working. The pandemic threatens to undo more than fifty years of progress for working women. For anyone who is not in denial, it is obvious that a significant part of K–12 as well as college education is going to be online when school starts in a little more than a month. Most families will not be able to manage this situation for a prolonged time and there is no prospect for public or private support. How are families going to manage this impossible situation?

Williamstown is a small town (seven thousand people) located in what is affectionately called the Purple Valley. Other than working at Williams College, there are few professional opportunities in the area. When Aaron and Kirsten were growing up, we not only assumed that they would leave the valley, but actively encouraged them to do so. College, graduate school, law school, and their chosen professions have taken them far from the Purple Valley. As the years have passed Dinny and I have become ambivalent about our advice and their success. When she took over as the head of information technology at Williams College, one of her colleagues gave her advice she never forgot: if you want to have a stable staff, find a well-qualified person whose mother lives in North Adams. She followed that advice and hired many such people. What most impressed her about these colleagues is the extraordinary networks of support they have—parents, grandparents, brothers, sisters, aunts, uncles, and cousins. People whose pursuit of education and career lead them to leave the valley don't have these networks. In the past when

Kirsten and Aaron have found themselves in a jam, Dinny has flown to DC or Chicago to help cover for them for a few days or weeks. But her time is always limited, and now such short visits are no longer possible.

What if the increasing virtualization of work creates new possibilities? When you work remotely, you can be anywhere. Perhaps the next great migration will be back to the future. Families in search of support neither the government nor the private sector is willing to provide might reverse demographic trajectories and return to the valley. But the valley to which they return will not be the same as the valley they left behind—both the world and they will have changed. Wired valleys are undeniably connected so people know what's on the other side of the mountain. If a new migration is beginning, it will be axiological as well as geographical and social. Paradoxically, the virtualization of reality in which place no longer matters might well lead to the recovery of the values and virtues of place. Social networks that once seemed confining might now appear to be liberating. It seems people are discovering that fetishizing disruption, mobility, and nomadism unsettle more than they settle. Perhaps modern disenchantment will be reversed through the reenchantment of the natural and the local. Urban emigrants returning to places they once fled might hear new messages from gods who once seemed silent.

The best time of the day for me is early morning. For the past three weeks, I have shared these quiet hours with Jackson and Taylor; this morning Taylor came up first. When she crawled onto my lap, she was crying, "I don't want to go home and leave Selma and Elsa. I want everybody to stay here." A few hours later, with both cars packed, Taylor and Jackson were crying, tears running down their faces, and everyone else was sobbing quietly. As both families pulled out the driveway, Dinny welled up and said, "I wish they didn't live so far away." So do I.

Mark

*July 6*

Dear Mark:

Where to begin? How to begin? Let me start with housing—with the apartment your son bought last week and the house my daughter did not buy.

Aaron and Frida had been reluctant but finally yielded to real estate force majeure and made a purchase for $885K or so: I don't remember exactly. On Tuesday of last week, Kathleen and Brian made a bid on a house but then, after a visit, backed out. Kathleen virtually lives at her computer, and so finding a place with a suitable home office has been housing priority number one for her. This house had only a depressing, closet-like space for an office and so just wouldn't do. But they are so very ready to leave their cramped apartment in a congested, down-market neighborhood that relief, once they pulled out, was blended with sadness. She phoned, facing up darkly to the reality that though she is a fiendishly hard worker and a relentless saver, she just could not get there.

Kathleen is as tuned in to what is going on in real estate both locally and globally as anybody I know. Before these latest troubles, she had sent me this link to an article in *Noēma* that, like every other article in that fat journal, she had edited:

https://www.noemamag.com/catering-to-a-contracting-middle-class/.

I read it, found it challenging, and said that I probably needed to read it more than once to really get it, but two factors I thought could well have been included were: 1) the place of foreign capital in the death of the prior market of private sellers and private buyers; 2) the goal of domestic as well as foreign capital to replace the erstwhile population of home-owners with a successor population of home-renters, renting henceforth from owners with the capital necessary to buy en masse and functionally monopolize the housing market. There has been some coverage of this in the press but not as much as the subject deserves.

One reason it deserves more is that the arrival in the real estate market of venture capital avid to turn owners into renters is among several factors that have led to a very short supply of houses coming available for private purchase and these few at exorbitant prices. Typically, a successful bidder bids over the asking price, and sales sometimes become like auctions. So, while still short of completion, this process is already driving thousands, probably millions, of would-be owners into the category of renters. And it is driving renters into smaller and smaller accommodations, with more and more people crowded in, and, of course, at the bottom producing mass homelessness. All this may well come to an explosive head at the end of this

very month. Congress has gone on recess for two weeks. The subsidies that
have given the economy what Paul Krugman calls a "dead cat bounce" are
about to end, and pandemonium may follow later or sooner.

COVID-19 is affecting African American and Latino Americans as
heavily as it does not only—and perhaps not even mainly because of—their
"front line" occupations: after all, a great many of them are unemployed. It
is affecting them disproportionately because they live crowded into spaces
where quarantine and social distancing are impossible and, of course,
because they are disproportionately represented among the homeless. One
physician was quoted in the press saying, "You can't be in quarantine in a
house with only one bathroom." Right, and try quarantining in a tent.
Today, I had a Zoom consultation with my pulmonologist (I'm provision-
ally OK), and he told me that St. Joseph's Hospital, where I had my cardiac
ablation, is "slammed" with COVID cases. As the skyrocketing rate of new
cases devolves into mass death for blacks and Hispanics, the current rage
over police violence could acquire a new platform. If Black lives matter,
then mass Black death has to matter massively.

It may be that some well-educated young professionals like your children
and their spouses may find it appealing to move from the cities to attractive
smaller towns. The Getty employs a professional oral historian (I was actually provided a bound copy of the one he did with me); he chooses to live in
Fargo, North Dakota, and just loves it. He'd be a good example of what you
envision. But a huge proportion of our country's overall African- and Hispanic American population is already in rural areas. In California, agribusiness in the San Joaquin Valley is overwhelmingly Latino. Look at the COVID

map today in the *New York Times*: rural Mississippi, Alabama, Georgia are heavily Black. And then there are the many pockets of Hispanics in chicken-processing plants in Arkansas or pork-processing plants in Iowa. ("Mechanization or Mexicanization" I once heard the phenomenon described.) These small towns are not where the well-off white Millennials will be heading, but the people who live there and live on the edge of dire want may be heard from when and if they are all pushed over the edge at once.

I take it that the fable (I would call it a parable) included in your letter is lifted from your earlier, half-forgotten "How the World Became a Real Fake." There is a good deal of overlap between your fable and the view of religion that I sketch in *Religion As We Know It*, but where you speak of real fakes, I speak of useful fictions—fictions recognized as fictitious but honored as useful, and indeed actively employed. And rather than speak of God or gods, I speak of our founding American political/religious fiction that "all men are created equal." It's true, of course, that some and perhaps most Americans fall short of recognizing that there is nothing "self-evident" about the assertion that all men are created equal. Many, like the "true believers" of your fable, simply take that hallowed line as true without further reflection, or, in your language, as a "real fake" unrecognized as such. But some do examine it without necessarily abandoning it. Today, Lucian K. Trescott IV, a descendant of Thomas Jefferson through Sally Hemmings, proposes that the Jefferson Monument in Washington, DC, be taken down. Monticello, including the slave quarters, is both a better monument, he says, and also all the monument needed. Or perhaps this temple of our civic religion could be retained but the towering Jefferson-idol within it correctively replaced by or joined by a statue of a Black woman. The ancient Greeks always made their god-statues larger than life-size, and that seemed as right and "natural" to them as our gigantic statues of Lincoln and Jefferson seem to us—at least to the True Believers among us. Lucian's word will not be the last word, of course, but it is a legitimate word and perhaps part of a painful journey toward the condition that Herbert Fingarette formulates (and you warmly approved when I placed it near the conclusion of my little book):

> It is the special fate of modern man that he has a "choice" of spiritual visions. The paradox is that although each requires complete

commitment for complete validity, we can today generate a context in which we see that no one of them is the sole vision. Thus we must learn to be naïve but undogmatic. That is, we must take the vision as it comes and trust ourselves to it, naively, as reality. Yet we must retain an openness to experience such that the dark shadows deep within one vision are the mute, stubborn messengers waiting to lead us to a new light and a new vision.

Isn't this fairly close to the happier half of the split ending in your fable? But then does Black Lives Matter—which has stimulated this daring suggestion from a Black descendant of the Thomas Jefferson who penned the Declaration of Independence—not call us to an "openness to experience such that the dark shadows deep within one [national religious] vision are the mute, stubborn messengers waiting to lead us to a new light and a new vision"? I doubt very much that Lucian K. Trescot IV wants to call us away from the faith of "all men are created equal," but he doesn't want that line or even that faith to live on just as they have lived, perhaps not even as quoted by Martin Luther King Jr. He wants the line and the related faith to change (*Du muss dein Leben ändern*) and in the process to change our lives and with them our language.

The final scene you described—and described beautifully and poignantly, I must add—struck a chord or two with me. Kathleen always struck me as a pretty verbal little girl, not that I really had a criterion to measure her by. What I am remembering, though, was a wondrous short period in which she was richly verbal but still only early in her formation of a self/other distinction. The result was that at certain moments when she was mentally alone though physically with me—classically, in her car seat in back while I drove along unaccompanied in the front seat—she would talk and talk and talk, and it was just a window right into her little brain. One of her soliloquies was a vision of something like a big family party, though it could as easily have been a big party of friendly adults, all with kids. The kids were all running around and playing together and it was "so much fun," but a part of the fun was that the adults were also there sitting and talking and looking on happily. She definitely included the adults. There were actually a couple long-lasting, all-afternoon parties like this at a swimming club we sometimes visited that may have met this

description. The mood she evoked brought me back to certain big family gatherings in my own past as well as to even bigger parish events that were a quintessence of happiness. But such also seem to have been these last days for your four grandchildren. Heaven is truly like this, I think, for a child, and so I can just all too easily imagine their tears at giving up your Stone Hill heaven, and your tears watching them. Paradise lost.

Years later, I told Kathleen that though it would be a financial stretch, if she wanted to apply to Harvard or another Ivy League school, we would make it happen. No, she said, instantly and adamantly. She had her eyes on UC Berkeley (which would become her alma mater)—with such a stellar option, why take on debt? But there was another factor. By going to college in California, she could build her childhood community into an adult community: a young adult hoping for a semblance of her girlish dream. If she went to Harvard, many of her friends and perhaps her partner would be from the East Coast, and that option was firmly rejected in advance: already considered, already rejected. Like her mother, another only child, Kathleen does not just make but cherishes her friends. A part of the appeal of the neighborhood where Brian and she almost bought was that they have friends there already and, casing it out, could imagine making more friends: the promise of a surrogate extended family. Choose a location and then plan to "be a neighbor to have a neighbor"—and, as with Dinny and North Adams, if you end up hiring (as Kathleen has), then hire a neighbor.

One last note on migration, and then I'm done (and I think this week we're both going to make do with just one letter each). Because our iPhone5s are about to become obsolete and unsupported, we masked up and gloved up and braved the cacophony of Best Buy to purchase two iPhoneSEs and to get our respective phone contents migrated over. I just loathe that store. With its glaring lights, blaring nightclub music, mural-sized product logos, hundreds of flashing screens wherever you look, and acres of latter-day electronic toys, it brings to mind the macabre Toyland in Carlo Collodi's original, long, picaresque but extremely dark novel *Pinocchio*. Collodi is no Disney; e.g., when Cricket (not "Jiminy") first chirps to Pinocchio about conscience, Pinocchio crushes the intrusive little bug with a brick! Anyway, we made our purchase, don't yet see any COVID symptoms, and the phones are working. Supplies were surprisingly short. One phone (Kitty's, I decided, and I was doing all the talking) can only be used in the United States. The other (mine) can be used overseas, but I know to a near certainty that I will never again leave the United States. That's one kind of big-to-small migration, no? I used to live in the world. Now I just live in the little United States, and the littler California, and the still littler Orange County, and finally I live here, possibly for good, in "Catherine's Grove," as I call this acre of fruit trees. Have phone, won't travel. But, hey, I'm not complaining: the oranges have never been juicier, and Kitty's tomato crop is also coming in with new fruit every day. Dinner tonight will be pasta with garlic, olive oil, and cherry tomatoes. Life goes on—at least through dinner.

Jack


*July 7*

Dear Jack:

It's 7:15. I've been awake since 4, and up since 5:30. Not much sleep the last two nights so my brain has been in a bit of fog as I read your letter. I have

always marveled at how a slight injury or disturbance can throw everything out of kilter. Friday I chipped a tooth and by Saturday the pain was excruciating. Though I have had several life-threatening illnesses, I have not suffered such pain. This is the worst pain I have had since I was in high school when I underwent surgery to fix my shoulder that I hurt when playing football. I called the dentist first thing Monday morning and the receptionist said the first appointment she could give me was July 23. I said I could not wait that long and eventually she relented and gave me an appointment at 8 a.m. today. When trying to explain to students how emotions color perception and cognition, I've often quoted Alexander Pope's "The world looks yellow to a jaundiced eye." Well, let me tell you, the world looks foggy when you have a toothache. There are, however, different kinds of fog; more about fog later.

Though much could be said in response to your letter, I will offer just a couple of comments. As we both know, money is never really about money, but is always about something else: deception, ego, security, power, control, mastery. Ever since Marcel Mauss's influential little book *The Gift*, anthropologists and eventually literary theorists and philosophers have been preoccupied with gift-giving. I have always been intrigued by the lack of any thoughtful discussion about the difficulty of giving a gift. Like you,

Dinny and I have offered Aaron and Kirsten financial support for their education, the education of their children, and major purchases like a car, an apartment, and a house. Giving without creating a sense of dependence or indebtedness that throws the relationship off balance, thereby creating something like a master/servant hierarchy, is difficult, perhaps impossible. More about this later, too. It is, I think, possible to express gratitude without a sense of encumbering indebtedness, but it's all too easy to say "no strings attached" when everyone knows that there is no greater string than the declaration of no strings.

Like your experience with Kathleen this week, our discussions with Aaron and Frida about whether or not to proceed with the purchase of the apartment drove home to me how much uncertainty they must deal with. With the war in Vietnam, social and political unrest, and the collapse of the job market in teaching, we had our share of uncertainty. As we've previously discussed, your professional life has had many more changes than mine. In spite of these vicissitudes, the future seems more daunting for our children than it did for us. I doubt Aaron and Kirsten will be able to support their kids as much as we have been able to support them. If Kathleen and Brian have kids, I suspect this will be true for them as well. Renting not buying is a metaphor for a life that is much more tenuous than we have known. Ownership is increasingly a thing of the past; most people don't own their car, they effectively rent it. And even when you seem to own a house you are renting. The bank doesn't even own it; indeed, with the sale of securitization of mortgages on global financial markets, it is impossible to know who really owns your house. In today's high-speed hypercapitalism, where commodification gives way to financialization everything and everyone is uprooted and set in motion, it is not only people living on deserted city streets who are homeless—everybody is.

I feel compelled to add a note about Aaron's visit that I did not include in my letter. We have previously discussed the interrelated questions of time and memory. Ever since he was a child, Aaron has had an unusual relationship to time. Dinny calls it "Aaron time." For quite a while when he was growing up, I thought he was just oblivious to time and was often frustrated when I could not get him to hurry up. Eventually, I began to understand that he is fully aware of the importance of time and deliberately cultivates a temporal rhythm that is at odds with the high-speed world around him. His temporal style, and it is a style, is a self-conscious strategy of resistance. This past week, it became clear that Selma has inherited or adopted Aaron's sense of time.

Yesterday after everybody left, I returned to rereading Thoreau's *A Week on the Concord and Merrimack Rivers,* which I will teach this fall in Recovering Place. Thoreau offers an apt description of Aaron time.

> Yet, after all, the truly efficient laborer will not crowd his day with work, but will saunter to his task surrounded by a wide halo of ease and leisure, and then do but what he loves best. He is anxious only about the fruitful kernels of time. Though the hen should sit all day, she could lay only one egg, and, besides, would not have picked up materials for another. Let a man take time enough for the most trivial deed, though it be but the paring of his nails. The buds swell imperceptibly, without hurry or confusion, as if the short spring days were an eternity.

> Then spend an age in whetting thy desire,
> Thou needs't not *hasten* if thou doest *stand fast.*

This book recounts a trip Thoreau and his brother John took from Concord, Massachusetts, to the White Mountains of New Hampshire. Written years after the excursion, the book is less a diary than a meditative act of mourning commemorating his brother, who had died at the age of twenty-seven. The river that preoccupies Thoreau is the river of life, which flows into death.

Ever since he was in high school, Thoreau has been important for Aaron. He would spend hours hiking and exploring the woods, and I have always believed that the lessons he learned led him to get his PhD in geology. Our house on Stone Hill is beside Route 2, and 132 miles to the east along the same highway is where Thoreau built his cabin beside Walden Pond. Thoreau once walked west to Williamstown and hiked up Mount Greylock. When he was in high school, Aaron would bike up Mount Greylock, which is the highest mountain in Massachusetts, every week. Saturday afternoon, Aaron insisted that everybody take a hike on Mount Greylock. We cheated and drove half way up to summit, where we found a mile-long trail leading to an overlook where you have a spectacular view of the Purple Valley. While not long, the last half of the trail is steep, but even Jackson and

Taylor managed to climb to the end. Jackson's reaction was unforgettable: "This view is amazing! Everything is so little. We have to do this every time we come; let's make it a family tradition."

This was not the first hike of the day for Selma and Aaron. All week Selma had been nagging her dad about hiking up a nearby mountain before dawn to see the sun rise. On their last day here, Aaron finally made time to do it. They got up at 4 and climbed up Berlin Mountain across the valley from our house in an astonishing forty-five minutes. When I awoke at 5, and saw that the mountain and valley were shrouded in fog, I thought to myself that Selma would be disappointed because she could not see the sunrise. However, when they returned a few hours later, Selma was radiant and exclaimed, "It was magical! The sun through the mist was amazing. It was like your head was in the clouds," as hers often really is. Far from disappointing, the fog had made the experience all the more special for Selma. What Selma does not know is that her father's hero also had a transformative experience in mist and fog while hiking up Mount Greylock.

In July 1844, Thoreau began a walking trip from Concord to the Catskills. He planned to meet Ellery Channing at the base of Saddleback Mountain, which was the name of Mount Greylock at the time. While Melville pondered through a window Mount Greylock while writing for long hours, he never climbed the mountain. An inveterate hiker, Thoreau relished the challenge of finding the most difficult route to the top of the highest mountain in Massachusetts. Though he recorded the climb in his journal, he did not publish his thoughts for five years, when he described the ascent in religious terms: "It seemed a road for the pilgrim to enter upon who would climb to the gates of heaven." Thoreau attended Harvard, but the woods and the mountains were the whaleship where he received his real education. Tired and thirsty, he arrived at the summit of Mount Greylock in the dark; with no blanket, he built a fire, ate some rice and fell asleep. He woke before dawn and climbed up an observation tower that had been "erected by the students of Williamstown College [i.e., Williams College]," and waited for the sun to rise. With light gradually falling on the Berkshire Mountains, Thoreau had a transformative epiphany.

As the light increased I discovered around me an ocean of mist, which by chance reached up exactly to the base of the tower, and shut out

every vestige of earth, while I was floating on this fragment of the wreck of a world, on my carved plank in cloudland; a situation which required no aid from the imagination to render it impressive. As the light in the east steadily increased, it revealed to me more clearly the new world into which I had risen in the night.... All around beneath me was spread for a hundred miles on every side, as far as the eye could reach, an undulating country of clouds, answering in the varied swell of its surface to the terrestrial world it veiled. It was such a country as we might see in dreams, with all the delights of paradise.... As there was wanting the symbol, so there was not the substance of impurity, no spot or stain. It was a favor for which to be forever silent to be shown this vision. The earth beneath had become such a flitting thing of lights and shadows as the clouds had been before. It was not merely veiled to me, but it had passed away like the phantom of a shadow..., and this new platform was gained. As I had climbed above storm and cloud, so by successive days' journeys I might reach the region of eternal day beyond the tapering shadow of the earth.

> "Heaven itself shall slide
> And roll away, like melting stars that glide
> Along their oily threads."

After recounting his experience, he adds one of the most revealing comments in all his works:

> The inhabitants of earth behold commonly but the dark and shadowy underside of heaven's pavement; it is only when seen at a favorable angle in the horizon, morning or evening, that some faint streaks of the rich lining of the clouds are revealed. But my muse would fail to convey an impression of the gorgeous tapestry by which I was surrounded, such as men see faintly reflected afar off in the chambers of the east. Here, as on earth, I saw the gracious God
> > "flatter the mountain tops with sovereign eye,
> > Gilding pale streams with heavenly alchemy."

When Thoreau returned to the valley, he brought his vision down to earth, where he "discovered God in flowing streams." If God is *in* the world, you can be at home anywhere. This is the lesson Aaron is teaching Selma and

Elsa. Such lessons not only take, but also give time, and what greater gift is there than the gift of time?

It is, perhaps, too simple to say that children live in the present, young adults live in the future, and old people live in the past. Life scrambles time in ways that blur the boundaries of its tenses. In your response to my parable, you rightly mentioned the image of Eden as the lost paradise to which we can never return. But paradise is not merely a phantom past, nor is it only a fanciful future that is never here and now. On rare occasions, it is briefly present and if you are quick, you realize its presence before it passes. I call the awareness of such moments "anticipatory memories" because I know that in empty days yet to come I will look back and recall that there was a time when little gods and goddesses romped in the green gardens I had cultivated.

Mark

## JULY 11–12: MARK BEGINS.

*Catching frogs . . . Thoreau,* A Week on the Concord and Merrimack Rivers *and* Walden *. . . Emerson, "Nature" . . . the tonic of wildness . . . Annie Dillard's* Pilgrim at Tinker Creek *. . . nature's excesses . . . memento mori . . . a gift is without why . . . humankind as an invasive species . . . man is not the measure of all things . . . who is master, who is slave? . . . Thoreau, "Civil Disobedience" . . . a seventies arrest at the Pentagon remembered on a seventy-fifth birthday . . . a new political oratorio, "Which Side Are You On?" . . . Thoreau's Hinduism . . . Pratapaditya Pal on Hindu wisdom in* In Quest of Coomaraswamy *. . . how Job defeated the Voice from the Whirlwind . . . "His eye is on the sparrow" . . . rethinking meat addiction . . . seventy-five kisses, spaced out.*

---

*July 11*

Dear Jack:

Ever since I dug the two ponds and created the stream between them, whenever our grandchildren come to visit, they spend hours trying to catch frogs. Their patience is endless and the whole time they are completely focused on capturing their prey. There are only 3–4 frogs in the upper pond and 4–5 in the lower pond, so they end up repeatedly catching the same frogs. Over the years Dinny has shown all our grandchildren how to hypnotize the frogs by gently rubbing their bellies. She taught Jackson and Taylor and now they do it to the frogs they catch. Having arrived a few weeks earlier than usual this year, there were still some clusters of frog eggs and thousands of tiny tadpoles swimming in the ponds. Jackson and Taylor knew about the life cycle from egg to tadpole to frog and had two larger tadpoles at home in Maryland. When Kirsten decided they needed clean water and replaced the pond water with water from the faucet, they died. Lesson learned: Purification and cleanliness can be dangerous.

As I said in the addendum to my previous letter, I reread Thoreau's *A Week on the Concord and Merrimack Rivers* in preparation for my Recovering Place seminar. This is a long work that often moves more slowly than the rivers it follows so I decided to reread *Walden* as well. These were the only

two books Thoreau ever wrote and neither sold very many copies. He was only twenty-eight years old when he withdrew from Concord to the woods around Walden Pond for two years; fifteen years later he was dead at the age of forty-four. While Thoreau was sauntering through the woods, building his cabin, and tending his beans, Kierkegaard was a world away roaming the streets of Copenhagen while completing his pseudonymous authorship. Six years after Thoreau left Walden and began writing *Walden*, Kierkegaard died at the age of forty-three.

Thoreau's writings have been romanticized by devotees of the Whole Earth Catalog, members of the Sierra Club, animal rights activists, vegetarians, New Agers, and countless others. Many of his most committed followers seem never to have read a word he wrote. Their rosy view of nature and of human beings' place in the natural order is more characteristic of his Concord neighbor Emerson than of Thoreau. In his essay "Nature," Emerson famously wrote, "I become a transparent eyeball; I am nothing; I see all; the currents of the Universal Being circulate through me; I am part of God." While Thoreau was overwhelmed by the beauty and even the sublimity of nature, neither he nor the world around him was ever completely transparent. There was always a residual darkness that was, like the navel of Freud's dream, the point of contact with the unknowable. The irreducible mystery of this dimension is what makes Thoreau's work so much richer than Emerson's.

The structure of *Walden* repeats the seasons of the year and hours of the day. "The night is the winter, the morning and evening are the spring and the fall, and the noon is the summer." Thoreau concludes with a meditation on spring. By entitling the preceding chapter, "The Pond in Winter," he makes the trajectory obvious—from night to day, darkness to light, sleep to awakening. It is the familiar story of death and rebirth, though his vision is more Eastern than Western. At the end of his thoughts on winter, he places his experience in a cosmic context. "In the morning I bathe my intellect in the stupendous and cosmogonal philosophy of the Bhagvat Geeta [*sic*]. . . . I lay down the book and go to my well for water, and lo! There I meet the servant of the Brahmin priest of Brahma and Vishnu and Indra, who still sits in his temple on the Ganges reading the Vedas, or dwells at the root of the tree with his crust and water jug."

Spring is undeniably the time of renewal when "fresh curls spring from the baldest brow" and, playing the role of a latter-day Champollion, he helps sojourners decipher the message in nature's hieroglyphics: "There is nothing inorganic." Even the light of this insight cannot dispel the darkness that not only surrounds but also indwells human life. Indeed, it is not clear whether darkness shadows light, or light shadows darkness. Once again it is a question of the intervolution of parasite and host. "Our village life would stagnate if it were not for the unexplored forests and meadows which surround it. We need the tonic of wildness. . . . We require that all things be mysterious and unexplorable, that land and sea be infinitely wild, unsurveyed and unfathomed by us because unfathomable. We can never have enough nature." And then in the closing lines of the book, his vision turns dark as he confronts the fact that the gift of life is inseparable from the gift of death.

We need to witness our own limits transgressed, and some life pasturing freely where we never wander. We are cheered when we observe the vulture feeding on the carrion which disgusts and disheartens us and deriving health and strength from the repast. There was a dead horse in the hollow by the path to my house, which compelled me sometimes to go out of my way, especially in the night when the air was heavy, but the assurance it gave me of the strong appetite and inviolable health of Nature was my compensation for this. I love to see

that Nature is so rife with life that myriads can be afforded to be sacrificed and suffered to prey on one another; that tender organizations
can be so serenely squashed out of existence like pulp,—tadpoles which
herons gobble up, and tortoises and toads run over in the road; and
that sometimes it has rained flesh and blood!

Tadpoles. So many tadpoles, so few frogs. "Nature so rife with life that
myriads can be afforded to be sacrificed." To be rife with life is to be rife
with death.

Today's Thoreau is Annie Dillard, who wrote her master's thesis on
*Walden*, and eventually married Thoreau's biographer Robert D. Richardson. I never met Annie, though she taught at my alma mater, Wesleyan
University, for twenty-one years and was a close friend of Steve Crites,
who launched me on the journey I am still pursuing. I don't think you ever
met her either, but you are good friends with Wendy Doniger, who is a
neighbor of Annie in Wellfleet on Cape Cod. Set in the mountains of Virginia rather than the woods of New England, *Pilgrim at Tinker Creek* is a
latter-day *Walden*. Dillard is more drawn to the sublime than the beautiful,
and, while reveling in the ecstasy of nature, her vision is consistently darker
than Thoreau's. I have always found the chapter "Fecundity" the most
revealing and most disturbing.

> I don't know what it is about fecundity that so appalls. I suppose it is
> the teeming evidence that birth and growth, which we value, are ubiq-
> uitous and blind, that life itself is so astonishingly cheap, that nature is
> as careless as it is bountiful, and that with extravagance goes a crush-
> ing waste that will one day include our own cheap lives, Henle's loops
> and all. Every glistening egg is a memento mori.

Every glistening egg, every dying tadpole a memento mori. Nature is "a
spendthrift genius"—such extravagance, such superfluity, such waste. So
many eggs, so few frogs. So many eggs, so few babies. What are the chances
that that I'm the one who is here and now? At birth a baby girl has about
one million eggs, by puberty 300,000 remain, and during a woman's reproductive lifetime, about 300–400 are released. A man's testicles make several
million sperm a day, and produce up to 8 billion sperm in his lifetime. A
fertile male ejaculates between 200 and 500 million sperm. One egg and

one sperm—what are the chances? What about all the other eggs and sperm? Who might they have been? They are like the countless seeds of trees and plants scattered on the ground without ever taking root. The story is the same everywhere you look in nature.

It is easy to forget that for a gift to be a true gift, it must be freely given and, thus, be "without why." To give a reason is to deny the gift. With this insight, we return to the valley of our ancestors, which we thought we had left.

> So I think about the valley. And it occurs to me more and more that everything I have seen is wholly gratuitous. The giant water bug's predations, the frog's croak, the tree with the lights in it are not in any real sense necessary per se to the world or to its creator. Nor am I. The creation in the first place, being itself, is the only necessity, for which I would die, and I shall. The point about that being, as I know it here and see it, is that, as I think about it, it accumulates in my mind as an extravagance of minutiae. The sheer fringe and network detail assumes primary importance. That there are so many details seems to be the most important and visible fact about creation. If you can't see the forest for the trees, then look at the trees; when you've looked at enough trees, you've seen the forest, you've got it. If the world is gratuitous, then the fringe of a goldfish's fin is a million times more so.

And so am I.

By what or by whose standard is nature's fecundity to be measured? What makes this excess so appalling? Why such extravagance, such "crushing waste that will one day include our own cheap lives"? These are urgent questions today, when it truly *is* raining flesh and blood, and the storm is getting worse as the virus continues to spread. Worldwide there have been 1.2 million cases so far and 555,000 deaths; in the United States, where every day marks a new record high, 3.17 million cases, and 135,000 deaths. Though propensities have been discerned, why one person falls ill and another does not remains as mysterious as why out of millions and millions of possibilities one egg and one sperm choose each other. For every individual, illness and death, like birth and life are without why. It is, after all, possible to know the cause of something without knowing the reason.

If, as Dillard suggests, you examine enough trees, a pattern in the forest begins to emerge. Consider the origin of the coronavirus as a metaphor for the interrelation of nature and humankind. A single individual in a distant Chinese city eats a bat and a few months later the world is ablaze with a fire that cannot be contained. It is a question of consumption—excessive consumption eventually consumes the consumer. As I suggested in my last letter, the ideology of incessant growth has turned humankind into an invasive species that destroys the wildness and wilderness without which people cannot survive. Cut down all the trees, plow all the meadows, drain all the aquifers, spray all the weeds and insects, and what is left but sand blowing in the wind?

> Interruption: Sometimes things become all too weird. Just as I fin-ished typing this sentence, I glanced out the window and beyond the stream joining the two ponds, a large black bear was sauntering across the lawn. This wasn't the huge bear that we saw two weeks ago or the small bear I saw scrambling up the tree in the woods, but a medium sized bear like the one that found Goldilocks sleeping in its bed. I kid you not, this is true.

Blowing sand and dust, however, are not the end of the story because nature is cunning and always has the last word. Once again, it is a question of mastery, control, domination, and slavery, deference, and servitude. But who or what is master and who or what is slave? Who is consumer and who is consumed? The pursuit of mastery leads to its own undoing. If man (NB) will not control his appetites and constrain his impulses, Mother Nature will. Since the earth is a sphere, there are limits to growth. What if the virus is a form of population control designed to subvert human hubris and to restore a balance in nature?

Protagoras was wrong, man is *not* the measure of all things, or, more precisely, man is the measure of all things *for man*. Not everything is designed to serve man's ends. If life is a web, neither nature (evolution) nor history is unilinear or teleological. If all forms of life could think, every species would assume it is special and would believe it should be preserved at the expense of others. We must rethink our place in the economy of creation in terms of webs, networks, and rhizomes, rather than lines, grids, and roots. In our webby world, the purpose of life is life itself rather than a particular form of life—human or otherwise. Dillard is right: "Nature is as careless as it is bountiful, and that with extravagance goes a crushing waste that one day will include our own cheap lives." Today there will be sixty thousand new cases of the coronavirus in the United States and who knows how many will die? Memento mori. Perhaps the next plague can be avoided if we stop destroying the rain forest, burning fossil fuels, and eating bats. In the meantime, we are left to ponder the beauty and the horror of it all—so many tadpoles sacrificed so that so few frogs can live.

An unconcluding postscript to the week's madness. There seems to be no end to the absurdity of the newly emergent cancel culture. This week representatives from the Black Lives Matter movement raised a furor in the tech community by demanding an end to the use of the terms "master" and "slave," which have been used for decades to designate situations in which one process or entity controls another. A *Wired* article reports that, since 1976, more than sixty-seven thousand patents using these terms have been issued in the United States. The article explains that "the 'master/slave' metaphor in technology dates back to at least 1904, describing a sidereal clock system at an observatory in Cape Town. . . . The concept of a free master that did no work and a slave that followed the master's orders made for a vivid, if ethically suspect technosocial metaphor"

(https://www.wired.com/story/tech-confronts-use-labels-master-slave/). This controversy split along predictable lines—people claiming to support racial equality called for banning the use of the terms, and three thousand members of the California tech community signing a petition opposing dropping the word "master."

Neither opponents nor proponents understand the history and philosophy behind the words about which they are arguing. The definitive interpretation of the master/slave relationship was developed by Hegel in his *Phenomenology of Spirit* (1807). In his dialectical analysis, everything is reversed. While the master appears to have all the power, which enables him (NB) to dominate the slave, he actually does nothing, and is, therefore, completely dependent on the labor of the slaves. Though initially unaware of his or her power, the slave is the really the master of the master. The dawning awareness of the power of the oppressed leads to a reversal of the hierarchical relation between the master and slave, which, for Hegel, eventually leads to a reconciliation between self and other that he defines as "an I that is a we, and a we that is an I." It is the slave who is progressive and drives history. This analysis of the master/slave relationship is the basis of Marx's entire critique of capitalism. When he declares in the *Communist Manifesto*, "Workers of the world, unite!," he is recasting Hegel's theoretical point in practical terms to inspire a revolution that he believes will lead to greater social justice and a more equitable redistribution of wealth. The irony about the call to reject the terms "master" and "slave" is that left-wing activists are trashing the very philosophy that grounds their call for social change. Marx was right when he wrote, "History repeats itself, first as tragedy, second as farce."

Mark


*July 12*

Dear Mark:

Yesterday was Kitty's seventy-fifth birthday. When I turned seventy-five, three years ago, I decided to have a substantial party with bingo as the entertainment and a set of silly prizes for the winners. There turn out to be seventy-five balls in a standard bingo set, or at least in the home bingo set I purchased—you know, with a wire sphere that you crank until it spits out a number, "B-15," or whatever. Among the guests was my former student Tae Sung, whose two little sons got so excited about the game that I should have given them the whole set as they left. I would have done something comparable this year for Kitty, but obviously the COVID-19 epidemic barred the path. However, I did cook dinner—pork chops sautéed in an apricot/wine/ginger glaze, roasted potatoes, and snap peas—followed by a chocolate éclair with three candles on it for the three elements in her birthday riddle. Each of three presents came with a piece of folded, colored paper with a clue to the riddle—namely, three numbers: a) 657,436; b) 900; and c) 27,393. She came so close to the answer that if it were *Jeopardy*, she would have won.

The first present was Max Bruch's very melodic "Scottish Fantasy," which we played while I cooked dinner and she helped. She responded to it much as I hoped she would. Bruch was popular at the turn of the twentieth century, then fell into obscurity, but this work, in four movements building on some lovely Scottish folk themes, has a lot of charm. I knew she'd go for it.

The second present began with the fact that her seventy-fifth birthday is, of course, the diamond anniversary of her birth, and diamonds are a girl's best friend. I went shopping for "diamonds" on Amazon but bought, instead, some very glittery, very elaborate "emeralds" instead, which I knew would be more becoming—OK, trashy but still becoming. Green in various shades is definitely her color, and with her hair growing longer, the long dangly, super-glittery earrings look terrific and make her eyes look green into the bargain. ("Bargain" is the word, too, for these jewels cost all of $19.95.)

The third present brings me to the central text of your letter—to *Walden,* on your mind, obviously, because you are about to teach it again. After the Kent State and Jackson State massacres, Kitty and a small group from St. Paul's Episcopal Church in Tustin went to Washington, demonstrated in front of the Pentagon, were arrested and jailed overnight, and then released after paying $25 each. The receipt ("Save this receipt for your records") turned up somehow on her desk. I stole it when she wasn't look-ing, bought a frame large enough for it and a photo, and finagled her into looking at some photos she had on hand from that period. One showed her standing next to Bill Persell, then Father Bill Persell, now Bishop Persell (ret.). She herself looks wonderfully pretty and also just spunky enough to do this. So their faces now look out from the top of the frame over the receipt at the bottom.

Which brings me to Thoreau. I'm sure you're right that, outrageously unread, he lives on less as the subtle philosopher of nature if not the nature mystic that he was than as the man who wrote "In wildness is the preserva-tion of the world" for the Sierra Club to put on its calendars. But as much can be said of the political Thoreau, who probably did *not* actually say, while locked up in jail, "Waldo, why are you *not* here." All the same, Tho-reau, like Lincoln, was appalled by the utterly gratuitous, imperialistic American invasion of Mexico, followed by our annexation of half of its territory. In full historical perspective, this was aggression by one white, European, postcolonial regime against another white, European, postcolo-nial regime in their contest to take territory from the American indigenes, but aggression our action definitely was. During the Vietnam War, there were those—always seen as the furthest-out, most unrealistic rebels—who called for withholding taxes in protest against the war. But tax resistance, in his day, was Henry David's chosen form of civil disobedience. His action was futile, but his fervor on the war issue and on abolition precipitated his "Civil Disobedience," a classic text of American resistance to the besetting American danger—namely, what Alexis de Tocqueville was the first to call "tyranny of the majority." Sacralized nationalism, even when democratic, believes that "vox populi vox Dei." Prophetic protest denies that equation: no, it says, the voice of the people is *not* the voice of God. The people are not divine but human, all too human, and not just fallible but also peccable. There are sins that are not mistakes, and mistakes that are not sins.

These matters are on my mind because whatever support Donald Trump may be losing in opinion polls, the American majority still respects as legitimate because legal the armed and dangerous political correctness of his administration. Beyond his own pardon of a criminal who aided and abetted the Russian meddling in our election that crucially helped put Trump in office, there is the Kremlin-style purge by Trump's attorney general of three different federal district attorneys in a position to continue investigations of the President for serious crimes. Yesterday, driving home from the supermarket, I heard a report on NPR of the deportation of a Mexican woman just *one hour* after she had given birth in a San Diego hospital. ICE waited just that one hour after her parturition to escort her to the border under armed guard where they gave her the compassionate choice to yield her citizen baby to them at that point and cross the border alone, or take the little citizen with her. Hearing that, I began to imagine a campaign commercial loosely in the vein of the recent Lincoln Project commercials, but with the refrain—in words coming up successively on the television screen—"un-Christian . . . un-American . . . *inhuman!*"

This is the face of the political correctness of the right, the political correctness of Stephen Miller. Left political correctness—like the objection to master/slave language in a set of computer programs or the looming objection to the same in Hegel—is a relatively impotent kind of extremism. Right political correctness is ferociously potent; it is extremism awash in wealth and heavily armed with both political and military weapons. On the eve of the Iraq War, there were *massive* peace demonstrations against it, including a truly gigantic one in New York, not to speak of major demonstrations in several European capitals. Then, the political correctness of the Left was "No blood for oil," and the demonstrators were correct on every count, whether of *Idealpolitik* or *Realpolitik*. But they had *no* effect, for the political correctness of the Right was entrenched in power and in the media, up to and including the *New York Times*, through at least the first several years of the conflict. As things turned so terribly destructive, the political correctness of the right became George W. Bush's claim that "the intelligence was wrong," when in fact the intelligence had been correct, but political correctness from the Right had cooked it to fit.

This past Friday, although the extended Miles family had already received the CD of brother Michael's "Mississippi River Suite" with his new word-and-music composition "Which Side Are You On?" We had never seen the latter performed live. That hap-

pened on Friday in the empty auditorium of the Old Town School of Folk Music as a bene-fit for the school. (I don't know whether it was recorded or not.) The beginning was acoustically a bit off, but I think the sound engineer may have made a cor-rection or two because the work built as it proceeded with aural as well as emotional power: four performers, two Black and two white. Mike introduced, as an unan-nounced interlude, a riveting instrumental duet between himself on banjo and Lloyd King on flute. As an encore, the ensemble did a composition that morphed by its final section into a throbbing "I Ain't A-gonna Study War No More." For me, it was particularly affecting to see my little brother at far stage-left, playing with such physical energy and with his eyes riveted on statuesque, queenly Zahra Glenda Baker, who was speaking all the lines at far stage right. In a few remarks that opened the performance, he cited Shondra, Zahra's partner, with a reminiscence about Duke Ellington and Ella Fitzgerald. The Duke could write a piece, but after Ella once sang it, "that piece belonged to Ella," Shondra said. Mike's quoting Shondra might seem just a generous gesture from composer to performer, but I know he meant it, for I know for a fact that as he wrote, he was thinking of Zahra all the way. The work has been in progress for about two years. With the slaying of Eric Garner, not George Floyd, on her mind, Zahra suggested early on inserting the words "I can't breathe" into (if I recall correctly) the "Destiny" section of "Which Side." Garner did speak those words, but it took another "I can't breathe," of course, to launch whatever may now have been launched. Only after the coronavirus slammed us all into involuntary confinement did Mike decide to marry "Which Side Are You On?" to a set of images with overprinted text for online access. He has been posting these one at a time on his website. You and Dinny have the link to one that gains hugely in impact from the visual alternation between two venues that alternate in the text: On July 4, a hokey Trump celebration at a dais built on and into the Lincoln Memorial and, at the other end of the Washington Mall, a Carole King concert full of simplicity and honest feeling.

Earlier in the week, I was thinking about your remarks one letter back on the complexity of gift-giving. The pure gift, I agree, is the gratuitous, the graced, the gracious, the gratis gift, but short of such purity there can be generosity, even grace, within something more transactional, and the more such generosity the better. Mercy is the act of not claiming what could be claimed; in that sense, it becomes the antithesis of justice by transcending justice. Mercy says, "You do *not* owe me," even when a debt could rightly be collected, even collected in the form of one hundred lashes, or in the form of deportation after parturition. Gifts can be gratuitous in the way that mercy is gratuitous, and I say again: the more such mercy and the more such giving, the better. American policy under Trump has become not just miserly and merciless but, by a further vile twist, gratuitously cruel.

One of your quotes from *Walden* finds Thoreau reading the *Bhagavad Gita*. The *Gita*, whose final message is that the soldier should do his duty and kill his relatives because, after all, the slain will be born again all in accord with their karma, is rather less Thoreauvian than the Daodejing, which we know he also read: Laozi was a loner and semidropout rather like Thoreau himself; in fact, he was more of a dropout, for, late in life, according to the legend, he actually left China for India.

I commented to Wendy Doniger at one point during our work on *The Norton Anthology of World Religions* that there seemed no religious possibility that Hinduism at one or another point in time, in one or another of its innumerable manifestations, had not activated. These days, I am slowly making my way through a book with many little fascinations along the way: Pratapaditya Pal's *In Quest of Coomaraswamy*. In his time, or, perhaps more accurately, slightly after his heyday, Ananda Coomaraswamy, who effectively introduced the United States to Indian art during his long tenure at the Boston Museum of Fine Art, was looked on askance by his fellow art historians because of his metaphysical ruminations. But Pal insists on the inseparability of art history and philosophy in Coomaraswamy's "dance with Shiva." He writes that "without the art historian the metaphysician would not have followed. Moreover, move on, move on (*charaiveti, charaiveti*) proclaims the Indian philosophical tradition, from the mundane to the spiritual!" The Hindu "stages of life" wisdom to which Pal alludes (*kama, artha, dharma, moksha*, or, very roughly, passion, ambition, devotion, liberation) has long had a powerful appeal for me, precisely because my own life path has been so violent a departure from that wisdom. Ten years of consecrated celibacy starting at age eighteen? How unnatural, how crazy! Reading Pratap, I was unexpectedly taken by that *charaiveti, charaiveti*. Where did these words, obviously a quote, come from? It suddenly occurred to me that while the Hindu gods are often portrayed dancing or otherwise in motion, Buddha—functionally, so nearly the Buddhist god—is always portrayed in beautiful stillness. Some connection, some significant contrast, here to be explored? Well, it turns out that the words conclude a Hindu hymn, later than the Upanishads, in which the ever-flitting honey-gathering bee; the ever-darting fruit-eating bird; and even the endlessly moving, life-giving sun are made to teach the prospective Hindu saint to keep moving, keep growing (*charaiveti, charaiveti*) onward toward spiritual perfection. But I note, as of special interest to you, perhaps, that either ideal is susceptible of powerful artistic expression.

The sense of passage is hardly unique to Hinduism. There's the Latin dictum *Per aspera ad astra*. And I think too of Samuel Beckett's mordant title, *I Can't Go On, I'll Go On*. But in my scouting around, I learned that the Sanskrit exhortation *charaiveti, charaiveti*, with or without the rest of the Hindu poem, is also used in Buddhism, and even attributed to the Buddha. For Buddhists, however, at least for those of the early centuries, the movement was to be entirely interior: dancing was associated with sensuality and was rejected as distracting illusion, thus the antithesis of enlightenment.

In our tradition, the climactic moment in the Book of Job comes when a Voice from the Whirlwind speaks contemptuously to Job, dismissing his petty moralistic demands with a recitation of the overwhelming physical power of the God of Nature ("Where were you when I," etc.) By one reading (for long, the more common reading), Job is humbled and stilled by this display. By another (mine, and more recently that of Edward L. Greenstein, an eminent Israeli American scholar), this performance by an unnamed power claiming to be the omnipotent creator is simply Job's last test, and he passes it: that is, he is impressed by the power but only *as* power. This bellowing braggart is clearly free to crush him at will, but so what? The braggart does not have the power to compel his respect. The only god who can do that is a god who combines moral and natural power.

Though Thoreau could invoke Christian tropes when it suited him, his was clearly a private sort of religiosity, eclectic at times in the way that Coomaraswamy's was eclectic, and yet it seems definitely to have been a religiosity that combined both the wisdom traditions (submission to nature) and the prophetic traditions (insistence on a morally better world). This combination is distinctive of the God of the Bible, Old Testament and New Testament both. Note in Psalm 65 (read in church today) how the emphasis at the start is entirely on morality, justice, sin, forgiveness, and worship and how at the end that emphasis yields to wonder at the power of nature, taken as a manifestation of God's power:

> You are to be praised, O God, in Zion; / to you shall vows be performed in Jerusalem.

> To you that hear prayer shall all flesh come, / because of their transgressions.

> Our sins are stronger than we are, / but you will blot them out.

> Happy are they whom you choose and draw to your courts to dwell there! / they will be satisfied by the beauty of your house, by the holiness of your temple.

Awesome things will you show us in your righteousness, O God of our salvation / O Hope of all the ends of the earth and of the seas that are far away.

*[here the theological volta from moral authority to physical prowess]*

You make fast the mountains by your power; / they are girded about with might.

You still the roaring of the seas, / the roaring of their waves, and the clamor of the peoples.

Those who dwell at the ends of the earth will tremble at your marvelous signs; / you make the dawn and the dusk to sing for joy.

*[and so on, easing into a hymn to the fruitfulness of the earth down to the last verse]*

May the meadows cover themselves with flocks, and the valleys cloak themselves with grain; / let them shout for joy and sing.

"You make the dawn and the dusk to sing for joy" is one helluva line, but poetry is not the subject just now. Against what I might wish to be the case, I always experience a change of gears, not to say a grinding of gears, when I move from considering, say, the pace of global aridification to considering the spread of juvenile malnutrition in the United States or worldwide. The shift from a problematic of resources and habitat preservation to the problematic of Black Lives Matter(ing) seems even sharper. But, in principle, I believe that these are all finally a single interlocking problematic. I grant (how can I deny?) that no single human agent or likely coalition of agents is likely ever to be equal to meeting the challenges that we face. All the same, rather than declare that finally there *is* no problem, only a single large fact in which, e.g., no one is homeless because everyone is homeless and no one is dying because everyone is always dying and someone is always being born, I am irresistibly drawn to a kind of resistance not altogether unlike my brother's: drawn to a taking of sides and a hope that I end up on the right side.

Random notes:

—*Thanatopsis*. You probably read it in school. William Cullen Bryant was Thoreau's exact contemporary. You would insist that Thoreau's "death-vision" is also a "life-vision," but, hey, "Biopsis" these days doesn't go down well as the title of a would-be visionary poem. You almost died of your biopsis, I mean biopsy.

—Annie Dillard. Actually, I have met her twice, both times in Wendy's company there in Truro. I also met her recently deceased husband, and it occurs to me now that I might drop her a line of condolence. She is an athletic woman, tall, rather fierce in manner, but her mind is slipping a bit, and she knows it and even, entirely in character, boldly alludes to it. She and he have both held private pilot's licenses in the past and once loved to fly. What she enjoyed most about pilot's training, she said, was a) flying upside down and b) stalling the engine, sending the plane into a spiral earthward, and then recovering in time. (Terrifying, but she implied that this was actually part of the training.) I have an inscribed copy of one of her later books; it galls her that they are all forgotten, and no one remembers any but *Tinker's Creek*.

And another tangent: on my second visit, the three of us were sitting on her little back porch when a sparrow fluttered in and settled into a nest under the eave. I started singing the lilting American folk hymn "His Eye Is on the Sparrow,"

> Why should I feel discouraged,
> Why should the shadows come,
> Why should my heart be lonely,
> And long for heaven and home?

And then the chorus:

> I sing because I'm happy
> I sing because I'm free
> For his eye is on the sparrow,
> And I know he watches me.

This is not a hymn I grew up with. I had learned it only a few years ago through my choir membership, but I needed only to begin it, and Annie took over. She knew all the words. Even more surprising, so did Wendy.

—About Thoreau's imagined Brahmin "sit[ting] still in his temple on the Ganges reading the Vedas . . ." Forgivably wrong, but still wrong: the Brahmin priests in those days resolutely insisted on *memorizing* the Vedas. The written word definitely did matter, but the spoken word—master to disciple—mattered more, and as late as the mid-nineteenth century, I think the private ownership of books was rare or confined to the wealthy. In the tropics, paper rots easily, and the earliest texts in any case were not written on either paper or parchment but on even more perishable palm leaves. As a result, the Brahmins became fabulously good at memorizing. When it came time to do a critical edition of the Vedas, it was discovered that all the Brahmins had memorized the very same version. Perhaps group recitation counts as a kind of true critical publication.

—"Protagoras was wrong, man is *not* the measure of all things, or, more precisely man is the measure of all things for *man*." True, and what you say of man is also necessarily true of all human products, including human thought, including philosophy and including science. Thus, science is not the measure of all things, and scientific proof is not *finally* probative—neither about life (vitality) nor about death (mortality), and leave aside "all things." All the same, the scope for scientific proof to matter quite decisively between now and when we can truly employ the adverb "finally" is gigantic.

—Pork chops. Mine were delicious, but I am thinking over my meat addiction, thanks partly to Kathleen and Brian, who are pescatarians (and were vegetarians for a time). In the short run, Kitty and I have tried—but, honestly, not very hard—to eat meat less often. Indian and Chinese cuisines excel at delicious vegetarian meals, but acquiring the skill to cook well in those traditions is no snap. Indian food, in particular, is just *hugely* complicated to prepare; I greatly admire those who have mastered it. But if the epidemic kills off enough slaughterhouse workers and bankrupts enough ranchers, maybe my conscience will get a little kick in the ass, and I'll try harder.

—(7/13) kisses. I forgot to mention my fourth gift to Kitty: 75 kisses, spaced throughout the day, with the last ten just before she fell asleep.

Jack

## JULY 19–20: JACK BEGINS.

*Mortgaging our future . . . white fragility . . . risking a haircut . . . politicizing masks . . . anti-vaxxers . . . better living through algorithms? . . . is forgiveness possible? . . . John Lewis's death . . . reading aloud to our spouses (or not) . . . Friedrich Nietzsche and Rudolf Otto . . . God's indifference . . . insurrection: Harvard Uprising, 1969.*

---

*July 19*

Dear Mark:

This morning, Kathleen forwarded to me an email sent to her at 7:12 a.m. by her realtor, who didn't want to phone her so early with the news that her house bid was unsuccessful. The message: "Ultimately, it came down to price, and the early determination shown by the accepted party." Kathleen will be crushed by that phrase "early determination." In the manipulative way the real estate game is currently played, at least in Los Angeles, a buyer often prices his property well below what he expects it to sell for. Why? Because in this way he can attract less affluent prospective buyers whose anticipated role is not to buy the property but rather to get caught up in competitive bidding long enough to force the more affluent buyer who is the real target buyer to pay more than he would otherwise have paid—more than he would have paid if he were in one-on-one negotiation with the seller.

Kathleen was in college when Ross Douthat was in college. He writes tellingly today, significantly out of his own experience, about the "overproduction of elites" (Peter Turchin's phrase) and what has lately been awaiting elite graduates:

A big-city ecosystem where the price of adult goods like schools and housing has been bid up dramatically, while important cultural industries—especially academia and journalism—supply fewer jobs even in good economic times. And they live half in these crowded, over-competitive worlds and half on the internet, which has extended the competition for status almost infinitely and weakened some of the normal ways that local prestige might compensate for disappointing income. These stresses have exposed the thinness of meritocracy as a culture, a Hogwarts with SATs instead of magic, a secular substitute for older forms of community, tradition or religion. If your bourgeois order is built on a cycle of competition and reward, and the competition gets fiercer while the rewards diminish, then instead of young people hooking up safely on the way to a lucrative job and a dual-income marriage with 2.1 kids, you'll get young people set adrift, unable to pair off, postponing marriage permanently while they wait for a stability that never comes.

From this point in his essay, Douthat veers off into a somewhat dubious meditation on the appeal of *White Fragility* to the demographic (roughly his own) that he writes about. His reservations about the book I might share; I just doubt that its purchase on his generation is as broad as he suspects. I myself, aware for years of how desperate the scramble is outside the West for every form of life-goods, have thought it inevitable that Americans' secular faith in cornucopian abundance would be eroded. Eroded, to be sure, in ways that to some degree are distinctly American—notably in American hostility to the welfare state and American tolerance of extreme concentrations of wealth. But eroded also, as North American natural abundance is steadily, painfully overtaken by world scarcity. Whatever the full story, and not yet having spoken at length to Kathleen, I am privately grieving with her.

By the way, though she has not joined a church and I don't expect her to, she does irregularly but frequently drop in at a Buddhist meditation center. I believe one makes a small good-faith donation at this center, hears a short talk, and then shares the quiet and the ambiance with others. She asked me awhile back to suggest a synagogue as well, and once in a while I believe she attends the ultraliberal All Saints Episcopal Church in Pasadena that her mother sometimes visits as well. At such a moment, meditation can't hurt.

Turning to your letter and to the politicization of mask wearing and social distancing even in California, I can say that in our quiet corner of polarized Orange County, I find no one unmasked in the supermarket that we favor and no service provider who has to come to house ever arriving unmasked. Unfortunately, a large and powerful minority, with influence reaching up to the level of the Orange County supervisors and the county school board, clearly is taking its lead from President Trump rather than from Governor Newsom. The *Washington Post* today posted the excerpts from an utterly appalling interview that Trump gave to Fox News's Chris Wallace. In it, speaking for "freedom of choice," he said that, no, he will not order the nationwide use of masks; he says this, and millions hear him. Nonetheless, freedom forgotten, he will indeed do all in his fiscal power to compel school districts to reopen even against their will, and the OC Board of Education has echoed his position: schools should open, no new restrictions. (Thank heaven, they did leave the ultimate responsibility up to each school district, but it's still an open question how or whether the districts will divide on the matter.) As for skyrocketing COVID cases, says Trump, it's all young people: "They get the sniffles, they're over it in a day, and they call it COVID." As for his repeated "It will go away," he stands by it: "I will be right eventually. It *will* go away." And as for accepting the results of the November election, "I won't say yes. I won't say no. We'll see." He reminded Wallace that he had refused to commit to accepting the results in 2016 as well. More exactly, he shouted that the election was rigged right down to the moment when the results came in making him the winner. Amid all this, Biden is pulling steadily ahead, but, per my earlier letter, who becomes president may depend on whose orders the army and the police departments and the other armed entities in our country choose to obey. And if it is they who determine who becomes a president, then our republic will have become a police state.

I hope you don't come to regret your haircut. Kitty and I had spoken to Andy, our longtime hair stylist, about either being his first client of the day or his coming to our house to cut our hair, but he finally declined and with poignant intensity. He thinks that no precautions taken in his salon and no protection we can afford at home during a haircut can obviate the danger that he himself carries with him. How can it be otherwise? With his only choices being contracting/spreading the infection, on the one hand, or going bankrupt, on the other, he chose to reopen when reopening became possible. (Gov. Newsom has now closed hair salons down again.) He took what precautions he could take, but he didn't think they were enough. He saw one client after another all day with no knowledge of their health or their habits of protection. He lived in fear of dying himself or infecting his partner—or us with our (mainly my) preexisting vulnerabilities. Because "I would just feel so terrible" if he infected Kitty, whom he has known since he was a teenager, he just couldn't bring himself to work on us. This quite likely has something to do with our advanced age and related vulnerability. I told him that I had done some trimming of my own hair. "Fine," he said, "or wear a hat. Whatever." Kitty's abundant hair will eventually grow long enough to braid, and I used to occasionally braid my sisters' hair. I even once knew how to do a French braid. Our caution and Andy's may be unwarranted: I read lately in an interview with Anthony Fauci that he has had a haircut. But for now, our hair is just growing freely.

You mentioned your surprise that your young North Adams stylist is an anti-vaxxer. When Kitty and I lived in Newton, our local congressman was an anti-vaxxer: Robert Kennedy Jr. One of my oldest friends and one of my first two close Jewish friends (we met as teenagers in Chicago) is an anti-vaxxer, a believer in tales of Fauci's dark collaboration with Bill Gates, and, lately, a skeptic of the *Washington Post* and the *New York Times*. Yet I'm sure she would vote for Biden over Trump . . . at least I think I'm sure. The *Times* today has a long feature on the national skepticism of vaccines, powerful in Black areas but by no means confined to them. Overall, only about half the country is sure it would get a vaccine if one is made available. Here, again, is an example of Trump's real, empirical influence over American opinion. There was skepticism of science before Trump. There was America's long-standing skepticism of all intellectuals and anyone, even physicians, who thinks he's smarter than you are. But Trump has poured real fuel on that long-smoldering fire, and he has scarcely been alone. Think of those many televised scenes of Congress in session: the Republicans unmasked, the Democrats masked. If Trump had been masking, those Republicans would have been masked as well. The pictures have been worth thousands and thousands of words.

Your riff beginning with Italo Calvino and ending with "The Professor Is In" has the brilliance of reference and the existential connection that so power and enliven *Intervolution: Smart Bodies Smart Things.* Just two or three tangential comments on all that.

First, hasn't the view been around for a long while—wasn't it argued by Paul Ricoeur, among others—that memory is not preserved but constructed? Your point stands, of course, that the way the wet, human brain constructs memory is different (above all, sensually different) from the way "MyLifeBit" constructs it. Your intriguing connection of algorithm and olfaction reminds me, too, that in the human brain, the amygdala, controlling olfaction, is close to the memory center, which is why scent is so powerfully able to evoke memory. Or so it has been argued. Will "affective computing" be able to duplicate this juxtaposition and its effects? Would its authors want to?

Second, the *Times*'s "Inside the News" feature today gives a glimpse inside the management of the *New York Times Book Review* now that nobody is any longer in the office to receive the uninterrupted onslaught of review copies, bound manuscripts, bound galleys, etc. I was accustomed back at the *Los Angeles Times Book Review* to cope with just the same flow, if at not quite the volume they face in New York. The *Times* staff are now working from home, and dealing electronically with the books that are to be (or not to be) reviewed, and they're coping as well as they can but feeling crippled by tactile and haptic deprivation. "Crippled" is not a word they use, but I do think it fits. And I felt my own haptic, tactile, and even olfactory memories welling up as I read of their struggles.

Third, about total recall, there are documented cases of individuals who are blessed or cursed with such recall. They are not necessarily idiot savants, either. After a *Times* feature on memory, one man made himself available to the newspaper for interviewing, testing, etc. His recall was simply astounding, but he himself clearly did not rejoice in his capacity. He did not seem tortured by it, but he was noncommittal about it to the point of seeming at least slightly glum. Minimally, this capacity seemed to mean absolutely nothing to him. It was there, simply there, and so what?

Learning of attacks like the ones you cite against Steven Pinker, I have two reactions. Call them the hopeless and the hopeful.

I feel hopeless when I see slander becoming efficaciously destructive by the operation of something like the ontological argument. That is, because the attack can be made, because a Pinker is conceivably a racist, there must be truth to it, he must *be* a racist. And if there is a little truth to the conception, that little is enough because a sinner cannot be slightly sinful: all sins are mortal, and no outcome is condign but damnation. *Malum in parte malum est*, as it was put at the Pontifical Gregorian University. I've mentioned former senator Bob Kerrey before. He was ambiguously involved in an action in Vietnam that eventuated in an atrocity. Was he, as a commanding officer, ultimately responsible? This lay beyond final determination, but suppose the worst. Suppose he was. Even then, Kerrey said, long after leaving office, "One would wish that a man could be judged not by the one worst moment in his whole life but by the whole of that life." I quote from memory and inexactly, but his point is yours about Pinker. His attackers disregard the full record and rest their case on the few scraps exhumed with the mnemonic aid of current technology. Such moments do begin to induce hopelessness.

I feel hopeful, however, when I observe that, at least some of the time, the frequency and the ease of making such attacks against almost anyone who has lived long and occupied any position of responsibility is beginning to have the effect of diluting their impact. In this connection, I derive an odd kind of optimism from the ability of Trump's supporters to stick with him no matter what crime he is found guilty of. I deplore that kind of loyalty, of course, but I once said of my own loyalty to Barry Munitz after he was found guilty of abusing his expense account, "He may not be a saint, but he is still my friend. If I confined my friendship to saints, I would be a lonely man indeed." My kind of loyalty entailed the kind of comprehensive judgment that Kerrey was calling for.

Finally, to your closing words about forgiveness, again, two associations.

First, on my one and only trip to Japan, I had a conversation with a member of a Japanese "new new" religion, one that was, as usual with these movements, heavily marked by Buddhism. He told me, through an interpreter, that he needed a heart transplant and that he and his wife had once waited for a few years for the needed heart to become available. (Aside: Japanese themselves do not normally make their organs available for transplant, so transplanted organs are normally imported from, usually, Thailand or elsewhere in South Asia.) After those few years of waiting, however, the man and his wife had decided to have themselves taken off the list of transplant candidates because they had discovered that they were hoping for some young healthy man to have the accident that would make his heart available, and this malignant hoping was harming the two of them spiritually more than the husband's heart disease was harming him physically. I repeated this episode to the late Bill LaFleur, who was with me on this trip, and he said that it was a classic Buddhist sentiment, or aspiration. On the Eightfold Path, it might be the equivalent of "right desiring." Buddhism deplores the holding of grudges. Hold a grudge, and you do yourself more harm than you do your begrudged brother.

Second, on the evening of the day when John Lewis died, MSNBC ran the special feature on him that they clearly had in the can, awaiting his passing. (It's been known for months that he was ill with pancreatic cancer.) An iconic moment in his career came when, wearing a cream-colored trench coat, he was among those savagely beaten by the Selma police as they walked across the famous bridge. A photograph exists of him in that coat, pushed to the ground as a policeman stands above him with a baton as long as a baseball bat, about to whale him with it. Well, that cop, at the time a member of the KKK, eventually contacted him to apologize and ask forgiveness, and Lewis forgave him. The two eventually appeared together in public to speak of their reconciliation, and the footage included in the memorial program was genuinely moving. So, yes, confession is good for the soul, but Alexander Pope's famous line also comes to mind: "To err is human, to forgive divine." The line you quote, one of Jesus's "seven last words" from the cross, was spoken by God Incarnate.

Jack


*July 20*

Dear Jack:

By a strange coincidence, immediately after reading your letter, I checked the headlines of the *New York Times*, *New York Post*, and Huffington Post. The lead story in Huffington read "Trump Won't Say Whether He Will Accept 2020 Election Results: 'I Have To See.'"

President Donald Trump wouldn't say whether he will accept the results of the general election in November during an interview with

"Fox News Sunday," claiming again without evidence that the process is rigged before any votes have been cast. Host Chris Wallace asked Trump if he was a good loser, to which the president responded that he is not. "But are you gracious?" Wallace pressed.

"You don't know until you see," Trump said. "It depends. I think mail-in voting is going to rig the election. I really do.

Asked if he's suggesting he might not accept the results of the election, Trump said, "I have to see."

It's beginning to seem that your friend Phillip had it right in *The Plot Against America*. The sentence in your letter that stopped me in my tracks was "Nothing Trump has done so far—Trump or the Trump Administration, and one increasingly wonders how fully the man is in charge—has so terrified me." Given the concerns we have shared over the past months, that is indeed a sobering statement. I have, of course, been following the events in Portland and, like you, have been puzzled by their persistence and volatility. While you have persuaded me that I need to take more seriously the possibility that Trump will not willingly leave office, I confess that I had not thought about your conspiratorial interpretation of what is happening in the streets. I continue to be frustrated by the unwillingness of retired military leaders to speak out forcefully against what Trump and Mike Pompeo are doing. There are important exceptions to be sure—James Mattis, David Petraeus, Stanley McChrystal, and Colin Powell among the most prominent—but where are the others? I would especially like to hear from Ash Carter, who was the secretary of defense under Obama. Ash was married to my former student Clayton Spence, who was the vice president at Harvard for years, and now is the president of Bates College. During her time in Washington, Clayton became Kirsten's mentor, and Kirsten would sometimes babysit for their children. Ash is literally a nuclear physicist (PhD from MIT) and spent years working on the problem of nuclear proliferation in Russia with another former secretary of defense William Perry, who has gone silent. Perhaps they are working quietly behind the scenes, but in the face of the recent developments you so graphically describe, that is not enough. What makes this all the more disconcerting is the complicity between Trump and Barr. Commentators endlessly repeat the suggestion that, in William Barr, Trump has found his Roy Cohn. But I think this gets it wrong—in Trump, Barr has found his Joe McCarthy. If, as you fear, Trump refuses to leave office, his enabler in chief will be William Barr.

Since we began our correspondence, I have marveled at the ritual of you and Kitty reading novels aloud to each other. And not just any novel, but an eight-hundred-page novel [S. Y. Agnon's *Shira*]! That's a commitment almost as serious as marriage itself. In all honesty, I simply cannot imagine doing that with Dinny, though I often discuss what I have read with her. For virtually my whole life, I have spent 10-12 hours a day, sometimes longer, silently reading alone. Since my interests range broadly, I've never been able to distinguish reading for work and reading for pleasure. If your goal is to develop a philosophy of culture, everything is fair game for interpretation and there is nothing that is not research. There is, however, something else that makes me resist reading aloud in a dialogical exchange. I read the books that matter to me very slowly, giving my mind ample time to wander. I always underline, often take notes, and usually jot down thoughts to which I return later. There is an unpredictable rhythm to such reading that would be disrupted by your practice. As I may have told you before, I've always remembered a conversation I had with my dissertation advisor at Harvard, Richard R. Niebuhr, when I asked him what he was reading. He responded that as he grew older he no longer was reading many new books or articles, but was returning to works to which he had devoted much of his life. In the past few years, I have found wisdom in what he did.

Though your literary and philosophical references are intriguing, I suspect you are right: S. Y. Agnon's *Shira* is not a novel for me. There is, however, one sentence that you quote from Robert Alter's afterword that drew my attention: "From one point of view, this is a novel about the impossibility of tragedy in the modern age, and especially after the advent of Hitler—that is to say, the impossibility of a literary form that assigns meaning to suffering, or represents an experience of transcendence through suffering." I have been intrigued by tragedy since I was a senior in high school, when I wrote my English term paper on Arthur Miller's transformation of the genre into the tale for everyman. Even at that young age, I was not sure that Willy Loman rose to the level of tragedy. Tragedy has always seemed to me to require that a person have a certain stature and, indeed, dignity that has never been more lacking in so many people as it is today. (A footnote: one of my most memorable experiences was hosting Arthur Miller for an event sponsored by the Center for the Humanities and Social Sciences, which I founded at Williams College. Though grander than life, he was completely down to earth, and what a showman! My mother taught *The Crucible* in junior English year after year, and I deeply regretted that she did not live to attend Miller's performance.) As for Nietzsche, whom you also mention, I have taught *The Birth of Tragedy* in various courses for years, and you are, of course, right when you suggest that his interpretation of the genre is grounded in "violent primal forces" often associated with the sacred. I usually read Nietzsche in conjunction with Rudolph Otto's *The Idea of the Holy*. As you know, Otto describes the holy as the "mysterium tremendum," which he characterizes as terrific power that is simultaneously destructive and creative. What is always most difficult to explain to students and, in all honesty, to myself is the absolute indifference of such power to human well-being and, indeed, existence. This indifference is what I hear in God's final words to Job, which we discussed without reaching agreement a few letters back. If, as Alter insists (or is it Agnon?), tragedy is impossible in the modern age, it is because suffering is not redemptive. We are part of a natural world in which everything and everybody suffers and dies; there is no escape, no solution, no cure, and there is no tragedy in that. As the kids say today, "It is what it is," and I would add, "Why should it be otherwise?"

Finally, your long, thoughtful, and, in many ways, provocative reflection on white privilege and white fragility. Though your comments come at the problem from a different perspective, they are not unrelated to my meditation on remembering and forgetting. I am not sure I have anything productive to add, but, given your continuing understandable concern about these issues, I feel compelled to offer a few thoughts, which I worry you will find insensitive. I have to admit that I found your friend's homily self-serving and naïve. I am tired of the public self-flagellation of people who fashion themselves liberals. Whom does it serve? Does anything productive come out of such public displays? All too often such exercises seem designed to assuage perceived guilt and gain acceptance, perhaps even praise, from like-minded people. I am also suspicious about the apparent widespread support of the BLM movement. Call me cynical, but so many of these gestures of apparent support are self-serving in different ways—politicians are scurrying to please voters, companies are trying to keep customers from defecting, cities and towns are trying to quell unrest, owners of sports teams are trying to placate both players and fans, celebrities are trying to curry favor and increase their social media footprint. It's all one big media show that reinforces the system the actors claim to reject. Yes, racism is systemic, everything is, but systems are more *complicated* than most people understand or are interested in understanding. In a polarized world, left and right, blue and red, liberal and conservative thrive on simplification. I've had too many conversations with students, colleagues, and friends who pose either/or questions. When I respond, "Well, it's not so simple, it's complicated," I am immediately dismissed and cast in the role of an adversary. Nowhere, absolutely nowhere do I see serious commitment to the kind of difficult analytical work that is necessary to understand the problem, to say nothing of beginning to design and implement solutions.

In letters several months ago, we discussed our experience during the student strike and takeover of University Hall at Harvard in the spring of 1969. You might also recall that faculty and students at the Divinity School, where most of my classes were held, voted to suspend classes. I was among the few who voted against that resolution, which was, to say the least, not a very popular position at the time. In subsequent years, there have been several occasions when classes have been suspended to support one or another social cause. Whenever possible, I have always held class in spite of the boycott. Again, this has not been an easy or popular decision, but my reason has always been the same. To suspend my classes has always seemed to me to suggest that what we do in the classroom is unrelated to what is happening on the street. I absolutely reject that disjunction. As I have previously written to you, I started on my lifetime intellectual journey by reading about Hegel and Kierkegaard in the fall of 1967 and spring of 1968 when both cities and draft cards were burning. I believed then and I believe now that these thinkers, as well as others I've studied along the way, help us understand what is going on and point toward possible solutions that comprehend and respect the extraordinary complexity of the interrelated systems and networks that make us who we are. Hegel and Kierkegaard, along with Nietzsche, Heidegger, and others are difficult, dead white guys. Did they have flaws? Do their writings contain disturbing racist, anti-Semitic, and anti-feminist passages? Yes, without a doubt, and those aspects of the texts must be addressed directly and responsibly. But it is, in my judgment, a mistake to tear down or even discard the works of the intellectual giants because of their shortcomings, and so I have continued teaching them year after year to generations of students, and in some cases to the children of my students. One never knows whether the seeds one spreads take root or if so where. Like everything else, teaching and writing are a leap of faith, which I regard as my social action. What is so discouraging as my career nears its end is that today more than ever before so few have the patience for the deliberate reflection and reasoned discussion necessary for effective policies and action. Last semester I taught my Hegel and Kierkegaard seminar, which I intended to follow up this fall with a seminar on Heidegger and Derrida. That sequence would provide a possible map for the uncharted territory we are struggling to navigate. Unfortunately, I had to cancel the seminar because of a lack of interest.

Eight hundred pages! Really? What page are you on?

Mark

## JULY 26–AUGUST 8: MARK BEGINS.

*View from the bike . . . insulin reaction . . . the contingency of birth . . . Lord Jeffrey Amherst's germ warfare . . . J. D. Vance's* Hillbilly Elegy *. . . Ashley York,* Hillbilly *. . . Peter Turchi and the art of editing . . . Lin-Manuel Miranda's* Hamilton *. . . Jorge Luis Borges's "The Exactitude of Science" . . . individuality as an illusion . . . bildungsroman . . . connecting the dots—space and time?. . . returning to New York City . . . spreading quarantines . . . Michael Lewis's* The Fifth Risk *. . . hot zones . . . Dixie Chicks, Toby Keith, and CD burnings . . . why tell stories?. . . frozen in time . . . The owl of Minerva . . . two sons of immigrants . . . real fakes; Mueller Report . . . programming, deprogramming, reprogramming . . . empty highways . . . trash on the streets . . . the tyranny of Microsoft Word . . . AI: promise or curse?*

---

*July 26*

Dear Jack:

Reconnected and back online after another week of Spectrum visits. How reliable is our communications network when it can be interrupted by clawing bears and gnawing mice?

I'm feeling virtuous this morning—just back from a twelve-mile bike ride with Dinny. She rides regularly, but this was my first time this year. Whenever I ride, I marvel at the remarkable ability and endurance of the Tour de France athletes. As I have told you, Aaron started riding seriously when he was eleven or twelve and continues to this day. When he was here a couple of weeks ago, he rode five miles straight up to the top of the mountain across the valley. Though I can no longer believe it, I also once rode to the top of the mountain, and even ran to the summit with Kirsten. Aaron is bringing up Selma and Elsa to ride—mountain trails as well as roads—with him and Frida. Herbert is also a dedicated biker who, though approaching eighty, rides ten to twenty miles almost every day. A couple of years ago, I was having trouble with my knees and he urged me to ride rather than run. As a gesture of encouragement, he gave me a bike a business associate had given him. Needless to say, it's much higher end than I would ever buy. It is as light as a feather and you can literally lift it with a single finger. What a strange world in which I'm the indirect beneficiary of a gift to Herbert Allen.

Even with such a fancy bike, I was uncertain I could handle the ride. A year older and different muscles, but the real problem is, as always, this damn diabetes. My digital pancreas gives me much tighter control over my blood glucose, but this makes managing exercise considerably harder. When I exercise for a prolonged period, my blood glucose drops and my muscles gradually shut down until I can hardly breathe or move my legs. I then have to eat something to raise my sugar level, which takes time. More often than not, my body responds by driving my blood glucose up too much. It's hard to convey how frustrating it is to try to manage this incessant roller coaster. As I am writing these words, my insulin pump is sending an alarm that my blood glucose is too low, so if my thoughts get jumbled you will know why!

The route we ride goes from dirt road to highway and back again. I'm always surprised by how different the world looks on the bike. On roads I've driven for years, I always discover twist and turns, bumps and dips that vanish when you are in the car. Hills you hardly notice when driving take more energy than you think your legs have. The sense of speed also changes significantly—fifty miles per hour seems much faster when a car passes you on a bike than when you pass a bike in a car. The lesson here is about more than biking.

I'm glad Dinny figured out why you could not post your letter yesterday. Who knew that there is a 1.5 million character limit on Google Drive? And even if we had known, would we ever have imagined that we would surpass it? Not to worry—now we've started volume 2 and have another 1.5 million character allotment. We did know that a serious editing challenge lies ahead, but we did not realize just how big a job it will be. As I mentioned in response to your email about WordPress, I've been thinking about a range of issues related to editing, but I'm not quite ready to write about all of this yet. Perhaps next week. My thoughts involve the relation of my reflections last week on remembering and forgetting to my ongoing reading about neuroscience and artificial intelligence. This, in turn, has me thinking about the interplay between reality TV and fake news. At this point one of my question is: Is all fiction a lie, or is narrative the only way to tell some kinds of truth? More later.

Among the many questions your letter raises, a single fragment offered in passing caught my attention: "I was conceived shortly before the bombing of Pearl Harbor and born into the middle of our country's frightened mobilization for war." Though your parents obviously could not have known what was coming, they chose to have a child in the midst of what was already a catastrophic global conflagration. What remarkable faith in the future! As you know, during the war, my parents left the Pennsylvania coal mining town where they met, married, and taught and moved to Kankakee, Illinois, where my father worked as a chemical engineer for DuPont in the factory that made TNT for the campaign in Africa. After trying to get pregnant for years, the change of scene brought success. On November 8, 1944, which was the birthday of my mother's father after whom I am named, their daughter—Baby Girl Taylor—was born and died. She was to have been named Noelle, after my father, Noel. One year later, on December 13, 1945, I was born. There is no doubt that if my sister had lived, I would not have been born. Once again, the utter contingency of life. I was supposed to be born in Chicago, but they moved to New Jersey earlier in the fall. The following is a picture of the hospital where I would have been born. Do you recognize it?

I was surprised by your dismissal of Andrew Sullivan's article "A Plague Is an Apocalypse. But It Can Bring a New World," which appears in the current issue of *New York Magazine*. There are, as you point out, overlaps with William McNeil's book *Plagues and People*, which we have previously discussed. But Sullivan's emphasis on the importance of smallpox in the American Revolution bears consideration. This is only one thread in the much larger story of the role of infectious disease in the making of the so-called "New World." This issue hits close to home. In the world of Division 3 sports, Williams-Amherst is the equivalent of Carolina-Duke. Amherst College, which is named after Lord Jeffrey Amherst, was founded by a group of students and faculty who fled Williams, following what is now known as the Mohawk Trail, and settled in the Connecticut River Valley. Lord Jeffrey Amherst was the commander in chief of the British forces that conquered New France during the Seven Years' War. He is best known for his support of chemical warfare to exterminate indigenous people during Pontiac's War. He allegedly sent blankets infected with smallpox to Native Americans. Amherst teams were long known as the Lord Jeffs, but a few years ago, they anticipated the Washington Redskins and Cleveland Indians by dropping that tag.

Sullivan's essay is interesting and important for other reasons as well. Though I rarely agree with him, I always find his writing thoughtful and well worth reading. Here, as elsewhere, his historical narrative serves an ethical and a political purpose, which is indicated by its subtitle: "But It Can Bring a New World." A similar hope is expressed by Gianna Potama, who is a retired professor of the History of Medicine, at Johns Hopkins Hospital. In the July 20 *New Yorker*, Lawrence Wright profiles her in an article entitled "Crossroads: A Scholar of the Plague Thinks That Pandemics Wreak Havoc—and Open Minds." While Sullivan draws comparisons between the current pandemic, the AIDS crisis, and subsequent political action and social reforms, Potama, who is Italian and has returned to Italy, remains historically focused and discusses how the Black Death in the fourteenth century prepared the way for the Renaissance and the Reformation. Wright relates Pomata's analysis to other similar events ranging from the Plague of Athens in 430 BC to the 1918 Spanish flu epidemic. He connects the dots in an illuminating way.

After the shock of the Second World War, America transformed itself into the strongest economic power in history, largely through an expansive middle class. But after 9/11 the United States forged a dark path. Instead of taking advantage of surging patriotism and heightened international good will, America invaded Iraq and tortured suspects at Guantanamo; at home, prosperous Americas essentially barricaded themselves off from their fellow-citizens, allowing racial and economic inequities to fester. The country we are now was formed in no small part by the fear and the anger that still linger from that tragic day.

Wright is, well, right—without George W. Bush, Dick Cheney, Donald Rumsfeld, George Tenet, and Colin Powell, there would be no Donald Trump. For this reason as well as others, I think Sullivan and Pomata are whistling as they walk through the graveyard.

A final point on Sullivan. It is noteworthy that a day after his essay appeared, he announced that he is resigning from *New York Magazine*. While expressing respect for his colleagues, he gave no details for his departure. Coming only days after conservative columnist Bari Weiss left the *New York Times* because of what she described as an "illiberal environment," Sullivan's departure suggests the political divisions in this country are growing deeper.

It might seem a long way from the *New York Times* and *New York Magazine* to the hills of eastern Kentucky, but there are important connections to be made. Having nearly exhausted Netflix, Dinny and I signed up for a free trial month of Hulu. Last night we stumbled on a fascinating documentary entitled *Hillbilly*, by Ashley York, who grew up in Meathouse Hollow, Kentucky. I never got around to reading J. D. Vance's *Hillbilly Elegy*, partly because after reading the reviews and listening to his interviews, I didn't think he had much left to say. Furthermore, there was something about him I didn't trust. York, by contrast, comes across as completely believable. After viewing her film, I'm more convinced than ever that we will never understand Trump and what is happening in America if we do not begin to understand why people like those living in Meathouse Hollow think the way they do. I am sure that, like me, you sometimes ask, "How can these people possibly support him, when everything he does is contrary to their best interests?" Now I learn that they ask, "And what makes you think you know what are my best interests?"

Though my mother's hometown in the coal mining mountains of Pennsylvania is not yet as devastated as sections of Appalachia, the closing of the mines and lack of new industry has been a crushing blow to the town and to the entire region. I have not been back there since we buried my father, and I have lost touch with the people I once knew and with whom I hunted so I don't know how political attitudes have changed. York, who is a progressive feminist, returns to her hometown in the weeks before the 2016 election and focuses primarily on her own family, all of whom were Trump supporters. The film begins with a flyover of the hills surrounding the town and zeroes in on a Walmart store. In the opening lines we learn that in this part of Kentucky the two largest employers are the coal industry and Walmart. The camera then isolates an older man struggling to push a string of shopping carts from the parking lot into the store.

Though York never mentions the news clips of Trump at rallies in West Virginia attended by thousands of MAGA true believers, where Trump declares he will bring back jobs by reviving the coal industry, this is the backdrop for the entire film. The interviews with her uncle are particularly revealing. Like many others in the town, he was a lifelong Democrat who had never voted for a Republican before 2016. He dismisses Trump's lies ("all politicians lie"), is not interested in Russia, and remains convinced that Trump is a good businessman. What drove him to flip was not just decades of empty promises, but, more important, the lack of respect, condescension, and even disdain by politicians as well as people he and his family describe as "know-it-all elites." And that, my friend, means us—yes, you and me. As York spins her tale, the issues become more rather than less complex until it no longer is clear what counts as condescension. Policies and programs going as far back as Roosevelt's New Deal and Johnson's war on poverty that seemed to be intended to help people by alleviating problems only compound the festering resentment that erupted in 2016.

As I have previously written, both giving and receiving a gift are difficult, perhaps impossible. How can a gift be given without creating a sense of indebtedness that breeds resentment? Claims to the contrary notwithstanding, there is no such thing as a gift with no strings attached. What the people York profiles want more than money, food, or clothes is respect and a sense of dignity. The baffling paradox for those of us who seem to be more privileged is how a faux billionaire who is so undignified and respects no one but himself can instill in these people the hope for the respect and dignity for which they long.

The most poignant moment is the film is when York returns to interview the older man pushing shopping carts in the Walmart parking lot with whom her story begins. The lines on his show a life of deprivation and defeat. As York lets him tell his story, he reveals that his name is Billy Redden, the young boy who played the unforgettable dueling banjo duet in the scene that is the pivot in the film adaptation of James Dickey's memorable novel *Deliverance*. He was only eight at the time and received a measly $500 for his performance. While actors Burt Reynolds, Jon Voigt, and Ned Beatty went on to fame and fortune, Billy never left Meathouse Hollow. Listen to the tune again on YouTube, where it is accompanied by clips from the film. You will see all the stereotypes, caricatures, and misunderstandings that are fueling the rage spreading like a virus through the body politic. After a shot of a golden record award for the duet hanging on the wall in some nameless executive's office, the scene shifts to Billy, weary and leaning on a shopping cart, saying, "All I ever wanted was to visit LA, but I guess that will never happen." If you and I can understand this episode in this documentary, we might begin to understand what is going on in this country. As I have said, the issues are not simply black or white, left or right, blue or red. There are multiple shades of white, black, blue, and red. I can't sing "I'm a coal miner's daughter" with Loretta Lynn, but I can say, my great grandfather, Aaron Cooper, was a coal miner, and my son is named after him.

Mark

P.S. Looks like it's time to return to the belly of the beast. I've not been back to New York since I left in March but have to go down to check the apartment and pick up some books I need to teach my fall courses. I think it's better to return before students start arriving, so with some trepidation I think we'll go down next Sunday. I have no idea what to expect.

*August 2*

Dear Mark:

Our subjects in this correspondence have been broadly three:

First, our lives during this plague.

Second, the life of our country during the same plague.

Third, reflexively, our correspondence itself.

Of these three signal subjects, the one clearly most on your mind through the past week has been the third, which you engage at length in yours of 7/30 under the heading "editing." I have said a little on this subject already, and in this response to your letter (written over three days) I will say more presently, but first let me quote from two works of art that your meditation on editing brought to my mind, or joined there under an unusual stimulus. When things come to mind this way, first, they're just there; only then, you start asking yourself why. So, after some more organized comments on the possible editorial servicing of our work, I'll return to these and see whether and how they connect. For now, let them speak—or suggest—for themselves.

The first of the two is a famous sonnet by John Keats:

> When I have fears that I may cease to be
>     Before my pen has gleaned my teeming brain,
> Before high-pilèd books, in charactery,
>     Hold like rich garners the full ripened grain;
> When I behold, upon the night's starred face,
>     Huge cloudy symbols of a high romance,
> And think that I may never live to trace
>     Their shadows with the magic hand of chance;
> And when I feel, fair creature of an hour,
>     That I shall never look upon thee more,
> Never have relish in the faery power
>     Of unreflecting love—then on the shore
> Of the wide world I stand alone, and think
> Till love and fame to nothingness do sink.

The second is Lin-Manuel Miranda's historical/musical play *Hamilton*. I am rarely sleepless. On 7/31, however, I awoke—clear-headed and untroubled but indeed quite awake—at 2 a.m. Our entertainment for my 7/30 birthday, ending about 9 p.m., had been our viewing, courtesy of Disney Plus, of the filmed original stage production of *Hamilton*. I had listened to the entire production on CD, twice, checking the libretto afterward and tracking down a couple of the more obscure historical references, but the live production pulses with the energy of brilliant nonstop choreography by Andy Blankenbuehler, a name I want to remember. We are accustomed to background music in film. This choreography is a fabulous visual equivalent. These wild but perfectly controlled dancers, many of them Black but all of them wearing white, create a compelling background mood behind the music and behind the acting. The film of the production appropriately focuses on the actors, and one sees them more clearly than one would have in the theater. But in the theater, viewing the entire stage at all times, one would have felt the presence of the dancers, who surround the actors on all sides, more powerfully, I'm sure, than in the film—and yet they were plenty powerful for me even in the film. In the wee hours, I was awakened mainly, I think, by a sheer overflow from their visual, physical, bodily energy.

All the same, while thinking back on the production, I was also thinking forward to my response to your letter, which began with a brotherly birthday letter (and thanks for that). *Hamilton* ends with Eliza, Hamilton's widow, alone on stage. She outlived him by fully fifty years, she tells us, was an abolitionist, a defender of orphans, a fund-raiser for the Washington Monument, and the curator of her husband's voluminous papers. But no one is, no one can be, the curator of anyone's reputation. Washington, already deceased as the play closes, speaks of this matter from beyond the grave to open the production's grand finale. We hear his words quoted again as we see Eliza for the last time. Washington says that he wishes he had known when he was young that he had no control over who would tell his story. As he speaks, Eliza is yearning to *see* Alexander again. She is nearing the end of her life. It is only a matter of . . . *time*, a word she starts to say, but then the chorus breaks in to join her at that word. In the manner of a Greek chorus, they sing *time* three times in the final seconds before the stage goes dark but for a spotlight on Eliza. She gasps as if seeing something or perhaps someone before complete darkness and silence descend.

I think I can draw a kind of line between Keats's "till love and fame to nothingness do sink" and Washington's posthumous recognition that no one has control of his own story once he is gone. Lin-Manuel Miranda makes room, through Eliza, in *Hamilton* for immortality that transcends any and all continuation on Earth. Through Washington, he makes room for the importance of storytelling, including his own in this musical drama and Ron Chernow's in his revisionist biography of Hamilton. One's true story, one's actual achievement, may be completely forgotten; Keats was sadly resigned to that. It may be remembered as other than you yourself knew it when you lived; Washington, in *Hamilton*, is belatedly resigned to that.

Let all this linger in the background as I now attempt a response to your much-pondered letter about editing. You begin noting our different experiences of editing. Yes, I have done more editing than you. I have also, on balance, received editing more than you have, though the reckoning would be close. You have written more than twice as many books as I have, but I wrote perhaps hundreds of pages of prose while at the *Los Angeles Times*. All of these pages were at least copyedited, and those for the editorial page were also edited closely for content by the opinion editors I reported to. The core difference between you and me, though, on the matter of editing—at least to judge from this letter—is that you are a theorist of editing, a philosopher or an epistemologist of the subject, and I am a practitioner, working always against the ticking clock of an implicit deadline. My late friend Richard Eder, the finest prose stylist I ever edited, taught a course at Princeton for several years after his retirement entitled Practical Criticism. I always thought of my reading and responding to Philip Roth's work as practical criticism in Richard's sense, by which I mean criticism while there is still time, criticism while a work is still in progress but, ideally, headed for publication—criticism before the deadline.

And for that task, as you move on to note, it's a rare or perhaps a vain writer who cannot be surprised by what a careful reader can note that the writer missed, even when the reader could never have produced what the writer delivered. Philip, certainly capable of narcissism, was the soul of humility when a page of prose was thus under double consideration. I have in my commonplace book the following aside by Edmund Burke in his *Reflections on the French Revolution*:

> If I might venture to appeal to what is so much out of fashion in Paris, I mean to experience, I should tell you, that in my course I have known, and, according to my measure, have co-operated with great men; and I have never yet seen any plan which has not been mended by observations of those who were much inferior in understanding to those who took the lead in the business. . . . From hence arises, not an excellence in simplicity, but one far superior, an excellence in composition. Where the great interests of mankind are concerned through a long succession of generations, that succession ought to be admitted into some share in the councils, which are so deeply to affect them.

Burke is arguing for the reasonability of granting voice to the common people in the deliberations of the state—a noteworthy qualification, coming as it does in a work essentially rejecting the idea of simply turning the state over to the common people. Down to the word "composition," however, his observation about the management of the state also applies to the management of any work of art while the work is still alive—that is, still in progress.

So, the suggestion for the practical criticism of our work that I infer just from your first two paragraphs is that we need to find an outside reader to both vet and edit our work. More before I conclude on who this might be and what his/her job description should be, but first let me proceed to the elaborate reflections that follow in your letter on these prologue paragraphs.

Yes, as you begin, "the issue of editing has broader significance than usually is recognized." But an engagement with that significance at its full breadth would yield not a critique of our unfinished but soon-to-be-finished plague diary but a philosophical study comparable to your *The Moment of Complexity: Emerging Network Culture*. Last week, as a kind of postscript to the connection game you had devised in a previous letter, you sent me the "mindmap" from Richard Hofstadter's *Gödel, Escher, Bach* that you reproduce in your 2003 book. I replied, "The mind is a very crowded room, and everyone is talking at once." You replied, "Precisely the way mine often feels." Mine, too, given the state of our world, although not long ago, in a quieter time, it had been my heartfelt ambition to clear out the room to some degree, and mute a few of the voices. I wanted to see myself not at the *moksha* stage in the Hindu life trajectory but at the *dharma* stage, with *kama* and *artha* (well, *artha* at any rate) behind me. I wanted to think of Kitty's orange grove as my Indian forest and retreat into it. But the election of Trump and then the descent of the COVID-19 pandemic forced a crowd of new voices upon me; the pullulating letter I sent you yesterday about the concerns of my past week is demonstration enough of that. So, Mark, both our minds are crowded now, but we cannot make understanding the place of editing in our respective minds or in mind in general (philosophy of mind) a prolegomenon to doing something or other (just the right practical phrase: "something or other") with what we have actually written.

As I read through your deep reflection on editing, I counted, as I recall, twenty-three questions, counting those that you quote. The answer to any question leads only to further questions, such that, quite literally, the more we know, the more remains to be known and so, proportionately, the less we know. Because I enjoyed your reflection for its own sake, apart from our task at hand, I would like to quickly move through it and offer a few ad hoc comments, but I have to insist at the start that, taken in its entirety, the philosophy of editing, valid in itself, is beside the point of practical editing.

So, then, ars gratia artis, on to a few comments.

I loved your discovering for me Jorge Luis Borges's "The Exactitude of Science." As you went further into your reflection on maps and territory, I couldn't help but think of Jonathan Z. Smith's collection *Map Is Not Territory*, though his point is not yours. As for Peter Turchi's *Maps of the Imagination*, though I can't be sure about my recollection, I seem to recall that I sponsored this work for the Guggenheim Fellowship that I do believe he won for it. While on the selection committee, I had the "general nonfiction" responsibility, which comprised everything that didn't quite fit anywhere else.

In any case, what your string of references—Calvino to Borges to Baudrillard to Blanchot and Lacan to Lewis Carroll to John Locke to Luce Ellmann to David Foster Wallace to Ove Knausgaard to Turchi—most strongly connects to in my own crowded room of a mind is the notion of distributed intelligence. We generally think of our intelligence as operating from our brains, but as you show in *Smart Bodies Smart Things* the human brain is just one system in a system of systems, and understanding of some sort cannot be denied altogether to those other systems. Ethology has contributed powerfully to reflection on this matter. The octopus brain—and octopi do have some remarkable abilities—is distributed down to the end of each tentacle. As a self-domesticating and social animal, *Homo sapiens* functions through intelligence vested in cultural knowledge that no one specimen possesses. Our contemporary use of the amazing prostheses that digital technology puts at our disposal only the more visibly confirms that this is so. I suspect that you saw in the business section of today's *New York Times* a piece by Kashmir Hill entitled "I Tried and Failed to Lose the Tech Giants." Hill discovered, in effect, that rather than using Google, Facebook, Apple, etc., she was hosted by them in a Hotel California from which there was no checking out.

There was a period of a few years in the late sixties and early seventies when, made aware of the harm that heavy human use of the automobile was doing to the world (most hideously in beautiful cities like Rome that are just defaced when their plazas and winding lanes become crowded with Fiats and Vespas), I determined that I would try to live on public transportation alone or on my bicycle. I couldn't do it, of course, not in the cultural world where I lived, and it was then, taking a broader point, that I realized how embedded we all are in the culture that science and technology have bestowed upon us, whatever the environmental consequences for even the physical survival of our species. That we are thus embedded means, for me, that our own thinking—by a further leap, even perhaps our own living—is not, is never, vested entirely in ourselves individually. We are not really individuals at all. Individuality is an illusion. We are "dividuals" from the moment of conception. We think of ourselves as we do only because, ineluctably, we must, and yet conceptually we can grasp the larger reality within which we are both more and less than the *we* that naïvely we begin our knowing with.

At one point in your letter, you open but do not close a quote from Peter Turchi that seems to begin your long approach to the practical task of editing our correspondence. Let me close the quote where I sense that it should be closed (talk about editing!) and then go on to make a larger point that will reprise an editorial suggestion I have already made to you in an email message from which I will then quote. You write:

> On the first page of his book, Turchi writes, "We organize information on maps in order to see our knowledge in a new way. Such organization does not have to be conscious; indeed, most mapping is preconscious, subconscious, or even unconscious. Maps suggest plot, which can be spatial or temporal. Plotting orients in a way that provides direction and can be reassuring. Plots lead us on and encourage us to ask what comes next, and to wonder if there are other possible maps and plots."

Postulating that the prime analogue for maps is the geographical map, I would further stipulate that such maps are the spatial fixing of a temporal process. Think of continental drift. The Earth is always in process, always in motion. The map halts time to fix that process, stay that motion, and map what then comes into view by whatever ratio of reduction is employed. A geographical map may, I think, legitimately be regarded as an index to the state of "geo-" (that is, Gaia) as frozen at that moment in time. This is particularly so, of course, if we imagine a political map, but even a geophysical map freezes Earth at what from a standpoint in geological time is still but an instant.

Toward the end of your letter, you assert that what we have been writing is "even if we have not realized it something like a bildungsroman of the 'present age,' which captures and extends the currents and countercurrents of time's eternal flow." To this, I reply that a bildsungsroman is not an index. If our work is conceptualized as a bildungsroman, and I concede that this is possible, then it can only be two bildungsromane. Two pages earlier, as you begin working toward this editorial suggestion, and such indeed it is, you write: "I am gradually beginning to grasp what we have been doing since we began, and through this to comprehend what I have been doing for many years without really appreciating it." But, not to speak at all querulously, Mark, what you have been doing for many years perhaps without really appreciating it is not what I have been doing. In either a vetting report or a for-quotation comment on your *Speed Limits*, I spoke of you as like a latter-day Hegel in your determination to address philosophically one domain after another after another in our contemporary world. Inasmuch as Hegel more than any modern thinker forced philosophy into history, into chronology, and forced philosophers to think, yes, across time, one might characterize him as having sought to write the great, comprehensive bildungsroman of his age (his being, of course, for him the culmination of all ages). I can stand in awe of such an achievement without regarding it for a moment as mine either in fact or by aspiration.

If it were possible for there to be a geographical map in the form of a bildungsroman of Earth, it would have to be—in a way that, having cited Calvino and Borges you can immediately grasp—a kind of mythically grand and endless motion picture of the planet's evolution. *Bildung* ("formation") is an apposite term for what this endless unscrolling screen would depict. The reason why "bildungsroman" falters as an editorial conception of our joint work, however, is that our work will shortly come to a conclusion, even though our respective lives, with any luck, not to speak of the life of our country (our other great subject), will likely extend beyond the end of our last works. So, large as it is, ramblingly complicated as it is, what we will have produced will be partial. As a story, life does not just begin *in medias res*, it will also end, full stop, *in mediis rebus*, and this can only be an infra-artistic conclusion. As such, as a necessarily broken-off narrative, I imagine our work pleasing scarcely any reader engaging it as such—that is, reading it from start to finish as narrative art. There are artful moments in it, I trust: after all, we have both given it careful thought as we went. It is not casually written. But taken in its entirety as a work of narrative art, it can only fail.

Here, I think, may be the preconscious, middle-of-the-night link from Keats and Miranda to your letter and my reply. You resist the thought of closing down our correspondence with so much left out, so long before our pens have gleaned our teaming brains. Theoretically, yes, we could go on; in fact, we will go on in one way or another until we die. But, practically, we have to determine what, if anything, our correspondence once halted adds up to or can be whittled down to. Does an editor, a publisher, have the final word? At least, in a milder form, I submit that s/he (whomever we choose) should at least have a decisive vote.

Thanks to your 7/30 }etter, I now know that the "deliverable" that you imagined proceeding from the act of drawing lines among the scattered words and phrases on a plane was, in fact, a set of open-ended narratives—open-ended not just in their respective interminability but also in the infinite number of possible narratives that the experiment would launch. If a bildungsroman in some form could result from this experiment, it could only be a roman that would defy practical editing, for practical as opposed to theoretical editing only begins when an editor knows the final dimensions of what s/he is editing. In your experiment, understood as a narration-generator to infinity, these dimensions can in principle never be known.

Nothing that I have written above gainsays my agreement with your assertion that editing is essential to thought. Indeed I quite agree with Turchi (if I have closed the quote correctly) when he says, "most mapping is preconscious, subconscious, even unconscious." The most profound and definitive form of pre-editing is species-specific editing. The brains of each species are designed to edit out what evolution has shaped the species to ignore. Frogs, famously, can see nothing that is not in motion. Because we humans can, at least, by comparing ourselves to other species, see that all knowledge is species-specific, we can escape the delusion that the form of knowledge specific to our species understands reality. The point is as old as Kant, isn't it? Our species, even in the person of our scientists, can understand only what evolution has shaped our species to understand, and from within our evolved limitations we cannot see what specifically as humans we have evolved to edit out. *Das Ding an sich* must ever escape us.

(Parenthetically, this is why I disagree with the rather abruptly arriving final sentence of your letter: "I see now more clearly than I have in the past that the fundamental difference between you and me is that for you the uncertainty of the moment makes belief possible, for me, it makes belief impossible." Foregoing for the moment any comment on you and belief, let me say of myself that what the invincible limits of human knowledge make impossible for me is, yes, the closure of certainty, and the impossibility of closure implies the possibility of aperture. Aperture to what? To what by definition we cannot know—namely, to mystery. And a hunger to acknowledge mystery and express our inadequacy before it not privately but communally, because, after all, human ignorance like human knowledge is collective, becomes, by a further step, an appetite for religion as ritual and moral practice. In the middle of page six of your letter, you ask: "Is all fiction a lie, or might narrative be the only way to tell some kinds of truth?" I reply, first, that not all fictions are narrative fictions; second, that, yes, there are some truths that can only be conveyed in narrative fiction; but, third, their untruth aside, fictions of any kind can be either enabling or disabling. I cherish certain religious fictions [dogmas, beliefs as well as narrative myths] for what they enable in me or—because I belong to a church—what they enable in us.)

The foregoing long parenthesis really and truly *is* parenthetical to this letter, Mark, to the extent that our target is conceiving how we might edit the text that we are jointly producing. To that end, I recur to my earlier comment that we need a third pair of eyes on what we are doing. I would want our designated reader to be someone with an education such that s/he could readily read and understand what we will have written. I would want him/her to be empowered to ask and answer unsparingly whether the work is publishable in any form; to imagine not just deletions from it but deletions to the point that only excerpts survive; and to take notes en route of recurring themes toward the creation of an analytical index that s/he might or might not proceed to create.

This letter does find you and me at odds, doesn't it? To quote Turchi, "Maps suggest plot, which can be either spatial or temporal." My preference is effectively spatial, yours temporal. And for now, I find us at that divide.

And, without knowing why, I find myself suddenly thinking of someone now deceased whom I dearly loved. The late Jean Wudke was a copyeditor assigned to the *Los Angeles Times Book Review* when I became its editor. She had been with the *Times* for years, was no intellectual, but was from the outset indispensable to my work in a way that Edmund Burke would appreciate. She would edit for superficial correctness and, if anything deeper was amiss, she would just in a very common-sense way "suss it out," bring it to me, and speak a sentence I recall so clearly, "This just doesn't *read.*" Though the soul of kindness, she could be plainspoken when the moment required plainness. She had two mottos stuck to the side of her desk, out there in the open-planning area: 1) "You have obviously confused me with someone who wants to help"; and 2) "You have clearly heard what I didn't say." I don't have that second saying quite right, but it bespoke a general awareness that there can emerge oh-so-easily a difference between what has been said and what is heard. Newspapers ignore that difference at their great peril, now more than ever, and Jean was an old-time newspaper pro.

A further association, now that it comes to me, is to Jean as my first computer tutor. The *Times* had computerized through a purchased proprietary system called "Coyote" only some months before my arrival. When I was hired, late in 1984, I had literally never touched a computer in my life. On my first day, I was scheduled to have a forty-five-minute introduction to Coyote, but I was called out of that class after just ten minutes because the Sunday section had to be closed, and there were decisions that only the editor could make. (Most likely, something had to be cut, and what to cut had to be my decision.) Well, those ten minutes of class constitute the sum total of my formal computer education. Everything else that I needed to keep from falling flat on my face, Jean taught me, and whatever else I know I have just had to learn on the fly since then, calling on the way upon a succession of generous IT tutors.

Jean's husband, whom she loved beyond measure, died while I was still at the *Times*, though no longer with the *Book Review*. I went to his funeral and burial in, as I recall, the Forest Lawn cemetery, which is the one that inspired Evelyn Waugh's *The Loved One*. (Have you ever come upon an actual lawn in a forest?) I think the service may have been in the Chapel of the Whispering Pines. Utterly "plastic" it was, and yet utterly authentic because, hey, we were in Los Angeles, where Angelenos have to be Angelenos to *be* authentic. In a note afterward, Jean thanked me for my condolence and my attendance and urged me to show my love to those who loved me because "they are with us for so short a time." Jean was a great golfer, quite good at the game, according to one of her regular partners on the links, a *Times* stalwart who was a former police woman. Jean died about a year after her husband's passing, in her sleep, only a matter of hours after her last round on the links.

Jack

*August 3*

Dear Jack:

Yesterday was a long day—we drove to New York down and back in the same day (320 miles). I was tired last night and resisted reading your two most recent letters until this morning, when I was more alert. In all honesty, I also needed more time to process our trip to the city. More about that after I respond to your latest.

I am going to focus primarily on your thoughtful response to my reflections on editing, but I have just a few comments on your careful analysis of what has happened during the past week. Trump wears you down; while it's hard to know if that is a self-conscious strategy, it's an undeniable effect. I find myself at a loss to find new words to express continuing concern and outrage. I realize the danger such fatigue poses and struggle to overcome it.

As always, your analysis is totally to the point. I usually listen to *Morning Joe* when I am eating breakfast, and am always interested to see what outrage they select for the lead story. This morning it was what's going on with the postal service—precisely the point you make. This might be Trump's most dangerous disruption, and there is little, perhaps too little, time to stop what he is doing. One of the many things that has puzzled me about his effort to discredit the media and the election process in both the last election and this one is that his claims effectively delegitimize the outcome even if he wins. I've not seen any commentator note this contradiction. All of this is, of course, part of his larger agenda, borrowed from Steven Bannon and promoted by his protégé Stephen Miller, of "deconstructing the administrative state." (Needless to say, I abhor this misappropriation of the word "deconstruction.") It's not just the postal service, the Department of Justice, and the judiciary Trump is subverting or dismantling, but the entire federal bureaucracy. In addition to George Packer's fine analysis, I would remind you of Michael Lewis's essential work on this problem. He started with a long analysis of the Agriculture Department, first published in *Vanity Fair*, which he expanded into *The Fifth Risk: Undoing Democracy*. Lewis is one of the very best observers of contemporary society and culture and he can flat-out write.

Dinny always says that when the calendar turns to August, she notices the days getting shorter. Last evening as the sun was setting so much farther south than in June, she said, "It's getting darker fast." Indeed, it *is* getting darker fast. While Nancy Pelosi is unwisely trashing Deborah Birx, Birx is breaking with Trump, who, predictably, trashed her as "pathetic," for warning the country that the pandemic has entered a new phase. The red states that were gloating over the virus infecting blue states are now being ravaged and are unable to cope with the disaster. In the absence of national leadership, responsibility devolves to the states, and then proceeds down to municipalities, and even different school districts in towns. This is creating countless disruptions at every level of life, which will only get worse in September. As you know, Aaron and family retreated to Wisconsin, where they have been living since March. With school approaching and work on their new apartment proceeding, they need to return to Chicago (a two-hour drive) more frequently. The incidence of infection in Wisconsin has been rising, and last week Illinois imposed a required two-week quarantine on people coming from hot zones, which includes Wisconsin. For the past week, their friends from DC have been visiting and were planning to leave yesterday, but have decided to stay longer because of restrictions imposed on places they were planning to stop on their way home. The fragmentation we are suffering is more than ideological and political.

As you know, I'm a country music fan even though the politics of people like Toby Keith and the recently departed Charlie Daniels are abhorrent to me. I've long been a fan of the Dixie Chicks. As I assume you know, success in the country music world has not come easily for women. Having won thirteen Grammy Awards and sold thirty-three million albums, they had become not only the bestselling female band, but also the bestselling country group in the U.S. All of this changed during a performance in London in 2003, when lead singer Natalie Maines criticized George W. Bush and the impending invasion of Iraq. Her outspoken opposition to the Bush agenda created a firestorm of protest—radio stations banned their music and erstwhile fans joined together to burn their CDs. As sales plummeted, Maines issued an apology that was about as convincing as Trump telling people to wear masks. By 2006, she finally felt free to tell the truth by reaffirming her criticism—she rescinded her apology insisting that Bush and his enablers deserved no respect in their defiant song "Not Ready to Back Down," declaring that she is still "mad as hell." This principled resistance is a reminder that the recent rehabilitation of George W's image obscures the *fact* that the lie about Iraq's weapons of mass destruction helped to prepare the way for Trump and the radical right's endless barrage of fake news. After the Dixie Chicks' defiance, silence from 2008 to 2014. Their comeback shifted into high gear with their European tour in 2016. In response to recent social protests, the trio has dropped "Dixie" and now are known simply as "The Chicks," which, of course, is not without problems. Concurrent with their name change, they released a new protest song, "March March." If you want to predict the outcome of the election, the response to this name change might be a better barometer than words of "wisdom" from clueless pundits who couldn't find the country station on their radios if their job depended on it.

Book burnings. CD burnings. The days are, indeed, getting darker. In your long and provocative letters, it is often a felicitous phrase, at which you are so adept, that sets my mind wandering. One such phrase in your recent letter was "lethal political orthodoxy." This really is *the* problem, isn't it? I have long said that I worry about true believers much more than unbelievers. Their unquestioning loyalty to ideas as well as people makes civil discourse and significant change impossible. However, I do not think it is correct to characterize such true believers, who are not the same as believers in truth, as holistic—I would call them totalizing and, thus, repressive. We need a revised notion of the whole that involves precisely the understanding of the interrelation and intervolution of apparent parts that overcomes the fragmentation currently threatening life on this planet. Not the absolutism of true believers, but the relativism of believers in the whole is what our age most needs. Once again I return to the importance of a relational ontology in and through which every subject as well as every object is individualized relationally. Such self-awareness requires self-reflexivity, which, as you point out, is one of the most important aspects of our correspondence.

The point of contact between your meditation on the events of the week and your more philosophical, dare I say theoretical, reflections on editing is your discussion of *Hamilton*, which I regret to say I've not yet seen. (Two asides: first, you know I deny the difference between theory and practice that you presuppose. Theorizing is a form of practice, and practice always entails implicitly or explicitly theoretical presuppositions. Second, did you know that Lin Manuel Miranda, who wrote *Hamilton*, went to Wesleyan? It would be interesting to know what his major was.) The lines you cited, so centered on the word and the reality of *time*, gave me much to think about.

Once again, we return to the question of time, or time returns to question us. Are we writing day and night because we're running out of time? If my memory is accurate, which is not a given, you suggested to me the subtitle for *Speed Limits—Where Time Went and Why We Have So Little Left*. Where, indeed, has time gone, and why do we have so little left? Time returns in the last lines you quote. "Time" *will* tell, time will always tell your story, my story, our story. In the long run, the story of our lives is not ours to tell because others must finish it for us.

Here I want to return to questions I raise in two of my books: *Journeys to Selfhood: Hegel and Kierkegaard*, for which you were the editor, and *Abiding Grace: Time, Modernity, Death*. To frame my thoughts, I want to edit my editor by commenting on your editing of my quotation from the first page of Turchi's book, *Maps of the Imagination: The Writer as Cartographer*.

> On the first page of his book, Turchi writes, "We organize information on maps in order to see our knowledge in a new way." Such organization does not have to be conscious; indeed, most mapping is preconscious, subconscious, or even unconscious. Maps suggest plot, which can be spatial or temporal. Plotting orients in a way that provides direction and can be reassuring. Plots lead us on and encourage us to ask what comes next, and to wonder if there are other possible maps and plots."

You insert not just one but two quotation marks—first after "way," and the second after "plots," with no quotation mark for the beginning of that text. Only the first insertion is correct. The rest of the words in this citation are my own. I stress this point because I don't think our differences are as great as you suggest when you argue that while I am more concerned with time and temporalization, you are more preoccupied with space and spatialization. You then turn to critical comments on my account of our work as a bildungsroman of our era. To explain my differences with you on this point (and the point is part of the point here), I will have to consider what is conspicuously missing from your letter—my discussion of the difference between the instant and the moment. This will show spatialization and temporalization are inseparable in narrative and the narrative quality of experience.

First bildungsroman. My comments here are directly related to *Journeys to Selfhood*, where, I am sure you recall, I argue that Hegel's *Phenomenology of Spirit* is, in effect, a bildungsroman. This argument is not original, but explicitly depends on Meyer Abrams's important book *Natural Supernaturalism*, where he maintains that Hegel's work is a philosophical version of two other bildungsromane—Wordsworth's "The Prelude" and St. Augustine's *Confessions*. There was no way I could have known at the time that a few years later, your erstwhile colleague at the University of California Irvine, J. Hillis Miller, would launch deconstruction in America with his trenchant criticism of Abrams and defense of Derrida. It has always seemed to me that Miller's criticism was misguided, and, in spite of my appreciation for Derrida's contributions, over the years I have repeatedly returned to Abrams's works for guidance. One of his most valuable insights is that every narrative is always nested in larger narratives that redraw the story line. Just as the meaning of each moment in "my own" story depends on its place in the whole, so the meaning of my life story depends on its place within the more encompassing story or stories of which it is a part. To complete his *Confessions*, Augustine had to write the *The City of God*, just as Hegel had to write his *Philosophy of History* to complete his *Phenomenology*. Since Hegel believed that the unity of God and man revealed in Jesus Christ is true not only for the historical figure of Jesus of Nazareth, but is the universal truth of all human beings, and, indeed, of nature as a whole, the *Phenomenology* and the *Philosophy of History* are nothing less than the autobiography of God.

And now my main point: your three-part chef d'oeuvre is thoroughly Hegelian. What you have done in *God: A Biography* is to have written the bildungsroman of God. As an erstwhile Jesuit, your story and God's story are one and the same. I know you will resist this reading, but pause to think about it. Furthermore, like Hegel, you could not stop with one story but had to finish God's (auto)biography by completing your holy trinity: *Christ: A Crisis in the Life of God*, and *God in the Qur'an*. But even this did not close the circle of the story you are telling; just as Hegel had to write his *Encyclopedia of Philosophical Sciences*, *History of Philosophy*, and *History of Religion*, you had to edit (NB) *The Norton Anthology of World Religions*. What a gloriously audacious project!

Stories within stories within stories return us to questions of space/spatialization and time/temporalization and to my reflections on the differences between "the instant" and "the moment." One could argue that narratives transform space into time by translating instants into moments. Inasmuch as the point is always already a counterpoint where accumulating past and approaching future intersect to form the moment, my point—in all senses of that term—here is Hegelian. Experience, be it personal or historical, is first undergone as an unreflected series of disconnected points whose interrelationship and perhaps even coherence become apparent, if at all, only retrospectively. In this sense, all knowledge is recollection or re-membering. Reflection gathers the remains of time to form a story that must constantly be revised as it continues to develop. Every event harbors the possible necessity of recasting and recontextualizing what has gone before. This means that "my" story can only be complete *after* I die. In the final analysis, "my" story is not my own because it must always be completed by an other, who must edit what "I" have written, what "you" have written, what "we" have written.

Even this does not bring the editing process full circle because the work is forever incomplete. Since all writing is rewriting and reediting, this process never ends. In *Abiding Grace*, I call this process "retro-reading." Rather than discovering the seeds of present and future works in the past (evolution), retro-reading demonstrates the ways in which later works transform earlier works to make them different from the author's original intention. For example, Hegel's works become different through the writings of Feuerbach and Marx, and Kierkegaard's works become different through the writings of Heidegger and Derrida. Later deeds by others actually transform what a person has done. Though Hegel never could have imagined Marxism, he is largely responsible for creating it as well as everything that followed in its wake. The past not only prefigures the present and the future, but the future also transforms and reconfigures the present and the past. In an important sense I/we do not know what we are writing because readers will edit and rewrite this work that was never really ours. The meaning of the work will never be known because it could be known after the end of history when there is no one left to read it or edit it.

\* \* \*

In concluding, let me return to my trip to New York, which I now discover is not unrelated to what we have been discussing. It was an utterly uncanny and, in many ways, unsettling experience. You will recall that I left the city abruptly on March 9 and had not returned since that time. Still wary of venturing into what had been such a hot zone, Dinny and I decided to go down and return on Sunday, when we thought the streets might be less congested. We left before 8 and, while I expected little traffic on the Taconic Parkway, I did not anticipate how few cars there would be on the usually busy Saw Mill River Parkway and West Side Highway. The road was as deserted as a ghost town. We got off at 125th Street and drove past the large Fairway Grocery under the highway, which had a large "Going Out of Business" covering the windows. A true sign of the times. Founded in 1933 and with five stores in the city, Fairway had long been the favorite grocery store on the Upper West Side for countless people. Problems began in 2007, when the business was taken over by the private equity firm Sterling Investment Partners. The rest is all-too-predictable history—borrowing, overleveraging, cutting pay and staff, bankruptcy, and generations of loyal customers left holding empty bags.

One of the first things that struck me was how filthy the streets were. Paper and debris scattered everywhere were blowing in the wind. On the other side of the West Side Highway, construction on Columbia's extensive expansion into Harlem seems to be advancing without interruption. The sight of impressive new buildings for the Law School, Business School, and School of the Arts rising amid growing poverty and homelessness seemed both untimely and unseemly. Our first stop was my office, where I needed to pick up some books and get my mail, which I assumed had been piling up since March. Not surprisingly, no one was in the building, but, surprisingly, there was no mail. I have no idea where any correspondence I might have received in the past five months might be, or who, if anyone, is waiting for a reply.

The strangest moment was when I entered the apartment—it was like stepping back into a moment frozen in time. Everything was exactly as I had left it expecting to start classes for the last week before spring break: the books on my shelf, the notes on my desk, the reminders on my calendar, though, fortunately not, as Dinny feared, any food I forgot to take out of the refrigerator. We have discussed the effect of aleatory memories at several points in our exchange. This was one of those moments. The sight, smell, and sound of the apartment created a sensory overload that set a melancholy tone for the few hours we were there. What was so unsettling was not so much the recollection of the past that had been so cruelly interrupted, but the realization that my teaching career will not end the way I had long imagined. I doubt I will ever again enter the classroom, and I am sure I will never again live in New York City as I once did. As I closed the door to the apartment, I thought to myself, what I will most miss when I stop teaching after nearly half a century is the ongoing conversation with students who have taught me so much and have kept me much younger than I have a right to be.

Mark


*August 8*

Dear Mark:

Your family's history coincides in your brief telling with three migrations: from Europe to the United States; from the farm to the city; and from still heavily manual labor of farming at the turn of the nineteenth century to digitally transformed labor at the turn of the twentieth. The Irish side of my family combined the first two migrations, moving from the fields of Ireland directly to the cities of America. The more buried history of the English/Welsh and the Polish sides of my family may have made a similar double migration, but my guess is that in these cases the migration was more likely urban-to-urban. What strikes me most strongly, though, as you raise this issue, crossing quickly as you do into the accelerating penetration of digital technology and artificial intelligence into every area of human life, is a related flow and ebb. At the turn of the nineteenth century, the flow of labor was toward the United States where remunerative employment was to be had. At the turn of the twentieth, this flow was reversed as employment flowed or, more accurately, was channeled from American labor to labor abroad. In both cases, these large movements were not driven by the workers alone but also, and sometimes primarily, by capital out to maximize profit by procuring labor when and where it was needed and paying as little to procure it as might be possible at any given time.

Capital has not needed digital technology to exploit foreign labor. I think, for example, of the pineapple industry in Hawaii, exploiting not just the native Hawaiians but importing impoverished Japanese for brutal plantation work. I think of the fruit industry, especially the banana trade, in Central America, not to speak of the horrific sugar/rum/slave triangle linking West Africa, the Caribbean, and New England during the nineteenth century. Examples are easily multiplied. And as for migration to the United States, obviously it still continues and does so at every level from the most brilliant medical and technological talent from China and India down to the most desperate asylum-seekers and "essential workers" in agribusiness and meatpacking flowing north across our southern border. And yet digital technology has been essential in the offshoring of at least certain crucial sectors of the American economy.

In the July 23 issue of the *New York Review of Books,* Daniel J. Kevles, whom I mentioned in my previous letter in a different connection, reviews Katherine Eban's *Bottle of Lies: The Inside Story of the Generic Drug Boom.* You are already highly sensitive, for personal reasons, to the consequences for Americans of the massive offshoring of the manufacture of pharmaceuticals. As much can be said of many other manufactured goods crucial to the practice of medicine, and the consequences have been painfully apparent through the course of the pandemic in our country. My family's parallel to the line you draw from your grandfather to his youngest great-grandchildren would be the story of my nephew, Gregory Vydra, whose Czech great-grandparents immigrated to the United States in the early 1900s and, after some time, set up their own butcher shop and grocery store/bakery in Chicago. Greg, with a master's degree in industrial engineering, rose through the ranks at GlaxoSmithKline until, at length, he was instructed to go to India and help set up an offshore analytical team that would replace some of the staff that Greg had been managing. He did that, and subsequently his own position was eliminated as part of the ensuing headcount reduction. So, the importation of Czech labor to the United States led, generations later, to the exportation of American employment to India. A strange tale, with digital technology crucial to it.

Now some more or less ad hoc reactions and associations to the latter half of your letter:

—Emojis. I still avoid them, but I don't recoil as much as I once did. They have a certain functionality within a mode of communication that excludes facial expressions, tones of voice, body language, and other in-person qualifiers of the spoken word. They can be the equivalent of "Hey, just kidding" after a spoken statement easily taken more seriously than the speaker intended. And there are times when they are scarcely worse than stereotyped congratulations or minor condolences: "Bummer" or "Sucks" or "Mazel Tov" and so forth. These are already, as it were, the verbal equivalent of emojis, so why not click the emoji? Six of one, half a dozen of the other, as I grew up hearing. (Is that expression still alive?) Out of curiosity, I looked up "emoji" in the 2011 *American Heritage Dictionary,* and there is no entry: it's that recent. There is an entry, though, for "emoticon," the typographic equivalent.

—*Gmail prompts.* Like you, I notice these but never use them, even when what I type is virtually identical to the prompt. What I do use, though, as I now have begun texting more frequently, is the word completions Apple offers. So, when I type "be in t" and Apple correctly completes to "touch," I do click the prompt. One little discovery I made as I began doing this is that *Jack* is becoming a surprisingly rare name. There are, to judge from the prompts I received when typing my name, more *Jacqueline*s out there texting than there are *Jack*s. But I have had many other *Ja* completions as well: *Jacob, Jason,* etc. The easier way to text is, of course, to use the dictation feature, but, despite the fact that I'm quite good at it, it feels so weird that I only sometimes resort to it.

—*Microsoft Word Editing.* I have had a couple hilarious corrections over the years, but I can't now call one to mind. "Head gear" for "Heidegger" really prompted a guffaw: it's just too, too apt! I once had a series of email exchanges with a Muslim writer named *Asma,* whose problem (you've guessed it already) was that Word constantly corrected her name to *Asthma.* What I find more interesting, and sometimes useful, is Word's color-coded underlining. You get a red underline if you insert a hyphen where none is necessary or, vice versa, omit one where one is required. (Later in this very letter, I got a red underline when I wrote "non-specialist.") These alerts invite correction to the statistical norm in American usage, and in general I prefer to follow such norms. (As I do below, where you will read "nonspecialist.") Not always, of course, and often one detects the program scratching its head, as it were in puzzlement. In the previous paragraph, I scored a red line under *Jacqueline*s, in which the name is italicized but the final "s" is in roman. But I did not get any red line under Jacks, where I perpetrate the same mix. Come on, Microsoft, make up your grammatical mind!

—*Renée de Resta on synthetic writing.* You have long been entranced with the nuances of the real fake, the fake real, the real real, and the fake fake, but you really floor me with the implications of this new technology. Garrison Keillor—now, sadly, all but silenced—popped up possibly two years ago with a wonderful one-liner: "The news is real, the president is fake." We know what he means, but your apposite comparison between photoshopped photography (and you could have added videoshopped video, as in the attack videos lately if clumsily produced to smear Nancy Pelosi) points to something much less easy to dismiss:

> If people assume that images and videos are routinely manipulated, why wouldn't they agree with Trump when he tells them not to believe what they see? Protests to the contrary notwithstanding, the war against "fake news" is more grounded in "reality" than the outcry to return to facts and let them speak for themselves.

You remind me that after Neil Armstrong walked on the moon, the view was surprisingly widespread in the African American population that the whole stunning video was just one more special effect. Hollywood's capacity for special visual effects is so amazing that you need to trust your mind (as your eyes read and trust print) or your ears (as you hear and trust speech) if you are also to believe your poor manipulated eyes as they view and begin to trust (but then hesitate) as a moving picture of a man allegedly walking (come *on*, man!) on the moon. Kinda looks like a Buck Rogers movie, don't it? But now, thanks to the new technology de Resta reports on, the explanatory prose, the delivery of the news of any sort, can also so easily be so readily fabricated that even the combination of eyes, ears, and mind can no longer be trusted. The whole thing might be just a *Gesamtkunstwerk*, a comprehensive artefact of fake news.

And yet the fact is evident even in the need you feel to reintroduce the term "reality" in quotes (which are not scare quotes) that the classic distinction between truth and illusion (innocent) or honesty and deceit (culpable) is still with us. I sense the same distinction—as old as Socrates referring in one of the dialogues to how a stick thrust into water appears bent at an angle—even in the air of worry behind de Resta's vision of ongoing debates, all fake:

> Indeed, it's possible that we'll soon have algorithms reading the web, forming "opinions," and then publishing their own responses. This boundless corpus of new content and comments, largely manufactured by machines, might then be processed by other machines, leading to a feedback loop that would significantly alter our information ecosystem.

Honestly, Mark, as you read this, can you avoid thinking about online Russian disinformation in the current presidential election? William Evanina, director of the National Counterintelligence and Security Center, published a report today—noted on the front page of the *New York Times*—that Russia is again trying to see to it that Donald J. Trump is elected. And with good reason, of course: anything, anyone that harms the United States helps Russia, at least in the evident Russian view of the matter.

In his preemptive summary of the Mueller Report, attorney general William Barr effectively glossed over the report's confirmation of earlier intelligence reports that, yes, Russia was trying to get Trump elected. Why? What was the Russians' motivation? Why did they prefer him? In all the brouhaha about the Mueller investigation, this question was almost never asked. More dismaying to me, the almost universal obsession—not just in the press but also in the congressional hearings—with whether or not Trump had cooperated with this effort obscured the importance of the Russian effort itself, whomever the Russians preferred. This effort itself, which in his testimony Mueller stated plainly was "continuing as we speak," surely ought to be our central concern.

You've noted in *Intervolution* how the newer kind of machine learning (the example you followed was the machine's mastery of the game Go) involved the machine-ingestion of thousands and thousands of actual Go games. Well, a comparable ingestion of thousands of conversations about, e.g., the theft of a presidential election might generate an apparent online tsunami of public concern, a virtual mass movement, might it not? Trump could then present himself as merely responding to this unprecedented outpouring of public concern as he sent out the paramilitary forces that do actually report to him to put down alleged anarchy and save "truth, justice, and the American way." I quote the beginning of the old *Superman* TV shows. That's what any American superman must present himself as fighting for, no? And, certainly adding to our concern, it is not as if there are no actual anarchists out there who might, some time in mid-November, be lending just enough on-the-ground verisimilitude to make Trump's claim as plausible as, say, the claim that Saddam Hussein had nuclear weapons ready to deploy against the United States.

You allude to the literary/philosophical debate over whether the author is, to use Foucault's famous phrase, the dummy at the bridge table. And I think you are right to speak of the debate in this form as now, effectively, in the past. It is not as if either side won, but somehow the debate itself did come to a kind of dead end. The very capitalized term "Theory," once so hot in English departments as the designation for an entire field of literary study, now has a distinctly passé ring to it. Publishers are no longer much interested because scholars, not to speak of nonspecialist readers, are no longer buying what the erstwhile theorists write. You deftly sketch the intellectual genealogy of the debate and then end your letter wondering, as it seems to me, whether this new technology will revive the debate. That's certainly a real question.

I can easily agree with you that a true transformation of authorship by AI could profoundly disrupt the practical task of higher education as you have understood it. I might further ask whether in such a debate the question of authorship might not shift to the authors, the artificers, of artificial intelligence. Once created, AI may perform wonders on its own, but theirs remains the *will* behind the performance. In itself, AI has no will to do what it does. Its will has been implanted, programmed, and it will act as it has been programmed to act until another will instructs it to turn itself off or, perhaps, dial itself down. A couple years ago, Kitty and I saw on Broadway *The Curious Incident of the Dog in the Night*, a play by Simon Stephens based on the novella by Mark Haddon, which I had earlier read. One scene from that play lingers in my memory. Some minor business or other is going on in the boy's home, and his parents tell him, "Be quiet." So the boy goes quiet—*permanently*. They don't know what's wrong, communication had seemed to be developing nicely, but now . . . nothing. Finally it comes out: "You told me to be quiet, but you never told me to stop being quiet." So, the boy was acting like one of our "intelligent" machines, wasn't he, but wasn't he also missing something crucial? They imposed their will upon him without really knowing what they wanted, and so, when he obeyed them, he ended up, in effect, disobeying them.

Latent function, unintended consequences—this afternoon these seem to me to guarantee that our chances of knowing where we are headed are just growing fainter and fainter and fainter. The little we know is dwarfed, engulfed, utterly swallowed up by all that we do not know. We have spun out of our own control.

Jack

* * *

## AUGUST 8–15: MARK BEGINS.

*New York City in decline: 140 hotels commandeered for 13,500 angry homeless . . . "gladness" defined and linked to the "creative effervescence" of Trump rallies . . . cooking—joy for some, chore for others.*

*Trump's germaphobia and narcissism understood through the counterintuitive complexity of the human immune/autoimmune system . . . pandemic denial as an autoimmune disorder, physiology and biology paralleling psychology and politics . . . narcissistic homeostasis as ultimately self-destructive.*

*The Stalinist cunning behind Trump's coup de poste . . . his relentless, quite unimpulsive reversal of environmental defense . . . the penetration of his ICE manhunt even into the smallest towns . . . capitalism's useful idiots in the Third Estate miss the crucial importance of labor organization . . . National Labor Relations Act of 1935 vs. Taft-Hartley Act of 1947 . . . Spiked prolabor editorials at the Los Angeles Times . . . why so many suddenly "essential" workers are still paid so little . . . the poignant German-Jewish dream of liberation through shared high culture and* Alle Menschen werden Brüder . . . *all this as tracking (or not) with Hegel-to-Nietzsche trajectory in philosophy.*

*Growing up anti-union amid tales of the Molly Maguires . . . Protestant rural anti-union red-state labor vs. Catholic urban union blue-state labor . . . Reagan vs. air traffic controllers and today's automated offshoring of white-collar labor . . . campus tuition rebellion among the disappointed . . . online instruction and the "end of higher education as we have known it," especially graduate education . . . seeing another's blind spot, missing one's own "deaf spot."*

---

*August 8*

Dear Jack:

Your sister's guidelines for her book club are a prudent way to impose discipline on wandering minds and chattering lips. While the first category (Take Away) is predictable, the other two (Gladness and Surprise) are, well, surprising, and, therefore, intriguing. Before commenting on them, a memory about William Styron and our mutual friend, the late John Maguire. Styron's *Darkness Visible* is a powerful and moving story of a journey through hidden corridors of the mind. It's been quite a few years since I read it, and, strangely, what I remember most vividly is his description of Martha's Vineyard, where he lived his last years before dying of pneumonia in 2006 at the age of eighty-one. Styron, like John, was a southerner who rose to fame with the publication of *The Confessions of Nat Turner*, which won the Pulitzer Prize in 1967. While I was an undergraduate at Wesleyan, John invited Styron to come to campus to discuss his work. I think it was before the Pulitzer was announced. As you know, John was a marvelous host and an unmatched raconteur, who was always upbeat and as far from depressed as anyone I then knew. He and Billie held a dinner party in their home for Styron. At that time, faculty dinner parties were common and not all of them turned into a *Who's Afraid of Virginia Woolf?* debacle. From time to time, John would ask Dinny and me to help with preparations, serving dinner, and clearing tables. Having grown up without ever having attended such a gathering, working these dinner parties provided an education that turned out to be as valuable as what I learned from John in the classroom when we arrived at Williams a few years later. My most vivid memory of the Styron party was the red wine. Not having mastered the art of the corkscrew, I messed up and got cork in the wine. I knew I absolutely could not serve the wine with cork in it, so spent much too long trying to fish out the fragments.

Your Take Away from articles that caught your attention is so thorough and thoughtful that I really have nothing more to say. I will, therefore, go bicoastal and add a few comments on an article about the Upper West Side neighborhood where I live in New York City. As I think I've told you, for the past several years, at the urging of a friend who is in finance I have been reading not only the *New York Times*, but also the *Wall Street Journal* and the *New York Post*. It is a helpful way to get out of my bubble for a short time. A few weeks ago this friend told me that his son, who now runs the family business, had contracted the virus and even after four months is still feeling its effects. He reported that his son, who is considerably more conservative than his father, is convinced that New York City is in sharp decline and will not recover for many years. In New York, as elsewhere, the virus is exposing long-festering problems at the local level that now are exacerbated by the ineptitude of the federal government. At first, I dismissed such doom and gloom as hyperbolic, but after this week, I am no longer so sure.

In New York, I live on the corner of West End Avenue and 89th Street; when Aaron and Frida lived in the city, they lived on 79th Street between Amsterdam and Columbus. When visiting them, I would walk down Broadway and across 79th past the stylish Lucerne Hotel. A couple of weeks ago, the *Post* ran an article with the headline "Hotel Lucerne on Upper West Side Converts to 'Temporary' Homeless Shelter.".

> The Hotel Lucerne at 201 W. 79th St. on Monday began welcoming the first of nearly 300 homeless men, many of them methadone users and "recovering" alcoholics. School buses dropped off the men and their makeshift bags at the hotel, whose website recently touted the inn as a "sophisticated" venue "imbued with European-inspired architectural charm and modern amenities."

The article reports that the Lucerne is one of 140 hotels the De Blasio administration has taken over to house 13,500 homeless people who are particularly vulnerable to infection. In the past week, 300 homeless people have been living in the Lucerne. Without tourists and with businesses fleeing the city, hotel managers welcome the $237 a night for each person. Seventy-five percent is being paid by FEMA and twenty-five percent by the city. Thursday the *Post* ran a follow-up article, "Hundreds of New Homeless Turn UWS into a Spectacle of Drugs and Harassment."

> Upper West Side residents say three hotels that are housing hundreds of homeless men during the coronavirus pandemic have turned the area into a spectacle of public urination, catcalling and open drug use. . . .

> Among those staying at the luxury Belleclaire on Broadway and the Lucerne on West 79th Street, and the more down-market Belnord on West 87th Street, are people who are mentally ill, recovering from drug addictions, and registered sex offenders.

> Ten sex offenders are staying in a single hotel—the Belleclaire, which is just one block from the playground of PS 87.

On Broadway between 80th and 79th as well as on the corner of Amsterdam and 79th, half a block from where Aaron and Frida used to live, there
have been repeated fights and there are reports of homeless people spitting
at passersby. One young woman spoke for many when she said, "It doesn't
feel safe anymore." My friend Wayne tells stories of the UWS during the
crack epidemic in the 1980s—needles everywhere on the sidewalk, junkies
prowling the streets, escalating crime. The situation became so bad that he
and his neighbors on 105th hired a private security company to patrol the
street. That past is beginning to look like the near future. This is the city
that awaits me if I ever return.

On a happier note, Gladness. But not quite happiness, which you and
Kitty explored at some length while reading Williams's *This Is Happiness*. Nor
is it precisely the same as joy, which I discuss in *Seeing Silence*. (BTW, after a
long delay due to the virus, printed books finally arrived this week; I'll send
you a copy soon.) The best discussion of gladness I know is developed by my
former teacher Richard Niebuhr in his book *Experiential Religion*. Drawing
on William James's distinction between the "sick soul" and "healthy-
mindedness" in *Varieties of Religious Experience*, Niebuhr contrasts gladness to
fear. In fear, the individual feels set against the world, other selves, and even
God. This is the mood Trump seeks to cultivate. To describe the condition
that is the polar opposite of fear, Niebuhr borrows a term from Samuel
Taylor Coleridge—"the gladness of joy." As an example of this mood, he cites
a passage from the former secretary-general of the United Nations, Dag
Hammarskjold: "To exist in the fleet joy of becoming, to be a channel for
life as it flashes by in its gaiety and courage, cool water glittering in the sunlight in a world of sloth, anxiety, and aggression." Niebuhr then proceeds to
explain that in gladness,

> the suggestion of motion, energy, power together with directionality
> of this energy as the felt content of the mood of rejoicing is unmistak-
> able. There is another feature here also: the apparent dependence of
> the sense of "fleet joy" upon the contrast with the "world of sloth, anxi-
> ety and aggression." . . . A third feature of the utterance only implied in
> the words "to be a channel for life as it flashes by," is that rejoicing
> discloses the sense and conviction of being part of something larger, in
> this case, the river of life.

Strange though it might seem to you and me, this "sense and conviction of being part of something larger" creates the euphoria of a Trump rally. And it is precisely the absence of this sense of what Durkheim so memorably labeled "creative effervescence" that so many people suffering social distancing and locked in isolation are feeling.

Surprise. To be surprised (*surprendre*, overtake -*sur*, over + *prendre*, to take) is to be overtaken by the unexpected. So understood, surprise is closely related to wonder, which, as you know, Aristotle argues is the beginning of philosophy. It is easy to forget that surprise and wonder can be terrifying and depressing as well as exhilarating and uplifting. Hence ambivalence invariably shrouds surprise and wonder. The expected, cultivated by routine, is the opposite of surprise, which is also fraught with ambivalence. There is something reassuring about predictable routines; this is why individuals and groups develop rituals they repeat again and again. Such rituals are often pleasurable: fine wine on a birthday, a special dinner on Sunday, popcorn and a movie Saturday night. But, of course, predictable routines eventually can become oppressive. When this occurs people long for the unexpected, the surprising, and the wonderful, which inevitably involve risks that often seem to make no sense. When everything appears to be prescribed and programmed in advance, it is precisely danger that is the draw. I think this is what Brian was feeling when he fled the security of home for a motel that might have harbored infection. This is also what draws people to bars and parties where danger lurks with every breath a person takes. As I am writing these words 250,000 bikers are gathering in Sturgis, South Dakota, without masks or social distancing. One biker, who rode his Harley from Arizona, explained, "I don't want to die, but I don't want to be cooped up all my life either." In a few weeks, I suspect these rebels who think they have a cause will discover that effervescence can be destructive as well as creative. While for those of us sitting on the sidelines, all of this seems completely unreasonable, for others, wearing seatbelts, helmets, and masks while remaining locked down in isolation is total madness. They believe there is a fate worse than death. Not quite Apollo vs. Dionysus, but not far from it.

Finally, a footnote in response to the recipe you sent. In the course of our correspondence, one of the things I have learned about you that I hadn't known is that, while not exactly a foodie, you are much more into food and cooking that I am, and, I must add, Dinny is. My cooking ability extends as far as scrambled eggs and rewarming what has already been prepared. Dinny is better but, in all honesty, cooking is more a necessary chore than a refined pleasure. The other day, she was having trouble measuring something for a recipe she was following, when she became exasperated and exclaimed, "I just don't understand why some people enjoy cooking!" Neither do I.

Mark


*August 14*

Dear Jack:

We should have seen it coming; it has been widely known for a long time that Trump is an extreme germaphobe. In a 2019 Politico article entitled "The Purell Presidency," Daniel Lippman reports:

> He asks visitors if they'd like to wash their hands in a bathroom near the Oval Office.

> He'll send a military doctor to help an aide caught coughing on Air Force One.

> And the first thing he often tells his body man upon entering the Beast after shaking countless hands at campaign events: "Give me the stuff"—an immediate squirt of Purell.

> Two and a half years into his term, President Donald Trump is solidifying his standing as the most germ-conscious man to ever lead the free world. His aversion shows up in meetings at the White House, on the campaign trail and at 30,000 feet. And everyone close to Trump knows the president's true red line.

Trump once went so far as to call shaking hands barbaric, and even avoided touching his son Barron when he was a baby for fear of becoming contaminated. The bitter irony is that just when the country needs him to be more germaphobic, the president is discouraging people to take steps necessary to curtail spreading deadly germs.

Trump's fear of contamination and infection is more than a personal bodily concern—it is the fundamental principle that shapes his worldview and guides his policies from anti-immigration and pronationalism to his trade war and racism. Though I had realized these different aspects of his agenda are related, I did not really understand the thread connecting it all until I read Ed Yong's outstanding article in the August *Atlantic*, "Immunology Is Where Intuition Goes to Die," which is an excellent scientific explanation of precisely how the coronavirus works and how the immune system responds to it. I was primed for Yong's analysis because I was finalizing page proofs for *Intervolution* at the time. When you read the manuscript, you found my explanation of the biochemistry of the immune system in diabetes tough going and urged me to simplify it. I demurred, insisting, as I often do. that it's complicated. Yong begins his discussion of the coronavirus by agreeing with me on this point.

> The thing is, the immune system is very complicated. Arguably the most complex part of the human body outside the brain, it's an absurdly intricate network of cells and molecules that protect us from dangerous viruses and other microbes. These components summon, amplify, rile, calm, and transform one another: Picture a thousand Rube Goldberg machines, some of which are aggressively smashing things to pieces. Now imagine that their components are labeled with what looks like a string of highly secure passwords: CD8+, IL-1$\beta$, IFN-$\gamma$. Immunology confuses even biology professors who aren't immunologists.

Yong then proceeds to explain how the immune system works and what makes COVID-19 an especially difficult case to solve as clearly and concisely as anything I've read.

To understand his explanation, it is helpful to recall the treatment I received when I suffered septic shock. When my blood pressure suddenly dropped to 50/20, the first thing the doctors did was to open an artery in my neck and started pumping in drugs known as "pressors," which were intended to raise my blood pressure. Speed was essential because the bacteria multiply very, very quickly. If drugs did not work quickly, my brain would have received insufficient blood and oxygen, and I would have died that night. Immediately after this procedure, doctors started an IV drip of an extremely potent global antibiotic. They cultured my blood to determine the precise cause of the infection, and then after almost two days began to administer an antibiotic that targeted the specific bacteria causing the infection. My survival depended on simultaneously maintaining adequate blood pressure and controlling the bacterial infection with extremely high doses of this global antibiotic until I could be given the specialized agent that would activate cells in my body that target the specific cause of the infection.

Yong explains that this is exactly how the immune system works when a virus invades the body. There are three stages in the immune system's response. When cells detect molecules characteristic of a pathogen, they produce proteins, known as cytokines, which transmit a signal that alerts a diverse collection of white blood cells to unleash a generalized counterattack. "This initial set of events," Yong writes,

> is part of what's called the innate immune system. It's quick, occurring within minutes of the virus's entry. It's ancient, using components that are shared among most animals. It's generic, acting in much the same way in everyone. And it's broad, lashing out at anything that seems both nonhuman and dangerous, without much caring about which *specific* pathogen is afoot. What the innate immune system lacks in precision, it makes up for in speed. Its job is to shut down an infection as soon as possible. Failing that, it buys time for the second phase of the immune response: bringing in the specialists.

There are two types of specialized cells, which, like the antibiotic designed to target a particular bacterium, are selective—preprogrammed and adaptive. One of the most remarkable features of the immune system is that during the fetus's embryonic development, the body trains millions of T-cells to attack specific pathogens that might be encountered during a person's lifetime. As a result of this process,

> for any new virus, you probably have a T-cell somewhere that could theoretically fight it. Your body just has to find and mobilize that cell. Picture the lymph nodes as bars full of grizzled T-cell mercenaries, each of which has just one type of target they're prepared to fight. The messenger cell bursts in with a grainy photo, showing it to each mercenary in turn, asking: *Is this your guy?* When a match is found, the

relevant merc [*sic*] arms up and clones itself into an entire battalion, which marches off to the airways.

The third phase of the response involves the adaptive immune system, which is considerably slower, but much more precise than the innate system. One of the most important features of these T-cells is that, unlike preprogrammed cells, adaptive cells have a memory. After the initial assault by the pathogen subsides, some of these T-cells survive and

remain on retainer—veterans of the COVID-19 war of 2020, bunkered within your organs and patrolling your bloodstream. This is the third and final phase of the immune response: Keep a few of the specialists on tap. If the same virus attacks again, these "memory cells" can spring into action and launch the adaptive branch of the immune system without the usual days-long delay. Memory is the basis of immunity as we colloquially know it—a lasting defense against whatever has previously ailed us.

One of the many remaining mysteries of the coronavirus is how widespread and how long lasting immunity is for people who contract the disease. Nor is it yet clear whether the antibodies produced to fight the disease can be used to create a vaccine.

In an earlier letter, I have discussed how military and espionage rhetoric have shaped our understanding of the immune system. While these tropes are understandable, the immune system is really better understood through the more contemporary metaphors of networks and webs. The so-called immune system is a network of networks that forms something like an intranet that functions as a body-wide web in which messages are sent, received, and translated or mistranslated, and responses chemically produced and transmitted. COVID-19 is a cagey virus that is a master of deceit; its different disguises enable it to interrupt the orderly flow of information through the bodily web. While precisely how this mechanism works is still not understood, it is clear that the ability of early invaders to avoid detection enables the virus to delay the innate immune response. This lag in response time is critical; it is as if the doctors had not

been able to detect my infection until it was too late to deliver the global
antibiotic that saved my life. According to Yale immunologist Akiko Iwasaki, this "creates a brief window of time in which the virus can replicate
unnoticed before the alarm bells start sounding. Those delays cascade: if
the innate branch is slow to mobilize, the adaptive branch will also lag."
Having been slow to get started, the immune network cannot catch up, but
keeps on trying. This leads to a further problem. Once turned on, the
immune system is not turned off and, in a manner similar to auto-immune
disease, the body starts destroying itself.

> "If you can't clear the virus quickly enough, you're susceptible to dam-
> age from the virus *and* the immune system," says Donna Farber, a
> microbiologist at Columbia. Many people in intensive-care units seem
> to succumb to the ravages of their own immune cells, even if they
> eventually beat the virus. Others suffer from lasting lung and heart
> problems, long after they are discharged. Such immune overreactions
> also happen in extreme cases of influenza, but they wreak greater
> damage in COVID-19.

At this point, a further complication, which can be fatal, develops.
What had been an immune response designed to protect the body from
invasion and infection becomes something like an autoimmune condition
in which the body attacks and destroys itself. As the immune response
goes haywire, the body's intranet cannot distinguish the viruses, microbes,
bacteria, and parasitic worms against which it is supposed to protect the
body. Iwasaki explains that in the worst cases "the immune system almost
seems confused as to what it's supposed to be making." In a manner similar
to cancer cells proliferating out of control, in some cases once the immune
response is switched on, it cannot be switched off. As a result of interference in the body's communication networks, strategies of self-protection
become self-destructive. Once again, "the thing is, the immune system is
very complicated."

This understanding of the immune system suggests that COVID-19 can
serve as an illuminating metaphor for our current psychological, social and
political impasse. While many people have long realized that Trump is a
germaphobic narcissist, they have not recognized the integral relationship

between immunology and narcissism. *Trump and his sycophantic followers are suffering from a generalized immune disorder that transforms healthy self-regard and reasonable defensive strategies into pathological personal and social narcissism that becomes self-destructive.* To defend this claim, I return to an essay I mentioned in a previous letter—Peter Sloterdijk's "Wounded by Machines: Toward the Epochal Significance of the Most Recent Medical Technology." I argued that Sloterdijk does not adequately distinguish immunity and autoimmunity. Having come to a very basic understanding of the immune response to the virus, I now think there is a way to rectify this shortcoming and salvage some of Sloterdijk's important insights. The *complexity* of COVID-19 and the body's response to it show the way the body's excessive immune response folds into (from the Latin *complicare*) and turns back on itself to become an autoimmune disorder. Sloterdijk writes,

> Recent biology has made us familiar with the thought that the physical life of the individual is synonymous with its fully developed immune system. In this light, life appears to be the wondrous drama of the successful delimitation of the organism from invasive environments. In extending this systemic approach it becomes apparent that the principle of immunity is not only to be understood in terms of biochemistry, but also psycho-dynamically and mentally.

In other words, it is necessary to translate physiological and biochemical processes into psychological and political processes.

The virus ravaging bodies reveals the virus infecting minds and poisoning the body politic. The health of every physical and social body requires the effective self-protection through the management of the boundaries that both distinguish the organism from and relate it to its surroundings. Since life depends on the osmotic exchange of bodily fluids, this boundary must be semipermeable rather than an impenetrable wall that functions as something like a "narcissistic shield." To recognize the importance of this point, it is necessary to stress that narcissism can be both individual and collective. For members of homogeneous self-enclosed groups as well as self-absorbed individuals, every way the narcissist turns he sees only himself. These two forms of narcissism create a positive feedback loop—when everybody at a rally is wearing a red hat, individual narcissism feeds collective narcissism, which, in turn, deepens individual narcissism. "From this angle," Sloterdijk explains,

> we should regard it as an accomplishment of organismic vitality in the human being that, as an individual and as a communal being, he is capable of a spontaneous and energetic privileging of his own way of life, of his own valuations, of his own convictions, and of his own stories that interpret the world. From the systemic vantage point, powerful narcissisms are a successful affective and cognitive integration of the human being into himself, into his moral and collective culture.... Where the narcissistic shield is intact the individual lives convinced of the unparalleled advantage of being itself. It can permanently celebrate its similarity with itself. The habitual form of this celebration is pride. Whoever takes pride in himself and his group endogenously produces a material-immaterial vitamin, as it were that protects the organism from invasive information.

"Narcissistic homeostasis" is, however, a fatal disease because, as I have suggested, every living organism requires osmotic processes that allow for the free flow of information between inside and outside. Paradoxically, the stronger the narcissistic shield, the weaker the body it is supposed to protect becomes. Once again the problem is an immune disorder caused by a malfunction in communication networks that results from the reaction to an attack on the organism's "cognitive immunity shield."

> Invasive information that breaks through the narcissistic shield of a psychical organism is called a "wound" in everyday speech. When the individual's pride is attacked, it has the experience that information which initially could not be warded off has invaded it and that it is thereby in a state of lost integrity. A wound is the pain of having something break through that for the moment or for a sustained period of time is stronger than the narcissistic homeostasis. If one understands primary narcissism as the psychical "organism's" operative phantasm of integrity, then the concept of wounding describes a pathogenic attack on the individual's shield of elation.

There is a paradox at the heart of narcissism that Sloterkijk overlooks and is rarely noticed: the narcissist's self-love is a symptom of a profound self-loathing. I was discussing some of the ideas in this letter with my former student and now colleague Jeff Kosky. His response clarifies the point I am making about the intertwining of immunity and autoimmunity.

> The germaphobe Trump perhaps fears his own autoimmune response, his germaphobia is rooted in self-hatred or a failure to accept his own nothingness, as is the case with most narcissists who populate their world with themselves not others like germs. The fear of his own autoimmune response turns that response into an autoimmune disorder. There is something about that in narcissism: the narcissist in fact has no self-regard, is hollow inside and unaccepting of that void, therefore is entirely dependent on others for his sense of self, but ends up hating those others because they make him dependent, and so is always trying to control others and reacts so meanly when they are critical or disappoint him.

As self-love becomes self-hatred, the immune system turns on itself. When the integrity of the organism is attacked, a virulent immune response is unleashed to protect organism's intranet—be it biological or social—from disruptive noise. If wily invaders are sufficiently skilled in the arts of deception to hack the system, they can confuse neural and political networks and trigger an overreaction that turns destructive. This immune disorder leads to paranoia, which, in turn, encourages belief in conspiracy theories. The paranoiac sees threats everywhere, and, therefore, cannot distinguish real from unreal dangers. To reinforce the narcissistic shield, the individual and/or the group lashes out at everybody and everything regarded as not-self or other. In an effort to explain proliferating threats, paranoiacs construct elaborate conspiracy theories to connect unrelated dots. When this is not sufficient, they consciously or subconsciously fabricate fake threats to sow doubt about what is true and what is false. This confusion is used to justify hostile reactions to enemies who appear to be everywhere. Just as noise coursing through the intranet of the body disrupts communications in the bodily web, so misinformation circulating in media and social networks through the World Wide Web creates an immune disorder that infects psyches and threatens to spread throughout the social organism. Since social as well as biological organisms are emergent complex adaptive system formed by positive feedback loops, viruses spread like wildfire and sometimes kill the bodies that feed them.

Yong concludes,

> Immune responses are inherently violent. Cells are destroyed. Harmful chemicals are unleashed. Ideally, that violence is targeted and restrained; as [Princeton immunologist Jessica] Metcalf puts it, "Half of the immune system is designed to turn the other half off." But if an infection is allowed to run amok, the immune system might do the same, causing a lot of collateral damage in its prolonged and flailing attempts to control the virus.

The coronavirus is running amok while the institutions designed to protect us have been perverted, and leaders responsible for serving the common good are wrapped in a cloak of narcissistic self-interest. The immune system that is supposed to protect us has turned against the body politic and become a virulent immunological ideology that is infecting our lungs and making it impossible for all of us to breathe. What we urgently need is not only a vaccine for COVID-19, but also a vaccine for the psychological, social, and political immune disorder that threatens to become fatal. As in all such critical cases, there is very little time to arrest the spread of the infection.

Mark

P.S. A very strange coincidence. Shortly after I finished writing this letter, I stumbled on a long and informative article in this weekend *New York Times Sunday Magazine* by Moises Velasquez-Manoff, "How COVID Sends Some Bodies to War with Themselves," which discusses debates among physicians and medical researchers about the role of the immune system in this virus. Velasquez-Manoff focuses on a rheumatologist who has been giving patients with COVID-19 drugs she usually uses to treat rheumatoid arthritis, which is an autoimmune disease.

> Navarro-Millán had unusual expertise for a hospitalist. Weill Cornell had asked her to move into that role when the pandemic hit, but she was a rheumatologist by training, a doctor whose specialty is autoimmune ailments in which the immune system, tasked with defending the self from invading pathogens, inexplicably turns on the body's own tissues. Now she drew on her experience to try to help this COVID-19 patient.

She suspected that the greatest danger here wasn't the coronavirus itself but an immune overreaction so severe that it could cause lungs to fill up with fluid and prompt organs to shut down, possibly killing the patient. Rheumatologists often describe this type of immune reaction as a "cytokine storm" or "cytokine release syndrome." Cytokines are proteins released by cells in order to send messages to other cells—signaling, for instance, that a viral invasion is underway. The number of different cytokines is large, perhaps exceeding 100, and each one calls for a specific response. To save her patient, Navarro-Millán decided that she would have to calm his immune system and prevent that storm from getting started.

It is increasingly clear to me that it is going to be very difficult to find an effective vaccine for this disease because of its uncanny ability to outsmart the body's immune system.

*August 14*

Dear Mark:

I intended to—and in part I will—write this letter following the "economy" format of my last letter: something gladdening, something surprising, something to take away or remember for future reference. In truth, however, one subject that scarcely qualifies under any one of those headings is crowding everything, even pressing personal matters, out of my mind— namely, the Republican *coup de poste*. Donald J. Trump is endlessly mocked for his ignorance, but I find him in certain key regards both consistent and cunning.

There is cunning in his recognition that the Homeland Security Act has created paramilitary armed forces that report directly to him. The legislators who created the Department of Homeland Security might have foreseen this abuse of what they created, but they didn't, as former senator Barbara Boxer recently ruefully conceded in the *Washington Post*. Past directors of DHS, including former governor Tom Ridge, the first of them, are appalled at this undreamed-of abuse. But if the harm can be undone at all, it can only be undone by a future Congress, and Congress is now in recess with only weeks to go before the election.

There is even greater cunning, even a kind of Stalinist genius, in Trump's recognition that the U.S. Postal Service is an Achilles heel that he can use to suppress Democratic voting and then invalidate many of the Democratic votes that actually are cast. He correctly asserted in an interview with Fox News that, casting COVID fears aside, Republican voters will reliably vote in person. Even now, as COVID deaths pass two hundred thousand, conservative voters do still minimize the danger and do continue to go maskless about their business. What a brilliant way to turn his very pandemic failure into electoral advantage! And the loyalist whom he has appointed as postmaster general has lately announced that all political mail, including ballots, will henceforth be treated as second-class mail, delaying or in many cases actually preventing the delivery of votes. This lackey of a postmaster general has ordered the removal of hundreds of mail-sorting machines with huge capacity—always without explanation and without notice. His deliberate tooling down of the USPS will, I fear, further cripple the casting and counting of votes by mail. I call this cunning "Stalinist," thinking of Stalin's notorious dictum "It doesn't matter who votes, it matters who counts the votes." Trump, like Stalin, has found the weak link in the chain that supports American elections, and I am in anguish at the thought that there is no way to stop him.

Under the heading of consistency, I would note the Trump administration's thoroughgoing reversal of previous measures taken to reduce American carbon emissions toward a mitigation of climate change. Trump's withdrawal from the Paris Climate Accord made major headlines; he announced that withdrawal on television from the Rose Garden itself. His regulatory move yesterday allowing an increase in hugely damaging methane emissions made only minor headlines—just more of the same, as far as the press is concerned. But that sameness is my point: he has been taking one measure like this after another after another through now nearly four years.

And under the same heading belongs the ongoing ICE manhunt for illegal immigrants, no matter how long their residence in the United States or their integration in their communities. Yesterday, ICE was noticed apprehending two longtime residents of Bend, Oregon (population a little over one hundred thousand). The two were clapped into an unmarked bus, which was driven to a parking lot. Because the two were well known and well liked in the community, an enormous flash mob surrounded the ICE bus to prevent the deportation, but, after a few hours, an armed, uniformed force arrived, tear-gassed and manhandled the demonstrators long enough to enable the targeted two to be removed, and transported them to who-knows-what undisclosed location. My point for the moment is only that this is a small town, that these were harmless longtime residents, and that only a thoroughgoing, determined, and consistent effort, backed whenever necessary by armed force, would ever have hunted these immigrants down and taken action to deport them. This particular action happened to be noticed because of the spectacular public resistance to it, but comparable actions, we can be sure, have been going on all the time and all over the place. Most of the time, the public feels impotent. But when it tries to step in, as in Bend, it discovers that, yeah, it is indeed impotent. Sic semper tyrannis.

Last week, I sent you "The Unraveling of America: Anthropologist Wade Davis on How the COVID-19 Pandemic Signals the End of the American Era" from *Rolling Stone*, care of my son-in-law. You countered with the much longer and searching Kurt Andersen in the August *Atlantic*: "College-Educated Professionals Are Capitalism's Useful Idiots. How I got Co-opted into Helping the Rich Prevail at the Expense of Everybody Else." I'll turn to my surprise in a moment. First a comment on this exchange between us.

I agree with you that, minus a few stats, our correspondence has covered very much of what is in Davis's tour de force for *Rolling Stone*. And you were right again to predict that Andersen, observing business and government from inside the third estate, would be reporting on a scene that I too have observed. He's a decade or so younger than I am, but I arrived late in journalism, so, yes, we were witnessing pretty much the same developments at the same time. But there is one key difference. I was, am, and always will be a supporter of unions, and that goes for my family as well.

Once, by exception, I went downtown to work in my editorial pages office on a Saturday, and Kathleen, maybe five or six years old at the time, came with me. My office was just a short walk away from the office of the publisher, and while Kathleen was singing, "Oh, you can't scare me, I'm stickin' with the union," which she had picked up from a Pete Seeger medley sent to us by my brother Michael, who should just then happen by but

the super-buttoned-down chief operating officer of the Times Mirror Corporation? A thin smile, and he moved on. Ever since anarchists bombed an
earlier Times building in the first decade of the twentieth century, the
Chandler family had been fiercely anti-union. Inscribed in the lintel above
the ceremonial entrance to the Times Building was (though one had to
hear in it a kind of code) the motto "True Industrial Freedom." Hear that
phrase as an ancestor of everything later called, so misleadingly, "right to
work."

You've read various columns by David Brooks, I'm sure, lamenting the
loss of the various middle-range societal vehicles, including the church and
a range of affinity groups, that used to anchor and strengthen American
lives by standing between them and the vastness and impersonality of government. Brooks, originally hired as a conservative voice, has drifted left-
ward over the years, but never far enough to include labor unions among
those lost forms of community strength and solidarity. In my 1992 *Atlantic*
article "Blacks vs. Browns" on immigration and its consequences in Los
Angeles, I noted that Times Mirror had cashiered all its Black janitorial
staff, all of them at the time on the payroll with pension and benefits, and
outsourced janitorial service to agencies that were hiring Mexican immigrants. Legal immigrants or not? At the time, nobody was looking too
closely. Years after that article, the now overwhelmingly Hispanic janitors
formed their own union without using the dread word "union." They called
it "Justice for Janitors."

Andersen has much to say about the white-collar, self-consciously "professional" and thus blithely above-all-that newsroom staff vs. the blue-
collar "slack-jawed cretins" of the pressroom staff. He is frank to confess
that he shared the mingled feelings of security and superiority that made
him, in the long run, a dupe of management and of the plutocracy that was
progressively taking over American life. I was of the same employment
stratum, perhaps for the most part bought off in the same way and, much
of the time, just thinking about other matters.

But I stress: much of the time but not all the time.

Unionization, initially regarded as simply and incontestably criminal
behavior in the United States, was licensed only after titanic struggles by
the National Labor Relations Act of 1935. It was this controversial and
fiercely contested law that made unions a growing power in American

political life. But union power, though it lingered long, was effectively emasculated by the Taft-Hartley Act of 1947, which introduced what was euphemistically called "the right to work" and massively hindered future labor organization. In the early 1990s, when I was on the *Times* editorial board, I wrote an annual editorial for two or three years running in support of the quixotic Democrat or two who would introduce every year a bill in Congress to amend the Taft-Hartley Act to enable easier organization. I would write the editorial favoring the bill, and my "coconspirator," the late Frank del Olmo, would schedule the editorial. It would be copyedited, all would be in order, but in the next day's paper the editorial would not appear. After we went home, management would yank the editorial ("Never apologize, never explain") and plug in something else. Frank and I would be chagrined but not surprised. We knew what had happened and why and that protest would be pointless. True Industrial Freedom.

Driving as much as I once did in LA and OC, I used to spend hours listening to the radio, and SoCal radio is really a pretty rich feast. One station is our Pacifica affiliate, KPFK, and the host of a call-in program on KPFK is Thom Hartmann. In his on-air manner, Thom Hartmann might put you in mind just a bit of the late conservative radio commentator Paul Harvey, whose show was *The Rest of the Story*. (I wonder if you ever caught it.) Thom's politics, of course, are the polar opposite of Paul's. Once in a while, he departs from the usual call-in format and just offers a kind of radio essay. The one I happened to catch this past week while driving to collect groceries was on "The Leisure Society." Do you even faintly remember when "the leisure society" was a buzz phrase? I do, but it was certainly a blast from the past.

Hartmann's contention in his essay is that wage increases had kept pace with increases in productivity so reliably for so long that economists in the 1950s and early 1960s found it plausible to extrapolate wage increases continuing to track with technologically enabled increases in productivity. On paper, it seemed quite foreseeable that the entire workforce would be well paid for far less actual work than was being done at the time of writing as each hour of work delivered more product. What happened, however, per Hartmann, is that capital simply pocketed the profit generated by increases in productivity while keeping wages effectively constant. (Andersen notes the neologism "high-net-worth individuals" for "rich people." Another such euphemism is "keeping labor costs under control" for "cutting pay.") Over time, obviously, income inequality does accrue to wealth inequality, and Andersen certainly does track this process. At a *Times* Christmas party one year, I was standing, cocktail in hand, with Art Seidenbaum, my mentor at the *Times*, while the late Robert Erburu, then the CEO, was giving a genial holiday speech. Art commented to me sotto voce at that moment that Erburu's salary was about thirty times mine—a differential that, as he conveyed more with a look than a word, was excessive. But that differential—well, consider it the good old days.

Let me mention one other writer alongside Davis and Andersen. This is Thomas B. Edsall. All through the Reagan-Bush years, Edsall was keenly aware of the conservative bait-and-switch strategy. The tactic was to foreground backyard conservatism during the election campaign—such simply grasped wedge issues as crime in the streets (Dukakis and parole policy in Massachusetts), the pledge of allegiance, race in coded terms ("silent majority"), prayer in the public schools, homosexuality ("family values" in 2012 with George W. Bush), and, of course, abortion—and then for the most part forget about these wedge issues once elected and concentrate on boardroom conservativism.

Well, Edsall is still around, and he did a rather long op-ed piece in the *New York Times*, one that may never have appeared in the print edition, entitled "Why Do We Pay So Many People So Little Money? The Coronavirus Pandemic Is Forcing America to Confront Its Epidemic Low-Wage Problem." Edsall opens his essay:

> With notable abruptness, thanks to the advent of the coronavirus, much of the public has become aware of its dependence on hospital orderlies, cleaners, trash collectors, grocery workers, food delivery drivers, paramedics, mortuary technicians, and postal, shipping maintenance, wastewater treatment, truck stop and mass transit employees—on what, to many, had been a largely invisible work force.

Because of my lower-working-class background or for whatever other mix of reasons, these workers have never been invisible to me, wherever I have ended up. My brief, two-year sojourn in New York sharply underscored my sense that, contrary to all talk of our moving from an industrial to an information economy, we were—we, right there in Manhattan—we were *surrounded* day by day and even hour by hour by manual labor in progress before our eyes. In this regard, Manhattan did not differ from the rest of the country, but, as you well know, everything in Manhattan is just more in-your-face than it is anywhere else in our country. It is only now, because of the pandemic, that we have begun to refer to these manual and variously high-skilled, mixed-manual workers as "essential," but essential they have always been and, unless robots come along in time and manual workers are, as it were, pulped for fuel, essential they always will be.

Changing the subject, but perhaps not entirely, I have mentioned to you that I am reading Jeremy Eichler's work in progress about music and memory. When I first characterized the book that way, I had read only his introduction and first chapter. This past week, I read his second and third chapters, in which we move into the later history of his real subject, which now seems to me to be the place of German high culture—*Bildung* culturally framed—in the story of the Jews of Germany from Moses Mendelssohn to Felix Mendelssohn and thereafter from Wagner to Richard Strauss + Arnold Schoenberg (the Gentile composer of *Mein Heldesleben* vs. the Jewish composer of *Moses und Aron*) and to Strauss, again, initially in collaboration with but later profoundly estranged from his librettist, the eminent German-Jewish writer Stefan Zweig. There are moments of deep poignancy in the story of how German and Austrian Jews, trusting that German thought and culture were on a path, through *Bildung,* to the transcendence of Christian prejudice, were finally and cruelly disappointed. This occurred even when, by a *sacrificium intellectus,* some of the most prominent Jewish composers converted to Lutheranism in the vain hope of removing the last barrier to their integration into a common German culture.

Jeremy is a fine writer, a writer whose talent I am only now beginning to fully appreciate, and some passages of his prose are truly eloquent. The broad outlines of the story he tells are not unfamiliar, and yet I have never been brought so deep inside it as I am through this work. What has struck me, too, in reading it is how it overlaps chronologically with the very period, the very Jena inflection point, that has left its mark on every part of your oeuvre. Jeremy Eichler has so far not mentioned, or barely mentioned, Hegel and never mentioned Kierkegaard at all in the story that he tells; Nietzsche, however, did play a decisive role in Strauss's developing conception of himself as an artist, a man of his time, and a heroic apostate from the faith of *Bildung*. You barely mention Goethe or Schubert or the Mendelssohns, father and son, in the story that you tell; Schiller's *Alle Menschen werden Brüder* in the poem *"An die Freude,"* which is the climax of Beethoven's Ninth Symphony, was for Germans of Schiller's and Beethoven's generation a sacred line and for Jews beginning with Mendelssohn a line salvific at least by their aspiration. On display is a single process doubly engaged, and so, I am mentally playing the one account off the other.

*Bildung* plays a role in Jeremy's book akin to the one that Newark plays in several of the novels of Philip Roth. It is, conceptually, the setting, and yet there is a dynamism about it that makes it almost like a character interacting with the human characters in the unfolding drama as they embrace it, reject it, or just, sadly, relinquish it. In any case, my experience as I read his work knowing yours is a bit like the reaction of an early Christian who had spent years reading only the Gospel According to Matthew and then, though he had loosely heard about the Gospel of Luke, was handed a copy of it. At one and the same time, déja vu and discovery. Knowledge has rarely made a less bloody entrance.

Jack


*August 15*

Dear Jack:

Let me begin at the end of your letter—*Bildung*. If it is possible to have a blind spot, is it also possible to have a deaf spot? I often see what others miss, but frequently do not hear what you and many others hear. I have long known that there is a musical version of the story of modernism and postmodernism that I have tried to tell, but I am not the person to write it. On more than one occasion, I've suggested to someone who hears what I don't hear that he or she write their own musical version of the narrative I have tried to compose. There are two sides to the *Bildung* story, and the obvious place where the dark side becomes undeniable is in the Nietzsche-Wagner relationship. As I am sure you know, Nietzsche actually composed some musical fragments, which you can find on YouTube. A former student of mine, Kimerer Lamothe, has written a book on Nietzsche and dance, and now is working on a musical about Nietzsche in which she is incorporating these fragments. To my knowledge, Hegel did not listen to music seriously, nor did he visit art galleries. Kierkegaard wrote about *Don Giovanni* at length in the first volume of *Either-Or*, but his real artistic interest was theater. Wouldn't it be fascinating to compose a musical or write a play about all of these characters attending a dinner party in Jena in 1807?

Your comments on the importance of unions not only for you, but also for your whole family have made the lingering importance of your blue collar identity clearer to me. As you know from what I have written, my working life from the time I could push a lawnmower and spade garden remains an important part of my identity. Looking back, I now realize that this experience was an extension of my father's childhood labor on the small family farm. It was the disaffected heirs of farmers like my ancestors who elected Trump. There is an important article on this subject by Dan Kaufman in this week's *New Yorker*, "The Last Stand: How Suffering Farmers May Determine Trump's Fate.". Kaufman focuses on a small number of Wisconsin dairy farmers of Scandinavian heritage who had been lifelong Democrats but became so frustrated with the lack of government support that in an act of desperation they voted for Trump. Trump's future as well as our own depends on these farmers recognizing their mistake. Farmers, of course, have traditionally been anti-union and are often staunch Republicans. My paternal grandfather was a farmer and my maternal grandfather was a small businessman; both were Republican and neither ever voted for a Democrat. The first time my father voted for a Democrat was in 1972 when he supported George McGovern and that was a big deal in our family. My earliest memory of thinking about unions was family discussions about the Molly Maguires. In the coal mining town where my mother grew up and where she and my father were married, there were countless stories about the Molly Maguires. I still have a vivid picture in my mind of a dilapidated shack on a twisting mountain road that was supposed to have been a hideout for the gang. At one point during my undergraduate years, I considered writing my senior thesis on the Molly Maguires and the rise of the labor movement. My only personal experience with unions was during the summer between my freshman and sophomore years in college when I

worked as what was called a "cable monkey" for Western Electric in the
AT&T building next to the site where the World Trade Center eventually
was built. A requirement for the job was joining the Communication
Workers of America union. Though there were never any union meetings,
the social hierarchy of union/nonunion was clear. The guys who ran the
cable wore "work" clothes and the guys who soldered the connections wore
ties but not jackets, and the two groups did not mix in the lunchroom or
anywhere else. I suspect our different experiences with and attitudes about
unions are closely related to your upbringing as a Catholic and mine as a
Protestant.

There are two other important factors in the growing disempowerment
of workers that you do not mention—automation and outsourcing—both of
which have been made possible by information technologies. Until
recently, the impact of these developments has been greatest on so-called
blue-collar jobs, but this is rapidly changing. With the increasing sophistication of artificial intelligence, many white-collar jobs are now being automated. This trend will accelerate in the coming years, creating widespread
unemployment among workers who thought their jobs were secure. When
this happens blue-collar and white-collar workers will discover that they
share more than they realize. As you rightly maintain in your letter, the
utopia of leisure society is vanishing in the dystopia of unemployment and
homelessness.

A final word on unions. As the Wade Davis article in *Rolling Stone* that
you sent me makes clear, many of the problems now tearing the country
apart can be traced to Ronald Reagan. Nowhere is this more evident than
in the demise of unions, which you trace. The turning point was August 5,
1981, when Reagan fired eleven thousand air traffic controllers who went
on strike. The collapse of PATCO began the decline of unions that continues to this day. As you suggest, the failure of working class people to recognize Republicans' repeated bait-and-switch tactics over the years is truly
astonishing. I think one of the reasons the Republicans have been so successful is that they have been able to divide the working class between cities (unions) and country (farmers). I suspect this opposition roughly maps
onto the Catholic/Protestant divide.

Since I posted my letter to you, there has been a major development
that merits reflection. Yesterday, Lee Bollinger, the president of Columbia,

sent a message to the entire university community informing everyone that all undergraduate courses this fall would be online, and, with a very few exceptions, no undergraduates would be permitted to return to campus. This represents a major reversal just a few weeks before the semester begins. The plan had been to allow up to 60 percent of the students to live on campus if they chose to do so. In making the decision to go virtual, Columbia is following other Ivy League schools like the University of Pennsylvania and Princeton. I think this is a major development for many reasons, not the least of which is that this move by such prominent universities will give other colleges and universities planning to open with in-person classes pause and cover to change their minds.

The dominoes have started to fall. We are seeing the beginning of the end of higher education as we have known it. I have, of course, been predicting this turn of events ever since I created Global Education Network. Indeed, concern about the collapse of higher education was one of the primary reasons I undertook that venture and wrote *Crisis on Campus*. We are now facing a perfect storm that will push higher education beyond the tipping point. To understand what is happening, it is necessary to consider the interrelationship of several converging factors. Even before the pandemic hit a survey by Moody's Investors Service reported that 30 percent of universities were running operating deficits. Most colleges and universities are highly dependent on tuition as well as income from room, board, and student fees. Going online not only cuts off badly needed revenue streams, but also creates additional costs. Shawn Hubler has an informative article in the *New York Times* today that is worth reading—"As Colleges Move Classes Online, Families Rebel Against the Cost." She reports that to reopen in the current situation adds 10 percent to operating expenses. For the industry as a whole, this amounts to a $70 billion increase.

At the same time that costs are going up, students and parents are understandably and predictably rebelling against paying the same amount for online as in-person classes. Huber reports that at Rutgers, thirty thousand people have signed a petition calling for a reduction in fees. Similar protest movements are popping up across the country. Colleges are in an impossible bind—they cannot survive without maintaining or increasing current levels of income, so they cannot decrease fees. However, if they don't lower the price for tuition for online classes and have no income from room, board, and fees, students will defer or even withdraw. The inevitable result of this looming financial crisis will be an explosion in college bankruptcies, and a drastic reduction in educational opportunities for future generations of students. It is important to realize that it is not only small, lesser-known colleges that are facing this grim future. Very few colleges and universities have endowments that are large enough to support their operations without income from students as well as significant contributions from federal and state governments and charitable donations from private individuals. As the unemployment economic crisis resulting from the pandemic deepens, all of these revenue streams will dry up. The failure of many colleges and universities will have a ripple effect throughout higher education and will have a negative impact on the economy. A little-noticed action by Columbia last week points to ominous developments. The administration announced a 60 percent reduction in graduate student admissions for at least the next two years. These cutbacks, which are long overdue, come at a particularly perilous moment. You might remember the opening paragraph of my 2009 *New York Times* op-ed "End the University as We Know It."

> Graduate education is the Detroit of higher learning. Most graduate programs in American universities produce a product for which there is no market (candidates for teaching positions that do not exist) and develop skills for which there is diminishing demand (research in subfields within subfields and publication in journals read by no one other than a few like-minded colleagues), all at a rapidly rising cost (sometimes well over $100,000 in student loans).

The situation has only grown worse in the twelve years since I wrote that article. The reason Bollinger gave for the cutbacks is financial. At Columbia every graduate student admitted is guaranteed tuition plus $35,000 for five years. According to responsible endowment management practices, this requires $700,000 of endowment for every stipend. With rising costs and declining income, this level of support is unstainable. Fewer graduate students means there will be fewer advanced seminars offered and more undergraduate courses will have to be taught. At the same time, there will be fewer graduate students to serve as teaching assistants to help with these courses. This will tip the balance between teaching and research.

Faculty members will have to spend more time teaching and working with undergraduates and will have less time to conduct research and write specialized articles and books. This will transform what had previously been known as research universities. At a school like Columbia, hiring, tenure, and promotion are based solely on research and publication. With fewer scholarly works being produced and declining support from universities, the academic publishing industry, which is currently hanging by a thread, will collapse. In my experience, most faculty members refuse to acknowledge this situation and assume that once we get through this difficult period, they will be able to return to business as usual. As I know all too well, it doesn't make you popular around the quad to tell colleagues that they are delusional.

As I have been writing to you this morning, my brother forwarded to me a copy of an email he sent to his grandson, Benjamin, who is starting his freshman year at the University of Georgia today.

> I have been thinking of you often these days as you get ready to head off to school. It is often said that these will be the best years of your life. I am not sure that is the case, but I am sure they will be the most consequential. The decisions you make and the effort you put forth will determine what kind of life you will be able to lead. That may seem like a heavy burden to have to assume so early in life, but it is indeed the reality. I hope you find a passion that will sustain you for many years to come, establish lifelong friendships, and have fun. Also, never forget that you have parents, siblings and grandparents that love you very much and will always be there for you.

For all those young people starting what is supposed to be the journey of a lifetime, what a disappointment this fall will be. I wonder whether there will be such a thing as a freshman year by the time Jackson and Taylor are ready for what once was called "college."

Mark

Labor Day

SEPTEMBER 12–13: MARK BEGINS.

*Wildfires in the West—200,000 acres/year in the 1970s, 4.7 million in 2020 . . . the end of the Anthropocene: war on fire as an unwinnable war on nature . . . the climate crisis meetable only by an impossible religious conversion . . . in Oregon, blaming the wildfires on Antifa . . . climate scientist Ram Ramanathan on a California of "houses lost, houses uninsurable, special heat shelters against now unimaginable heat waves, and crippling new mass migration" . . . a father's letter to his daughter about/against buying property in inhabit-at-your-own risk California . . . life with grab 'n' go bags packed for evacuation at any hour in any season . . . troubling resignations-on-principle from the Department of Justice . . . William Barr as a "culture war Catholic" committed politically to the "unitary executive" theory of presidential authority . . . how is either God or nature to be obeyed? Who gets to tell us? . . . Biden's teflon—tougher than Trump's?*

---

*September 12*

Dear Jack:

> In this story of the outside world and the inside world with fire between, the outside world of little screwups recedes now for a few hours to be taken over by the inside world of blowups, this time by a colossal blowup but shaped by little screwups that fitted together tighter and tighter until all became one and the same things—the fateful blowup. Such is much of tragedy in modern times and probably always has been except that past tragedy refrained from speaking of its association with screwups and blowups.
>
> —Norman Maclean, *Young Men and Fire*

The world shrinking down about a raw core of parsible entities. The names of things slowly following those things into oblivion. Colors.

The names of birds. Things to eat. Finally the names of things one believed to be true. More fragile than he would have thought. How much was gone already? The sacred idiom shorn of its referents and so of its reality.

—Cormac McCarthy, The Road

Last week we had friends over for the first time since March. I had worked with Kathy on my Stone Hill exhibition at the Clark Art Institute and was eager to hear how the museum was dealing with the pandemic. Judging by Peter Schjeldahl's review of the new exhibition in this week's *New Yorker*, they are doing just fine ("Lineage: French Drawings from the Nineteenth Century"). We sat around a fire I started in our firepit and drank wine long into the night. It was a beautiful late summer evening with a magnificent sunset and later a clear night sky with a dazzling display of the Milky Way, which can only be seen in remote areas where it is truly dark.

When I turned on the news this morning, I was met with horrifying yet strangely beautiful images of raging fires and apocalyptic images of cities glowing brilliant red and orange, and smoldering remains of what until a few hours before had been homes. Orange County, it seems, has literally turned orange. We have discussed the fires in connection with Dan Hirsch's home, but it is unbelievable how they continue to spread. Thirty major fires are now burning in California, six of which are the largest in the state's history. And still Trump has said absolutely nothing about the disaster—not a single word to acknowledge what is happening. No federal assistance, no troops to help contain the fires. Maybe he thinks the fires will also miraculously disappear, or maybe he wants the fires to burn—especially in reliably blue states.

The banner headline in the *New York Times* this morning reads "Oregon Orders 500,000 to Evacuate as Fires Near Portland Suburbs." The governor is warning of a "mass fatality incident." In his column "I've Never Seen the West in Such Deep Distress," Timothy Egan writes, "The West of 2020 is very sick. Like much of the country, we Westerners are at each other's throats, struggling to put our lives back together under a madman for a president. But unlike the rest of the country, we're also choking on smoke and staring out at Martian-red skies in a world becoming uninhabitable."

A world . . . our world is becoming uninhabitable. The West, not just California, Oregon, Washington, Idaho, and Montana, but the West is in such deep distress. The temperature is rising everywhere as never before.

On September 8, 2014, Kathryn Schultz published in *New York Magazine* an article on Norman Maclean's *Young Men and Fire* entitled "The Story That Tore Through the Trees" in which she writes, "In the years since that book came out, the cost of controlling wildfire in the United States has risen from $240 million to almost $2 billion. When Maclean began working on it in the 1970s, fires burned an average of 200,000 acres per year. So far in 2014, they have burned 2.7 million." That was six years ago; today, with three or four more months of the fire season remaining, 3.5 million acres in California and 4.7 million acres nationwide have already burned this year. The fires and the virus are symptoms of the disease plaguing the West. But what is this disease and how can it be controlled?

To begin to understand what is happening, it is necessary to shift the angle of vision. What if the Anthropocene is ending? What if humankind has become the disease by morphing into an invasive species prone to toxic biological and economic growth? When growth becomes excessive, it turns cancerous. As people expand into territories previously inhabited by different plant and animal species, conflicts inevitably develop. Closer contact between humans and so-called "exotic" animals like bats and pangolins create an increased likelihood that viruses and bacteria can jump from animals to humans. In a similar manner, as people build houses and neighborhoods expand into previously forested areas, the possibility of fires and the inevitable damage they cause increases. "A fire is only a disaster," Ron Steffens explains, "if there is a house there."

There is a profound irony in these developments. As everyone knows, the trickster Prometheus stole fire from the gods and gave it to human beings. This gift, however, turned out to be a poison (*ein Gift*). The invention of the internal combustion engine led to the domestication of fire and the excavation and commodification of fossil fuels. The more coal, oil, and gas that burns, the higher the temperatures rise, and the higher the temperatures, the more fires burn. Schultz writes, "The National Council reports that for every 1.8 degree rise, the amount of western land that burns could quadruple." Loops within loops—fire raises the temperature, which creates more fires, which raise the temperature . . . What had been a gift from the gods becomes a danger that must be contained or preferably extinguished. When confronting such a threat mankind does what men always do—declare war, war on fire.

From 1935 to 1978, the federal government followed a strict policy of suppressing wildfires, which created financial incentives that actually exacerbated the problem it was intended to solve. Stephen Pyne, author of *Fire in America*, points out that "there are whole industries now that depend on fire-fighting . . : air tankers, helicopters, contractors—a whole private workforce of crews and engines and support services. These are the mercenaries, and they don't want the firefight to end." The suppression of fire leads to the excessive growth of underbrush, which creates fuel for bigger fires. Increasing temperatures lead to shifting weather patterns, which create widespread drought that turns forests into tinderboxes waiting for a spark to ignite them. Worldwide lightning strikes the earth 100 times a second, 8 million times a day, and 3 billion times a year. Fire is inevitable.

It's elemental: earth, air, water, fire. Wildfire is a natural phenomenon that plays an essential role in the health of ecosystems. The war on fire is part of the broader war on nature that is inseparable from modern man's incessant will to mastery and control. Once again apparent self-defense is actually self-destructive. What appears to be an immune response to an external threat turns back on the organism it is supposed to protect to create an autoimmune disease. In recent years, there has been a growing consensus that the policy of suppressing forest fires is misguided. Tucked away in the back pages of the *Times*, there is a less obvious but no less important article by Brad Plumer and John Schwartz, "These Changes Are Needed Amid Worsening Wildfires, Experts Say—The Blazes Scorching the West Highlight the Urgency of Rethinking Fire Management Policies, as Climate Change Threatens to Make Things Worse." "A century of federal policy to aggressively extinguish all wildfires rather than letting some burn at low levels, an approach now seen as misguided, has left forests with plenty of fuel for especially destructive blazes. This is all in an era when global warming is creating a hotter, drier environment, loading the dice for more extensive fires" (September 10, 2020). Photographs and an animation of smoke spreading across the state provide a graphic depiction of the magnitude of the damage.

Though short-term measures like revised zoning laws and stricter building codes might limit some destruction, the only long-term solution is to
curb climate change by extinguishing the fires consuming fossil fuels. It
has long been clear that this requires a change in human self-understanding
and values that is so profound that it amounts to nothing less than a religious conversion. Rather than separate from and at war with the natural
world, human beings must come to accept the *fact* that we are integral
members of an infinitely complex and frightfully fragile organism that is
now gasping for breath.

(Aside: At four years old, I think Taylor might be a budding Hegelian
philosopher, who understands the importance of double negation. Yesterday she asked Kirsten: "Mom, what if the coronovirus gets the
coronavirus?")

In today's hyperpoliticized world where, paradoxically, both everything
and nothing is believable, a conversion to such a vision of the world is
impossible. In the hours since I've been writing to you, a new article
appeared on the *Times* website—"As Antifa Rumors Spread in Oregon, Residents Defied Evacuation Orders." With a major fire fast approaching the
town, local officials in Milalla, Oregon trying to get residents to evacuate
were met with resistance.

"There's already reports that antifa's in town, going down the streets
looting," he said, echoing widely discredited rumors on Twitter and
Facebook that left-wing activists had been systematically setting
blazes. "I'm getting texts."

Every natural disaster has its holdouts. But the political fear-stoking
that accompanied a tumultuous summer of racial-justice protests in
Oregon has become a volatile new complication in the catastrophic
wildfires that pushed closer to Portland on Friday, as authorities try to
evacuate hundreds of thousands of people.

Law-enforcement officials across the state said they had been swamped
with calls about social-media misinformation and begged people to
"STOP. SPREADING. RUMORS!" In the line of fire, the swirl of rumors

actually helped goad some people into defying evacuation orders so they could stay and guard their homes.

While some burn to death protecting themselves from phantom conspirators, others die from a virus deemed fake. This *is* the fire next time and it's real; ignore it at your own risk.

Mark


*September 13*

Dear Mark:

For a long while now, I have regarded the United States as equivalently an overvalued stock whose valuation was overdue for a sharp correction. In saying that, I'm using the stock market, obviously, as a metaphor, but the stock market itself is implicated. The market's continuing strength has been remarkable, but a quarter of its value and much more than a quarter of its growth has come from the computer technology behemoths, but all of them are finally parasitic on the real economy, so it does stand to reason that they may be overvalued as or if the real economy is poised to collapse. We were seeing possible signs of that last week, but for me the overvaluation metaphor applies with particular severity to the California real estate market.

Below, I am going to quote from a very long, very complicated letter that I wrote to Kathleen and Brian on August 5, 2019—two months after their marriage on June 22, 2019.

Background for this letter was, first, the catastrophic Northern California fires of the summer of 2018 and, second, my education, through Ram Ramanathan, in the connection between global warming and fire. Though Ram has rightly seen me as his ally in attempting to rally organized religion around the cause of climate stabilization, I have presented myself to him as also a writer practiced in the op-ed genre and otherwise at his service. He is fluent in English and quietly charismatic in person, but English is still his second language, and he does not write it with what I view as rhetorical bite. I saw no better opening in the various aspects of the global warming that he, as an atmospheric scientist, explains so well, no aspect of the

complex scientific picture likelier to galvanize a sea change in public attitudes in California than the risk of catastrophic fire. So, he and I worked
for a while on a couple draft op-ed pieces, but somehow they were overtaken by events and never appeared or even quite reached final form. In a
nutshell, their core message was that warming air is thirsty air that, under
drought conditions, accelerates and exacerbates drought by "drinking"
moisture from vegetation on the ground and from any other water sources
on the ground, thus preparing dry tinder for catastrophic fires that, at
lower temperatures, would not be catastrophic at all. I wanted our op-ed to
show that global warming truly did make the difference between the livable
old normal in California and the emerging, unlivable new normal.

At the time, I had heard a sobering presentation at the Pacific Council
on International Policy by a former speaker of the California Assembly
(lower house) and the then-CEO of Southern California Edison. Their
point: set aside the dire future consequences of global warming; look only
at actual consequences of warming to this point; and now recognize, people, that historical strategies for fighting mass conflagrations are about to
cease working as large portions of the state have become effectively inde-
fensible and therefore uninhabitable or uninsurable and thus inhabit-at-
your-own risk.

There is a third element of background that I should mention. Kathleen
is very project-oriented and very intense in her application to whatever her
current project is. Over the past year or so, her project has been seeing
*Noēma* through to its successful launch. Earlier, it was simultaneously (at
the start) managing their wedding and buying their first house. As the
enormous scope of managing a DIY wedding for about 150 guests when
you have never managed one before became clear, Kathleen and Brian
decided to postpone buying a house until after the wedding. The wedding
was a splendid success, but I did indeed anticipate that her/their next challenge would be the house purchase, and so I wrote the letter that I quote
below in preparation for that development. In fact, the next project after
the wedding turned out, instead, to be *Noēma*, and so the real estate project has surged back into the lead only recently, as you know from previous
correspondence.

Taking the view that their lives are theirs to live and that I will not be
around for that much longer, I have been willing to assist them in purchasing

a house that I myself, if buying for myself, would never purchase. But I am tempted again and again to resurrect my earlier argument and urge renting or another expedient suggested by her considering herself, her mother, and me as a single economic unit. As both her mother's heir and mine, Kathleen should regard herself as heading an economic unit defined by our collective wealth (hers and her parents'), or so I argue, and her wiser decision as the manager of this wealth should be to invest as little of it as possible in endangered California real estate, consistent with her acquiring adequate housing for herself, her husband, and the child they yearn to have. I have outlined at different times several different scenarios to this end, within which my preference was that Kathleen and Brian should rent until, as was then already foreseeable, her mother moved to a retirement community and that they should then move into her house and pay her the rent they would otherwise be paying a landlord. This scenario, I already knew, was emotionally out of the question for Kathleen, and, of course, COVID at least temporarily made me glad about that for her mother's sake. Just lately, however, Kathleen's mother has expressed interest in moving sooner rather than later (sooner for now means two years) to a CCRC, and the CCRCs are far better prepared than they were months ago to keep their residents COVID-protected. I am resigned to not having my advice taken, but I think you still might find interesting what I wrote to them back in 2018, where "you" refers to the couple and the partners appear by name:

> The decisions ahead are yours to make, and I want to help in the best way I can. The more trust and openness we can have among us, the wiser our decisions are likely to be. Lately, some of the reading I have been doing about real estate, especially in California and especially at just this point in our history, has left me anxious on your behalf about the risks that I fear you face. So, just as "deep background," let me begin, referring as I go to one or another of three enclosures. [Mark, I have omitted the enclosures.]

> Why are prices so high in California? The prices are not to be explained by supply and demand as we have known it in the past, as Mom and I knew it, for example, when we bought our Pasadena house in 1986. Then, we were bidding against other individual buyers. Now, you two are bidding against investment bankers capitalized not just by

American but also by foreign capital and selling American residential real estate to foreigners as well as Americans. [See appendix to enclosure #1.] Back then, one always bid below the asking price, and if one were a seller, one was ecstatic if one sold for the asking price. Now, you two are expected to bid above the asking price and to rejoice if you get your house for *only* the asking price. Why? Why the big change? At least very significantly because of whom you are bidding against.

What does it mean now for a young couple to buy a house in California for $1 million? Does it mean that their investment will climb in value to $2 million? Or that it will drop to $.5 million, leaving them owing, say, $.75 million on a house now worth much less? The answer [enclosure #1, especially the latter paragraphs] is that we don't know because the market could go *radically* in either direction. In short, the future is hugely more unpredictable than ever because of these unprecedented disruptions. You might think, *Well, this won't matter too much if we have bought our forever house and are still just happily living there.* But can you really say that? You two face more than just the usual unpredictability in American work life. (Without stopping to do a really exact count, I would say that I thought I was permanently employed five times in my work life and five times discovered that I was wrong.) No, you also face a new factor of California unpredictability, which is, in a word, fire. [See enclosure #2.]

Professor Veerabhadran "Ram" Ramanathan is a super-distinguished climate scientist, former director of the Scripps Institution's Department of Oceanic and Atmospheric Sciences, and the expert tapped by Janet Napolitano to lead a UC-wide (and successful) effort to prepare a set of "scalable solutions" for then-governor Brown to take to the COP 21 Climate Conference in Paris [Mark, the COP 21 agreement is the one that President Trump, of course, has now repudiated]. In a recent article in *Nature*, Ram and two colleagues report on ominous data indicating a serious *acceleration* in climate change. Ram, who also worked with the Vatican on Pope Francis's climate encyclical, though he is a Hindu by birth, hopes to bring about a mobilization of religious leadership on behalf of climate education, and I am a collaborator in that. But his 8/1/19 private email to his California collaborators addresses immediate implications for our state: houses lost, houses uninsurable, special heat shelters against now unimaginable heat waves, crippling new mass migration, etc. A colleague of mine at Yale told me recently that scientists working at the National Center for Climate and Atmospheric Research, sponsored by the National Science Foundation, have been so disturbed by their own findings that they have had to seek psychotherapy to keep working.

Confidence that real estate in any area will basically at least retain its value rests on an assumption that the future will be in basic regards like the past. *But what if this ceases to be true in a given region?* What if California itself begins to become undesirable to almost uninhabitable over the next generation? The Camp Fire in Northern California left San Francisco with air quality worse than that of New Delhi and more than wiped out the positive effect of *everything else* that California did in 2018 to reduce emissions and mitigate global warming. Nobody's house burned down in San Francisco, but everybody's sense there about the future changed on the day when because of the smoke, it was as if the sun never came up. A long article last Sunday in the *New York Times Magazine* on that fire ended (I quote almost verbatim), "As for how it all ended, it didn't. It won't." So, climate, which adds a degree of risk to all investments, adds an especially large degree of risk and unpredictability to real estate investment in California. We could be facing not just a decline but even a *collapse* of real estate values in California.

A basic principle—for practical purposes, *the* basic principle—of sound investment is diversification: don't put all your eggs in one basket, or even half your eggs. And if the basket in question is a fragile basket, one that might leave a bunch of your eggs smashed on the sidewalk? Unless you are super-wealthy and can handle big risks in the hope of big profits, that kind of investment is not for you. Now, some of the big money now investing in California can very easily handle big reversals in the hope of an incalculably large pot of gold at the end of the investment rainbow—namely, the transformation of millions of would-be home owners into lifelong renters at the investors' mercy in a now effectively monopolized market. This is the Amazon model transferred to housing: drive out the retail real estate investors and then, effectively, own the real estate market. The potential picture along the way is already pretty ugly: sales remain steady at the top (see enclosure #3) but are declining sharply at the bottom, as the number of potential buyers resigned to being permanent renters grows. Down at the very bottom, of course, are those who cannot afford even to rent and so are homeless and living on the street. Enclosure #3 shows how this broad picture is now spreading inland from the coastal cities where real estate is scarcest and most in demand.

So, it would seem highly imprudent to sink a very large chunk of all your available capital, counting not just your own but everything that your parents' can spare, to buy in at what might just be the very top of the California real estate market and then be stuck with a colossal debt as property value in the state—and surely much else along the way—starts to *really* go to hell because of a factor independent of supply and demand. This is why, as you know too well, I keep trying to push you toward waiting until you can move into Mom's Pasadena house. Doing that would permit you to keep all or much of the wealth that you have accumulated *out* of California real estate. If proceeding thus meant that I was called on to assist in funding Mom's move into an attractive retirement community, the outlay might be roughly what we foresee in my helping you two buy a house in NELA [Northeastern LA—then but no longer their target area]. The difference? That, at the end of the day she would be well cared for, but, crucially, all three of you would be housed *without* taking on any new real estate debt at all.

I take it that this "Scenario #3" is DOA, and so be it. I am in agreement with Kathleen that Mom should be allowed to take whatever risks she wants, within some very broad limits, and to age in place and live just where she wants. It's her life, after all, as Kathleen keeps reminding me. By the same token, it's your life as well, and you two have the right to assume whatever debt you want to assume and run whatever risks you want to assume to live the life you dream of. Kathleen, you may or may not remember that for years I had on display on my UCI office a photo of you at about six years of age in your bright blue bathing suit with wet red hair at the top of a water slide, just poised to push yourself off. In the

background, partly obscured, one can read in
this snapshot "...AT YOUR OWN RISK." I
loved that slide because it was so completely
you: a little scared but finally ready to take
the plunge into the pool at the bottom of the
slide...at your own risk. What I loved then I
still have to respect now.

Love,

And then, of course, I signed my name and didn't type it. Nils Gilman, a
Berkeley social scientist and administrator now with the Berggruen Institute,
told Kathleen that he expects California's forest to be effectively gone by
2080, making Alta California (the state) look like Baja California but that he
does not expect this change to bring about a total collapse in real estate
because "people have to live somewhere." That's true, but what I find equally
plausible is that people with portable wealth will leave the state, while people
without it will have no choice but to stay and to become that population of
captive renters that I envision above. My widowed sister Mary Anne lives
alone in a long-paid-for brick house in Chicago. I've said in her presence that
if our house burns down here in Santa Ana, what Kitty and I will do is "move
in with Mary Anne," and I know she would take us in. When in Chicago, we
usually stay in her finished basement, which has a hide-a-bed and its own
bathroom. This would be temporary, of course, but since I no longer have any
money in real estate at all and Kitty has wealth beyond this residence (itself
now worth plenty), we will be able to buy or rent in Chicago. This is whistling
in the dark, of course, for the shock to Kitty of losing this house, where she
has lived since 1971, and the ongoing strain of feeling herself so much more a
guest in Chicago than I ever could or would—well, I need not go on.

This has been, of course, a week of new and disturbing revelations about
Trump and contempt for the American military; Trump and his duplicity
about the pandemic (but do check out "If Trump Lied, So Did Fauci" by
Trump apologist Marc A. Thiessen in the 9/10 *Washington Post*); Trump and
Russian intrusion into our election; Trump as financially compromised
and a hostage to Russia (Peter Strzok); and, despite these revelations, a
narrowing of Biden's lead over Trump that brings the spectre of 2016 to the

front of the mind. Perhaps the one piece of ironic good news has been that the existential threat to Portland, Oregon, posed by raging wildfire there has smothered the directionless autopilot protests in downtown Portland.

On Monday of this past week, I had a "Zio" patch placed on my chest above my heart, where it will remain for two weeks monitoring my every heartbeat. This is simply part of the process of ascertaining, now as we approach the four-month mark since my cardiac ablation, whether normal sinus rhythm has been restored. *Zio* in Italian means "uncle," so I am wondering whether "Uncle Patch" can detect my anxiety about the collapse of so much of America as we have known it and depended upon it.

Kitty and I are planning to pack suitcases, medications, the other survival items recommended on various grab 'n' go checklists that we have, have followed in the past, but now need to redo just in case. She asked me the other day, "Suppose we finally get the grab part done, where can we go?" Imagine how many thousands on the West Coast are now asking just that question. We are making other anti-fire preparations (sprinkler checks, raking around the house, keeping car gas tanks full), but meanwhile normal life continues—e.g., a church silent auction by Zoom this week and the skin cancer surgery that I have scheduled for the end of this month. One lives not so much in reality and illusion but rather in a doubled reality—the nearer and ongoing old normal and the farther or intruding/impending/menacing new normal. In one way, the fearful doubling concentrates the mind (cf. Dr. Johnson); in another, it tends to paralyze it by overload.

I speak grandly of "the" mind. My own Jack Miles mind? Well, not so far gone that I was not able to acquire a terrifically jolly and confidence-exuding "JOE" sign and attach it, perhaps illegally, to the reverse side of a tall traffic sign, so high up (I used a ladder to place it) that Trump trolls in our neighborhood will not easily remove or deface it.

Act 1: Jack the Democrat climbs the beanstalk.

Act 2: "Fee-fie-fo-fat, I smell the blood of a Democrat."

Act 3: In pursuit of Jack the Democrat, the Giant pursues him up the beanstalk, but nimble Jack has chopped the beanstalk down at the bottom, the Giant falls to earth, is deported to Russia, and never tweets again.

Jack

*September 13*

Dear Jack:

I have to be brief this morning because I must finish reading your book *Religion As We Know It* for the first class in my undergraduate Theory seminar tomorrow. While the fires continue to burn out of control, another smoldering fire is flaring up, and I want to register my concern and solicit your take on what is happening. On September 11, the *Hartford Courant* ran an article: "Nora Dannehy, Connecticut Prosecutor Who Was a Top Aide to John Durham's Trump-Russia Investigation, Resigns amid Concern About Pressure from Attorney General William Barr." In the past couple of months, I have become convinced that Barr is as great, if not a greater, threat to our democracy than Donald Trump. Durham has been the U.S. attorney for the District of Columbia since February 2018, where he has worked for thirty-five years. A year and a half ago, Barr appointed him to investigate the legal justification for the FBI's counterintelligence investigation that looked into ties between Trump and the Russians. Dannehy, who is widely respected across the political spectrum, was Durham's lead investigator in this case. Though she has not yet offered any public explanation for her departure, reliable sources report that her action was prompted by pressure from the attorney general to issue a preliminary report on the investigation's findings before the presidential election.

I am sure you will recall that my former student, Jonathan Kravis, was the first attorney in the Department of Justice to resign over pressure from Barr. In his case, it was Barr's intervention to reduce the sentence of Roger Stone. As you know, I do not read the *Washington Post* regularly so I missed his May 11 op-ed, "I Left the Justice Department After it Made a Disastrous Mistake. It Just Happened Again." Jonathan had not intended to go public, but when Barr stepped in again on behalf of Flynn, he felt a moral obligation to speak out on behalf of his former colleagues at the DoJ. Jonathan writes,

> In both cases, the department undercut the work of career employees to protect an ally of the president, an abdication of the commitment to equal justice under the law. Prosecutors must make decisions based on facts and law, not on the defendant's political connections. When

the department takes steps that it would never take in any other case to protect an ally of the president, it betrays this principle. Indeed, the department chose to assign these matters to a special counsel precisely to avoid the appearance of political influence. For the attorney general now to directly intervene to benefit the president's associates makes this betrayal of the rule of law even more egregious.

While I have not communicated with Jonathan since Dannehy's resignation, I am sure he is more freaked out than ever by Barr's escalating interference. From the beginning of this debacle, it has been clear that Barr has been planning his own October surprise to help Trump get reelected. I believe his intention all along has been to release a report he believes will be damaging to Biden and the Democrats just before the election, and I suspect this is what Dannehy finally had to admit to herself. Now I am discovering that, as so often, it all comes down to religion.

Like others, I have been both intrigued and puzzled by Barr's repeated dubious actions to support the president, but I think I am finally beginning to figure out what he is up to. Much has been written about white Evangelicals support of Trump, but very little about the support he receives from conservative and right-wing Catholics. As long as Barr is attorney general, this is where the real danger lies. If you have not read the address he gave on October 11, 2019, at the Notre Dame Law School, I would encourage you to do so. It is a remarkable statement that lays bare the ideology behind his agenda. While framed as a defense of religious freedom, the speech is a diatribe against what Barr labels "militant secularism," which, he argues, the Founders anticipated. "They never thought the main danger to the republic came from external foes. The central question was whether over the long haul, we could handle freedom. The question was whether the citizens in such a free society could maintain the moral discipline and virtue necessary for the survival of free institutions."

Cathleen Kaveny, who holds joint positions in the Law School and Department of Theology at Boston College, describes Barr as having "a kind of authoritarian Catholic thought and an elitist vision that is not particularly comfortable with the give and take of a democracy." Far more than the latest episode in the endless culture wars, the Notre Dame address is a diatribe in which Barr rages against the "sins" of modernity that threaten civilization itself. "Unless you have some effective restraint," he warns, "you will end up with something equally dangerous—licentiousness, the unbridled pursuit of personal appetites at the expense of the common good. This is just another form of tyranny—where the individual is enslaved by his appetites, and the possibility of any healthy community crumbles."

It's hard to imagine a better description of his boss. What is Barr's solution to personal and social disintegration? Abject deference to the highest authority of all.

> But what is the source of this internal controlling power? In a free republic, those restraints could not be handed down from above by philosopher kings. Instead, social order must flow from the people themselves—freely obeying the dictates of inwardly possessed and commonly-shared moral values. And to control willful human beings, with an infinite capacity to rationalize, those moral values must rest on authority independent of men's will—they must flow from a transcendent Supreme Being.
>
> For many years I have said that I fear true believers much more than nonbelievers. Barr *is* a true believer.

Several canny commentators have noted Barr's association with the notorious right-wing Catholic organization known as Opus Dei. You know more about this than I do, and I would be interested in your thoughts about this group. The *National Catholic Reporter* ran an article a few months ago entitled "William Barr, Nation's Top Lawyer, Is a Culture Warrior Catholic," which reported:

> While Barr is not a member of Opus Dei, according to his Senate questionairre, from 2014 to 2017 he served on the board of the Catholic Information Center, an Opus Dei-affiliated bookstore and chapel a few blocks from the White House that is a longtime hub for conservative intellectuals, Republican politicians and other well-connected Catholics in the nation's capital.
>
> Other prominent board members at the center have included Leonard Leo, co-chairman of the Federalist Society, which helped shepherd the Supreme Court nominations of Brett Kavanaugh and Neil Gorsuch through the Senate confirmation process. White House counsel

Pat Cipollone, who led Trump's defense during the Senate impeachment trial, also previously served on the Catholic Information Center's board. Cipollone was a speechwriter for Barr during the first Bush administration.

When pundits speculate about the reason Republicans and Evangelicals continue to support Trump even as he obviously betrays many of their most fundamental beliefs, they always answer, "It's all about the judges." They have made a pact with the devil to stack the court and influence policy for decades to come. While Don McGahn might be doing the legwork, it is increasingly clear that Barr is pulling the strings. This is a very, very dangerous situation.

In Trump, Barr has found the Manchurian candidate he has been seeking since his early days in the George H. W. Bush administration. Jimmy Lohman, one of Barr's Horace Mann high school classmates, sounded the alarm when he recently remarked, "The only thing that really makes sense to me is that Barr clearly wanted to get in on all the power and he saw Trump as someone he could manipulate and be a kind of Robespierre to a [foolish] king ... in effect the most powerful person in the country by manipulating this man." It's time to wake up to what's going on behind the charade of deceit and reflection that is the Trump Show. All of this needs more digging and deserves more attention, but I don't have time now.

Mark


*September 14*

Dear Mark:

You've changed the subject, but so be it. The subject concerns you deeply, and I respect that. I learned of and quickly read William Barr's Notre Dame Law School speech at the time when he delivered it last year. It had aroused incensed and alarmed reactions outside conservative circles at the time. I could easily understand how his words offended liberals and secularists, but I did not find them dangerous until something else about Barr came to my attention somewhat later. This was the fact that Barr is a leading adherent to the "unitary executive" theory of the American executive branch—namely, the view that the full authority and all the privileges of the presidency inhere in any action taken by any employee of the executive branch. That's doubtless an oversimplification, but such at least is the thrust.

Rereading the speech this morning at your instigation, I wrote down the one sentence that I thought best captured the moral philosophy to which Barr adheres: "In fact, Judeo-Christian moral standards are the ultimate utilitarian rules for human conduct." This was his conclusion from his prior claim that Judeo-Christian moral standards rest not on revelation but on nature itself. He does not misquote the Founding Fathers. A belief in natural religion and, within it, natural morality, both resting upon nature itself, was widespread in the late eighteenth century, and the Founders shared that belief. But comparative religion and comparative morality were then still in their infancy. It is the case, inconveniently for Barr's claim, that Islam too claims that it is humankind's natural religion and, thus, that "imposing" it on others is really no imposition; rather, it is a boon, even a liberation. The Native American religions—now often celebrated for their respect for the land, for biological diversity, for sustainable use of natural resources, and so forth—implicitly entertain the same self-understanding. Why otherwise would religion scholars call them "nature religions?"

Crucial, of course, is the fact that nature does not announce itself as a morally obligatory law but only as a fact. It is only as interpreted that the facts of nature can be fashioned into an ethical command or an obligation. The Christian moral understanding that sperm and egg are destined by the creator to join and become a new human (an understanding by no means confined to Roman Catholicism at its origin) and that therefore God is disobeyed when the two are artificially kept apart is such an interpretation. A parallel interpretation leads, however, to no parallel obligation when it comes to hen's eggs for breakfast. Why not? God did not create humans alone; he also created chickens. Does God not wish the hen's egg to be fertilized and become another chicken? The facts would seem to speak as loudly. Ah, comes the objection, but human beings are created in the image and likeness of God; chickens are not. At just that point, of course, we leave nature and enter the realm of biblical revelation. And no secular morality supposedly based on nature alone has any better chance of dispensing with the need for interpretation if it is somehow to lead to civil law.

From all this it follows that when Barr argues that his ultimate utilitarian authority is nature, he is arguing inescapably for his own authority or for some other authority that he might designate to tell us what nature is saying. When he writes that "to control willful human beings, with an infinite capacity to rationalize, those moral values must rest on authority independent of men's will—they must flow from a transcendent Supreme Being," he invites inescapably the question of who will speak for that transcendent Supreme Being. It is at this point that his espousal of the unitary executive theory of the authority of the American president makes his views seriously consequential. It is inconceivable that he would intend matters of such moment to be settled by plebiscite, never mind his adducing the Founding Fathers' experiment in trusting to the morality of the American people. It is at this point, in other words, that he becomes a kind of American Thomas Hobbes, arguing that only a presidential Leviathan can restrain the wolves of American lust and rampant hedonism from undermining the Republic. That Trump should occupy the White House as he argues this case might seem to be ipso facto its refutation, but there are those, I gather, who, like Jimmy Lohman, Barr's schoolmate, see Barr as entertaining grand ambitions for the pursuit of which Trump would be merely a temporary expedient. The presidency as an office can be the needed American Leviathan, but when it comes to how in practice the morality and the law of the land shall be enforced, the unitary authority of the presidency must be extended to the Department of Justice. What looms as that happens is morality by executive order.

I am never easily convinced by "slippery slope" arguments. Sisela Bok has a persuasive and important book arguing against such arguments. Often, a prudential decision can be made that, extrapolated, could wreak great damage but, shy of such extrapolation, does none. And prudential decisions can be wholly benign. It took a prudential decision in favor of the constitutional neutrality in religion to extend it to Catholics and to Jews when, for decades, it had practically extended only to denominations of Protestantism. Just now, our country teeters back and forth between extending and denying to Islam the same constitutional protection that Judaism and Catholicism now enjoy. In the concrete instances of federal impingement on religious liberty that Barr adduced in his Notre Dame speech, I myself was inclined in 2019 to allow prudential exceptions to be made for Evangelical bakers disinclined to decorate cakes for gay weddings and for nun-run institutions disinclined to make even any reference to artificial birth control when providing health insurance to their employees. Why allow these? Because they are so few and because by allowing them, contention can be put to rest and the country can go forward in peace, having made an undeniably large but also sufficiently large change without requiring every last baker to honor it. Prudentially, in other words, a double standard can indeed be allowed in a few, limited cases without, in practice, jeopardizing the majority—the majority, here, of bakers who will bake whatever for whomever and the majority of even Catholic and Evangelical employers who will either insure contraception for their employees or notify them of how they may avail themselves of government insurance to procure what they need. Allowing for such discretionary exceptions is the very definition of what we mean in everyday conversation by "good judgment."

It is only when the moral philosophy that Barr espouses in theory becomes linked in practice to a grossly inflated understanding of the presidency that prudence dictates a very different reaction. But what should it be? When the news of Nora Dannehy's resignation was announced, I was dismayed that she did not go public with her reasons. It is all well and good that she has followed her conscience, but what of her duty to the public? Might her conscience not dictate that she do as your student Jonathan Kravis did? Are you thinking of reaching out to him with the suggestion that he reach out to her?

With so very Irish a name, Nora Dannehy may well be a Catholic, may well be conservative politically, but may be a conservative in the Cathleen Kaveny mold. I had been reading Kaveny for years and reached out to her even before I arrived on the Boston College campus to recruit her to speak at the conference I was to organize there (and did) for spring 2019 (and she did speak). As an expert in the rich Catholic judicial and ethical tradition, Kaveny will know that the tradition honors the notion of "subsidiarity," which is the principle that decisions and policies that can be handled at a lower level should *not* be transferred to an upper level. (The pyramidal ecclesial authority structure centered on the papacy itself violates this principle, but that's another story.) The remark of hers that you quote, in which she describes Barr as having "a kind of authoritarian Catholic thought and an elitist vision that is not particularly comfortable with the give and take of a democracy," implies minimally that she is well aware of *other* kinds of Catholic thought. See her most recent book, *Prophecy Without Contempt*. I can only guess here, but Cathy Kaveny is someone who might be able to reach out to Nora Dannehy at this juncture. Harvard, too, is a link between the two.

Such are my darkest thoughts, but let me balance them with one lighter one. There is an assumption among liberals, I suspect, that Trump like Reagan is a Teflon president (nothing sticks to him) while Biden like Clinton is the opposite (everything sticks to him). At this late point in the campaign, I suspect that Biden may be as Teflon-coated as Trump when it comes to arcane charges linked to Ukraine, China, recorded conversations, and so forth. Your most concrete fear is of a Barr-launched October surprise, and one may well be coming, but will it matter? Perhaps not. Barr has a "record" now that will tend to impugn anything he serves up at the last minute rather more, I think, than Comey's did with his last-minute attempt to torpedo the Clinton campaign. Comey had much more credibility at that point than Barr may have just now with prospective Biden voters.

What I do hope, now that I think of it, is that Dannehy may have resigned so as to be free to alert the Biden campaign to the bombshell the Trump campaign and Barr in particular may plan to drop just before the upcoming debates. At this point, the debates would appear to be Trump's best hope of a turnaround. I worry about them, but I also have an increasing sense that Biden is quite good at being forearmed with some basic forewarning. He has often insisted that he is positively itching to debate Trump, and Trump's debate style is so well known that he can be forearmed against it. The audience for these debates is likely to break all records, and they may be historic indeed.

Jack

P.S. There is another aspect to the American experiment that bears mentioning. When the Constitution was ratified in 1787, Venice was the only republic in Europe, and a broad consensus obtained that no major nation could function without a monarch. There were those who thought that, yes, America could become independent from Britain but, no, it could not dispense with a hereditary executive. There were those at the time who wanted to make George Washington our first king. But the Founders, with the memory of royal oppression firmly in mind, were on guard against risking such oppression in the governance of the newly independent and united American states. The inflation of the American presidency via a theory of the "unitary executive" into a monstrous Hobbesian monarchy would seem to be, almost by definition, the failure of the experiment that they launched with our post-monarchy, "post-monacracy" American Democratic Republic.

* * *

## SEPTEMBER 26–28: MARK BEGINS.

*Taylor and Miles as, respectively, Protestant and Catholic "at heart" . . . secularism to be understood as a religious phenomenon . . . media attention to conservative Evangelicals more than to conservative Catholics . . . Supreme Court with ethnic and gender diversity, yes, but with academic uniformity and a 6–3 Catholic religious majority . . . poet Todd Boss on bees, humans, and gynarchy as the best defense against extinction . . . Luther vs. Confucius on preparing for the long term—or for the end . . . Ram Ramanathan on 2020–2030 as a last chance to forestall "an extinction event" . . . his work as an Indian scientist at the Vatican . . . the tragedy of Pope Francis . . . Wittgenstein's greatest line and the lack of a true English equivalent for the German verb* schweigen.

---

*September 26*

Dear Jack:

In a recent letter, I mentioned that church plays a much larger role in your life than in mine. Nonetheless, we both know how deeply early experiences shape our lives. Though you now identify yourself as an Episcopalian, you are, of course, still a Catholic at heart. And while I do not identify with any particular religious denomination, I am still a Protestant at heart.

Catholicism is implicitly and explicitly present everywhere in your letter this week—from your opening reflections on Pope Francis's forthcoming encyclical on climate change to your response to Joseph Henrich's *The* WEIRDest *People in the World: How the West Became Psychologically Peculiar and Particularly Prosperous.* As I was reading your letter, the *New York Times* confirmed that Trump is nominating Amy Barrett to fill RBG's position on the Supreme Court. After finishing your letter early this morning, I reread Weber's *The Protestant Ethic and the Spirit of Capitalism* in preparation for my seminar on Monday. When I finished reading, I emailed a question to the class with the subject heading "Religion Matters." With Trump's nomination of Amy Barrett for the Supreme Court, what will be the religious affiliation of each of the justices? An interesting question to ponder in light of Weber's argument. Later today I plan to send a second email to the class with the subject heading "Education Matters." What college and law school did each of the justices attend?

While Weber is most often remembered for his argument about the way Protestant—more specifically, Calvinist—religious beliefs and practices created the conditions for the emergence of capitalism, his analysis of how Calvinist values and disciplinary practices regularized and rationalized behavior led to what became a view of the disenchantment of the world. This insight became the foundation of the popular secularization theory according to which societies become less religious and more secular as they modernize. With the continued flourishing of Fundamentalism and Evangelicalism in this country, and the eruption of so-called Islamic and Hindu fundamentalism, there has been a reevaluation of the secularization theory. I never accepted this line of argument because it sets up a specious opposition between religion and secularity. In the West, which is what secularization theory is supposed to explain, secularism is a *religious* phenomenon. For Luther and for Calvin, the so-called secular world has religious value. This is the basis of Luther's doctrine of vocation, which informs Calvin's argument about the importance of Protestantism for capitalism. In ways it took me a while to understand, my conviction that religion is most influential where it is least obvious is a Protestant insight.

Ever since the rise of the religious right in the late 1960s, commentators have focused on the influence of Protestant Evangelicals. While Evangelicals have tended to support Republicans, Protestant pastors like Timothy LaHaye and Ted Haggard initially supported Jimmy Carter. When Carter supported the Equal Rights Amendment, the religious right broke with him and threw their support to Reagan. The rest is history—neither Bush II nor Trump would have been elected without the support of Evangelicals, and, indeed, they might decide the coming election. No less important, though much less noted, is the enormous impact of conservative Catholics. I have already discussed the importance of Barr's Catholicism for his ideological agenda. With the nomination of Barrett, not only conservatives but also Catholics have a majority on the Supreme Court. This is no accident—rather, it is the result of a decades-long covert campaign. It would be interesting to know the religious dynamics of the Federalist Society. In all likelihood both *Roe vs. Wade* and Obamacare will be overturned and who knows what else will change.

The current constitution of the Supreme Court raises profound questions about how diversity is defined. With the new appointment, there will be one African American, one Hispanic, and three women. In matters of religion and education, however, as distinct from race or ethnicity, the Supreme Court is one of the least diverse institutions in the country. What would Weber say about this?

| | College | Law School | Religion |
|---|---|---|---|
| Roberts | Harvard | Harvard | Catholic |
| Thomas | Holy Cross | Yale | Catholic |
| Breyer | Stanford | Harvard | Jewish |
| Alioto | Princeton | Yale | Catholic |
| Sotomayor | Princeton | Yale | Catholic |
| Kavanaugh | Yale | Yale | Catholic |
| Kagan | Princeton | Harvard | Jewish |
| Gorsuch | Columbia | Harvard | Raised Catholic, Episcopalian |
| Ginsburg | Cornell | Harvard-Columbia | Jewish |
| Barrett | Rhodes | Notre-Dame | Catholic |

Before class tomorrow morning, I will send a third email: How is diversity defined?

Mark


*September 27*

Dear Mark:

There are those who deny or cannot even conceive the possibility of human extinction. There are others, however, and their number seems to be growing, who, faced with the mounting evidence of this possibility, are prepared preemptively to embrace it. Today, Todd Boss sent his supporters a new poem with a cover note confessing his own preemptive despair. The poem, entitled "Haplodiploidy," is about the likelihood that bees, as a species, may outlive the human species. Todd's poem, playful in a way that belies his declared ecodespair, suggests that bees will outlive us because

their mode of reproduction, the haplodiploidy of the title, results in queen
bees who relate more closely to one another than to their own children. A
major formal strength of his is internal rhyme, and the closely calculated
spacing in this poem highlights the internal rhymes for anyone reading it
aloud, as I discovered reading it aloud to Kitty last night. Here are the final
two stanzas:

> Imagine
> a civilization
> run
> by terrifying
> women
> who love one
>   another more
> than they love their
> own
> children.
>
>   A species
> that preceded ours
>   (by a hundred
> thirty millions years)
> —a sisterhood
>   hung
> in honey
>   and flowers—
>   clinging
> to temporal matters—
>   will,
> a hundred
>   million more
> after ours is in
>   tatters,
> by sheer
>   sororal powers
>     still
>     thrive.

The poem delights me, I confess. Alas, I myself am not at all sure that bees will survive the human species. We seem to have been making fair progress of late in wiping them out, despite our extreme dependence upon them and their pollination. We might take them down with us, or vice versa. The spectacle lately before us has been the ongoing mass extinction of other species through our actions. To be sure, the inference that our turn may come is hard to avoid, although, obviously, millions do avoid it or, in a more day-to-day struggle to keep body and soul together, scarcely have a moment free to think about such a question. But if the bees are as doomed as we are, then the ecodespair that provoked Todd to write this poem is only the more deeply warranted.

You write this week in a vein of similar despair about surveillance capitalism at its perhaps irremediable Marxist/Hegelian logical and malignant extreme: "I have no idea how to fix it; nor does anybody else." But earlier in the synthesis that you limn in this week's report, you do see fit to write rather less bleakly: "The real problem is that the design of the entire infrastructure *as well as the business model that keeps it running* makes it impossible to regulate the media virus infecting the global body politic." But business models made by men can be unmade by men. Infrastructure designed to serve the goals stipulated in the models can be dismantled and rebuilt to serve another model business model, can they not—to serve even, conceivably, a nonprofit, regulated-public-utility model. If the prospect of that happening seems slight, there is still no reason to regard it as somehow a logical impossibility.

The odds that a business model and its servant technology can be revised certainly seem higher than the odds that accelerating natural processes set in motion by centuries of human activity can be slowed or paused within just a few years by countervailing human activity. Have you ever heard quoted the following line, perhaps apocryphal, attributed to Martin Luther? Asked as he was planting an apple tree what he would do if told that the world would end tomorrow, he said, after a pause, that he would proceed to plant the apple tree. I thought of that line as I listened yesterday to a talk Ram Ramanathan delivered to a "climate summit" of K–12 teachers gathered at UCSD. He began his remarks with a saying of Confucius (possibly also apocryphal, I venture to guess) that went approximately as follows:

If you are planning for next year, plant rice.
If you are planning for ten years hence, plant a tree.
If you are planning for one hundred years hence, educate
children.

No one is more aware than Ram of how little time remains to stabilize the
climate. In the same talk, he cited a brief paper of his published in *Nature* in
2018 noting that it had taken two hundred years of the Industrial Revolution (1780–1980) to raise the global temperature by one degree. But, citing
new research not then included in IPCC estimates, he and his coauthors
predicted the rise of another half degree within just fifty years—in other
words, by 2030. From this, he and his colleagues inferred that the decade
2020–2030 is a kind of last chance to slow the acceleration before it becomes
unstoppable to even the point of an "extinction event." In his talk to the
teachers, Ram also included a remarkably detailed pie chart indicating the
percentage of slowing to be realized from each of several needed and technically quite possible measures during the coming decade. The cost is undeniably enormous, but the alternative is a worse enormity. And I know, from
hearing him respond ex tempore to questioners asking the basis for one or
another of his claims, that he ventures nothing for which he does not have
fullest backing. (He is scornful of Al Gore for making certain claims in *An
Inconvenient Truth* for which there was no adequate backing.)

Some claims, of course, he makes at a relatively low level of probability.
But regarding the likelihood of runaway global warming, supposing that
likelihood to be reckoned as low as 5 percent, he asks, "Would you board a
plane with a one-in-twenty chance of crashing?" And then he goes on:
"You're putting your grandchildren on that global-warming plane, and
they won't have the option of getting off."

From these last considerations, you would expect him to be utterly given
over to lobbying for immediate policy changes in a mood of national and
global emergency. He is, to be sure, always included at the successive COP
conferences, and yet his vision makes room for *kindergarten* education in
environmental protection! That's why he was addressing (and probably
helped provoke) this gathering of K-12 teachers. I find in his optimism a kind
of secular faith that, perhaps because it can *only* be a matter of faith, fosters
his openness to partnerships between organized religion and environmental

science. His is clearly more than a hold-your-nose expediency, but just where it comes from is a bit of a mystery—this despite the fact that he is nonchalantly open about his personal history, beginning in an impoverished village in Tamil Nadu. He was once admittedly happy, for example, to use his brilliance to live large in the American manner. He loved his sleek seventies Impala until—the expression seems only too appropriate—he got religion. He underwent a Jamesian conversion experience. But his is a kind of religion that feeds primarily upon his scientific research and what it has done to him as a man.

As for his cooperation with the Vatican, he did not seek it out. It turns out that the Pontifical Academy of the Sciences is a group of only some seventy scientists, by no means all Catholics but all members by invitation only. Becoming a member is like becoming a MacArthur Fellow. There is no way to apply, but one day you may get an unexpected call. His came when he was lecturing at the University of Kenya, where an Indian friend and colleague of his, also a scientist, is a professor. But the experience of thus being invited in seems to have engendered in him a vision of religion/science alliances, beginning with Catholicism, that he fearlessly professes and not without some negative feedback from colleagues who, however, cannot deny his scientific brilliance.

I feel honestly that I have very little to offer Ram other than my services, if he finds them useful, as a ghostwriter for popular work. I have long thought, as you know from an earlier letter linked to real estate, that it could be acceleration in the rate and severity of wildfire in California that would convert the climate-change deniers in this state into believers. And as goes California in such matters, so often goes the United States. The imminent (10/3) papal encyclical *Fratelli tutti* provided me a handy news hook for a piece with this as my real agenda, and I have now drafted an op-ed that Ram may or may not find acceptable. It is very difficult, I think, for any full-fledged intellectual to accept another's words as his own. Even when there is no substantive disagreement, there is an attachment to nuances that only the man or woman in question knows enough to be fully aware of.

So, we'll see what happens to what I've written. What I find rather sadly telling, however, is that though I propose that Ram and I give the piece a final revision once the encyclical is in hand, I found it possible so easily to

LABOR DAY

anticipate the thrust of the encyclical that I could write a complete and plausible piece in advance. Perhaps I overestimate the predictability of the pope; perhaps I am even insulting him. *Laudato si'*, its content aside, was profoundly different in style from any twentieth-/twenty-first-century encyclical that I have read. But I think that my hunch will prove correct and that I have guessed the thrust from the minimally announced content and just the detail that its inspiration is, again, St. Francis of Assisi. The tragedy, meanwhile, is that the pope's attachment to the unbearable sexual regimen of the church or, in any case, his failure to bring about any revision in that area has by now grievously shrunk the high hopes that were entertained for him at the start along with the wide and warm reception that for a time he was receiving beyond the church. He can still speak on the environment and be heard but not nearly so well as several years ago.

You will have seen the monster headline (I grow tired of these games with giant type) yesterday in the *New York Times* "Sunday Review" section: "AMERICA IS UNGOVERNABLE." As it happens, this message lands at a moment when I find myself almost sneakily optimistic. The Republicans will, yes, put Professor Coney Barrett on the Supreme Court, but the extremity of their action will both enable and justify a Democratic counteraction, if the election goes as it well may, that will include abolishing the filibuster, enlarging the court by four new justices, and going on from there in reformist ways for which we have an early draft c/o Adam Schiff. Ross Douthat confesses a similar optimism, arriving at it from a different starting point than mine, in his exceptionally thoughtful essay in the same section of the Sunday *Times*.

And it matters, too, that the Republicans are going to such extremes in their attempt to suppress the vote that, as these virulently antidemocratic measures come fully to light, they may further warrant Democratic reforms that could accrue to a major new departure for our country, from its electoral system on up. I am thinking of the fact that when Michael Bloomberg announced his willingness to pay the court debts of any and every Florida ex-felon with court debts barring his path to the voting booth, Florida Republicans immediately sued to block his generosity. When the Republican Senate blocked funds for the states in support of the elections and private donors stepped in to help, Republicans elsewhere again sued to impede this private and patriotic generosity. All this does seem to me to be the Right taking just enough rope to hang itself.

I had decided to make *Seeing Silence* my reading through a four-hour skin surgery procedure today (brief surgeries interrupted by long waits for on-the-spot biopsies of the excised cancerous tissue). The choice was a good one, and I was quite engrossed. I had just barely begun the book as of last night. Checking the spot where I would resume just before I went to bed, I happened on p.17 upon Ludwig Wittgenstein's most famous line, which, in the Ogden translation you quote is "Whereof one cannot speak, thereof one must be silent." But I have long thought that this and other similar translations of *Worüber man nicht sprechen kann, daran muss man schweigen* miss a nuance in the German verb *mussen*, which typically expresses logical necessity rather than moral obligation: for moral obligation, *sollen* is the modal verb of choice, as in Kant's famous *Du kannst weil du sollst*. Thus, if you say in German, *Dass möchte sein, aber es muss nicht*, the idiomatic translation in English would be, "That could be, but not necessarily." So, a translation that I suspect would be closer to Wittgenstein's intent would be "Of necessity, one does not speak of that of which one is incapable of speaking." The *Tractatus*, after all, is about logic rather than morality, and this remains true when, as you remind us, logic for Wittgenstein apprehends what logic cannot comprehend, growing mystical at its limit. This may easily be granted, and yet we need not hear him delivering any kind of exhortation.

This matter, I regret to say, troubled my sleep last night. Or perhaps I was just a bit sleepless, as anyone might be on the eve of surgery, and the last item of the day, this little conundrum, happened to be there to fill the wakeful spaces. I find it interesting, by the way, just to linger a moment longer on the linguistics of silence, that English has no verb available to translate the German *schweigen*—that is, no verb "to sile." English could have developed such a verb: our "silent" comes from the Latin verb *silere*, but from that antecedent only the participle survives as a participial adjective in our language. German expresses silence through an active, intransitive verb, making silence an action, which is signaled also by its using the verb *sein* rather than *haben* as an auxiliary. French and Italian express silence through a reflexive verb: one is silent by silencing oneself. We do have in

English the transitive verb "to silence," but we never use it reflexively. The English speaker silences others but never him/herself!

Or so, ruminatively, one could begin to speculate, but the conventions of language are arbitrary, while the underlying philosophical problems—the ones you address in this book—are really common across language barriers. Fascinating as the language differences are, they can bear only a very little weight.

One final, airy note:

My "Mr. Rogers" video on Noah (at emir-stein.org) has now attracted more than 100,000 views [updated in January 2021: 360,000]. My hunch is that these are disproportionately Muslim views and that the reason is that I say near the end that God in the Bible is a more fearful figure than God in the Qur'an because he plays fair and gives people a chance to escape the Great Flood, while God in the Bible does not. My intent is irenic, but my audience may appreciate me for other than irenic reasons.

Jack

\* \* \*

## OCTOBER 4: MARK BEGINS.

*Autumn on Stone Hill and* Autumn *in Karl Ove Knausgaard's seasons quartet: "Silence, eternity, nothingness" . . . Depression—or deflation—as the climate-change tipping point passes before our eyes . . . chthonic webs (of death) within cosmic webs (of birth) . . . the edge of time as the edge of knowability . . . physical inconsequence, psychic grandeur.*

*Elon Musk: Are we living in a computer simulation? Can we know? . . . Descartes: the same question three centuries ago . . . evolution as Descartes's demon . . . how mortality, once recognized, fosters reproductive success . . . the depersonalization (now, with Tinder) and the robotification (soon, with AI) of sexual pleasure . . . cui bono? . . . attendance, twice, at a drag show as a latter-day courtship ritual.*

---

*October 4*

Dear Jack:

This is peak foliage time in the Berkshires and the reds and yellows of the maple trees' leaves are brilliant this year. It's always easy to remember the date because peak color is the weekend of Aaron's birthday. He turns forty-eight on Tuesday, which is hard to believe. The *New York Times* today has an article on leaf-viewing road trips and our neighborhood is ranked number one. In a normal time, the roads would be jammed with leaf viewers, but not this year. Yesterday Dinny and I hiked up a nearby ridge where there is an outlook that affords a spectacular view of the valley. Each weekday in the late afternoon, I run back the woodland trail along Stone Hill. In a few weeks when we go off daylight savings time, it will be too dark to run and I will have to exercise inside on treadmill and elliptical. On Sundays, I run in the morning, and I just returned from today's jog. I am always intrigued by how different the light in the forest is at different times of day. As the sun drifts south and falls lower in the sky, the differences between morning and afternoon light become more pronounced.

We have discussed Knausgaard's *My Struggle* and even noted certain similarities and differences between his chronicling of the everyday and ours.

While I was intrigued enough by this work to complete more of it than I
had time to read, I really prefer his four brief volumes on the seasons,
where he, in effect, creates a calendar of moods. I have described the sweet
melancholy of autumn on Stone Hill in a previous letter. In ways that I
cannot describe, sound and its absence change with the seasons. Regard-
less of the time of year, I am always absorbed by the silence along Stone
Hill; rarely do I hear a sound—no birds, no animals, no human voices, only
rarely the rustling of leaves. In *Autumn*, Knausgaard comes close to capturing this silence.

> The silence does something to the landscape and, through it, to us. All
> sounds are linked to the moment, they belong to the present, that
> which changes, while silence is connected with the changeless, in
> which time does not exist. It is eternity but also nothingness, which
> are two sides of the same coin.

Eternity and nothingness—two sides of the same coin.

Your letter this week expresses a mood I have not previously detected.
I've been trying to figure out the right word for it, and the closest I can
come is "deflated." Given the accelerating downward spiral of world events
and the endless serious medical issues with which you are dealing, this
mood is completely understandable. Nonetheless, the change in mood
from earlier letters is noteworthy. You ended your last letter with the op-
ed on the climate crisis you wrote with Ram Ramanathan. The tone of
your words was full of energy and even, I dare say, hope. Since you have
now submitted it to the *Washington Post*, I assume the *Times* didn't work
out. The Trump nonsense is drowning out discussion of so much that matters. Though you have long been deeply concerned about climate change, it
was the publication of Pope Francis's encyclical this week that moved you
to action and made you think the time might be right for a strategic intervention. It now seems that the Pope's statement was not all you had hoped
it would be, and your disappointment was deepened by the attack on the
encyclical by a branch of the Catholic radical right, which we discussed in
relation to William Barr and Amy Coney Barrett.

The timing of your letter was uncanny. This week I am teaching my
friend Elizabeth Kolbert's book *Field Notes from a Catastrophe* in my Recovering Place seminar. Betsy lives across the valley and I have long admired

her important work. After reading your letter early this morning, I checked my email and discovered David Remnick's weekend mailing of *New Yorker*'s classics. The topic this week is The Global Climate Crisis and the last article he includes is Betsy's essay "Greenland Is Melting." I then proceeded to my Sunday morning ritual of reading the *New York Times*, where I found an article entitled "A Satellite Lets Scientists See Antarctica's Melting Like Never Before" (originally published April 30, 2020). The color picture that appears with the article leaves absolutely no doubt that we are at or have passed the tipping point. When the South Pole glows red, you know you are in deep trouble. Most people simply do not understand the importance of glacial melting. In *Field Notes*, Betsy explains with admirable clarity and concision the way the combination of the disappearance of sea ice and the melting of glaciers increases greenhouse gases and alters ocean currents in a way that changes weather patterns across the globe.

In preparation for class on Wednesday, I have also been rereading Betsy's Pulitzer Prize–winning book, *The Sixth Extinction*, which should be mandatory reading for every CEO and member of Congress. The scale, rate, and implications of species extinction that she describes are chilling. What I find most intriguing in her account, however, is the intricacy of the web of life she describes. In the course of our correspondence, we have discussed networks, webs, connectivity, and relativity or relationality in abstract philosophical terms. In her account of flora and fauna from the Arctic and deserts to coral reefs and rain forests, Betsy tells the story of astonishing interrelation and intervolution. In countless instances, the difference between survival and extinction is a few milligrams of a chemical or a fraction of a degree in temperature. The slightest alteration ripples through the entire ecosystem with cascading effects that are completely unpredictable. Coral reefs, like forests, function as a single organism. According to reliable estimates, four thousand species of fish and an estimated 25 percent of all marine life depend on coral reefs for their survival. Furthermore, oceans absorb carbon dioxide from the air. When more greenhouse gases are emitted into the atmosphere, oceans absorb more carbon dioxide and seawater becomes more acidic. This increase in acidity interrupts the production of calcium necessary to produce the coral that protects the vital organs of the reef. As bleaching occurs, the reef slowly dies and the marine species that depend on it become extinct. Though our ancestors left water for land millions of years ago, we are still part of the web that is bound to ocean depths.

 The webs within which we are suspended are not merely planetary, they are also cosmic. Another article in the *Times* today boggles the mind: "At the Edge of Time, a Litter of Galactic Puppies—The Discovery of a Black Hole Surrounded by Protogalaxies Provides Astronomers with a Rare Glimpse of the Web of Matter Permeating the Cosmos." Dennis Overbye reports,

> Astronomers announced on Thursday that they had discovered a giant black hole surrounded by a litter of young protogalaxies that date to the early universe—the beginning of time.
>
> The black hole, which powers a quasar known as SDSS J1030+0524, weighed in at a billion solar masses when the universe was only 900 million years old. It and its brood, the astronomers said, represented the infant core of what became a vast cluster of galaxies millions of light years across and encompassing a trillion suns worth of matter. The discovery should help astronomers understand the origins of galactic clusters— the largest structures in the universe—and how supermassive black holes could have grown so quickly in the early universe. And it provides a rare glimpse of the cosmic web, a network of filaments spanning the cosmos that determine the large-scale distribution of matter in the universe.

Is it really possible for finite minds to comprehend this infinity? Does even the smartest scientist truly understand black holes, or is this merely a different name for the navel of Freud's dream, which, he claims, is the point of contact with the unknowable? Who really can explain distances measuring millions of light years or volumes encompassing a trillion suns worth of matter? I had never even heard of this cosmic web of matter that I now learn is widely accepted by scientists. We are indeed nodes in a web that is spatially and temporally incomprehensible. As I struggled to understand this article, I once again returned to the question, "What, then, is time?," from St. Augustine's *Confessions* that I quoted in the first paragraph of the first book I ever published.

"The quasar SDSS J1030+0524," Overbye writes,

> clocked in with a redshift of 6.31, meaning that light waves from it—indeed,
> the size of the whole universe—have been stretched by a factor of 7.31 since
> the time of the quasar. That corresponds to when the universe was 900
> million years old, according to conventional cosmological calculations.
> That means it took 12.9 billion years for the light from that quasar to reach
> Earth, making it one of the most distant quasars ever discovered.

Pause to ponder this statement—what scientists are now observing
occurred 12.9 billion years ago! Now try to imagine 12.9 billion years into
the future. That puts climate change, to say nothing of the juvenile political circus swirling around us, in a totally different perspective.

Knausgaard concludes a section of *Autumn* entitled "Daguerrotype"
with a meditation on photographs similar to my account of old photographs in the first chapter of *Seeing Silence*.

> That there is something ghostly about all photographs from this early
> period is due not merely to the haziness and indistinctness of their
> subject matter, which seems almost to hover, as if the material objects
> depicted belonged to another dimension, but also because they don't
> portray people. The exposure time was several hours, so that only
> unmoving objects were fixed to the plate. That is perhaps the most
> incredible thing about these early photographs, that they related to
> time in such a way that only the most lasting of appearances are visible
> and the human form is shown to be so fleeting and ephemeral that it
> leaves no trace anywhere.

Whether the seventh, the eighth, the ninth, or the tenth extinction, the
human race will pass away, but the cosmic web that momentarily sustains
us will not. Deflation or inflation? Accepting this fact that you are part of
a cosmic web can either make you feel very small and insignificant, or very
large because you are part of the Infinite itself.

Eternity but also nothingness—two sides of the same coin. That is what
I see in the silence of the light on Stone Hill on these precious autumn days
just before the maple trees lose their glowing red leaves and stand bare for
the harsh winter that lies ahead.

Mark

*October 4*

Dear Mark:

We've agreed that although the COVID-19 plague is still with us, our "plague diary," to use its original and still working title, will end with the 2020 election.

Two observations about that:

First, we didn't call it "election diary" and yet we're allowing the election to close it.

Second, the election will not end on election day, November 3rd, 2020.

So, we are left with a degree of uncertainty about the duration of this correspondence. My sense is that we will continue until, at some point after election day, some kind of resolution has been achieved about the course our country is to follow into its immediate future. I am staggered to have just written and meant such a sentence, but such just now is our American world.

Your intellectual bias is always away from individual agency and toward large processes, either imponderable in principle or else perceptible only by a visionary few. In a previous letter, rather than see fascism as the work of fascists, you elaborated a vision of technological determinism yielding political outcomes that, after the fact, some might choose to see as descriptively fascist but that, essentially, are another phenomenon entirely. This week, the visionary few are those attending the (annual?) Code Conference sponsored in 2016 by Vox Media. I can't tell from your letter whether the proceedings of the conference are available at its website. This seems doubtful, a priori, given the character of the participants and their discussions. But you have at least read an account or comment on the conference by Joshua Rothman, who singled out Elon Musk's answer to an audience member's question about the "possibility that we are actually living in a computer simulation."

You say that this question "was motivated by a 2003 paper written by the influential Swedish-born Oxford philosopher Nick Bostrom...'Are You Living in a Computer Simulation?'" I may be wrong, but I will guess that no

philosopher asking that question could easily avoid René Descartes specu-
lating, as part of his systematic-doubt self-interrogation, about whether an
"evil demon" had not arranged for his or our entire human perceptual apparatus and all that we *think* we see to be an elaborate demonic illusion. For
me and I am sure for many others, that seventeenth-century question has
been reinscribed in our current understanding of the evolution of intelligence. All intelligence is species-specific, and each species perceives only its
own reality; evolution is, in effect, the demon that brings about this relationship between the perceiving animal and what the animal perceives as
"the world" in each specific case. It is thus an act of Cartesian faith, not of
observation, to postulate that our species perceives reality as it is.

Let me suggest one example—namely, the commonplace that only our
species understands that it is mortal. In functional, evolutionary perspective, the reproductive success of our species is powerfully fostered by our
age-old perception that the progenitor dies while the offspring live on and
by the related distribution of identity across generations. Death thus recognized has been hugely adaptive for the human species by maximizing the
survival of offspring. It's clear that the ancient Israelites did not believe in
individual immortality at all but did believe that reproductive success was
its one available equivalent. Believing in mortality thus motivated them to
breed and to care for their offspring as for their greatest treasures. But one
may now ask, "Why should my children be my greatest treasures?" Why,
logically, should you care more about them than about yourself? Or more
about them than about anybody else you might choose to care about?
Questions at least adjacent to these animate Thomas Nagel's 1974 paper,
"What Is It Like to Be a Bat?" But if I were more widely read, I suspect I
could identify much earlier thinkers.

Your letter, in any case, takes the literal simulation that the Code Conference speculated about technologically, and (I would say) Descartes
anticipated conceptually, and employs it metaphorically. You write elo-
quently: "The digital technological miracles that were supposed to facilitate communication have, paradoxically, made communication virtually
impossible. When all media are customized and all news is personalized,
everyone becomes isolated in solipsistic bubbles." While I would argue
that, in fact, not *all* media are customized and not *all* news is personalized,
plenty is—easily enough, in fact, that the first of your sentences as I just

quoted them can be matched quite closely by a sentence in the papal encyclical that I skimmed and partially read in Spanish yesterday. The pope's
exhortation to the world is that its warring communities come out of their
respective solipsistic bubbles, Weber's iron cages, and recognize that common threats like the pandemic can only be met collectively.

My own bias if I can be trusted to identify it or confess to it is toward
personal rather than impersonal agency but not to the exclusion of large,
collective, often hidden, but nonetheless finally personal agency. So, in the
present instance, rather than speak of Trump as a symptom, I would speak
of him as a tool in the hands of those who, for empirically identifiable reasons of their own, want him reelected and by careful prior calculation are
attempting to invalidate the next election in advance so as to preserve
themselves in power through ensuing parliamentary manipulation. This
scheme may not work out, of course, but the cover story in today's *New
York Times Magazine*—"The Attack on Voting: How the False Claim of Voter
Fraud Is Being Used by Republicans to Disenfranchise Americans"—
details a well-planned effort operating on many fronts. The chaos that
swirls around Trump is partly real chaos and partly instrumental chaos in
the service of this group effort. It is because we cannot begin to guess at
this point how the election struggle will be resolved that you and I must
regard our correspondence as beyond conclusion on a date certain.

The speculations about gender and identity in my previous letter and
yours about artificial intelligence and identity in *Intervolution* intersect to
a degree in a double review today in the *New York Times Book Review*. The
two books under review are *Work Mate Marry Love: How Machines Shape
Our Human Destiny* by Debora L. Spar and *Sex Robots and Vegan Meat:
Adventures at the Frontier of Birth, Food, Sex, and Death* by Jenny Kleeman.
Claiming that hookup apps like Tinder have already made sex an impersonal matter for millions even as gender difference has been blurred down
to triviality, Spar pulls these social trends together and takes the further
technical step: "Because if we can love across gender and sex, if we can
harness technology to build bodies that defy reproductive logic, then we
can build bodies and intimacies that cross species as well." The reviewer is
unpersuaded by this vision, but you do see the connection, I'm sure. The
second book actually seems both more mind-blowing in its talk of sexual

robots, assisted suicide machines, and artificial wombs and more realistic in its attention to the *who* behind the *what*. Or, as in the classic Latin query, *Cui bono?* The reviewer comments that Kleeman "seems less invested in predicting the future than she is in questioning the people who are so obsessed with shaping it. Kleeman recognizes that technology has the power to shape human life, of course, but she is also interested in interrogating that power, and understanding who exactly gets to wield it." This turn toward the personal strikes me as archetypally a female move. The reviewer and both the writers are women: not so frequent a lineup in this realm so dominated by male venture capital and males in computer science.

And a final, perhaps bizarre item from the *Times* but one that seems somehow relevant to the foregoing. Kitty finds it fun to read the "Vows" feature in the Style section of the Sunday paper—vignettes of couples married in the previous week and how they found each other—and I have started doing so too. ("Vows" is a far cry from the little wedding write-ups that I did, precociously enough, for the *Northwest Times*, the neighborhood newspaper I worked for between eighth grade and high school!) The feature is evidently very popular, by the way: the *Times* gives it three full pages.

Today, one item is headed "The Second Drag Show Was Just to Make Sure." Lindsay and Sandy (guess which one is male and which female) met on Tinder and had a fairly promising first date. She wasn't sure where this would go, however, so she invited him to go to a drag show with her for their second date. He enjoyed it; "that was an important sign for me, that he was able to love a drag show, too." But then, just to be sure, she tested him further with a third date at a different drag show. They were married on the steps of the Second Bank of the United States, in Independence Park, on September 18. The Reverend Dr. Susan Richardson, an Episcopal priest, officiated. A socially distanced reception followed in another park. For the report in "Vows," the bride expressed her great joy in their wedding as follows: "Life is about making lemonade when life hands you lemons. And we're trying to embrace that." Lemons joined in love . . . with years of drag shows still ahead.

Jack

\* \* \*

## OCTOBER 10–11: MARK BEGINS.

*In the Berkshires, power outages frequent, cell phone reliability poor, dependency on both now extreme . . . contemporary bibliography for a climate-crisis course beginning with Empedocles's classic quartet: Earth, Air, Fire, Water . . . pro and con the razing and possible rising of the Los Angeles County Museum of Art . . . Louise Glück on her receipt of the Nobel Prize for literature . . . her "The Red Poppy" . . . Billy Collins's "Forgetfulness" . . . collating great horror movies for Halloween . . . Jacques Demy in the carefree Umbrellas of Cherbourg, vs. same director in the noir Model Shop . . . Wired magazine mirroring the indomitable optimism of the young?. . . Jane Smiley's A Thousand Acres as collateral reading for any Earth, Air, Fire, Water course . . . why, COVID aside, "Americans should stay the hell home" . . . how the Catholic Church (and Jesus himself) led the West into kinship relationships beyond the family.*

---

*October 10*

Dear Jack:

### *Interruption about Interruptions*

I'm thinking about the weather—your weather and mine. Yesterday afternoon a violent thunderstorm tore through town and knocked out power for the fourth time in the last month. Whenever there are such extreme weather events, I am always impressed by how much damage is done in such a short time. The most severe winds lasted no more than 4–5 minutes. Limbs and trees were down all over town. When electricity was restored 5 hours later, the cable and Internet remained out for another 17 hours. Completely cut off from the world, I finally dug out a radio, which I had not used for years, and tuned in to *NPR* to discover that two hundred thousand are without power in western Massachusetts and the Albany area. No word on how many are without Internet. With people working at home and school children in class online, this is a total mess. I emailed my friend H., complaining about living in a fourth world country. His consolation was, get used to it, because it's going to get much worse. Power outages in the Northeast are going to become much more frequent due to refusal to grant permits for pipelines and transmission lines. Our problems on Stone Hill are compounded because we have very unreliable cell phone coverage. Our NIMBY neighbors have delayed the construction of a cell tower that would improve reception. We now have to rely on Wi-Fi for our cellphones so when the Internet goes, we have no phone service.

You will recall that I had this problem last spring when the bear tore apart the cable running to the barn. That only took a day to repair; I fear this will take much longer. In *Speed Limits: Where Time Went and Why We Have So Little Left*, I examined the perils of connectivity. As networks have expanded and our lives have accelerated, there has been a widespread romanticization of the prewired world. Unplugging, however, is no longer possible. Fortunately, I do not teach until Monday and hopefully will be back online before then. Not being able to communicate with students and colleagues, to say nothing of family and friends, creates endless complications.

I had been planning to try to watch the Harris-Pence debate, but, of course, could not. I'm sure that would have been good for my blood pressure. I've not been able to read or listen to any of the commentators, so I have no idea how it went. Ever since I heard Kamala take on Biden in the primary and grill Barr during his confirmation hearings, I have wished she could debate Trump. To say Trump has a problem with women—especially strong women—is a vast understatement. I suspect Kamala would crush him in a one-on-one exchange. After the Biden-Trump farce, I really don't have anything else to add. The image of Trump with pumped-up chest wheezing, thick makeup appearing more orange than ever, standing at attention and saluting the military he disparages and actually endangers says it all. I sometimes get angry that this charade occupies so much of our mental energy when there are so many other things crying out for attention.

Let me withdraw from the endless buzz of the news to comment on my reading, teaching, and thinking this week. As I have mentioned, in my Recovering Place course, we discussed Elizabeth Kolbert's *Field Notes from a Catastrophe*. By coincidence, she has a short piece in this week's *New Yorker* outlining three possible responses to the climate crisis. As you noted, she appears to be more optimistic than you and Ram Ramanathan are in your op-ed. Her vision is, in fact, much darker, and I know from personal conversations that she expects the worst. Remember how she ends *The Sixth Extinction*:

> Right now, in the amazing moment that to us counts as the present, we are deciding, without quite meaning to, which evolutionary pathways will remain open and which will forever be closed. No other creature has ever managed this, and it will, unfortunately, be our most enduring legacy. The Sixth Extinction will continue to determine the course of life long after everything people have written and painted and built has been ground into dust and the giant rats have—or have not- inherited the earth.

In an earlier letter, I mentioned that if I teach Recovering Place next year, I am going to begin by reading books on the four elements that philosophers ever since Empedocles have argued comprise the universe. I have already discussed David Montgomery's book *Dirt*. When considering Betsy's book, I focused on water, which includes not only rainfall, flooding, and drought, but also the melting of glaciers, rivers, and oceans. Turning to air and fire, this week I read Tim Smedly's *Clearing the Air: The Beginning and End of Air Pollution*, and Stephen Pyne's *Fire: A Brief History*. While Smedly's study focuses on the UK, his data and conclusions readily apply to the United States. His argument clarifies that which is often overlooked—there is a distinction between the deleterious effects of greenhouse gases and air pollution. Pyne's study of fire is a shorter version of his opus *Fire in America: A Cultural History of Wildland and Rural Fire*, which is an extraordinary book. Needless to say, one of the reasons I have been so intrigued by fire is the ongoing threat you face. Your report that you are cutting back trees and shrubs around your house made the gravity of the situation all the more real.

Taken together, these books point to the wisdom of the ancient Greeks: the four elements continue to interact to make, unmake, and remake the world we live in. Montgomery focuses on the way different agriculture technologies and methods transform the earth and soil. He gives special attention to way plowing methods, pesticides, and fertilizers used in industrial farming destroy the structure and architecture of soil. This has a negative effect on both the air and water—wind-blown pulverized soil pollutes the air, and excessive fertilizers and pesticides pollute groundwater. Somewhere I read—might have been in Jared Diamond's *Collapse*—that for every one bushel of corn produced, seven bushels of topsoil are lost. In addition to polluting and destroying the soil to raise crops, the extensive use of antibiotics to fatten chickens, cattle, and hogs is destroying the biome upon which life depends. Antibiotics and pesticides also contaminate groundwater. Furthermore, industrial farming is draining aquifers dry. Whose bright idea was it to raise rice in the desert? I'm sure you know that the economics of water in Southern California are unsustainable.

Pyne's account of fire artfully crafts a story of the interplay of technology, culture, and history to create a narrative of the way fire has changed the world and shaped our lives. He explains the significance of the transition from natural to anthropogenic fire by following human development from the time of the Neanderthals to the present day. Changing sources of fuel and farming methods are central to the story he tells. Fire directly impacts the other three elements, even as they condition fire. Scorched earth alters the soil, which changes fauna, which, in turn, transforms the kind of fires that burn and their frequency. All fires obviously contribute to atmospheric warming and pollution.

The pollution of earth, air, and water, is not, of course, new. Some of the stories Smedly tells of nineteenth-century London are as dark as daily reports coming from Beijing, Delhi, and Los Angeles today. The difficulties with asthma you recently reported are without a doubt related to the pollution the fires are causing. I know this is a problem that has long worried you, even to the extent of arguing for the cancellation of conferences and professional meetings as a way of cutting down on air travel. In the category of facts you sorta know but prefer to know for sure—every gallon of gasoline burnt releases 5 pounds of $CO_2$ into the atmosphere. A 747 plane, which uses approximately 1 gallon of fuel per second, burns about 36,000 gallons of fuel during a ten hour flight. If these estimates are correct, then one ten-hour flight would emit 180,000 pounds or 90 tons of carbon dioxide. There are two relevant factors to analyze when considering the implications of this fact. First, the most dangerous emissions are not visible particulate matter that most people associate with air pollution, but invisible gases that both damage the lungs when inhaled and interact with other atmospheric gases in ways that are not fully understood; second, the widely acknowledged effect of high levels of $CO_2$ on atmospheric temperatures and hence the impact on climate change. An unexpected benefit from the pandemic is that the decrease in land and air travel across the world has led to a drop in air pollution.

No less important is the way fire, air, and water interact. The carbon emitted by the burning of fossil fuels creates massive amounts of $CO_2$ in the air, much of which is absorbed by the world's oceans, where it initiates a chemical reaction that leads to the increased acidity of seawater. The change in the composition of seawater alters ocean ecology. Higher levels of acidity inhibit the production of calcium, which coral reefs depend on to produce the shells that protect the organism. Increased acidity triggers a bleaching process that eventually kills reefs. Twenty-five percent of all marine life, including four thousand species of fish depend on coral reefs. This means that every time you fly on a plane, drive a car, or cut your lawn with a gas-fueled lawnmower, you are contributing to the death of coral reefs and accelerate a major extinction event.

A second way air and water interact actually changes ocean currents. Atmospheric warming leads to the disappearance of sea ice and accelerates glacial melting. By reflecting the sun's rays back into the atmosphere (the albedo effect), sea ice plays a significant role in regulating ocean temperatures. As air temperature increases, sea ice melts, triggering a positive feedback loop. The warmer the water, the more sea ice melts, and the more sea ice melts, the warmer the atmosphere gets. A second effect of warmer air temperatures is that glaciers melt faster. The current rate of glacial melting is alarming. According to reliable estimates, all the glaciers in Glacier National Park will be gone by 2030, and all sea ice in the world will disappear by 2080. As I'm sure you know, glaciers are made of fresh water rather than salt water. On land, melting glaciers provide fresh water for agricultural and domestic purposes as well as supplying drinking water for much of the world's population. For example, water from glaciers in Tibet feed the four major rivers in Asia. When these glaciers disappear, millions of people will not have enough potable water. The effect of melting glaciers on the sea is no less significant. Since fresh water and saltwater are different weights, when there is major melting, ocean currents change. This affects what scientists label the oceanic conveyor belt. This enormously important phenomenon is not well known, so it's worth quoting Kolbert's description.

> Owing both to evaporation and cooling, water from the tropics becomes denser as it drifts toward the Arctic; near Greenland a tremendous volume of seawater is constantly sinking toward the ocean floor. As a result of this process, still more warm water is drawn from the tropics toward the poles, setting up what is often referred to as a "conveyor belt" that moves vast amounts of heat around the globe.
>
> "This is the energy engine for the world climate," [Konrad] Steffen went on. "And it has just one source: the water that sinks down. And if you just turn the knob a little bit . . . we can expect significant temperature changes based on the redistribution of energy." One way to turn the knob is to heat the oceans, which is already happening. Another is to pour more freshwater into the polar seas. This is also occurring. . . . A total shutdown of the thermohaline circulation is considered extremely unlikely in the coming century. But, if the Greenland ice sheet were to start to disintegrate, the possibility of such a shutdown could not be ruled out. Wallace Broecker. . . . has labeled the thermohaline circulation the "Achilles' heel of the climate system: Were it to halt, places like Britain, whose climate is heavily influenced by the Gulf Stream, could become much colder, even as the planet as a whole continued to warm up.

In the few years since these words were published, melting in Greenland, Iceland, the Arctic and Antarctica has accelerated.

To grasp the significance of what is going on, it is necessary to understand the interrelation of fire, air, and water. The burning of fossil fuels as well as the forest fires raging around you dump millions of tons of greenhouse gasses into the atmosphere, which increases atmospheric temperatures. Oceans absorb $CO_2$, while at the same time warming temperatures melt sea ice and glaciers, thereby increasing freshwater and altering ocean currents. Shifting ocean currents alter the circulation of air, and shifting air currents change weather patterns. As a result of changing air currents, the distribution of water across the globe shifts, leading to droughts in some areas and floods in other areas. In California, drier air absorbs more moisture from the earth and trees, and hence increases the likelihood of forest fires. Once again, loops within loops within loops, all caught in accelerating positive feedback cycles. Sitting in the dark without power and cut off from communication with the outside world by increasingly violent storms, this is what I am worrying about, while the country is preoccupied with a buffoon who rejects the science that might save us.

Two unrelated but noteworthy points. The first concerns the Los Angeles County Museum of Art (LACMA), which, I know, you have been following. There is a long and informative article in the October 12 *New Yorker* by Dana Goodyear—"From the Ground Up; Will an L.A. Project Be Peter Zumthor's Masterpiece or a Fiasco?" For many years, Michael Govan, who is the director of the museum, has been a good friend of mine. Michael went to Williams and is a protégé of my erstwhile friend, Tom Krens. When Tom began planning what eventually became the Massachusetts Museum of Contemporary Art (Mass MoCA), Michael left the University of California San Diego, where he was studying for his MFA, and returned to Williamstown to help Tom. He moved with Tom when he went to the Guggenheim, where he was the deputy director at the ripe old age of twenty-four. From the Guggenheim, he moved to the DIA Foundation, where he created his version of Mass MoCA—Dia Beacon. Michael has always favored DIA-type artists—Michael Heizer, Walter De Maira, James Turrell, and Robert Irwin. Irwin designed both DIA Beacon and the gardens of the Getty, which I am sure you enjoyed when you worked there. For my money, Irwin's gardens eclipse Richard Meier's austere and uninviting structures. Meier and the Getty always seemed a mismatch to me. Michael is every bit as smart as Krens, and has considerably more social skill. I should also add that over the years he has been generous enough to help me arrange contacts with Heizer and Turrell.

Michael's charm initially took LA by storm and created high expectations, but recently he has run into serious problems. I was surprised by his choice of Peter Zumthor to design the new museum and by the decision to circumvent the customary solicitation of proposals from multiple architects. I suspect that I am not the only one who had never heard of Zumthor, and assume that much of the resistance the revised plans has encountered is a result of his obscurity and his lack of experience with major projects. I have not talked to Michael since the controversy has heated up so I have no idea how serious the problems are. Goodyear's article is quite informative and gives hints about what seems to be the heart of the problem. Michael knows art history cold and has a definite aesthetic. He is not interested in creating yet another encyclopedic museum, which, he knows, will never be able to compete with other such museums in this country and in Europe. In addition to this, he rightly thinks this model for a museum is a vestige of the past and is ill suited for the twenty-first century. From what I understand, he wants to create novel spaces in which it will be possible to retell the story of modern and contemporary art in a way that complicates the narrative Alfred H. Barr defined and the Museum of Modern Art canonized. It is noteworthy that MoMA's recent reinstallation of its collection recognizes this problem and has been designed to retell the story of modern art in a way that is more appropriate for our time. The problem MoMA faces is that the architectural design of the display spaces as rectilinear white boxes necessitates a linear structure that makes a teleological narrative unavoidable. Michael and Zumthor seem to be trying to create new spaces for a different way to encounter works of art. I would not bet against Michael. If the project is not derailed, I expect LACMA to have a world-class building that will do for LA what Gehry's Guggenheim did for Bilbao.

The second point, and much more briefly. I was delighted to hear that Louise Glück has received the Nobel Prize for literature. Though I admire Bob Dylan, he did not deserve the Nobel Prize, and his refusal to attend the award ceremony was arrogant and embarrassing. When was the last time a poet received the prize? I knew Louise a bit when she taught at Williams years ago and was always impressed by her thoughtfulness and willingness to engage in serious conversation. So often this award seems to be decided as much for political as for literary reasons. It seems everyone was pleasantly surprised by her selection, and I have yet to hear any objections. Her response to the announcement was telling in personal as well as political ways.

Completely flabbergasted that they would choose a white American lyric poet. It doesn't make sense. Now my street is covered with journalists. People keep telling me how humble I am. I'm not humble. But I thought, I come from a country that is not thought fondly of now, and I'm white, and we've had all the prizes. So it seemed to be extremely unlikely that I would ever have this particular event to deal with in my life.

I'm not sure if I ever told you the story about Aaron and the Nobel Prize in literature. A few years ago several books by Doris Lessing arrived from Amazon several days before Christmas. I had not ordered them and figured they were for Aaron to give to Frida. I put them aside and when I gave them to him, he said, "No, they are for me. A few years ago, I decided to read a couple of books by every author who has received the Nobel Prize in Literature since the year I was born [1972]." This from my son with a PhD in geochemistry who understands earth, air, fire, and water much better than I do. It seems my quant son understood some of the lessons his nonquant father tried to teach him. I am glad Aaron now will be reading Louise's poetry.

Mark

*October 11*

Dear Mark:

Let's begin with Louise Glück. I believe she's been a guest in the UCI MFA poetry program at one point or another. My good friend Michael Ryan, who retires as director of the program on 11/1/20, is a friend of hers. So, when the news broke, I sent him a quick message with a link to the *New York Times* story. He replied:

> Dear Jack:
> I trust you voted for our great Commander in Chief— or else we'll have to banish you forever from People of Praise. As well as kidnap you and hide you in our underground concrete bunker in Travers City and torture you mercilessly by playing 24/7 loudspeaker MAGA rally tapes. Like The Commander, I myself am a perfect physical specimen and I'm extremely young. That's why those commie Swedes picked Wheezie for the Nobel Prize, although I couldn't get them to release Hillary Clinton's emails or suspend the requirement for the winner to grow eyebrows like Coleslaw Miloscz.
>
> Such fun days, eh? Who coulda thunk it?
> November one is my official exit date, after fifty years in this racket. After schlepping 8–5 his whole life, my dad would have said it was "a racket" and he was right. I caught the wave and thank you Jesus.

Happily, all that education almost made me able to negotiate the labyrinth of UC retirement and insurance-with-Medicare, which made the great mythic tasks feel like a slow dance with a gentle lady.

Speaking of which, I hope you and Kitty are well. O Lord deliver us on November 3.

M

All of my poetry books, which amount to quite a few boxes, are still in storage, but Kay Ryan, when poet laureate, did the laureate's usual "Poem in Your Pocket" anthology, where you can peel off a poem and put it on your refrigerator if so moved. Kay did a fabulous job, and fortunately Kitty had that collection on her shelves, so on our refrigerator just now is this by Louise:

"The Red Poppy"

The great thing
Is not having
A mind. Feelings:
Oh, I have those; they
Govern me. I have
A lord in heaven
Called the sun, and open
For him, showing him
The fire of my own heart, fire
Like his presence.
What could such glory be
If not a heart? Oh my brothers and sisters,
Were you like me once, long ago,
Before you were human? Did you
Permit yourselves to open once, who would never
Open again? Because in truth
I am speaking now
The way you do. I speak
Because I am shattered.

This is a wonderful poem for almost any day, but I was reading it, of course, just after the implosion of my little project to write, with

Ramanathan, of a brotherhood among humans and trees. *Shattered* . . . the
trees are shattered indeed in California, by the millions. The wildfires
constitute less their execution than their postmortem cremation. We have
all been their executioners. I think of Robert Oppenheimer at the first
nuclear detonation: "I am become Shiva, the destroyer; Death, the shat-
terer of worlds." But I also think of Shakespeare: "How with this wrack
shall beauty hold a plea/ Whose action is no stronger than a flower?"
Glück wrote a poem about the wrack by way of the flower. She deserves
the prize.

You and I have both been coping with our respective mixes of environmental threat and infrastructure weakness. Yours led you to a long reflection
on Elizabeth Kolbert's latest in the *New Yorker*, "Three Scenarios for the
Future of Climate Change," with further particulars from your own wide
and general reading. More about that in a moment, but first I want to mention Kitty's wry delight in a Billy Collins poem that came to her via her
subscription to the American Poetry Society's "Poem of the Day" program.
The poem happened to land the day after a long and ultimately calming
conference call that she and I had with her primary care physician and just
as the news of Louise's Nobel was landing.

"Forgetfulness"

The name of the author is the first to go
followed obediently by the title, the plot,
the heartbreaking conclusion, the entire novel
which suddenly becomes one you have never read,
never even heard of,

as if, one by one, the memories you used to harbor
decided to retire to the southern hemisphere of the brain,
to a little fishing village where there are no phones.

Long ago you kissed the names of the nine muses goodbye
and watched the quadratic equation pack its bag,
and even now as you memorize the order of the planets,

something else is slipping away, a state flower perhaps,
the address of an uncle, the capital of Paraguay.

Whatever it is you are struggling to remember,
it is not poised on the tip of your tongue
or even lurking in some obscure corner of your spleen.

It has floated away down a dark mythological river
whose name begins with an L as far as you can recall

well on your own way to oblivion where you will join those
who have even forgotten how to swim and how to ride a bicycle.

No wonder you rise in the middle of the night
To look up the date of a famous battle in a book on war.
No wonder the moon in the window seems to have drifted
Out of a love poem that you used to know by heart.

Funnily enough, I actually thought of Billy Collins when I read in the
*Times*'s first comment on Glück's Nobel that hers was an accessible poetry,
not one dauntingly intellectual in content or obscure in manner. I also
thought of Jorie Graham as a much admired poet of whom no such comment will ever be made. Of Collins, I thought, first, "Yes, they are both
accessible, but her subject matter is often so much darker than his." But
then I read her own report of her reaction as she heard the news: she
thought of all the other fine American poets who could as easily and wor-
thily won as she. So true, of course, and I have thought such thoughts
myself as I have won my own few prizes and never doubted that certain
others were thinking them ungenerously of me. Collins has often been
faulted as a lightweight because his work is indeed unusually popular, but
no, he does not dodge the more difficult questions. In the end, my favorite
sentence on these competitions and their criteria was spoken by Saul Bel-
low, when asked of his reaction to the Nobel news: "The child in me is
delighted, the adult is skeptical."

Kathleen and Brian were here last night, as aware as either you or I of all
that faces our country and our world just now, with the added intensity
that comes from youth and the certainty that they will be coping with the
current crises long after we are gone. Yet their mood was the antithesis of
dejection. They were full of laughter and bursting with talk. We spoke of
the pros and cons of two or three of the dozen California voter initiatives

on the ballot. They spoke with pleasure and amusement of Pete Buttigieg's new chapter as designated liberal on Fox News, how he has repeatedly tied his hosts in knots to the point that they must cut to commercials rather than attempt a riposte. Fox evidently keeps him on, political embarrassment be damned, because he's proving great for ratings.

Brian writes for Fandango, which has regularly sent him off to Toronto or Telluride or Vienna or wherever to write on the major film festivals. But now? Few new films opening. Virtual film festivals a pale shadow of what actual film festivals were. What is left for him to do? What is left turns out to be curating the huge but almost entirely uncurated libraries of online film providers. Fandango, which owns Vudu, is in that game itself but apparently can benefit from the attention that Brian pays even to films streaming elsewhere. As I learned of his current work, I thought of the French circumlocution for what we call an editor, as, for example, Jon Segal at Knopf or Alan Thomas at Chicago; the phrase is *directeur de collection*. That phrase came to mind because, for example, this month Brian has pulled together a collection of haunted house films just in time for Halloween viewing. After Kitty and I enjoyed the late Jacques Démy's *The Umbrellas of Cherbourg*, I asked Brian if he knew of another film, not an opera, like that one, in which every word is sung. He knew of none but went on to tell me of Démy's other, nonmusical, black-and-white work, utterly different in mood, often bleak, never popular but, in his view, searching and still worth watching. I am hoping to find online one among these entitled *Model Shop*, a noir film set in Los Angeles during the 1960s and featuring Anouk Aimée as a woman forced by penury to work as a nude model in a down-market studio. Backdrop to the film is race relations and antiwar activism in the LA of that decade. I am getting "into" film in new ways.

Kathleen brought along two items for our edification. One is a copy of the London magazine *Monocle*, which at a quick glance seems very roughly like a British version of *New York Magazine*, with a little less politics and a little more culture/ideas. Unprompted, *Monocle* chose to do a little feature on the debut of *Noēma*, interviewing Nathan Gardels and Kathleen for the occasion. In the article, Kathleen is photographed at full length, looking rather like a high-polish New York editor. She mentioned that Nathan shrewdly and successfully lobbied against any heavy Berggruen Institute publicity for the *Noēma* launch. You never know, as you start a new magazine, he argued, whether your first issue will put your best foot forward. Best to let the world find a new magazine on its merits alone, and then, once you're sure you know what you're doing and what works, risk a little pump-priming.

Dad's other reading assignment from his daughter was the 28.13 issue of *Wired* magazine. (I did not know she was a subscriber, but she is.) This issue bears the headline "AMERICAN HUSTLE. U.S. Elections Are in the Middle of a Major Reboot. Our Democracy Will Come Out Stronger." And the contents, article after article, just exude optimism and confidence. Silicon Valley whistling in the dark? Irrational exuberance from inside a bubble? I have yet to dip in, but I am prepared to be cheered.

Perhaps the most interesting discussion of our evening was about the novel *Stoner* by the late John Williams. Brian included in his wedding vows an excerpt from *Stoner* on the discovery of love, its power, and its meaning. As it happens, the title character in the novel, an unhappily married professor of English, discovers the meaning of love with his mistress, but Kathleen took no umbrage over that detail. What most intrigued me is that, as I learned from them, fully three long central chapters in the book are devoted to a doctoral dissertation defense on the subject of medieval grammar. Defending intellectual standards with passion, Professor Stoner wants to deny the candidate his doctorate. But Professor Stoner is, otherwise and to this point in the book, an intelligent, decent, but generally passive-to-apathetic fellow. Life has dealt him one bad break after another, and he is, as it were, just serving out his life term—honorably but most unspectacularly. The dissertation controversy rouses him to unwonted passion; his unexpected love affair does as well. But that's it.

*Stoner* wrote only three novels. One was short-listed for the Pulitzer but did not win. None of the three sold well or were widely reviewed. He died in complete obscurity, but then, years after his death, *Stoner* became an improbable sensation in France, then in England, and very belatedly, around 2011–2012, in the United States. It was then that Brian read the novel, which clearly has strong autobiographical elements, and was captured by it. I myself was simply astonished at the thought of a novel building (as they report) enormous suspense in the protracted presentation of a doctoral defense, so I intend to read it or perhaps, with Kitty, listen to an audiobooks version if one is to be had.

I am intrigued if left just a bit dubious by the readings that you plan on assembling for an iteration of your Recovering Place course, now to be elaborated along the classical categories of earth, air, fire, and water. A number of other works popped into my mind as I read your bibliography for this course. One was Jane Smiley's novel *A Thousand Acres*, which is set in Iowa and in which the pollution of Iowa groundwater by pesticides becomes finally decisive in a story that initially seems to be one of sibling rivalry among three sisters, all heirs to the same farm. When I think of "rice in the desert," I think of the book *Cadillac Desert* and of the reclaimed delta of the Sacramento River, protected by levees that enable rice cultivation fed by the river's diverted water. Those levees are now superannuated, and many reports at the time of Hurricane Katrina warned of the catastrophe that will result if and when they break.

As for monstrously polluting international jet travel, especially that done for purely recreational purposes, I thought of my own op-ed in the *Washington Post* against it, of the 10,000+ hits it drew, and of the flow of hostile letters denouncing this outrageous indictment of every American's right to travel where and how they choose. COVID-19 has spread a huge cloud over the planet, but the silver lining in that cloud has been the happy collapse of recreational air travel. Americans should stay the hell home, if you ask me.

You mention Jared Diamond at one point, and I will be mentioning him myself later in this letter, but with regard to the pollution of the oceans, he once commented to me that he thought what would trigger a major shift in the world's awareness of or belief in the reality of climate change—if any such shift truly ever will occur—would be the collapse of the world's ocean fisheries and the ensuing hunger among those (largely South Asians, I suspect) who depend on the seas for food so much more heavily than we do.

My dubiety about this makeover of your Recovering Place course stems simply from what seems a major shift in mood away from the experience of the unique local, of locatedness, placement, rootedness, and that entire set of subjective or experiential topics and toward the vast, the global, the impersonal, and necessarily the morally confrontational. Your students have less need, I suspect, of your take on that latter set of topics than of your invitation to the former set.

Your climate change reflections were significantly prompted by Elizabeth Kolbert's "Three Scenarios," about which I believe I said in an email that she was more optimistic than Ram Ramanathan. Saying that, I meant to refer only to the fact that he sees global warming as accelerating at .5 degree Celsius every fifteen years, starting now, unless drastic action is taken—a more rapid rate of acceleration than she reports. Temperamentally, he is a pronounced optimist. Having heard her speak, I easily believe your report that she is a pessimist, though she cannot have given up completely if she still bothers to write. You used the word "deflated" of me in a discouraged mood a letter or two back. Deflated is just how I found her when she spoke at UCI, as if it was just too depressingly futile for her to recite the grim facts yet again, knowing that no meaningful action would ensue.

In this connection, her article on James Hanson, entitled "The Catastrophist," in the 7/27 *New Yorker*, makes interesting reading just now. In the chaos of the Trump/Biden "debate," Joe did manage at one point to make a surprisingly specific comment about climate change. If we are truly at the "reboot" that *Wired* sees or an "inflection point," to use the phrase you prefer, then perhaps a Democratic landslide could make Hansen, whom Kolbert finds prophetic but impolitic (and so doomed to irrelevance) politic as well as prophetic. One might say that *unless* this can happen, the inflection point will inflect nothing and the reboot will crash.

In an earlier letter, you found my reaction to the *Atlantic's* review of Joseph Henrich's *The WEIRDest People in the World* revealingly Catholic. This may or may not be true of my reaction, but the book would scarcely seem aimed at a Catholic readership. In today's *New York Times Book Review*, Daniel Dennett, no Catholic he, reviews it with enthusiasm and compares it in scope and ambition to Jared Diamond's *Guns, Germs, and Steel*. Here's how Catholicism appears in Dennett's review:

> The centerpiece of Henrich's theory is the role played by what he calls the Roman Catholic Church's Marriage and Family Program, featuring prohibitions of polygamy, divorce, marriage to first cousins, and even to such distant blood relatives as sixth cousins, while discouraging adoption and arranged marriages and the strict norms of inheritance tha prevailed in extended families, clans and tribes. "The accidental genius of Western Christianity was in 'figuring out' how to dismantle kin-based institutions while at the same time catalyzing its own spread."

The genius was accidental, according to Henrich, because the church authorities who laid down the laws had little or no insight into what they were setting in motion, aside from noticing that by weakening the traditional bonds of kinship, the church got rich fast.

I can easily concede that "the church authorities who laid down the laws had little or no insight into what they were setting in motion." As much could easily be said of the Founding Fathers of the United States of America. My objection—tentative until I have delved into the book—is to Henrich's elision or outright omission of Jesus's radical dissolution of family as foundational to Israel's covenant with God. "Who is my mother, who are my brothers?" he asked, and much indeed flowed from that dissolution in the genesis of the religion that, a thousand years later, was making the institutional moves that Henrich finds so unforeseeably consequential. A covenant there still was; it was just no longer founded on family and genealogy.

I found Dana Goodyear in the *New Yorker* on Govan and Zumthor rather a valentine. A remarkable building may yet be built; but if so, the intellectual and cultural result for Los Angeles will nonetheless be a foreshortening of temporal vision to the present and of spatial vision to the United States. The maligned (and misnamed) "encyclopedic" museum took the visitor to other times and distant places. LACMA was doing just that when Govan arrived. I doubt that it will still be doing so when he leaves.

Oh, and the Lakers did not win the championship in the fourth game, but the fifth is on as I speak, the Lakers are off to a roaring start, and so off now to the second half.

Jack

\* \* \*

## OCTOBER 29–NOVEMBER 1: MARK BEGINS.

*Ending . . . Jersey guys . . . Bruce Springsteen's "Letter to You" . . . indirect communication . . . ghost stories . . . prayer . . . vocation—burning need to communicate . . . it's always been about death. . . . logic of life . . . interruption: insulin reaction . . . see you in my dreams . . . fire breaks out nearby . . . mandatory evacuation . . . camping out . . . passing the tipping point for climate change . . . Orange County Trumpublicans . . . wild horses . . . history awaiting thought . . . leaving life's work unfinished, perhaps unremembered. . . . the West's on fire . . . searching for patterns . . . being is relational . . . will to power . . . "Eve of Destruction."*

---

*October 29*

Dear Jack:

The end is approaching. The end of the campaign. The end of our conversation. But other ends, countless ends as well. The end of the line. The end of teaching. The end of writing. The end of life—not merely our lives, but, perhaps, the end of human life itself. Will this be a book? If so, will it be our last book? When to end? How to end? The pages have grown far beyond what we imagined when we began—approaching 1,700—and now it is time to pause and look back to ask if there is a thread running through this text we have woven together.

Reading and writing have been our lives—our lives both separately and together. Never more so than for the past seven and a half months. Yes, seven and a half months—every day, every week for seven and a half months without either of us ever missing a single letter. Quite a commitment. How many couples are that devoted to each other so long? It will take us a while to understand what we have done; who knows whether anyone else will ever understand or will even care to try to understand. Reading and writing stitched together by art—for me painting, photography, and sculpture, for you music. Today as I write what was to have been my last letter and still might be because the future is always unknowable, I am thinking about reading and writing through your art rather than mine.

Like many Jersey guys of my generation, I've long been a huge Bruce
Springsteen fan. When I was a kid, my grandfather would take my brother,
mother, and me to the Wildwood on the New Jersey shore for a week's
vacation. My father never came with us because he had to work during the
summer. We stayed at the Manor Hotel, which was an unheard-of treat.
Our routine was always the same—after a pancake breakfast, it was the
beach during the day, and the boardwalk at night. Skee ball for junky
prizes, bumper cars, Ferris wheel, merry-go-round, and the shooting gallery where I first shot a gun. The Boss's Jersey shore was not exactly mine,
but it was close enough for his lyrics and music to resonate at a level deeper
than memory. I have heard him in concert only once and it was the longest
and most explosive show I've ever attended. Durkheim's "creative effervescence" on steroids.

While I was teaching at Williams, one of the presidents was also a Jersey
guy who was a big Springsteen fan. When I proposed giving the Boss an
honorary degree, Morty didn't need much persuading. The problem was
how to get through his agent to the man himself. I hit on a solution when I
remembered that my brother lives near Freehold, where Bruce has lived for
years. As I've previously mentioned, Beryl is an equine vet and he knows
the vet who takes care of Springsteen's horses. I wrote a letter of invitation
to Springsteen, which the president signed. I then sent the letter to my
brother and he arranged to meet his colleague to give him the letter to
deliver personally to Springsteen. I was frankly surprised and disappointed
he didn't have the courtesy to respond to Morty. I suspect Williams was
not blue collar enough for him. Though I'm not big on forgiveness, I found
a way to excuse his less than classy move.

Last year, Dinny and I splurged spending far more than we should have
to attend Springsteen's Broadway one-man show. It was a fascinating experience that provided added depth to his already personal songs. Springsteen has recently released a new album—*Letter to You*, which is different in
tone from his signature bombastic songs. It's much more introspective and
quietly reflective than many of his best-known albums. Some of the most
poignant tunes border on the melancholy of late autumn days. He is only
three years younger than I am, and, as in my *Last Works: Lessons in Leaving*
and *Seeing Silence*, he is looking back over a long career and asking what it
has all added up to. This is not to suggest that the private crowds out the

public. As always, his lyrics provide powerful social analysis and penetrating political commentary that has more of an edge than anything you read or hear in the media today. With the presidential election in a week, two songs—"Rainmaker" and "House of a Thousand Guitars"—seemed to me to be timely, so I sent them to my undergraduate Theory class without any comment. The song seems to have been written for this climactic week. "The house is on fire," Bruce sings, and the Rainmaker is telling us that black is white and black is white. But this singing troubadour who has the uncanny ability to capture the moment in his unforgettable lyrics refuses to despair and promises to light up the house with the music of a thousand guitars. I have no idea if the students listened to the tunes, and if they did listen, I don't know whether they understood what I was trying to say to them through Springsteen's words and voice.

Springsteen also knows the end is drawing near, and freely admits that he is the "Last Man Standing." *Letter to You* is haunted by ghosts, some named—his legendary sax player Clarence Clemons, George Theiss, and other members of his first band, the Castiles (1965–1968)—as well as unnamed predecessors without whom he would not have created his music. Neither present nor absent, these ghosts are shades that lend his music depth and create resonances that extend beyond the present moment. This is an afterlife in which I can believe.

Springsteen had planned to tour with his legendary E Street Band this spring, but cannot do so because of the pandemic. In place of the tour, he has released a remarkable film, which also bears the title *Letter to You*. The film was shot in Springsteen's production studio on his horse farm in Freehold and features the band of brothers (and one sister) while they are producing the album. Springsteen has said that it is a celebration of the "collective soul" of the band. But it is more than that—much more. The film is shot in exquisite black-and-white with winter scenes of snow-covered woods, fields, and barns interspersed between the recording sessions. Having reached the age when every song might be his last, Springsteen and his brothers know winter is coming. The cover image for the album CD is a close-up sepia photograph of half of Springsteen's face with snow falling.

What has made Springsteen's music so compelling for all these years is his ability to enter into the lives of people and give voice to their

worlds—the down-and-out at the edge of town, the orphan, the unemployed factory worker, the forgotten Vietnam veteran, the aging pitcher
reliving his glory days. In *Letter to You* he seems to have stepped out of character and to be singing in his own voice about himself. What most surprised me about his Broadway show was how important a role religion
played in his upbringing. Religion returns in both the album and the film
*Letter to You*, now in the form of a deep spirituality. With an end that might
be more than personal approaching, the Boss in his signature black jeans
and a tight black T-shirt is no longer embarrassed by his beliefs and turns
the stage into a pulpit singing "The Power of Prayer." Prayer: an ode to the
power of prayer from the greatest rock musician of his generation.

Springsteen actually talks about prayer in the film. He frames his reflections by recalling attending funeral services with his parents. An old,
slightly out-of-focus color film of him standing in line outside a church
waiting to kneel beside an open casket, a ritual I too knew as a child, interrupts the present of *Letter to You*. Shifting from color back to black-and-
white, the camera focuses on a close-up of Bruce's face as he recites the
prayer he offered every night as a child.

> Now I lay me down to sleep.
> I pray the Lord my soul to keep.
> If I should die before I wake,
> I pray the Lord my soul to take.

His words startled me—though he, like you, is Catholic and I am Protestant, this is precisely the same prayer I was taught to repeat every night as
a child. As soon as he uttered the first three words, I spoke the rest of the
prayer with him. "If I should die before I wake, I pray the Lord my soul to
take!" Who teaches a child to repeat that prayer night after night? And you
wonder why I've spent most my professional life thinking about death!

Like those who seek comfort from the Rainmaker, Springsteen needs "to
believe in something so bad, so bad, so bad." But he knows a con man when he
sees one, and no longer believes in a God who takes the souls of innocent children while they sleep. So what is left—where can he turn? His answer in *Letter
to You* is music; though his songs are not always a joyful noise offered to the
Lord, Springsteen believes in the redemptive power of rock and roll. Singing
alone, however, is not enough, singing with his brothers is not enough—he

must share the gospel that has found him with others. Springsteen reflects, "After all this time, I still feel the burning need to communicate. It's there when I wake every morning. It walks alongside of me throughout the day.... Over the past fifty years, it has never ceased. Is it loneliness, hunger, ego, ambition, desire, a need to be felt and heard, recognized, all of the above? All I know, it is one of the most consistent impulses of my life."

In these words I hear echoes of my own life. "The burning need to communicate" that's why I have taught and written for more than fifty years. I am still enough of a Protestant to believe that teaching and writing are a vocation. In *Field Notes from Elsewhere: Reflections on Dying and Living*, I asked, "Is it possible to believe in vocation, if you do not believe in one who calls?" I proceeded to respond to my own question: "The vocation of the person called by the silence of the Word is not to expose the impossibility of faith but to show the inescapability of faith for those who believe it impossible." But what about communication? How can this faith, this belief—if that is what it is—be communicated to others?

To try to answer this question, I turn to my second preoccupation this week, which helped to distract me from the election cacophony. I have been reading a recently published book by Derrida—*Life Death*, which is the transcript of a seminar he gave at École normale supérieure in the fall semester of 1975. From Springsteen to Derrida—I imagine you shaking your head, but you know by now that this is how my mind works. I have long told my students that how you understand a book is in large measure a function of when and where you read it. That is why I write the date and place inside the front cover of every book I read. With twilight beginning to fall, reading *Life Death* is like taking flight with the owl of Minerva. At the time Derrida was delivering this seminar, I had just finished *Kierkegaard's Pseudonymous Authorship* and was beginning *Journeys to Selfhood: Hegel and Kierkegaard*. I had no idea about the content of Derrida's seminar until I started reading this book this week. As I think I've mentioned in a previous letter, Derrida once said to me, "It's always been about death." I wonder what bedtime prayer his mother taught him when he was a child. In this posthumous book it's still all about death, but now death appears to be inseparable from life.

Though his philosophical preoccupations remain, Derrida ventures into new territory by exploring molecular biology and genetics through a careful reading of François Jacob's *The Logic of Life: A History of Heredity*. I first read Jacob's book in 1998 when I was researching what became *The Moment of Complexity: Emerging Network Culture*. I recently returned to it while I was studying artificial intelligence in preparation for writing *Intervolution: Smart Bodies Smart Things*. In ways that are not immediately obvious, I think Hegel's logic suggests a way to integrate genetics (body, nature), consciousness (mind, culture), and artificial intelligence (technology). Alternatively contemporary science and technology disclose the far-reaching implications and abiding importance of Hegel's complex system. Hegel and AI—not quite Springsteen and Derrida, but not really that far from it. Though I did not realize it when all of this began in those undergraduate Hegel and Kierkegaard seminars in 1968 while war was raging and Springsteen was singing with the Castiles in bars on the Jersey Shore, I have, in fact, been developing something like a philosophy of culture that extends Hegel's analysis—with modifications and corrections from Kierkegaard—into the twenty-first century. Imagine, then, how surprised I was to discover that Derrida begins his analysis of Jacob's "textualization," which I describe as the informatization, of biological organisms with a meticulous interpretation of Hegel's account of life in his *Science of Logic*.

> *I just had a very bad insulin reaction. Saw the white bagel. Had to take a break.*

In this notoriously difficult text, which has been so important for my intellectual development, Hegel argues that the essence of life is constituted by the dialectical relation of identity and difference. Since opposites are inextricably interrelated and, thus, intervolve, such a structure is self-referential, self-organizing, autopoietic, and autotelic. For Jacob what distinguishes living organisms from nonliving entities is the capacity for *self*-reproduction. Derrida concisely explains this difficult but important insight. "Self-reproducibility is the living itself [*le vivant*], insofar as (1) there is no living being that is not capable of it, and (2) there is no self-reproducibility that is not qualified as living. Self-reproducibility belongs only to the living."

I realize you will find it incongruous, but reading those lines and the following pages was a "Eureka!" moment for me. I could try to explain why I think this idea is so important, but that's not the point in this context. Rather, the point is that this insight draws together the threads of the diverse classes I have been teaching and books I have been writing for more than fifty years. The reason I have been drawn to the writings of Derrida is that we were asking the same questions and tracing the same issues through the same writers at the same time without either of us knowing it. Sadly, we never had the chance to discuss this because I did not realize the depth of this connection until after he died. In the end, we both discovered that our obsession with death is really a preoccupation with life.

This brings me back to Springsteen. "After all this time, I still feel the burning need to communicate. It's there when I wake every morning. It walks alongside of me throughout the day. . . . Over the past fifty years, it has never ceased." This is what I share with Bruce, and this is what draws me into his music and won't let me go. My deepest belief is that ideas matter—indeed, they are nothing less than a matter of death and life. The burning desire to communicate is why I have taught and written all these years and what makes it so hard for me to stop. Like the Boss, I've been preaching without a pulpit. But there is a difference in our sermons, and this difference enables him to communicate in a way I cannot.

It's complicated, always so complicated. What if the final piece that makes all the pieces of the puzzle fall into place is too complicated to explain in anything less than a lifetime? What if people don't have the interest, time, or patience to listen to what I have struggled so long to say? Is it possible to communicate complexity in an age that reveres simplicity? I believe the writers to whom I have devoted my life have created the world in which we dwell and have profound lessons for the worlds into which we are moving—Kant, Hegel, Schelling, Kierkegaard, Marx, Nietzsche, Freud, Heidegger, Derrida, Melville, Poe, Thoreau. In today's high-speed ADD world, philosophical fashions change as fast as haute couture on Paris runways. I too am the last man standing—when I retire most, if not all, these difficult dead white guys will no longer be taught in the Religion Department at Columbia University. They have not been taught at Williams since I left fifteen years ago. Facing that reality, I decided to lodge a protest by teaching a seminar sequence featuring my most important ghosts—Hegel and Kierkegaard last spring, and Heidegger and Derrida this fall. The Hegel-Kierkegaard went well—or as well as it could have after being disrupted by the pandemic. But when only two people signed up for the Heidegger-Derrida seminar this fall, I had to cancel the course. So the story I had hoped to tell remains incomplete and the keystone securing the arc of time is missing. Unless, unless, unless completion and closure are death and incompletion and opening are life. "The artists who hold our attention," Springsteen avers, "have something eating away at them, and they never quite define it, but it's always there." Yes, it really has always been about death—and about life. Satisfaction is death and dissatisfaction is life. Paradoxically, I find satisfaction in that insight perhaps because I now understand what Hegel understood from his earliest theological writings—another name for life is love. "In love the separate does still remain, but as something united and no longer something separate; life senses life."

Though "the road is long," it's getting shorter fast. I misread the clock this morning and got up at 4:30 rather than my usual 5:30. I suspect I was composing these words in my troubled sleep. When light dawned, I discovered the first snow of winter. More snow is predicted tomorrow.

Mark


*October 29*

Dear Mark:

Fire broke out in open country north of us—you'd be amazed at how much open country there actually is just north of us—early on Monday morning of the past week just as Santa Ana winds, east winds, sprang up as predicted. Mandatory evacuation orders quickly went into effect for the most immediately adjacent residential areas or about sixty thousand people. Shortly thereafter voluntary evacuation areas went into effect for larger, less immediately adjacent residential areas, including ours. We neither saw nor smelled smoke through Monday—largely, I think, because the wind was blowing straight west. Rather than be surprised by a wind shift during the night, we spent that night in the guest room of an old friend of Kitty's, Lorna Adkins, and left after a quick breakfast on Tuesday with a key to her house, should we need it again and should she not be home. Her son Greg (Kitty's godson), daughter-in-law, Rebecca, and three-year-old granddaughter, Dancer, live in Pasadena, and Lorna spends roughly half the week with them.

Nighttime temperatures here are now into the low fifties, with some related dampness. Perhaps for that reason, through the slightly open bedroom window at Lorna's, I seemed to detect the acrid smell of wet ash, as from a doused campfire, through the night. In the morning, that smell was gone, but the air-quality was worsening. Looking north, I could see that the bulk of the fire from twenty-seven thousand burning acres (at last report, and including a second fire slightly further north) was indeed blowing straight west. We were thus spared the very worst of it, and yet, according to the *Los Angeles Times* this morning, air in our entire area is "unhealthful for all," and I do notice that I am bringing up phlegm as when my allergies are activated. (They don't test for smoke or vehicle-emission allergies, by the way, because, in effect, all humans if not all sentient beings are allergic.)

As you know, we have lately updated our sprinkler system and done serious preventive bush- and tree-trimming. The house has a fair chance, then, of coming through a fire, but the garage-plus-shed building does not, and it houses the bulk of my books, all still boxed up. I am looking into renting some off-site storage, but the sensible and cost-effective way to do this would have been, long since, to do the remaining severe triage and library reorganization that is called for. Unfortunately, for reasons I won't linger over, much of most days for me is now taken up with house maintenance that used to fall to Kitty.

I have an air-filtration machine in my office and may invest in a second for our bedroom, but as important or more so is the attic furnace. So, earlier today, I made an appointment for it to receive routine annual maintenance—maintenance, however, that it actually hasn't had in two years. More worrisome, our pool is badly fouled with blown-down leaves (as is the whole property), our pool man has not shown up this week, and the pool pump has stopped working, perhaps because it burned out when the outflow of circulating pool water became jammed solid with vegetation. I can hope that it just shut down automatically, but if nothing is done soon the pool will begin to grow algae, the leaves sinking to its bottom will rot away, and so forth.

I phoned Joel Moreno to inquire when he might next be coming and found his phone out of service. My immediate fear was that this quiet, intelligent, skillful, and knowledgeable Hispanic gentleman may have been deported. Kitty weakly objected, "But he has a son at Tustin High School."

But we both know that the savage Stephen Miller/Donald Trump man-hunt has never been slowed by a consideration like that one. A regime of matchless cruelty.

When the *New York Times* reported the creation of the new Earthshot Prize on 10/11/20, it commented, "The goal is no less than 'to repair our planet by 2030.' That might be a tad overly ambitious." But 2030 is just the year that Ram Ramanathan thinks will mark a point of no return, and I have intended to attempt a second draft of our op-ed noting this agree-ment. It was gratifying to receive so many messages from friends inquiring about our well-being. Ram was one, and he replied to my reply as follows:

> I nowadays say in my talk: When the warming hits 1.5C by 2030, cli-mate change will move into everyone's living room. I then define what I mean by that: either you will be personally affected or you will know someone (family or friends) who has been affected. By that definition, climate change, by affecting you, has moved into my living room.

He wants me to draw this latest personal experience of ours into whatever I write. A bit tricky, but doable.

A bit of local political color: today's mail brought two of the Biden/Harris fly swatters with the motto, on the handle, "Truth before Flies." Our vener-able house flyswatter has gone missing, so we did need a replacement, but I bought two—one for us and the other for Brian and Kathleen. In my early enthusiasm for Elizabeth Warren, I provided her campaign my cell phone number, and today they texted me asking if I had voted for our congress-woman, Rep. Katie Porter, who upset a longtime GOP incumbent in 2018, and for other down-ticket Democrats. I replied that I had, that Kitty had, and that we had also contributed financial support. I was then asked to do some phone-bank work over the weekend, and I may do that. Kathleen and Brian have done a ton of such volunteering.

We all hope that dedication like this will pay off, but my anxiety about the upcoming election remains. It has very little to do with Trump's alleged continuing appeal to ill-educated white males and even equally ill-educated nonwhite males and very much to do with the Trumpublicans' canny sabo-tage of the postal service. Rachel Maddow has been astute to report on how the most serious delays in mail delivery have been targeted in major

metropolitan areas in swing states and how the USPS has grounded its
police force, the officers who otherwise would be out there defending us all
against mail theft. The sentence echoing in my head continues to be Stalin's
"It doesn't matter who casts the votes. It matters who counts the votes."

Amid all this, I was surprised and not displeased to hear from Costica
Bradatan this week, whom we both know from Columbia University Press
and I knew earlier through the *Los Angeles Review of Books*. Costica and a
colleague, Ed Simon, have edited a collection of what their publisher,
Broadleaf Books, bills as "personal, subjective, voice-driven New Religion
Journalism . . . by young writers willing to scrutinize questions of faith and
doubt while taking God-talk seriously." Twenty-six selections including a
few names you'll recognize and more that I don't and guess you won't either
are divided into sections: Personal Agon: Experience and Identity; Political
Agon: Politics & Society; Natural Agon: Science & Technology; and Divine
Agon: Theology & Philosophy. Costica wrote to request a blurb, and though
I did read the authors' introduction to *The God Beat: What Journalism Says
About Faith and Why It Matters*, my blurb was more than half-written before
I did even that much. Here it is:

> During ten years ending in 1995, I was repeatedly invited and repeat-
> edly declined to be the religion editor of the *Los Angeles Times*. Reading
> this anthology, I understand both why I was right to decline the gig
> back then and why today another reporter might jump at it. The reli-
> gion beat of old has become what Bradatan and Simon call "the God
> beat"—an exciting new, freestyle game still learning its own rules.
> —Jack Miles, Pulitzer Prize winner for *God: A Biography*

I have it secondhand that Alfred North Whitehead once said, "Only
journalism lasts." If he did say that, what he must have meant is that ideas
last if and when they enter the common sense of a literate culture and that
this has happened when they enter the life of journalism, the readiest
expression of a literate culture's common sense. It may matter considerably, then, that a new, agonistic form of religion journalism is coming into
existence, though, tragically, it also matters for that and many other reasons that journalism itself is dying before our eyes.

So often the assumption is made that religion is dying because more
people reply "none" to the question "What is your religious affiliation?"

David Biale, interestingly, ends *The Norton Anthology of World Religions/Judaism* with a section entitled "Secular Jews Confront the Tradition." None of the other component anthologies has a comparable section, and David maintains that the Jewish role in the rise of secularism is pivotal; he is the author of an entire book on that subject, *Not in the Heavens*. In that final section of the Judaism anthology, my favorite contribution is a long excerpt from the poet Yehuda Amichai, but I love it partly because it subverts the section in which it is placed. I may have quoted it before, but here is just a stanza:

> Tombstones crumble, they say, words tumble, words fade away,
> the tongues that spoke them turn to dust,
> languages die as people do,
> some languages rise again,
> gods change up in heaven, gods get replaced,
> prayers are here to stay.

That prayers (religion by metonymy) are here to stay while gods change and are replaced means, for me, that religion is more durable than God or the gods, that it is irreplaceable or somehow ineradicable from the human condition. Declare it gone, and you merely inaugurate its reconstruction. You have not escaped it, even if, for the fleeting moment of a single lifetime, it may have escaped you.

Final item, mostly though perhaps not entirely by association to the word "escape": I heard today from Michael C. Miles of Montana, for whose book—about recovering from the untimely death of his son, Sean—I will write a foreword. Mike wrote:

> Hopefully this finds you well. How often have we extended such salutation without giving it a second thought? COVID has changed all that.
>
> I couldn't resist sending the attached photo. We had a few horses get away on Sunday following a major snowfall and frigid nights. We have some idea where they are but it is no easy task since it's in a wilderness area. Yesterday we were flying around in the Cessna 180 searching for the three escapees. During part of the flight we passed alongside Sphinx Mountain (elevation 10,850) and the Helmet. The

Sphinx is obvious in the photo (left) and Helmet is on the right. (If you zoom up on it you will see why the name.)

Abraham Heschel's most influential book was entitled *God in Search of Man*—a transparent rejoinder, of course, to the more usual notion of man in search of God. Imagining the search going in either direction, I am in love with this metaphor for it—namely, the metaphor of hunting in a Cessna for an unruly horse escaped into the snowy wilderness of a mountain forest.

Jack


*October 30*

Dear Mark:

Later in this letter, I will do as I usually do and react to a few particulars in your letter by associating them to other particulars drawn from my memory or experience, but let me begin with a more general comment. Your vocation—and I use that word thinking of how you define it in this letter—is to draw together everything, or as near to everything as you can manage, into a synthesis both artistic and intellectual. The word "religion" is rendered superfluous because for you religion has long since been subsumed into art, but into your kind of highly intellectual, serious, *consequential* art.

As a philosophy student at the Pontifical Gregorian University, I particularly enjoyed the lectures on the history of philosophy delivered by a younger German Jesuit who seemed to speak to us from somewhere far outside the scholastic philosophy that defined our curriculum. Speaking of German idealistic philosophy, he said that its defining aspiration, equivalent to Springsteen's and your "burning need to communicate," was a drive to completeness. He wrote on the blackboard *Die Wahrheit ist das Ganze*, a sentence that, he said, he could not find anywhere in the canonical works (and he had searched) but one that captured what he saw formatively enacted throughout the canon. He saw *das Ganze* as the ever-receding goal that philosophers in that tradition—in some ways, clearly, his own and, I believe, yours—were ever driven to pursue. I have written, long before this letter, that your ambition is Hegelian. By an alternate formulation, your ambition is Hegel's to comprehend your historical moment in thought.

In this letter, then, out of the same impulse, you are trying on the eve of the American presidential election to draw our correspondence over the past plagued months, voluminous as it has become, into your always-ending/always-beginning Hegelian synthesis. Our correspondence is no more than a small part of the American historical moment that still awaits its comprehension in thought, but because the Great World, as Philip Roth liked to call it, must be included if the moment is to be included in its entirety, the megapopular Bruce Springsteen is an apt vehicle. He speaks to you personally because of what his songs say; he is anonymously Hegelian, partly via Jacques Derrida, because his late work, like your late work (including this late correspondence) and like Derrida's is all about death; and finally through his popularity he builds into the synthesis a cross-section of the entire American population.

What to say? The phlegm that I was bringing up as I began this response on Friday morning, October 30, was clotted, dark, and spotted with black flecks that I take to be ash or other particulate spewed by the local wildfires, still only partly contained. My existing pulmonary comorbidity is only exacerbated by the interaction between the SARS-CoV-2 pandemic and the climate crisis that guarantees future, more dangerous wildfires and quite possibly future pandemics complicating my last years. I, too, then, have death on my mind—my muddy spat-out counterpart to your white bagel of insulin imbalance. But just such a comment as this one risks leading me off into my usual skein of associative comments that do not cohere and cannot reasonably aspire to cohere as the kind of synthesis that calls so loudly to you. I expressed my disclaimer in *Religion As We Know It* when I wrote,

> Just as an individual man may conclude that life is too short for him to answer the larger questions that loom around him—whose answers, for all he knows, may impinge quite directly on his most personal decisions—so it may be for the human species as a whole. You may die never having learned the one fact that would have changed everything for you. In just the same way, extinction may befall the human species as a whole with key questions still unanswered and perhaps even unasked.

I recognize, Mark, that these comments of mine scarcely leave us at intellectual loggerheads, for your letter includes very comparable lines:

> What if the final piece that makes all the pieces of the puzzle fall into place is too complicated to explain in anything less than a lifetime? What if people don't have the interest, time, or patience to listen to what I have struggled so long to say? Is it possible to communicate complexity in an age that reveres simplicity?

But these elegiac lines of yours and the discouraged or discouraging words in the paragraph that immediately follows only confirm the anterior ambition.

As this epistolary diary nears its appointed end, let me suggest that we now separately commence a pair of postelection diaries and that we continue these two diaries until the political future of our country becomes clear to us both. Like a river becoming a delta as it nears the ocean, we can flow down separate channels as we conclude, keeping in touch informally by email, until our two channels trail off into the oceanic *Ganze*. At an agreed-upon point, we will conclude this twofold epilogue by exchanging what we have written, but neither will then reply to the other's closing words, at least not in writing or as a part of this opus. We may want to speak, but we will conclude what we will have written with a doubled diminuendo into silence.

In previous replies to your letters, I have sometimes felt myself a kind of vandal. That is, you offer a splendid summation, and then I snipe at particulars. I point to something left out by bringing up something, anything, and my doing so seems gratuitous, uncalled for, unsporting or, as I say, almost vandalistic on the part of someone who doesn't now and never will have any comparably deep, philosophically and historically grounded edifice to offer. But after making this confession, let me now sink into vandalism for one last, brief round:

Item: There is obviously a point of contact between Springsteen on the "Power of Prayer" and Yehuda Amichai as I quote him in my last letter.

Item: Springsteen is clearly an artist working creatively in his late music well beyond the confines of his early music and working, in other media, beyond rock music itself. He first broke through to me with what I believe was his breakthrough hit, "Born to Run" with the refrain "Tramps like us / Baby, we were born to run." Or that and his later "My Little Town," which was coincidentally my first wife's hometown. But for indefinable reasons, perhaps musical but I can't really say, both of these tunes somehow rubbed me the wrong way, and thereafter I was mostly tuned out. Emotionally, as a result, Bruce is available to you for the large purposes that shape this culminating letter, but he isn't to me.

Item: that said about Bruce Springsteen, and not hearing him actually perform the words with which you conclude, I can yield to them easily enough simply through their honest content—a lost friend (lost love?), a past summer, and an intimation of immortality. To this content, I have two minor, perhaps almost trivial associations—the first an association by reversion to the thought of leaving one's work unfinished and perhaps unremembered; the second, more simply and perhaps just by way of sequential reaction to the first, a musical association to past summers of my own and my own lost loves.

The first association, then is to Longfellow's oft-quoted (more likely, *once* oft-quoted) quatrain—namely, the preachy, singsongy

> The lives of great men all remind us
> We can make our lives sublime

And, departing, leave behind us
Footsteps in the sands of time.

I recoil from that, don't you? But *why* do we? We might ask why.

The second association is to the lines that close the wistful French original of the song we know (and I love) as "Autumn Leaves." The French
original—*Feuilles morts*: not "autumn" leaves but "dead" leaves—ends:

*Et la mer efface sur la sable*
*Les pas des amants désunis.*

"The sea erases from the sand the footprints of lovers parted." So much more
could be said about all that these words evoke in the present moment, but
let me end, for now, my half of our correspondence to date simply with that
seashore image: waves washing across footprints, softly wiping them away.

Jack


*November 1*

Dear Jack:

Fire lives in the death of earth, air lives in the death of fire, water lives
in the death of air, and earth in the death of water.
—Heraclitus

My internal clock doesn't automatically reset nor can I correct it. The term
"daylight savings time" has always puzzled me—nothing is saved by moving
clocks ahead one hour. What is "saved" in the morning is "lost" in the afternoon, and there is a lesson in that that extends far beyond clocks. As long
as there are twenty-four hours in a day, time is never saved nor lost, it is
only redistributed. When I awoke today, it was brighter than it had been in
recent weeks. Light breaking in the eastern sky shone a brilliant reddish
purple. On such mornings, a childhood jingle always pops into my mind:
"Red in the morning sailors take warning, red at night, sailors' delight." I
wonder what coming storm this "rosy fingered dawn" portends.

While the light of the Berkshire sky was not the same as the yellowish
orange glow of the skies above LA and so many other places out west, it was

close enough to call them to mind. You conclude without concluding, "Let me end, for now, my half of our correspondence simply with that seashore image: waves washing across footprints, softly wiping them away." But it is fire not water that threatens to wipe away our footprints and so much else. An infinite loop in which alpha and omega become one. The spark that brings light also brings death. Check out the frontispiece in *Erring: A Postmodern A/Theology*. It was a gift from the once-boyhood preacher Barry Moser, who became the country's most accomplished printmaker. While you were at the University of California Press, he did memorable illustrations for *Moby-Dick*, *Alice in Wonderland*, and the Bible. Barry lives near us in Massachusetts and when we visited him years ago, he gave me that image for *Erring*. A bolt of lightning strikes a land bridge suspended over a black void that is a tear in mother earth. Is this tear a womb, a tomb, or both?

As Heraclitus teaches us in fragments not even Heidegger can make whole, fire was with us before the beginning. It all began with a spark, a heavenly spark that ignited the primal soup and brought together the ancient molecules that are still circulating somewhere in the cosmos. But the spark of life is also the spark of death. The fires raging around your house were also caused by a bolt of lightning from the sky. Hundreds, thousands of bolts of lightning every day igniting fires humans no longer can control. Prometheus's gift to man has turned against him.

"The house is on fire," sings the Boss. And we are led by a Rainmaker, who is a confidence man. *The Fire Next Time* has become The Fire This Time. Our time, our moment, our present, which is turning our future and the future of our children and grandchildren to ash. The temperature keeps rising and more than houses are burning—forests, towns, cities, and bodies—yes, bodies burning with fever and already turning to ash—230,000 bodies and counting in the U.S. alone. The trees and houses burning around you are fouling the air that is clogging your lungs. That black gunk you are coughing up brings with it the smell of death, your death, my death, humanity's death. You have done all you can: raked the leaves, trimmed the trees and bushes, and hosed the roof, but we both know that in the long run, however long that might be, it will not be enough. And so you keep your bags packed and borrow your neighbor's key. Springsteen's "Born to Run," you say, finally broke through to you, a lover of Bach, Beethoven, and opera. But where can we run when the planet is on fire?

Fire, fire, fire, everywhere fire, fire and more fire. The story about your friend hunting for lost horses in a Cessna plane and the accompanying picture of Sphinx Mountain are a reminder of just how vast and varied this country is. The spectacular aerial photograph could just as well be the Himalayas, Alps, or Andes. As always, the larger the mountains, the smaller human presence appears to be. I was surprised you didn't mention your years in Missoula, Montana, with our dear friend Ray Hart. As I recalled in an earlier letter, fire haunts Missoula. Norman Maclean's *Young Men and Fire* tells the story of tragic fires that are still burning. Nor did you mention the trip to the North Fork to visit with Ray that we had to cancel because of the pandemic. We promised to go there next summer, but I suspect we know we never will. Like so much else, the final rendezvous of the three amigos is another casualty of the plague. Fire is a constant threat in the North Country, and Ray has had to flee for his life as often as you have. Nowhere is there a better gauge of climate change than Glacier National Park. Experts predict that all the glaciers will be gone by 2030, if not sooner—just like the glaciers in the Andes, Alps, and Himalayas.

Today the calendar flipped—November 1. Two articles in the *New York Times* caught my attention. The first brought back memories of the chant on the streets of Chicago in August 1968—"The whole world is watching": "A Frazzled World Holds Its Breath While the U.S. Chooses Its Leader" (David Halbfinger).

> American presidential elections always seize international attention, but this year is exceptional: Mr. Trump has dominated news cycles and frayed nerves in almost every corner of the earth like few leaders in history. Having lived through his impulsiveness, and his disdain for allies and dalliances with adversaries, the world is on tenterhooks waiting to see whether the United States will choose to stay that rocky course.

As you have insisted for months, Tuesday might be the beginning rather than the end. The fires raging on the streets of New York, Philadelphia, Kenosha, Charlottesville, Richmond, Denver, Minneapolis, Seattle, Portland, Los Angeles, and countless other towns and cities foreshadow more devastating violence lurking on the horizon. Your fears are echoed by some of the people who are closest to Trump. The second article was by Ron

Suskind, "The Day After Election Day." Suskind writes, "I've spent the last
month interviewing some two dozen officials and aides, several of whom
are still serving in the Trump administration. The central sources in this
story are or were senior officials, mainly in jobs that require Senate confirmation. They have had regular access to the president and to briefings at
the highest level." He proceeds to report a surprising and disturbing consensus among these officials.

> Many of the officials I spoke to came back to one idea: You don't
> know Donald Trump like we do. Even though they can't predict
> exactly what will happen, their concerns range from the president
> welcoming, then leveraging, foreign interference in the election, to
> encouraging havoc that grows into conflagrations that would merit
> his calling upon U.S. forces. Because he is now surrounded by loyal-
> ists, they say, there is no one to try to tell an impulsive man what he
> should or shouldn't do.
>
> "That guy you saw in the debate," a second former senior intelli-
> gence official told me, after the first debate, when the president offered
> one of the most astonishing performances of any leader in modern
> American history—bullying, ridiculing, manic, boasting, fabricating,
> relentlessly interrupting and talking over his opponent. "That's really
> him. Not the myth that's been created. That's Trump."

It will not be over on Tuesday as we naïvely assumed when we began our
exchange. And so what to do?

You are right when you claim that I search for larger patterns in everyday events—this is my Hegelian moment. Truth, Hegel insists, "is the
whole." This conviction is the result of an insight that I have discussed
repeatedly in my letters. Being, I have insisted, is relational—to be is to be
related, or, in a contemporary idiom, to be is to be connected. All relations
are interrelations and all connectivity is interconnectivity. These relations
and connections are, in linguistic and philosophical jargon, both syn-
chronic and diachronic. That is to say, everything, everybody is what it is
by virtue of its, his, or her interrelation with everything and everybody
else at a given moment as well as its, his, or her relation to the accumulating past and impending future. The truth of anything and anybody is constituted by these interrelations taken as a whole.

But we can never know the whole because the whole, which is temporal as well as spatial, thus, is always incomplete. This is my Kierkegaardian moment. There is no Archimedean point, Kierkegaard insists, from which we can survey and comprehend the whole. To the contrary, truth is not the whole, he argues; rather, "truth is subjectivity." If, however, truth is subjectivity, then we are all trapped in filter bubbles and echo chambers where we can hear no one but ourselves. What Hegel understood that Kierkegaard did not is that our relations with others make us who we are and allow us to know whatever we can know. This knowledge, however, is always incomplete and, therefore, must constantly be revised. Unanticipated events and unexpected decisions shatter narratives and reveal new patterns. Just because we cannot know the final pattern does not mean that we should stop writing and rewriting our stories, and just because the truth is incomplete does not mean that it is not true.

Fire, fire, the house is on fire. Your house, my house, our house. The planet is burning and there is nowhere to run and nowhere to hide. Prometheus's gift has turned to poison. The Anthropocene is the practical outcome of the theory that "truth is subjectivity." Or, in Nietzsche's memorable words with which *The Will to Power* concludes, "A *solution* for all its riddles? *A light* for you, too, you best-concealed, strongest, most intrepid, most midnightly men?—*This world is the will to power—and nothing besides!* And you yourselves are also this will to power and nothing besides!" The will to power and nothing besides—all-consuming subjectivity. The world's on fire. Are we "midnightly men?" We are learning that midday is midnight, the burning question that remains is whether midnight is also midday.

In a previous letter, I have referred to Heidegger's essay "The Question Concerning Technology." Heidegger devoted a four-volume study to Nietzsche's philosophy. His obsession with Nietzsche reflected his conviction that his philosophy represents the catastrophic conclusion of the entire western theological and philosophical tradition. Heidegger anticipated the end of the Anthropocene long before Eugene Stoermer invented the term in the late 1980s. His language is obtuse, but his meaning is clear.

Yet when destining reigns in the mode of Enframing, it is the supreme danger. This danger attests itself to us in two ways. As soon as what is unconcealed no longer concerns man even as object, but does so, rather, exclusively as standing-reserve, and man in the midst of object-lessness is nothing but the orderer of the standing-reserve, then he comes to the very brink of a precipitous fall; that I, he comes to the point where he himself will have to be taken as standing-reserve. Meanwhile man, precisely as the one so threatened, exalts himself to the posture of lord of the earth. In this way the impression comes to prevail that everything man encounters exists only insofar as it is his construct. This illusion gives rise in turn to one final delusion: It seems as though man hears everywhere and always encounters only himself.

We are now on the brink of this precipitous fall because we have forgotten how listen. Bombarded by noise 24/7 and bewitched by a con man who has turned the world into a stage for his incessant reality TV show, we have forgotten how to listen to each other, to the world around us, and to ourselves. The virus is a symptom of a much deeper fire consuming us—we are destroying each other as well as the world without which we cannot survive, and, by so doing, we are destroying ourselves. The only important question on the ballot Tuesday is whether we will turn away from this self-destructive path, or whether, in the memorable words of the long-forgotten sixties rock group, the Turtles, we are on the "eve of destruction" and yet more fires will break out.

Mark

*Epiphany*

## MARK: NOVEMBER 3–12

*National Guard activated to defend polling places . . . continuing isolation, mounting fear . . . GOP wins even if it loses . . . anger at the Trump attention tax . . . midnight on election: "I don't think it looks good" . . . three days later, a four-year-old's reading: "Mom, Biden and Trump both have the most votes" . . . Biden gains, Trump rages . . . black crows in white snow augur death . . . Bannon calls for "heads on a pike" . . . 11/8: the next seventy-five days the most dangerous of all . . . home delivery of a skeleton . . . as the end nears, "I'm going to miss our visits."*

---

*November 3*

Dear Jack:

6 a.m.

On March 15 I began my first letter by writing, "Midnight is also midday." Today we will see whether Nietzsche was right. The early signs are not encouraging. This morning when I awoke, I was greeted once again by snow. Living in the Berkshires for nearly half a century, I have never seen snow twice this early in the season. When I checked my email, I found a message from Kirsten sent late last night. She attached a picture of her with Taylor, who was six months old, in a BabyBjörn standing outside the place where she voted. Kirsten had gotten up early to vote and took Taylor with her because she wanted to be with her when she cast her vote for the first woman president. Her message accompanying the photo: "Remember hope?"

I then checked my newsfeed and stumbled on a Fox News report: "Massachusetts Gov. Charlie Baker Activates National Guard Ahead of Election Day as a Precautionary Measure." Reading this headline, my mind wandered back to Election Day fifty-two years ago, when we were

both in Cambridge. We have discussed that pivotal year and its after-
math in previous letters. This morning I marvel at how 1968 continues to
reverberate throughout the body politic. It is painful to acknowledge
that Donald Trump graduated with us in 1968. As for sex, drugs, and
rock and roll, he's batting one for three. In the state of my youth Trump
is best known for his failed attempt to turn Springsteen's Jersey shore
into an East-Coast Las Vegas. In the remarkable fall of 1968, how could
we have imagined that the baby boomer generation—our generation—
would not end with Bill and Hillary, but with two old men fighting battles even more divisive than those that divided Nixon/Agnew and John-
son/Humphrey?

Even in what we once thought were normal times, I am isolated; sitting
alone in the barn reading and writing, I am not in a position to take the
pulse of anything or anyone other than myself. As I read, watch, and listen
to a broad spectrum of media, the mood I hear most often expressed is
fear—fear of losing jobs, fear of hunger, fear of homelessness, fear of racial
minorities, fear of foreigners, fear of losing guns, fear of a changing America, fear of another four years, fear of not having another four years, fear of
deception, fear of a rigged election, and, above all else, the fear of violence.
When fear displaces hope, violence is not far behind. In recent months,
violence on the left and the right has fed on each other, and the escalating
cycle has played right into Trump's hands by providing a justification for
his obviously racist "law and order" campaign.

What I feel this morning is not so much fear and anxiety as anger,
resentment, shame, and guilt. My anger comes from the realization that
Trump and the Republicans have already won even if they lose, and Biden
and the Democrats lose even if they win. Trumpism has already triumphed
and will not disappear even if Trump is defeated. His successors are already
lining up for 2024—Mike Pence, Nikki Haley, Mike Pompeo, Josh Hawley,
Ted Cruz, Tom Cotton, Ron DeSantis, Don Jr., Ivanka, and who knows
who else is waiting in the wings. Even if Democrats win, they are in a more
precarious position than the Republicans. Biden is at best a transitional
figure who might not be strong enough to survive one term, to say nothing
of two terms. While Trump revealed social, political, and economic
fissures that had been growing for decades, it was the election of the
first African American president that marked the tipping point. With

Trumpism victorious even in defeat, a woman of color, no matter how qualified, charismatic, and talented, is very unlikely to be elected the next president. Furthermore, divisions in the Democratic Party are even deeper than in the Republican Party. If Biden wins, pressure from the Left will come fast and furious, and without an effective leader these fissures will shatter the party. Furthermore, Trump's refusal to contain the virus and the economic fallout of the pandemic combined with his dismantling of the federal bureaucracy, or, in Steve Bannon's misleading terms, the "deconstruction of the administrative state" have created pervasive problems that cannot be solved in the next four years. The 2024 campaign has already begun and the Democrats are behind once again.

Trump has stolen not only our future but also our present. He has actually succeeded in making it all about him—not just the election, but the last four years have been all Trump all the time. Life is imitating so-called art—the Truman Show has become the Trump Show, which runs on multiple channels all day and all night. My anger provokes resentment that Trump and his antics have stolen so much of our time, as well as the time of people across the country, and, indeed, throughout the world when there are so many more important things to think about. Nothing is more precious than time and too many people have wasted too much time on Trump. This is all the more infuriating when one has as little time left as you and I. In addition to anger and resentment, I feel shame and guilt. I am ashamed that our generation has not done better than it has and feel guilty that we are not leaving a better world for our children, grandchildren, students, and, future generations.

In the final analysis—as if any analysis could be final—today it comes down to a clear choice: hope or fear? This time Kierkegaard is right—it *is* Either/Or. I have decided to write to you four times today: morning, noon, evening, night. I am sure my mood will change with events of the day. We already know that neither the election nor the madness will end today. In between, I am going to read Don DeLillo's new book, *The Silence*. Having just published *Seeing Silence*, I will be interested in what he has to say and hope I am not disappointed again. In contrast to his epic novel *Underworld*, his recent works have been slight in more than page numbers. DeLillo is eighty-three and probably should stop writing, but like Trump, Biden, and, perhaps, you and me, he is having trouble letting go.

It is light now and the mountains blanketed in snow against a deep blue sky make a perfect scene. In the east, the sun is just above the horizon, and in the west above the mountains the pale nearly full moon shines. In between east and west, sun and moon, day and night, hope and fear, I am writing to you.

Late evening—midnight approaching.

The *New York Times* has reported early results: Kentucky Trump, Vermont Biden. Totally predictable. But something is going on that was not so predictable. It seems Trump's relentless attack on voting by mail is having the unexpected (at least by most commentators as well as by me) effect of tilting early returns toward Biden and masking Trump's strength. Same-day voting seems to be breaking decisively for Trump. At 8:45 I emailed Aaron, Kirsten, and Beryl, "I don't think it looks good." At 9:10 Aaron replied, "It isn't a good vibe." It's 10 and I'm going to bed; I have class in the morning, and I'm not looking forward to the news tomorrow.

Mark


*November 6*

Dear Jack:

Perspective. Perspective. Perspective.

Yesterday the snow disappeared and the temperature soared to the low sixties. It looks like the next few days are going to be an unexpected respite from the beginning of the long winter. About mid-morning I noticed dozens—perhaps a hundred—crows riding the air currents high in a cloudless blue sky. I often see crows around the barn and sometimes their relentless cawing is distracting. I have never before seen so many crows in the sky at the same time. Needless to say, lines from Poe's "The Raven" ran through my mind.

Four days and counting. I have more or less tuned out the news because there is nothing to say, yet pundits and commentators drone on endlessly trying to fill the time. This is like watching the last quarter mile of a marathon with Biden slowly, relentlessly picking off one state after another. The only question is whether he can pass Trump before they reach the finish line. No matter who wins, we are living in a house divided and both parties are to blame for the crisis we will continue to face. Trump's mad rants are sowing the seeds for disruption, which might turn violent, and Biden's talk of unifying the country rings hollow. The Republicans gained seats in the House of Representatives, and I suspect they will retain control of the Senate. Equally important, the Democrats failed to make gains in any state legislature races. With impending battles for redistricting, this will have major repercussions for at least a decade.

Time. It's always a question of time. The clock is ticking–ticking for you, for me, for people lying in hospital beds, and ticking for the planet.

Kirsten had not sent us any additions to her journal for months and I thought life had become overwhelming and she had to stop writing. It turns out she has been writing all along and two days ago sent us what she has completed so far. I spent most of yesterday reading her journal. Her writing continues to be remarkably insightful, engaging, and, most surprising, humorous. Indeed, at many points I literally laughed out loud, and, trust me, that doesn't happen often. She reports that, on Wednesday, Taylor ran up to her and said, "Mom, Biden and Trump both have the most votes." That sums it up better than the pundits.

Kirsten's reflections offer a window into the ongoing tensions people—especially mothers with young children—are facing as they try to cope with the virus, homeschooling, and work while keeping the household running. For me, some of her most insightful comments focus on the question of time. Pushed to the limit by the impossible demands of daily life, she is acutely aware of never having enough time for Jackson and Taylor, for Jonathan, her friends and family, work, and for herself. Though she never phrases it in quite this way, the recurrent question she is asking is: How can you live in the present when the future keeps crashing in on you?

In all of these pages, it was a brief remark in her very long text that gave me pause: "The uncertainty about the duration of this moment hits me hardest with my parents right now. My life, what's a year? My kids' lives, they are young. That's naïve in this day and age, but a safer bet. With my parents, it feels less fair. There are many things this virus will take from me, has taken from many, will take from more. But time with my parents, that one is hard."} After a long discussion earlier this week, Dinny wrote to Aaron and Kirsten saying that we think we should skip our family gathering at Thanksgiving this year. That will be the first time we are not together for the holiday. We hope we will be able to gather for Christmas but who knows? Dinny's comments became all the more poignant when she reported that her niece Betsy's condition has taken a turn for the worse. Her brain tumor has returned and is spreading rapidly. I doubt she will live until Christmas.

The count goes on and the more Biden gains, the more Trump rages. The outcome is vitally important for this country and, indeed, for the entire world. And yet this morning none of it seems to matter.

Mark


*November 8*

Dear Jack:

The dozens of crows that a few days ago were soaring on changing wind currents high in the sky have landed on the lawn and in the gardens outside the window where I am writing. I have never seen so many in one place on the ground. Some of these harbingers of death are lined up like soldiers on patrol, some are searching for food alone, and others are engaged in combat to stake out their own territory.

While the world anxiously awaited the final vote count on Thursday and the weather suddenly threw off the premature winter chill and turned unseasonably warm, it seemed as if nature itself were anticipating a victory for the climate. Unable to resist the lure of the sun's warmth, I decided to walk—not run—on Stone Hill this morning. I wanted to give myself time to gather my thoughts and compose my final letter to you. Though the trees are bare and the golden glow of autumn has faded, it was a glorious walk. The path was covered with oak and beech leaves colored many shades of brown. I saw no one and the woods were completely silent—not a squirrel scampering or a bird chirping.

The celebrations that spontaneously erupted yesterday were unlike anything I've seen since the Red Sox win the World Series after years of frustration. It seemed as if half the country and a good part of the world were

finally breathing a huge sigh of relief. When a crowd of supporters gathered to welcome the president and vice president elect in the parking lot of a minor league baseball club in Wilmington that I pass every time I take the train from New York to Washington, it was tempting to hope that the country's long nightmare was over. Kamala Harris's election as the first woman vice president appeared to turn a new page in history. Her radiant smile, boundless energy, and electric presence contrasted sharply with Biden's slow, hesitant, sometimes tottering pace. This was not just a juxtaposition of woman and man, young and old, but, more important, a contrast between the future and the past. Almost seventy-eight years old, Biden was first elected to the Senate forty-eight years ago and first ran for the president thirty-two years ago. Throughout the campaign, his message of unity and reconciliation did not change and he repeated it more forcefully than ever last night.

There is no doubt that the nation, indeed, the world desperately needs to heal, but pious calls for unity will not cure the ills infecting the body politic. Watching the celebration and fireworks last night, it was impossible not to imagine Trump raging and plotting in the White House. He still has not conceded defeat and probably never will. Nor has he tweeted in more than twenty-four hours. Only two Republicans have publicly acknowledged Biden's victory. Ted Cruz and Lindsey Graham, chairman of the Senate Judiciary Committee, are getting a head start on the 2024 presidential election by continuing to spread false conspiracy theories about the legitimacy of the election. Once again, where is John McCain when we need him? While Biden was announcing that he will name his pandemic advisory board on Monday, Trump's erstwhile advisor Steve Bannon's lawyer, who was once Kirsten's husband's boss, announced that he was no longer representing his client. Thursday Bannon suggested that Anthony Fauci and FBI director Christopher Wray should be beheaded. "I'd actually like to go back to the old times of Tudor England," Bannon said. "I'd put the heads on pikes, right? I'd put them at the two corners of the White House as a warning to federal bureaucrats: You either get with the program or you're gone." As always, Dylan is right: "You don't need to be a weatherman/To know which way the wind blows." I don't think this crew is going to sit around a table in the White House with Joe and Kamala singing "Kumbaya."

Difficult though it is to believe, more people voted for Trump than have voted for any presidential candidate in history—except Joe Biden. This means that on average almost every other person you meet is a Trump supporter. The Republicans gained in the House and most likely will retain control of the Senate. From state legislatures to governorships, the Republicans outperformed the Democrats everywhere. It ain't over until it's over, and even then it might not be over. The Electoral College doesn't meet until December, and who knows what will happen then? There have been 165 "faithless electors" who have voted for someone the majority in their state did not support. In 2016, Trump lost two electors and Clinton lost five. Behind closed doors in the White House, are Trump and his henchmen plotting a coup? Even if Trump leaves office on January 20, the next seventy-five days will be among the most dangerous in American history. This victory may turn out to be pyrrhic; the cooperation Biden calls for cooperation will not occur and the unity he seeks is a pipe dream. It is fortunate that the violence we both feared has not erupted, but it is too early to be sure it won't.

And yet, and yet, and yet. On Friday, while I was washing the dinner dishes, the doorbell rang, which almost never happens. It was our neighbor

Bruce Goff, who is a bigtime hunter. He had just gotten back from Colorado where he had shot an eight-hundred-pound elk and a huge mule deer. Bruce also flies a small airplane and yesterday when taking off at the nearby airport noticed a deer skeleton along the runway and, knowing my fascination with bones, immediately thought of me. After he landed, he retrieved the skeleton; he concluded the deer had been killed and eaten by coyotes. When I opened the door, there was Bruce with an ear-to-ear smile holding the skeleton draped over his arms. He also brought me a beautiful elk skull with huge antlers that he found in Colorado. It was covered with

leaves and Bruce surmised that it had been killed by a mountain lion and the carcass had been hidden so he could eat it over a period of time.

It took me a while to figure out how to display the skeleton in my bone garden. I finally decided to mount it on a piece of plywood painted black and hang it between two trees. Rather than placing the skeleton upright, I twisted it in a way to suggest some kind of ancient sea creature from which we might all have evolved. When the work was finished, I called Bruce to ask him if he could come down to see what I had done with his gift and help me hang it in the bone garden. He said it had to be quick because he was leaving to drive to western Pennsylvania, where he and his cousin are going to hunt deer with his crossbow. He has a different weapon for each hunt—rifle, shotgun, black powder muzzleloader, bow, crossbow. I was trying to decide whether to screw or nail the plywood to the trees. Bruce said, "Don't do that, it won't give when the wind blows. Whenever I build a deer tree stand, I make it flexible. Let's hang it on hooks with wire." While we were working, I asked if he had heard the election results and, sticking with the hunting theme, said, "We dodged a bullet." Bruce replied, "You're talking to the wrong guy." I've lived in Williamstown more than fifty years and when I need help with something I cannot do by myself, he's the only person I can call for help and he always comes immediately.

*Memento Mori*

Two photographs.
COVID-19
10,000,000 Cases
238,000 Deaths
138,000 New cases yesterday

And so it begins, always begins again and again and again. There are only two, maybe three presidential elections for you and me. Though it has sometimes been a challenge to keep up with you every day, I'm going to miss our visits. You have taken me places I would not have ventured and made me think thoughts I could not have imagined by myself. Our correspondence started with death and disease, which, unbelievably, are worse now than when we began. Through all these days, through all these pages, our rare friendship has deepened immeasurably, and for that, I am eternally grateful. While this phase of our conversation is ending, our struggle continues.

Mark

## JACK: NOVEMBER 3–12

*Trump people "tired of being good"? . . . cruelty as television entertainment and the tenor of 2020 politics . . . Election Day cake . . . a quadrennial emptying of the septic tank . . . annals of late phone-banking . . . a shuttered campus like Sleeping Beauty's castle under a spell . . . Hispanic and Asian Trump voters resisting "people of color" label . . . fieldwork among Christians who believe Democrats are literal demons . . . the relevance of Milton's "On the Eve of Christ's Nativity" . . . a prematurely relieved Irish cousin . . . Biden at graveside: "He will bear you up on eagle's wings" . . . analyzing the vote in Los Angeles . . . Auden: "What needn't have happened did" . . . diapering babies as the world ends.*

---

*November 12*

Dear Mark:

I did not attempt as you did during election week to keep a daily diary. All I managed to do was take notes for the letter that I am writing now. My notes begin not on Election Day but on October 31, and so let me start with the following few pre-election jottings.

10/31     It was on Halloween, I believe, that my old friend Larry Christon forwarded to me Wallace Shawn's long reminiscence in the *New York Review of Books* about how the moods of America have changed during his lifetime, from his earliest boyhood memories of New York in the 1940s to the present. His sharpest contrast is between the elation and optimism of 1960 and the very different mood of 2020: "I was seventeen when John Kennedy was elected president, and I was thrilled by his speeches promising the total eradication of poverty on earth and peace between nations, self-government, and economic growth across the globe." The fifteen years that followed came quickly under the shadow of the Vietnam War. As regarded America's purity of intention and honor in execution, the scales fell from Shawn's eyes as happened for so many in our generation.

Now that I'm seventy-six, when I remember the way I used to feel— when I think about how important it once seemed to me to tell people the truth about the crimes in which we all were implicated—well, that all seems quaint and sad. It turns out that by the time the American public learned the sorts of things I'd felt they needed to learn, by the time they came to look in the mirror, what they saw there didn't look so bad to them. And so, yes, an awful lot of people don't get upset when they hear talk.

And then there follows immediately what strikes me as Shawn's real insight:

> On the contrary, they seem to feel a great sense of relief. Trump has liberated a lot of people from the last vestiges of the Sermon on the Mount. A lot of people turn out to have been sick and tired of pretending to be good. The fact that the leader of one of our two parties—the party, in fact that has for many decades represented what was normal, acceptable, and respectable—was not ashamed to reveal his own selfishness, was not ashamed to reveal his own indifference to the suffering of others, was not even ashamed to reveal his own cheerful enjoyment of cruelty . . . all of this helped people to feel that they no longer needed to be ashamed of those qualities in themselves either.

It certainly has been striking in the extreme that at a time of national agony, the president has never once addressed himself to what our people have been suffering or expressed gratitude to those who have been laboring, often at the cost of their own health or their own lives, to save the lives of their fellow Americans or to relieve their suffering. As with that form of distress, so also, of course, for the distress of Black people at the unending sequence of police killings of unarmed Black men and sometimes women. Lyndon Johnson—in domestic matters, probably more liberal than John Kennedy—made "war on poverty" a centerpiece of his administration, thus admitting that America does not just have a middle class, it also has a lower class, a large class of people living in true poverty. Trump could never bring himself to speak of the plight of millions of Americans plunged suddenly into destitution by the economic collapse triggered by the pandemic. He could only boast of the strength of the economy and declare, right down to the election, that the pandemic was about to vanish. Shawn's point, though, is not just to indict Trump once again. That exercise at this point would be beyond superfluous. No, it is that millions of Americans want to *join* him in these and other ways in excusing themselves from "pretending to be good," as Shawn puts it.

This is by no means a full explanation of the Trump phenomenon (and what a phenomenon it is!), but it is a partial explanation. And rather than contextualize this change exclusively in political and economic terms, I see it at least partly in the context of popular entertainments like *South Park* and *Beavis and Butthead* celebrating sexism, racism, ignorance, and the grossest sort of boorishness. Trump starred in *The Apprentice*, which gave people the pleasure of vicarious cruelty as Trump, the boss, fired people. Being fired—ousted, eased out, let go—is an experience I have had several times, and it's a brutal experience. To actually take *pleasure* in vicariously inflicting this pain on another? What does that tell us about Trump's fans and, now, his constituency? The various other reality TV programs that involve somebody being publicly hurt—girls not chosen by the eligible bachelor, singers ousted from *American Idol*, and so forth—are part of the same cultural shift. Being "thrown off the island" has become a cliché because of the great popularity of the show for which the appeal was the sick excitement of trying to guess who would be scorned and dismissed next.

You've probably seen a few vindictive Democratic "You're Fired" posters in the wake of Biden's victory. Even they bespeak the cultural effect of Trump's formative run as the star of *The Apprentice*, but so also does his string of firings while in office, all done with the least possible notice and otherwise timed for maximum humiliation of the associate and maximum schadenfreude for Trump. Comey learned that he was fired just as he took the stage to deliver a speech. Mattis resigned effective as of a date in the near future; Trump retaliated with an effective-immediately firing that took Mattis down just as he was headed for a crucial meeting with NATO allies about bolstering the Baltic states against a possible Russian invasion. A Trump crowd in Pennsylvania, just a few days before the election, began chanting, "Fire Fauci!" and the president just basked in that chant. Finally he said something like, "We'll see—after the election. He's a nice guy. Wrong about a lot of things, but a nice guy. But don't tell anyone, OK, after the election . . ." Apparently, Fauci as part of the civil service is beyond Trump's reach, but I won't be surprised if Trump tries somehow to at least humiliate him. And, though my stomach turns at thought, this seems pretty clearly to be a part of his appeal.

11/2    Kitty does two things every four years: 1) she has the septic tank drained; 2) she bakes Election Day cake from an old Connecticut recipe that includes a full cup of whisky. In the evening, her son Edward called us from Brooklyn in a state of serious angst over the prospect that Trump might be reelected. I quieted him and perhaps myself by citing the respected Charlie Cook, who had just lately written, after reviewing both published and unpublished polls, that the only question was whether Biden would win a "skinny" victory or a fat landslide of a victory. Cook also thought it quite likely that the Democrats would control both houses of Congress. Kathleen, who with Brian had done hours of phone-banking, phoned earlier that day to say that the fun part of phone-banking always came after a session had closed when the volunteers had the option of staying Zoomed in and exchanging memorable experiences. One phonebanker working North Florida reported a woman who said, "I'm ninety-two years old, and I am going to vote for Joe Biden if I have to walk on broken glass through fire buck naked." The phone-banking itself she characterized as sifting for gold—most calls find either nobody home, somebody already voted, or somebody declining to speak—but then every so often a voter who needed the reminder, was pro-Biden, and now, thanks to the phone-banker, came away with a specific polling place to go to, or that plus a ride. And then, once in a great while, there was the mother lode, the big strike of a nursing home with sixty Biden voters but no transportation to the polling place.

11/3    The day was eerily quiet—gray, cool, and calm with a kind of the eye-of-the-hurricane feel about it. At 8 a.m., I had, of all things, a dermatology followup appointment at UCI medical offices adjacent to campus. The mood of Sleeping Beauty's castle with everybody asleep was especially pronounced on the deserted campus. I took the occasion to return a few books through the dropbox at the closed and silent Langson Library. Once again, there was the mingled sense of wonder and mourning that perhaps the colossal, generations-long investment in our brick-and-mortar campuses might leave them finally as empty and barren as the cathedrals of the Netherlands, whose air of utter abandonment exceeds that of any European cathedrals I have ever visited.

Diagnosis of the results became nonstop on television even while the results were still coming in. As it became apparent that the Hispanic vote had not gone massively to Biden, two thoughts came to mind together. The first was of the fact that Mexico's presidents have always been white men. Benito Juarez, a Zapotec who became president around the time of our Civil War, was an exception, but I believe he remains the one and only exception. Much of Mexico's mestizo population identifies upward toward white rather than downward toward Indian, much less toward African. The second was mostly just a memory, the memory of a story told me in the seventies with some amusement by my Cuban-born Chicago girlfriend. She attended with a girlfriend, also Cuban, a Spanish-language documentary about Peru. My girlfriend laughed as she recalled that at a certain point in the documentary, her pal had blurted out loud, "Ahí, esta gente! Son todos Indios!" (These people! They're all Indians!) My brother Terry's partner is half-Nicaraguan and regards Nicaraguan society as classist first and, when racist, racist by prejudice against those of native blood. Considerations like these blur and skew the now nearly standard "people of color" label, especially when every indication at the Democratic Convention was that the concern was for African Americans or for the "browner" element of the Mexican American population, not the rest of it. Excluded, in other words, were not just Asians but also lighter-skinned Hispanics happy to be identified as white, and, among these, standing in the forefront, are Cubans and South Americans who join classist antagonism toward anything called socialism to their self-identification as white. Cuba has a huge Afro-Hispanic population, but it was not that part of the population that fled from Cuba when Fidel Castro's socialist dictatorship began. *Al contrario!*

As further results accumulated on the evening of the 3rd, other diagnoses were offered. Chris Hayes on MSNBC said that the clearest, most consistent across-the-board criterion was education. Those with more education vote Democratic, those with less Republican. A later analysis nicknamed "density and diplomas" linked the urban/rural divide to higher/lower educational attainment. Lucrative employment opportunities, requiring more education, are to be had in the cities, and so the educated congregate there and in the suburbs.

As the evening wore on and it became evident that four years of Trump's abysmal performance had not nearly sufficed to crush his electoral appeal and as, above all, it became clear that Republicans were likely to retain control of the Senate, I went to bed feeling only marginally better than I had on Election Day, 2016. In the middle of the night, I woke up thinking, "America cannot be better than the Americans." A great many Trump voters, despite some who say they don't like him but do like his policies, are voting for him in fact because they are indeed like him—far more like him than like Biden and quite probably little attracted if not actually repelled by Biden's calls to decency, honor, respect, and interracial collegiality. On 11/5, Nicholas Goldberg wrote in the *Los Angeles Times*:

> For the United States to have elected Donald Trump once can perhaps be written off as an aberration, a dreadful mistake.... But for tens of millions of people to double down and vote for him *again* in 2020 is entirely different. It is an assertion by those voters that, yes, this is who we really are—and what the United States has become over the last four years is really what we want it to be. Their votes send a message to the world that this bizarre and untrustworthy man didn't weasel his way into the most powerful job in the world by fooling the great American people. Rather, he was—and remains—the conscious choice of too many of them.
>
> That does not bode well for the months and years ahead. Even if Trump is gone, Trumpism, I'm afraid, is not going away.

11/4-6    As I write, despite many reassurances that the Republicans have no chance to overturn the election, I am still not quite at ease. (Of passing note: Republicans are in one case or another challenging the validity of the presidential election result while accepting Senate and House results achieved *on the same ballots*.)

On 11/4, I had my usual weekly Zoom meeting with my siblings. The mood was optimistic but still guarded. My sister Cathy said that we had to meet for a toast if and when the election was called for Joe, but we did not feel safe in doing that until Friday 11/6 in the afternoon. This time, spouses and kids were welcome, and some of them did turn up to join us. At Brian's request, I invited his mother as well, a beleaguered Democrat in violently red Coeur d'Alene, Idaho. By the time we lifted our glasses, I was finding some other grounds for hope. I had feared, earlier in our correspondence, that Trump's paramilitary intervention in Portland was rehearsal for something comparable after the election. That did not happen, and my anxiety began to abate, but the sudden replacement of the secretary of defense and several other top Pentagon officials, including, notably, its chief counsel, with Trump loyalists all sharing with Trump a penchant for ignoring established protocols and chains of command brought the anxiety back in a hurry. Everyone knows that Trump "might do anything," and he seemed to install a team prepared to do the same. There are many ways that the commander in chief might attempt to bend the military to his own ends, and I am far from alone in wondering fearfully what he or unknown associates/advisors may be planning. A key count against ousted Secretary Esper quite likely was his declared opposition to any such use of the American military.

On Friday morning, 11/6, at 8:45 a.m., I interviewed anthropologist Tanya Luhrmann (T. M. Luhrmann) about her new book from Princeton University Press, *How God Becomes Real.* I had earlier read a long excerpt in the *Atlantic* from her earlier book *When God Talks Back.* Our host was the Harvard Bookstore.

The new book may not be a masterpiece, but it does have the core strength of taking an obvious question, lying there in plain view yet all but never actually answered, and setting out to answer it. The book has a handsome blurb from Pascal Boyer, and early on she offers an apposite quote from him, much in the anthropological, fieldwork-based vein: "Observing rituals in the flesh, so to speak, one is bound to derive the impression that beliefs are often an occasional and elusive consequence of ceremonies rather than their foundation." But it is certainly not as if Luhrmann wants to "bless" religion. Before the Zoom session began, I raised with her the possibility that Donald Trump's following had begun to resemble a cult more than a political party in that his followers seemed scarcely any longer to expect the material goods that a party can deliver, when effective, but seemed rather to be devoted to him for more "spiritual" reasons. Trump's supreme failure as president has been his failure to lead the nation in dealing with the SARS-CoV-2 epidemic, but, as Nicholas Kristof pointed out in a recent column, nine of the ten states with the worst rates of coronavirus infection and COVID-19 death voted GOP. What explains their loyalty despite their suffering? I rather expected that some question about the Trump cult and how it sustains itself might come during the Q&A, but I did not intend to raise it myself in interviewing her. No one did ask that question, as it happened, but she had already been thinking along such lines and commented to me, before our public session began, that in her most recent research, among American Pentecostals, she has observed that the terms "demon" and "Democrat" are entirely interchangeable. I would love to have heard more, but the implication seemed to be that Pentecostals are attributing otherworldly and evil powers to Democrats even as empirical effects have always been attributed to demons.

John Milton wrote a great, long poem, "On the Eve of Christ's Nativity," in which he imagines that as Christ is born, the myriad false gods and demiurges and satyrs and what-have-you of antiquity (and Milton being Milton, he calls them all by name) are driven into outer darkness by the brilliance of the infant God Incarnate. The converse can be true and may be unfolding before us—namely, that the failure of organized Christianity is being followed not by some triumph of rationality but by this efflorescence of weird new superstitions.

Later on 11/6, my notes say a Los Angeles man was arrested after posting on Instagram as follows: "If Biden gets in, I'm just going to do like a school shooter, just take out all of these Democrats." In Philadelphia, two heavily armed men whose vehicle contained some bit of QAnon paraphernalia were intercepted as they headed toward the vote counting taking place in the Philly convention center.

On about 11/7, I heard again from Eamonn Cannon in Galway:

Dear Jack,

The calm after the storm. Quiet joy, and great relief, and pride too at the gracious demeanour of Joe Biden and Kamala Harris as they waited and waited., and when they spoke to America. It's difficult to adjust to the lack of bluster. Kathleen [his wife] heard a replay of John McCain's concession speech on John Bowman's programme this morning, and was greatly taken with it. Little chance of a repeat in this instance.

And, of course, the discomfiture of Boris Johnson—Trump's brother in bluster—is a source of quiet pleasure to us; the election result will, hopefully, have a beneficial effect on Brexit negotiations—well, from our point of view.

Joe Biden has a cousin in Ballina, Co. Mayo—also Joe—who for some months has been driving around with a picture of Biden on his van, and the slogan: "Joe Biden for the White House; Joe Blewitt (plumbing and heating contractor) for your house!"

Will try to find some news and write when I adjust to the new reality.

Best regards to you all,
Eamonn

11/7   This evening, Biden gave his first speech as the presumed winner of the election, recognized as such by all the states and by all major media. I had to notice that he entered actually *running* down the sloping entry ramp—if Trump was watching, he of the infamous runway stumble, I'm sure he did not miss the point being made. I found the speech vigorous, dignified, as gracious as the circumstances allowed, and moving near the end when he quoted his family's favorite hymn, whose chorus is

> And he will bear you up on eagle's wings
> Bear you on the breath of dawn
> Make you to shine like the sun
> And hold you in the palm of his hand.

This is not a classic sixteenth- or seventeenth-century hymn. It's a twentieth-century composition that we sing at our church, and I will be rather surprised if it isn't also familiar to Evangelicals. Obviously, it must be in use among Catholics. The gesture was one inconceivable in the mouth of Donald Trump, as inconceivable as Biden's early expression of shared grief in the colossal loss of American life to the coronavirus. But I have to say that nothing delighted me more than the terrific rock song played at the end to cheer the crowd gathered mostly in parked cars and, most of all, the flashiest fireworks that I have seen in many, many years. I'm not the biggest of fireworks fans; we hear them in the distance from Disneyland every night during the summer. But these were witty and thrilling all at once. And on the Sunday after the election, after going to Mass, Biden went alone to the graves of his first wife and his dead children. As a Catholic, he might have done that on the previous Sunday, All Saints' Day, but surely couldn't, so, as I imagine, he was catching up. Again, an action inconceivable as performed by the man soon to be (Deo volente) his predecessor.

11/8-10 As the days pass, Trump secludes himself in the White House tweeting outrageous claims and charges, key Republican leaders (McConnell, Graham, Barr, Pompeo) rally round him, recounts commence, and conservative lawsuits proliferate, analysis also continues apace. I have found my daily read of the *Los Angeles Times* rewarding during these days. Gustavo Arellano, a lively Chicano columnist only lately added to the *Times* team but bringing a wide following with him, wrote that, hey, Latinos voting Republican were a sideshow. They still came through 70 percent for the Democrats. The group everyone should be talking about is whites, who supported Trump 58 percent. Erika Smith, a Black columnist who appeared opposite him on the same page, took a somewhat different tack, one rather more akin to that earlier taken by Nick Goldberg and even by Tom Friedman, in a column Smith headed "Millions in California Voted for Trump. This Is Deeper Than White Grievance Politics." She didn't deny the white grievance factor but she went on:

> I can't help but wonder if there's more to the call of Trumpism. Exit polls show that Trump, in addition to his usual base of white voters, also managed to nab a not insignificant number of Black, Latino, Asian American and even LGBTQ voters. And these voters are real people. Real Californians. Real Angelenos. I spoke to several of them on Tuesday evening, while polls were closing on the East Coast, as they gathered for yet another Trump rally in Beverly Hills. The diversity of the crowd was as surprising as it was disturbing.

The end of our correspondence, Mark, if here is where we end it, could scarcely be more palpably a beginning than it is. The virus that set us in motion has got its lethal second wind and is tearing through the country as never before. We began in March, and it is effectively March again or worse. Biden has put together a team to fight it, but Trump's failures to date will continue to exact their early toll, and now worse, through two full months before Biden's team can begin to implement their plans. It is more likely than not that the government aid to millions of our unemployed citizens will end at the end of December and not resume until some

time after Biden's inauguration, if then. Unless the Democrats win both of
the two Senate seats open in Georgia, Biden's first one hundred days will
be as besieged by Republican intransigence and vindictiveness as Obama's
were in 2008. When my friend Mustafa Akyol shared with me the news
that his wife is pregnant with their third son, I went looking for W. H.
Auden's wonderful poem "Mundus et Infans" to send him and Riada, his
wife, by way of prenatal congratulations. When I found that poem, somehow it was paired with Auden's 1949 poem "A Walk After Dark," which
ends speaking of an old menace returning:

> For this moment stalks abroad
> Like the last, and its wronged again
> Whimper and are ignored,
> And the truth cannot be hid;
> Somebody chose their pain,
> What needn't have happened did.

Auden walks after dark, you run at dawn, but I can effortlessly insert
you into this poem in my imagination. This morning, as I sat down to conclude this long, pullulating, agitated report on election week as I had lived
through it, I found a message awaiting me from my former student Sam
Mowe, who after years in New York City, mostly in Brooklyn, married and
returned home with his wife and first child to Portland, Oregon, where he
grew up:

Hi Jack,

I enjoyed your conversation with James on the Tricycle Talks podcast.
I am always interested when Tricycle considers religion broadly and
how Buddhism fits into this bigger picture.

How did you find the process and outcome of working on this
interview?

I hope that you and Kitty are well. What a year! The two little ones
keep me grounded in my little world, so I don't drown in the news of
COVID, wildfires, social unrest, and the ongoing political chaos. Of
course, I still worry about all of these things but I feel lucky to have
diapers to change and lunches to make. Yesterday, I took Lila to the

zoo and watching her take in the majesty and mystery of the elephants made me grateful to be alive.

Sam

Dear Sam:

Your message is a breath of fresh air. A brilliant professor of Russian literature at Northwestern once pointed out in a lecture that Tolstoy's masterpiece *War and Peace* ends with a dirty diaper. A happy ending? Not exactly, but a profound return to the deeper realities that remain through all political vicissitudes, all wars and every peace.

Give your kids a kiss from Uncle Jack.

11/12    Your report of election week, Mark, and mine, much belated as it is, tell the same story and even end on a similar note. I link Taylor's delightful "Mom, Trump and Biden both have the most votes," which gave me a good laugh, with Sam's glimpse of paternity at the other end of the continent. Meanwhile, as our own lives, yours and mine, near their end, we find ourselves surrounded by death, threatened by it as never before in our lives. COVID-19 will undoubtedly end by taking more American lives than World War II did. That was a war that we knew of only because our parents' generation fought it, and even for them it was mostly "over there." But now the slaughter is occurring right here where we live, and any phone call may bring the kind of news that reached you and Dinny about her niece during election week.

And then . . . the macabre delivery of a skeleton to your back door. I know: you have your own substantial bone exhibition up and running—your ongoing, artistic memento mori. But I must confess that this particular surprise struck me as a shock straight out of a horror movie. Yet death is now our familiar, isn't it? It terrifies us, but not the way it once did. And meanwhile, however long it lasts, I can so easily, so very easily, make my own the words that close your letter: "Through all these days, though all these pages, our rare friendship has deepened immeasurably, and for that, I am eternally grateful. Though this phase of our conversation is ending, our struggle continues."

Jack

## JACK: JANUARY 6–7

*Epiphany: how the denied reality of electoral defeat and the denied reality of pandemic are a single issue . . . "We will never give up" vs. "We shall never surrender"— Trump vs. Churchill . . . Republicans ostentatiously unmasked and formally backing "Stop the Steal" lend the cover of patriotism to the Capitol assault . . . in Beverly Hills, a demonstrator's double sign: "Stop the Steal" and "Take off Face Diaper" . . . constant claim of "fake news" as Trump's most brilliant move: a disabling of fact . . . two cohabiting populations living on in two contending "realities" . . . last words of last letter: all hope rests on power of truth.*

---

*January 6–7*

Dear Mark:

When we began our epistolary "plague diary" nearly nine months ago, we expected the plague to be our central and principal subject. Nearer the end of our correspondence, a second topic—the impending political danger to our country rather than the threatening new disease—seemed increasingly to displace the original topic. We even agreed to conclude our correspondence with the November 2020 election. Did that mean that the plague diary had become an election diary? Had we lost our way? It might seem so, but on the day after a Trump mob stormed the Capitol Building and temporarily halted the formal election of Joe Biden as the forty-sixth president of the United States, I see more clearly now than ever how the two dangers became and remain a single danger. Call this my epiphany.

If it were really true that an American presidential election had been stolen, then it would indeed be the case that no option remained for patriotic Americans but insurrection. Think about it: Harvard alumni of our vintage can scarcely be surprised at building takeovers by political dissidents with "nonnegotiable demands." Timothy Snyder recognizes taking to the streets *en masse* as democracy's court of last resort in his books *On Tyranny: Twenty Lessons from the Twentieth Century* (2017) and *The Road to Unfreedom: Russia, Europe, America* (2019). Snyder in that second book was out to prepare liberal and patriotic Americans for what they might face when and if Donald J. Trump were able to consolidate authoritarian rule over our country in a second four-year term that then might not end in four years. But what is sauce for the liberal goose is sauce for the conservative gander.

Speaking to his militant supporters yesterday before they had quite congealed into a mob, Trump said: "We will never give up. We will never concede. It will never happen. You don't concede when there's theft involved. Our country has had enough. We will not take it anymore. . . . We fight like hell, and if you don't fight like hell, you're not going to have a country anymore." I am quoting from a *New York Times* article this morning, " 'Be There. Will Be Wild!' A Date Trump All but Circled," by Dan Barry and Sheera Frenkel. Trump was speaking to militant followers whom he had publicly summoned to Washington for a last stand against the election of his opponent. The reporters end their article as follows:

> Mr. Trump concluded his 70-minute [!] exhortation by encouraging everyone to walk down Pennsylvania Avenue to give Republicans at the Capitol "the kind of pride and boldness that they need to take back our country." Then the president returned to the White House, at safe distance from the mayhem to unfold.

A comparison here to Churchill may seem grotesque—"Hyperion to a satyr," to quote Hamlet—but Trump's "We will never give up" does call Churchill's most thrilling speech to my mind. In the immortal peroration to that speech, Churchill thundered: "We shall fight on the beaches, we shall fight on the landing grounds, we shall fight in the fields and in the streets, we shall fight in the hills; we shall never surrender."

If the election of Joe Biden truly meant the end of America as Americans have known it for 240 years, then insurrection would be justified along with the rhetoric of a fight to the death. It matters substantially, though, that in making the fraudulent claim that the presidential election had been stolen, Trump's audience knew that he was by no means speaking for himself alone. 147 Republican senators and representatives had gone on record through formal legal or political actions as well as a steady flow of rhetorical denunciations to support that lie. Could all those lawmakers *plus* the president be just making it up?

But, of course, the election had *not* been stolen, those Republicans were indeed making it up, and therein lies the link between the political threat you and I have lately been writing about and the medical threat that we began writing about. The political threat has lain crucially in the fraudulent claim of fraud. The medical threat now worsening exponentially has lain crucially in the fraudulent claim that the threat was not a threat or, if a threat, that it would disappear by April, or by Easter, or by Memorial Day, or after an undated but imminent turning of the corner, or that masking did not help, or made things worse. The very same people who have made—publicly and repeatedly and for months—the fraudulent claim of electoral fraud were those minimizing the pandemic threat by, most visibly and performatively, refusing to wear a mask or maintain physical distance or cancel mass gatherings to prevent the spread of contagion. In the earlier months, one was accustomed to see televised congressional hearings at which the Republicans would be unmasked, the Democrats masked. Although little by little, Republican politicians did begin to mask up, Mike Pompeo was announcing as late as December huge Christmas parties for diplomats stationed in the capital. Collectively, then, the Republican leadership that, beginning with the president, has lately been denying the reality of Democratic electoral victory has been for months demonstratively denying the reality of the pandemic, and both times the leaders' message has stuck with the followers.

Last week, Kitty asked that we take our exercise walk through Old Town Tustin, dotted with shops and restaurants that we once happily frequented. Late on a bright, cool morning, we took that walk, and as we neared noon I saw restaurants opening for lunch and serving unmasked clients in blatant defiance of the state ban. A few days later, I decided to order takeout seafood dinner from the Black Marlin, an Old Town place we hadn't visited in a year but had passed on our walk. Unfortunately, when I got to the Black Marlin in early evening, my order wasn't ready, there was no curbside service, maybe twenty or more diners were on the scene, and I was instructed to take a seat at the bar and wait. Instead, I just walked out. Evidence like this that the Republican denial of medical reality has stuck with many people greets one on every side in our vicinity. Yes, of course, one sees masks everywhere as well. But this is, in a way, the point. Two populations live alongside each other, one accepting the reality, the other denying it. And the same two populations accept and deny, respectively, the political reality that—officially and under duress—official Washington did finally accept yesterday.

So, yes, there is hope, but the double reality lives on. Again from today's *LA Times*, one learns that the leader of the California state senate Republicans "posted, then quickly deleted, a tweet Wednesday accusing the mob that overran the U.S. Capitol of being led by the leftist, anti-fascist group known as antifa and not by supporters of President Trump." The same lady

> ... has also opposed the state's public health restrictions on businesses as coronavirus cases spread.

> "Zero data!!! No science behind the decisions @GavinNewsom makes against our small businesses," [Shannon] Grove tweeted Dec. 24.

In linking these two denials, I am making no novel linkage. The Republican leadership has been making the same two denials, and moreover turning them into marks of Republican membership, for so long that the linkage is now deeply embedded—at times almost comically embedded—in the Republican faithful. A team of *LA Times* reporters wrote in an article today entitled "Protests and Clashes in LA":

> In Beverly Hills, about 50 peopled gathered at Canon Drive and Santa Monica Boulevard, barraging motorists idling in luxury cars at the intersection with megaphone-amplified theories that COVID-19 was a concept invented to achieve totalitarian control, unfounded accusations of voter fraud and predictions that Trump would remain in office for another four years....

> "Stop the Steal!" one woman repeated as she crossed back and forth across Santa Monica Boulevard, holding a large sign above her head that read, "End the Lockdown, Take Off Face Diaper."

This scene is just one tiny, ludicrous, even grotesque moment from within the reality we are living through and, variously, either accepting or denying, yet it neatly makes my point. For the lady with the sign, as evidently for tens of millions among us, stopping the steal and taking off the face diaper are two facets of the same cause, twin denials of the two realities that the president and his loyalists have linked to the collective peril even of those among us who accept the realities.

What remains, thus, as the last topic in this, my last letter in the series, is for you a perennial topic—namely, the fake and the real, and the real fake, and the fake real. Yesterday, you included me in an email message that you sent to our friend David Schulte that included this:

> At this moment in France there is a raging debate in which the Right is blaming Foucault, Derrida, Deleuze, and company for the ills of cancel culture and political correctness. There are also elements of this in the States. It's complicated because there is a trace of truth in it, though this is distorted. I have always said that you cannot understand Derrida without understanding the importance of the fact that he was an Algerian Jew—hence in Paris and elsewhere he was an outsider twice over. His preoccupation with otherness, difference, marginality, etc. is a direct reflection of his experience as an outsider wherever he went. What happened was that marginal groups—women, gays, African Americans, Latinos, etc., etc., seized on the language of otherness and difference and turned it into a politics of identity, which is the exact opposite of what Derrida was arguing for. It is less clear that Foucault would disagree with this development. Unless you are in the university, it is hard to appreciate how deep and pernicious this ideology of identity has become.
>
> More than you wanted, but not more than you should know.

As I see it, Mark, the "politics of identity," as you call it, is a political judo by which those treated as *other* reactively insist on their own *otherness* and in the process *other* the initial *other*-er, as in the reported T-shirt motto "It's a black thing . . . you wouldn't understand." But comparable and indeed more powerful processes of identity-formation occur far from the university even if, as always, university influence can usually be shown to have affected them indirectly. Trump's signature phrase, "fake news," his most brilliant political maneuver of all, has the effect of turning "the" news, which for so long has effectively been "our" news in an uncomplicated way, into "their" news. Where there was once only a universal *us*, vis-à-vis the news, there is now both an *us* and an othered *them*. And if and when *they* have their news and *we* ours, over here in our alternate media, then they begin to have their realities as well, and we to have ours.

You call the ideology of identity "deep and pernicious." I would distinguish: yes, pernicious when artificial—introducing division where none need exist or divided commitment where by rights there should be common commitment; but no, salubrious when natural—recognizing and defending the legitimacy and dignity of natural differences against invidious attempts to either exaggerate and exploit these, as by segregation, or obliterate them in the name of an enforced and artificially homogeneous unity. The attempt to create two distinct political identities vis-à-vis SARS-CoV-2 has been as deep and pernicious a politics of identity as we are ever likely to face because these are supremely and viciously artificial identities: before this novel coronavirus, we are truly all alike; pretending otherwise can have murderous effects.

As for the transformation of two erstwhile mere political parties with a once-shared American identity into one party with, allegedly, a legitimate American identity and one with, allegedly, only an illegitimate claim to American identity—respectively, of course, the Republicans and the Democrats—this transformation has been almost entirely an invidious Republican project. A pernicious example of this kind of political identity politics in early formation would be the "Hastert Rule." Dennis Hastert, who served several terms as Republican Speaker of the House under George W. Bush (and who was later condemned for bank fraud and still later imprisoned for sexual molestation), followed during his terms as Speaker the "rule" that no bill would be brought to the floor for a vote that did not enjoy majority Republican support. It was, for him, as if Democratic support was not real support, not legitimate, not American. But this was, of course, to fly in the face of the reality that, like it or not, Democrats are just as American as Republicans.

When a difference is natural rather than artificial, it takes no great effort to maintain it. When it is artificial, sustained efforts, even brutally aggressive efforts are always required. Such aggressions include, for example, the career ruination that we, and you more often than I, have seen imposed on academics who did not pay adequate obeisance to one embattled ethnic or gender difference or another. Over the past four years, Trump was quick to fire anyone who spoke too plainly about either the virulence of the virus or the legitimacy of the election. Turkish nationalists vacillate between demonizing the Kurds and denying that there even exist any Kurds (they are all just "Mountain Turks"). Israeli Jewish nationalists vacillate between demonizing the Palestinians and denying that there even exist any Palestinians. (As I heard the latter referred to in Israel in the

1960s, it was *'ein plishtiyim, yesh raq 'aravim*, "There are no Palestinians, there are only Arabs," the point being something like "Go back to Arabia"). In *Age of Ambition: Chasing Fortune, Truth, and Faith in the New China*, Evan Osnos has written tellingly of the scarcely believable lengths to which the PRC's Communist regime goes in suppressing even the most indirect online reference to Tiananmen Square.

With regard to the use or misuse of twentieth-century reflection on Derrida, Heidegger, and Hegel, let me mention again Lee McIntyre's little book *Post-Truth*. That term, "post-truth," isn't used on campus unless perhaps in discussing its emergence in popular discourse, especially popular political commentary. But because of that popular currency, it scarcely requires academe for its functioning. Cf. Stephen Colbert's related coinage of "truthiness." Truthiness isn't either plausibility or verisimilitude, both of which have their long-established and legitimate places; it comes rather out of what I have been discussing throughout this letter—namely, the attempt to foist and foster warring truth-identities for invidious gain. The attempt may succeed for a while, even for a very long while, but does it not always fail in the end?

Just now, the interim consequences for Americans caught in the middle of the salient frauds linked above are doubt and often anguished confusion. Whom can people trust? What institutions deserve their respect? As you write, "there is a trace of truth" in the claim that the dissolution of supposedly indissoluble truths through Derridian deconstruction or of supposedly natural facts or through Foucauldian poststructuralism has fed the growing popular anomie, distrust, and withdrawal into defensive silos. One can hardly be surprised that the hermeneutics of suspicion, once universalized, might lead to such a result. But in taking a stand for the truth, one must stand also for the truth about, so to call them, these dissident epistemologies. And post-truth has many more parents than Derrida.

The relevant chapter in *Post-Truth* carries, appropriately, a question for a title: "Did Postmodernism Lead to Post-Truth?" McIntyre answers that, yes, it did so but only by "a complete misfire of the politics that motivated postmodernism, which was to protect the poor and vulnerable from being exploited by those in authority!" But now that his has happened, what are liberals to do? The poor and vulnerable will suffer most from climate

change, "but how does the left fight back against right-wing ideology climate change denial] without using facts?"

This is the cost of playing with ideas as if they had no consequences.
It's all fun and games to attack truth in the academy, but what happens when one's tactics leak out into the hands of science deniers and
conspiracy theorists, or thin-skinned politicians who insist that their
instincts are better than any evidence?

Journalism matters enormously to me, as the whole run of these letters
makes obvious. As I conclude this letter and this final intensification of
our decades-long conversation, I am hopeful that the truth about the raging pandemic will gradually win out over denial of the truth and that the
truth about Donald Trump and his Trumpublican enablers will win out as
well. "Truth will out," to quote Shakespeare again; and when it does, we
will find that journalism in one form or another will have delivered it. I
have used to great, crowd-pleasing effect the line "The Jesuits made me an
intellectual, and then the intellectuals made me an ex-Jesuit." A less crowd-
pleasing but more accurate confession mimics Macaulay about Steele: "He
was a rake among scholars and a scholar among rakes." My confession (or

brag) is that I have been a scholar among journalists and a journalist among scholars—too deep in one company, too shallow in the other.

The perils that faced us when we began writing to each other, Mark, face us still and will grow worse before they grow better, but I end my last letter in hope and base my hope, as I know you do too, on the power of truth.

Jack

## MARK: JANUARY 7, 2021

*Jimmy Carter and the power of political music . . ."The devil went down to Georgia / He was lookin' for a soul to steal" . . . revival there of a Christian-Jewish alliance . . . stunning electoral victory swallowed up in sudden terror . . . a father to his children at the fall of the Berlin Wall, "Remember this day" vs. Trump to his followers at the assault on the Capitol, "Remember this day forever" . . . unrest in Kenosha, Wisconsin, and fear of insurrection around the country . . . distress because, after the storming of the Capitol, "no handcuffs, no police vans to carry criminals to jails" . . . ahead "neither cooperation nor reconciliation," only an "autoimmune disease infecting the body politic" . . . final faint hope: learning to listen because "we can't go on, we'll go on."*

---

*January 7*

Dear Jack:

How could we have imagined when we began writing to each other on March 15, 2020 (the Ides of March), that this is where we would be on January 6, 2021 (the Feast of the Epiphany)? Weeks, months, years were compressed into the last forty-eight hours, and it will take far longer than our remaining lifetimes to unravel what has occurred. From political betrayal to epiphany, questions linger. Was yesterday the beginning of a civil war that, as in ancient Rome, will bring the end of the American republic? What is the epiphany? What has been revealed to us? What do we know now that we did not know last March?

Several days ago, I was channel surfing and stumbled on a CNN special, "Jimmy Carter: Rock and Roll President." The peanut farmer from Plains, Georgia, the Rock and Roll President? I never realized how important music was for former President Carter, nor did I realize how much he used music—all kinds of music from country and folk to blues, jazz, and rock and roll—to advance his progressive political agenda. Jimmy Carter remains the most misunderstood and underappreciated politician of the last several decades. It is important to remember that Carter was the first truly Evangelical president and his life after leaving office is a testament to the depth of his faith and moral conviction. The world changed for the worse when Evangelicals shifted their support from Carter to Reagan in the 1980 election. This set the course for the so-called Reagan Revolution and the rise of neoliberal economic policies inspired by Milton Friedman. There would have been no Trump or Trumpism without Reagan and Reaganism.

Tuesday night I went to bed depressed because I was convinced that the Democrats could not sweep Georgia, and this morning I awoke with a sense of dread. Then I turned on *Morning Joe* and before the picture filled the screen heard the late great Charlie Daniels singing "The Devil Went Down to Georgia." For the past seventy-seven days, the Devil has been "in a bind 'cause he was way behind," and he was looking for votes to steal. When I heard the tune, I knew the Devil lost because Georgia turned the crimson tide blue deep in the heart of Dixie. Little did I know that later in the day, the Devil would return to collect what he thought he was due.

How did this unexpected development occur? The initial commentary and analysis have been typically unhelpful because they simply repeat what is obvious. While there has been ample discussion of the role of race in these elections, there has been no recognition of the important role religion continues to play in the political process. For too many years, the alliance between the political Right and the likes of Franklin Graham, Jerry Falwell, Jerry Falwell Jr., Timothy LaHaye, Jim and Tammy Faye Baker, Ted Haggard, and Joel Osteenhas overshadowed the important role that the liberal African American church hasplayed in the civil rights movement and continues to play today. The Democratic victory in Georgia last night revived the Christian-Jewish alliance that was crucial to the socially and politically transformative events during the 1960s. Raphael Warnock went to Union Theological Seminary, where I was once on the faculty. Since 2005, he has been the pastor in Ebenezer Baptist Church in Atlanta, where Martin Luther King Jr. and his father before him once preached. Jon Ossoff was raised Jewish and entered politics as an intern for the legendary Georgia congressman John Lewis, who attended Warnock's church. When Congressman Lewis died in July, he was honored as the first African American to lie in state in the rotunda of the United States capitol. President Trump, who had viciously attacked Lewis in his tweets, refused to pay his respects. I suspect that somewhere John Lewis is smiling today.

Even as I was feeling relief because of the Georgia victories, I had a gnawing awareness that more trouble was brewing, but little did I realize what the day would bring. Just as Trump and Trumpism can be largely explained as a reaction to Obama and all his presidency represented, so the election in Georgia can be largely explained as a reaction to Trump and all his presidency represented. I had no doubt that there would be yet another reaction to the reaction. The morning's headlines about the growing crowd in Washington overshadowed reports that the governor of Wisconsin had called out the National Guard in anticipation of violence in response to the refusal of the district attorney of Kenosha to bring charges against the police officer who shot Jacob Blake in front of his children, leaving him paralyzed from the waist down. The same day the first African American was elected to the Senate in the Deep South, the questionable assault on yet another Black man went uninvestigated. Protests that would quickly turn violent seemed inevitable to a Republican governor.

All of this was, of course, occurring as Congress was convening for the traditionally ceremonial confirmation of the election of Biden and Harris. Trump's months-long assault on democracy culminated in his speech before twenty thousand of his supporters who had answered his call to come to Washington to protest the "rigged election." What followed was as astonishing as it was predictable.

On November 9, 1989, the collapse of the Berlin Wall was broadcast around the world. Aaron, who was seventeen, and Kirsten, who was thirteen, were in bed, but I woke them up so they could watch this world-historical event. For the first time since that day, I called them yesterday to be sure they were watching what was happening and encouraged them to record it for Selma, Elsa, Jackson, and Taylor. I said to them, "Remember this day. Remember this day. The axis of the world has shifted, and life will never be the same again." In a mere three decades, history has turned upside down. While the fall of the Berlin Wall seemed to signal the triumph of liberal democracy and global capitalism, the treasonous assault on the U.S. Capitol is a troubling symptom of the drift toward hegemonic authoritarianism and the death of democracy.

As I watched the siege of the capitol unfold, my thoughts drifted back to Kenosha, which had faded from the daily news feed; I wondered what was happening there. Had violence broken out and if so, how had police and the National Guard responded? I was struck by how different the MAGA riot and the police response were to the countless demonstrations that have taken place on streets throughout the country in the past year. In his speech to the crowd, Rudy Guilliani explicitly incited violence when he called for "trial by combat." Trump proceeded to throw gasoline on the fire by continuing to promote conspiracy theories, and even at 3:49 a.m. this morning, after Congress had confirmed the outcome of the election, he tweeted on the account of an aide because Twitter and Facebook had finally suspended his accounts, "While this represents the greatest first term in presidential history, it's only the beginning of our fight to Make America Great Again," and, of the assault, "Remember this day forever!" The MAGA insurrectionists came to Washington looking for a fight. While it is difficult to know how organized the uprising was, they had a plan and their actions were clearly coordinated. What was most startling was the tepid response of the Capitol police. Where were other law enforcement authorities—the DC police, the state police, National Guard, Homeland Security, FBI? Everyone knew something like this was likely to happen, everyone should have been prepared for it, but no one was. Was this an accident? Rather than forcibly resisting the rebels, some of the police seemed to welcome the assault by holding open doors and even taking self-ies with the intruders. Most distressing of all, I did not see a single arrest—with hundreds, perhaps thousands of criminals rampaging through the capitol invading congressional chambers and offices, no handcuffs, no police vans to carry criminals to jails.

How many of the police are Trump sympathizers? This is not conspira-torial speculation, because the Secret Service recently reassigned agents who were to be responsible for protecting President Biden and Vice President Harris because they were suspected of being Trump loyalists. Imag-ine, just try to imagine what would have happened if the crowd had been Black, brown, or Muslim! The seditious seven wear white shirts and ties rather than white sheets or brown shirts, but true colors are red and black. The most dangerous threats always come from within.

All of this is occurring while the plague continues to rage throughout the country and across the world. Not only spread, but mutate—not once, not twice, but multiple times with no end in sight. The numbers continue to surpass comprehension. There have been 21.4 million cases of the coronavirus and 361,000 deaths in the United States. Today the number of deaths increased by a record 3,865. The much-touted vaccine remains bottled up by political obstructionism and bureaucratic ineptitude with no relief is in sight.

Once again a new semester is beginning—the *third* semester online. On Monday, I will face thirty disappointed and anxious young people, who long to be hopeful, and, on Tuesday, twenty more. As I finalize the syllabi, once again I am asking myself, how honest should I be, how far into the darkness dare I take them? My students are very smart and they will know if I try to reassure them with empty platitudes. If I am honest, I must tell them that the coming regime change will bring no closure, and, olive branches notwithstanding, there will be neither cooperation nor reconciliation. The divisions are growing deeper not only between, but also within the two parties that have provided the structural foundation of our governmental system for more than a century. The autoimmune disease infecting the body politic is getting worse and there is as yet no vaccine. This excessively contagious virus respects no boundaries and is rapidly spreading across the world. To make matters even worse, this crisis is unfolding at the worst possible moment—not only are global political and economic systems in meltdown, but the planet is on fire and the temperature continues to rise. Yesterday was the country's down payment on its pact with the Devil, more pain lies ahead.

> "Fire on the Mountain," run, boys, run
> The Devil's in the house of the risin' sun

The past year we have been writing has been a prolonged lesson in loss—the loss of health, the loss of life, the loss of reason, the loss of facts, the loss of truth, the loss of morality, the loss of beauty, the loss of civility, the loss of community, the loss of care, the loss of time, the loss of faith, the loss of hope. Is recovery possible? The plague is telling us something, but we are not listening. Paradoxically, disease can be therapeutic—it is a humbling experience, which exposes everyone's unavoidable vulnerability. We are all patients who are infected even when we seem to be healthy. Far from masters of the universe, we are entangled in complex systems and networks that exceed our understanding and control. Within these intricate webs, all life is a gift, which disease reveals can be taken away at any moment.

Dust to dust...ashes to ashes. "Human" and "humility" both derive from the Latin word *humus*, which means "ground," "earth," "soil." To be human is to be of the earth, and to be of the earth is to be humble. Humility opens one to the other always lurking within ourselves as well as silently sounding through all others. Only a humble person can shatter the silos of self-enclosure and self-assertion and listen to what she or he neither knows nor wants to hear. Truly listening requires time and patience—*if* we can learn once again how to listen to each other, we might be able to accept those we do not understand.

We have not heard from Jimmy Carter during this escalating crisis, but I am sure he would appreciate Joe's predawn tune this morning—Johnny Cash singing his version of the Nine Inch Nails tune "Hurt." Recorded late in life when his health, his voice were failing, and everyone he knew going away, this is his most soulful song. His words are full of regret for past shortcomings, and yet with twilight fast fading into night, he promises to find a way.

> What have I become?
> My sweetest friend
> Everyone I know goes away
> In the end
> And you could have it all
> My empire of dirt
> I will let you down
> I will make you hurt
> If I could start again
> A million miles away
> I would keep myself
> I would find a way

But can we? Can we find a way, or is it too late?

Last words are never final. Beckett once again beckons:

> I can't go on, you must go on, I'll go on, you must say words, as long as there are any, until they find me, until they say me, strange pain strange sin, you must go on, perhaps they have carried me to the threshold of my story, before the door that opens on my story, that

would surprise me, if it opens, it would be I, it will be silence, where I am, I don't know, I'll never know, in the silence you don't know, you must go on, I can't go on, I'll go on.

And so I'll go on for those who come after—my students, for my children, my grandchildren, and their children and grandchildren. And, I'll go on for you, dear friend. I have not written this work, nor have you; *we* have written it together; rather, for more than half a century, this work has been writing itself through us. Point and counterpoint, like notes in an antiphonal chorus. Our conversation has changed us—neither of us would have become what we are without the other. Even though we are once again ending, I wager our conversation will continue to change us after one of us, perhaps both of us dies. Though ghosts are not holy, they are, I believe,... real.

Mark

# Works Cited

Amichai, Yehuda. "Gods Change, Prayers Are Here to Stay." In *Judaism, The Norton Anthology of World Religions*, general editor, Jack Miles; associate editor for Judaism, David Biale. New York: Norton, 2015.

Auden, W.H. *Collected Poems*. New York: Vintage, 1991.

Augustine. *Confessions*. Translated by Rex Warner. New York: Mentor-Omega, 1963.

Bates, Gregory. *Steps Toward an Ecology of Mind*. New York: Ballantine, 1972.

Beckett, Samuel. *The Unnamable*. New York: Grove, 1958.

Bellah, Robert M. *Religion in Human Evolution, From the Palaeolithic to the Axial Age*. Princeton, NJ: Princeton University Press, 2011.

Bergman, Ingmar. *Four Screenplays*. New York: Garland, 1985.

Boss, Todd. "Haplodiploidy." In *Someday the Plan of a Town: Poems*. New York: Norton, 2022.

Bostrom, Nick. *Superintelligence: Paths, Dangers, Strategies*. New York: Oxford University Press, 2014.

Bryant, William Logan. *Dirt: The Ecstatic Skin of the Earth*. New York: Norton, 1995.

Burke, Edmund. *Reflections on the French Revolution*. Cambridge, MA: Harvard University Press, 1909-1914.

Camus, Albert. *The Plague*. New York: Knopf, 1957.

Carter, Robert. *The Kyoto School: An Introduction*. Albany: State University of New York Press, 2013.

Clooney, Francis X., S.J. *His Hiding Place Is Darkness: A Hindu-Catholic Poetics of Divine Absence*. Stanford, CA: Stanford University Press, 2013.

Collins, Billy. "Forgetfulness." Poetry Foundation. Accessed October 8, 2020. https://www.poetryfoundation.org.

Corballis, Michael. *The Recursive Mind: The Origins of Human Language, Thought, and Civilization*. Princeton, NJ: Princeton University Press, 2011.

Csikszentmihalyi, Mihalyi. *Flow:The Psychology of Optimal Experience*. New York: Harper and Row, 1990.

Defoe, Daniel. *A Journal of the Plague Year*. New York: Norton, 1992.

Derrida, Jacques. *Life Death*. Translated by Pascale-Anne Brault and Michael Haas. Chicago: University of Chicago Press, 2020.

Dillard, Annie. *Pilgrim at Tinker Creek*. New York: Harper, 1988.

Eliade, Mircea. *The Sacred and the Profane: The Nature of Religion*. New York: Harper and Row, 1961.

Emerson, Ralph Waldo. "Nature." In *Selected Writings of Ralph Waldo Emerson*. New York: Modern Library, 1950.

Ghosh, Amitav. *The Great Derangement*. Chicago: University of Chicago Press, 2017.

Gibson, William. *Neuromancer*. New York: Penguin, 2003.

Glück, Louise. "The Red Poppy." In *Poem in Your Pocket: 200 Poems to Read and Carry*, edited by Kay Ryan. New York: Academy of American Poets, 2009.

Hardison, O. B. *Disappearing Through the Skylight: Culture and Technology in the Twentieth Century*. New York: Viking, 1989.

Harari, Yuval Noah. *Homo Deus: A Brief History of Tomorrow*. New York: Harper Perennial, 2018.

Hegel, G. W. F. "Love." In *Early Theological Writings*, translated by T. M. Knox. Philadelphia: University of Pennsylvania Press, 1971.

Heidegger, Martin. *The Question Concerning Technology and Other Essays*. New York: Harper Torchbooks, 1977.

Heinegg, Peter. *Mortalism: Readings on the Meaning of Life*. Amherst, NY: Prometheus, 2003.

Kant, Immanuel. *The Critique of Judgment*. Translated by James Meredith. New York: Oxford University Press, 1973.

Kaveny, Cathleen. *Prophecy Without Contempt: Religious Discourse in the Public Square*. Cambridge, MA: Harvard University Press, 2018.

Keiji, Nishitani. *Religion and Nothingness*. Berkeley: University of California Press, 1983.

Kierkegaard, Søren. *Either-Or*. Vols. 1-2. Translated by Howard and Edna Hong. Princeton, NJ: Princeton University Press, 1987.

Knausgaard, Karl Ove. *Autumn*. New York: Penguin, 2015.

Kolbert, Elizabeth. *Field Notes from a Catastrophe*. New York: Bloomsbury, 2015.

——. *The Sixth Extinction*. New York: Picador, 2015.

Kurzweil, Ray. *The Singularity Is Near*. New York: Viking, 2005.

Maclean, Norman. *A River Runs Through It*. Chicago: University of Chicago Press, 1989.

Miles, Jack. *Christ: A Crisis in the Life of God*. New York: Knopf, 2001.

——. *God: A Biography*. New York: Knopf, 1995.

——. *God in the Qur'an*. New York: Knopf, 2018.

——. *Religion As We Know It: An Origin Story*. New York: Norton, 2019.

Miles, Jack, gen. ed. *The Norton Anthology of World Religions*. New York: Norton, 2015.

Niebuhr, Richard. *Experiential Religion*. New York: Harper and Row, 1977.

Nietzsche, Friedrich. "The Twilight of the Idol." In *The Portable Nietzsche*, translated by Walter Kaufmann. New York: Penguin, 1968.

——. *The Will to Power*. Translated by Walter Kaufmann. New York: Random House, 1968.

Otto, Rudolf. *The Idea of the Holy*. New York: Oxford University Press, 1958.

Pal, Pratapaditya. *Quest for Coomaraswamy: A Life in the Arts*. Calgary: Bayeux Arts, 2020.

Pyne, Stephen. *Fire in America: A Cultural History of Wildland and Rural Fire*. Seattle: University of Washington Press, Weyerhaeuser Environmental Books, 1997.

Serres, Michel. *The Parasite*. Translated by Lawrence Schehr. Baltimore, MD: Johns Hopkins University Press, 1982.

Shah, Sonia. *The Next Great Migration: The Beauty and Terror of Life on the Move*. New York: Bloomsbury, 2020.

Sloterdijk, Peter. *Not Saved: Essays After Heidegger*. New York: Polity, 2016.

Springsteen, Bruce. *Born to Run*. New York: Simon and Schuster, 2016.

Stevens, Wallace. "The Snow Man." In *The Collected Poems of Wallace Stevens*. New York: Knopf, 1981.

Taylor, Mark C. *Abiding Grace: Time, Modernity, Death*. Chicago: University of Chicago Press, 2018.

——. *Field Notes from Elsewhere: Reflections on Dying and Living*. New York: Columbia University Press, 2009.

——. *Intervolution: Smart Bodies Smart Things*. New York: Columbia University Press, 2020.

——. *Journeys to Selfhood: Hegel and Kierkegaard*. Berkeley: University of California Press, 1980.

——. *Seeing Silence*. Chicago: University of Chicago Press, 2020.

——. *Speed Limits: Where Time Went and Why We Have So Little Left*. New Haven, CT: Yale University Press, 2014.

Thoreau, Henry David. *Walden*. Princeton, NJ: Princeton University Press, 1971.

——. *A Week on the Concord and Merrimack Rivers*. Princeton, NJ: Princeton University Press, 2004.

Turchi, Peter. *Maps of the Imagination: The Writer as Cartographer*. San Antonio, TX: Trinity University Press, 2007.

Williams, Niall. *This Is Happiness*. New York: Bloomsbury, 2019.

13, 25, 278,